Southern Illinois University Press
Carbondale and Edwardsville

WRITING

Unheard Voices

OURSELVES

from

INTO

Composition

THE

Studies

STORY

Edited by

Sheryl I. Fontaine & Susan Hunter

96 95 94 93   4 3 2 1

Library of Congress Cataloging-in-Publication Data

Writing ourselves into the story : unheard voices from composition
    studies / edited by Sheryl I. Fontaine and Susan Hunter.
        p.   cm.
    Includes bibliographical references.
      1. English language — Composition and exercises — Study and
    teaching.   2. English language — Rhetoric — Study and teaching.
    I. Fontaine, Sheryl I., 1955–   .   II. Hunter, Susan, 1948–   .
    PE1404.W729   1993   92-10625
    808'.042'07 — dc20   CIP
        ISBN 0-8093-1826-1
        ISBN 0-8093-1827-X (pb)

The paper used in this publication meets the minimum requirements of
American National Standard for Information Sciences
— Permanence of Paper for Printed Library Materials, ANSI Z39.48-1984. ∞

Excerpts from *A Wrinkle in Time* by Madeleine L'Engle. Copyright © 1962
and renewal copyright © 1990 by Crosswicks Ltd. Reprinted by permission
of Farrar, Straus & Giroux, Inc.

Contents

Acknowledgments

We express our appreciation to the many individuals who supported our project by sharing their unheard stories with us in proposals they submitted and in personal letters and phone calls. We hope to have included the spirit of all their voices in this book. Our thanks also to Fay Hicks for her secretarial assistance and to Jeff Adams and Richard Boyd for their ever-candid responses and words of advice and their seldom-waning good humor.

Writing
Ourselves
into the Story

Introduction: Taking the Risk to Be Heard

Sheryl I. Fontaine/California State University, Fullerton
Susan Hunter/Kennesaw State College, Marietta, Georgia

Stories and Storytellers from Composition Studies

One of the most influential positions from which to speak in our discipline is the lectern in the grand ballroom of the Hilton or Marriott or whatever metropolitan hotel has won the bid to host the annual Conference on College Composition and Communication (CCCC). Delivered to an audience of hundreds and published a year later to a *College Composition and Communication (CCC)* readership of thousands more, the chair's address is among the most well-circulated texts in composition. One unspoken rhetorical purpose of the address is to galvanize this diverse constituency with a shared focus, to touch the professional lives of every listener and reader: the teachers who gather from all over the country to attend the CCCC, bringing heads full of their most recent classroom experiences and faculty debates, and the teachers who are seated alone reading *CCC* in their offices or studies, trying to close the door on the daily successes and problems that speak more insistently than the voices in their journals. Directed to every member of the profession, the chair's address introduces new conceptual terms, suggests the most pressing agenda, and seeks to direct the collective intellectual gaze of composition professionals at colleges and universities, in classrooms, offices, and libraries.

Looking at just three examples of recent addresses, we can see the speakers directing and redirecting the gaze of the audience: from disciplinary autonomy to disciplinary integration, from conceptual grounding in the past to conceptual grounding in the present, from overarching characterizations of the discipline to highly focused descriptions of individual practices.

Begin with the address that received a standing ovation at the 1985 conference. In "Breaking Our Bonds and Reaffirming Our Connections," Maxine Hairston declared that "as rhetoricians and writing teachers we will come of age and become autonomous professionals with a discipline of our own only if we can make a psychological break with the literary critics who today dominate the profession of English studies" (273). Hairston goes on to describe our colleagues in literature as being the "mandarins" from whom we should be "breaking our bonds . . . emotionally and intellectually" (273). Her impassioned words gave composition professionals permission to consider seriously an action that many had timidly dismissed: forming departments of composition separate from literature's disciplinary purview, defining ourselves according to our own set of values about scholarship and teaching.

In 1989, Andrea Lunsford shifted attention away from attempts, like Hairston's, to "define" composition in terms of oppositions: as "a science, or an art," "part of literary studies, or . . . against the literary 'mandarins,'" "theorists or practitioners," "classicists, cognitivists, or epistemic rhetoricians" (72). Lunsford's address, "Composing Ourselves: Politics, Commitment, and the Teaching of Writing," urges composition teachers to resist the "lure of crisp definition" that is "too often limiting and constricting." She proposes that, instead, "we attend closely to *composing ourselves*" (72) historically and subjectively (her emphasis). After first discouraging the audience from defining composition according to rigid meanings grounded in preexisting, fixed categories, Lunsford encourages her listeners to take advantage of the fluidity of composing, drawing from various disciplinary sources to construct notions of what it means to teach and study composition. Then she identifies the historical context in which such constructing or composing should occur: "into and around and within" the history of rhetoric and "in terms of those who have been the teachers of writing" (72).

The next year, in a speech entitled "Valuing Teaching: Assumptions, Problems, and Possibilities," Jane Peterson shifted our intellectual gaze away from the past and its significance for disciplinary characterizations toward the present and its importance to the practice of teaching. Grounding herself in what we currently know about reading, writing, and learning, Peterson maintains that while our profession has contributed to improving the teaching of composition, there is "evidence that a hierarchy exists within the profession, evidence that we consider teaching far less important than research or scholarship, evidence that our understanding of the value of teaching remains limited" (27). Peterson urges that the profession draw on its wealth of knowledge about reading, writing, and learning to deepen its understanding of teaching as a "transformation into a genuine way of learning and knowing" (33).

Throughout the four days of CCCC and well afterwards, when we have returned to the colleges and universities where we teach, we hear echoes of the counsel and warning offered in the chair's address. Interestingly, though this is not true of all CCCC chair's addresses, the three titles in these examples use the present participle, a verb form that in this case seems to presume the actions of "breaking," "composing," and "valuing" are already in progress, giving the listener the impression that the speaker is describing the way things *are*, not the way they *should* or *will* be. Indeed, to be rhetorically effective, to galvanize the gaze of so many diverse professionals, every chair's address must imply this kind of consensus—as if the audience needn't be convinced that this description is correct, just excited by its existence. And later, when the members of the audience are alone to face their own departments, we often unconsciously gauge our professional behavior against the standard implied by the chair's description: Am I adequately challenging the literature-based syllabus of my senior colleague's section of freshman composition? Do I know enough medieval and classical rhetoric to call myself a "specialist in composition and rhetoric"? Does my teaching engage students, making them reflective readers and writers? And many individuals find, to their disappointment, that they cannot measure up. One *CCC* reader described his vain attempt to respond to Lunsford's request to "compose" himself: "I spent much of last year *trying* to compose a wholesome self amid these conflicting demands. I *wanted* to be dialogic, multi-voiced, and heteroglossic. But I failed, and lamented my failure" (Burton 337).

Put another way, each conference chair tells what she or he believes to be the story of composition, the central narrative into which the members of the discipline are to enter. The audience's attention is directed to a particular part of the composition world: an exclusive group of ancestors, allies, or enemies; a particular call to action; a singular moment in its history. And a good storyteller has the ability to make the listeners forget all other stories, hear only one voice, see only one set of characters, seek—too often in vain—their place in the narrative being unfolded for them.

The chairs of our national conventions are not the only ones with the opportunity to direct our gaze, telling the composition story as they would like it told. Recent books, either commissioned or approved by our professional organizations and edited by well-recognized scholars, describe their vision of the current status of composition and their prescription for its future.

The English Coalition Conference: Democracy Through Language and *What Is English?*, published by NCTE and MLA, were written as a result of discussions at the 1987 English Coalition Conference. Scheduled twenty years after the Dartmouth Conference, the ECC included sixty-one elementary, secondary, and college teachers who were invited to the Wye Plantation in Maryland to "see if a consensus about the teaching of English could be achieved; and to identify solutions to the problems that teachers of English have been encountering" (Elbow, *What is English?* 5). The original voices includes a select chorus of fifteen elementary teachers, seventeen secondary teachers, and twenty-seven college teachers, all of whom contributed to discussions with personal "position papers" that were submitted and distributed before the conference along with process pieces, stories, and reports written during the conference. The chorus became three collaborative voices as each section compiled a draft of their final report. And the number of voices was reduced twice more: Richard Lloyd-Jones and Andrea Lunsford were elected to edit and summarize these reports through their own voices for the official publication, *De-*

mocracy Through Language, and Peter Elbow was invited by the MLA Executive Council to write *What Is English?*, "a series of professional and personal ruminations on the conference and . . . sometimes on the profession of English itself" (v). Though Elbow does "get the voices of many of the conference participants into [his] book" (vii) by including quotations from their formal and informal writing, his recurring solo interpretation dominates.

The Future of Doctoral Studies in English represents the "dominant view" (Lunsford, Moglen, and Slevin vi) about "the present state and future shape of doctoral studies in English" (v) as shared by "invited representatives from eighty Ph.D.-granting departments" at the Wayzata Conference. The twenty contributors to the book—three of whom were also the book's editors—tell the story of what "can now be said to constitute our discipline: The connections among the subjects we teach and the foci of our scholarly efforts; the nature of the profession for which we train and into which we socialize our graduate students, a profession that they, in turn, will define through their own theoretical interest, institutional assumptions, and pedagogical practices" (v).

Like the CCCC address, these collections serve as standards against which the readers who were not invited to attend the initiating conferences judge their beliefs, their programs, their own stories of composition. And while the authors' words imply that the essays are representative of the constituency (recall that one stated goal of the ECC was to "see if a consensus . . . could be achieved" and that the Wayzata documents claim to describe what "can now be said to constitute our discipline"), undoubtedly, they do not, cannot represent everyone.[1]

Stories of our discipline are being told not only by the representatives who have been selected or elected by our professional organizations. Certainly, there are many composition scholars who have, themselves, chosen to narrate our evolving story, directing our intellectual gaze toward certain theoretical frameworks or research rubrics. Books such as *Composition as a Human Science* by Louise Wetherbee Phelps and *Textual Carnivals: The Politics of Composition* by Susan Miller set out, quite explicitly, to "define, locate, and legitimize composition as a discipline" (Phelps vii) or to "reread [its] denigrating tale" (Miller, *Textual Carnivals* 1) from particular theoretical perspectives. George Hillocks, Jr., in *Research on Written Composition* and Stephen North in *The Making of Knowledge in Composition: Portrait of an Emerging Discipline* map out the research territory of composition. They are among a group of scholars (e.g., Beach and Bridwell, Lauer and Asher, Odell and Cooper) who have created categories and designed rubrics that narrate the research stories of composition, telling who is doing research worth valuing, how they are doing it, and what it means for the future.

And finally, we hear in commissioned collections such as *An Introduction to Composition Studies* edited by Erika Lindemann and Gary Tate or *The Politics of Writing Instruction: Postsecondary* edited by Richard Bullock, John Trimbur, and Charles Schuster, not one voice, but many voices telling the story of the discipline. Lindemann and Tate asked "nine knowledgeable people, all of whom have demonstrated their commitment to the field" (vi), each in his or her own voice to "introduce" readers who are unfamiliar with composition as well as those uncertain about its disciplinary status to what it means to do work in composition. Bullock, Trimbur, and Schuster, in the first volume in a series called for by the NCTE Commission on Composition, compile eighteen essays by well-known scholars that advance their familiar stories about the political state and status of composition.

For each book on composition theory or research or pedagogy, there are tens or hundreds of researchers or teachers searching for their place in the stories, wondering how each version applies to their lives. And often, the search ends with some doubt: "Wait, you forgot something; that could never happen in my classroom; that would never work in my department; that's not the *only* way to tell the story."

Contradiction and Illusion

The point in naming these authors and editors is not to criticize them for being the "storytellers" of composition, a role many of them did not consciously assume, or to take issue with any particular version of the story. Rather, we use these authors and their texts as examples that will help call attention to a serious contradiction between the vision described in journals and books and the reality told through much of our professional behavior.

Composition has been described as "multivocal, dialogical," a discipline that "reflects in its actions its theoretical opposition to a unifying, dominant discourse" (Bartholomae 49), and is "non-hierarchical" and "intensely collaborative" (Lunsford 76). The quintessential composition classrooms have been characterized as "sites for dialogues and polyphonic choruses" (Lunsford 76), places where students are "active learners, engaged in conscious theorizing and open to being transformed" (Peterson 32). Yet this discipline, which loudly distinguishes itself from others by its alleged tolerance of plurality and heteroglossia, is systematically reducing its members' opportunities to be heard and promoting notions of hierarchy.

Consider, for example, that one elected member of our constituency is in the position to direct the discussions of so many people, not only through the chair's address, but through the theme he or she selects for the conference and the areas of discussion selected to be emphasized and listed on the CCCC proposal form mailed to NCTE members. However engaging this theme and its subsequent areas of discussion may be, they serve on one level as predetermined conceptual structures into which writers must accommodate their proposed panels. And even after panels have been accepted, the program chair may reorganize them.

Can we call ourselves "non-hierarchical" when selected individuals — sixty-one teachers attended ECC; eighty doctoral institutions were represented at Wayzata — are invited by our professional organizations to describe the status and future of our discipline and then to publicly assert this description in commissioned books as if it represented the views of all ten thousand members? In addition to these selected representatives, other self-appointed ones have created hierarchies in teaching where pedagogies are valued according to their implicit theoretical framework (what are the consequences of being labeled expressivist, current traditionalist, or social constructionist?) and in research where investigators are valued in relation to the kind of inquiry they conduct (how is my work valued if I am a practitioner instead of a scholar or a researcher?).

Can we claim we are opposed "to a unifying dominant discourse" or that we are multivocal at the same time that our journals assert increasing control over the content and form of submitted essays and that the authorship of published essays represents such a small percentage of the composition membership? "Gender, Writing, and Pedagogy"; "Race, Writing, and Pedagogy"; "Rediscovering Lost Rhetorics"; and "Implementing the CCCC's Statement of Principles and Standards for the Postsecondary Teaching of Writing" have appeared in a *CCC* list of desirable topics ("Call for Submissions" 150). There is nothing actually *wrong* with a list that could serve to create thematic structure in future issues of the journal. But, nonetheless, it implicitly validates the issues it names while invalidating those not listed. The editor of *CCC* in the February 1991 issue informed contributors that submissions should either "explore an issue, describe a problem, etc.—with the aid of or in the context of an empirical study." They should be either "compact descriptions of specific instructional or administrative practices" or "fuller essays of application, speculation, and introspection" ("Information" 110).[2] Book reviews, subjective summaries that are often as close as many of us come to reading the exploding number of books in composition, are assigned or solicited by journal editors. And even editors whose journals are committed to the "nondominant discourse" publish only solicited essays or characterize the voice they want essays to have. A reviewer of one such journal criticized a submission for being insufficiently "lively" and "personal."

The ratio of male to female publications in our scholarly journals, which is more than two to one (Enos 213), certainly doesn't reflect the overall ratio of male to female composition professionals. Sue Ellen Holbrook claims that our field is dominated by a traditional gender hierarchy in which men develop knowledge at conferences and in print and women apply it in the classroom (205–11). And although M. Elizabeth Wallace has collected essays on *Part-time Academic Employment in the Humanities*, no studies that we know of document the ratio of part-time to full-time or tenured faculty publications. We suspect the ratio is most probably similar to or possibly even more uneven than the male/female ratio, in no way representative of the fact that "more than half the English faculty in two-year colleges, and nearly one-third of the English faculty at four-year colleges and universities, work on part-time and/or temporary appointments" (CCCC's *Statement* 330).

It's not that the discipline *can't* be nonhierarchical and multivocal or *doesn't* in many ways promote collaboration and dialogue. But we composition teachers are living an illusion if we believe that the present state of our discipline will naturally and necessarily unfold into a future without hierarchies, one where all members speak to and among one another. Certainly the national organizations, journals, and published writers of composition are not setting out to jeopardize such a future. But in the process of "professionalization," of working toward disciplinary autonomy, composition has begun to promote an illusion about itself.

In his critique of professionalization, Richard Ohmann cautions that as a group becomes a profession at the same time that it "appropriates, shares, and develops a body of knowledge," it also "discredits other practitioners performing similar work" (250). Seemingly aware of this danger, Lee Odell urged composition specialists not to "compartmentalize our knowledge about our profession" (397), to "become better able to make connections among apparently disparate elements of our discipline" (398). Four years later, Odell's advice goes unheeded, compelling Janet Emig to describe an unhealthy tendency among compositionists to shift intellectual allegiances. Instead of seeking out connections, we declare interest in a new idea and simultaneously debunk and discard all those that preceded it. Composition professionals have the opportunity to act out among themselves, at conferences and in publications, the tolerance implied by the most current theory and encouraged by our most respected scholars. But it becomes increasingly difficult for individuals to be heard in the rush of strengthening academic hierarchies.

Making Illusion Reality

This book is our response to the serious contradiction we have found in the self-perception of composition, a response to Ohmann's warnings and to Odell's and Emig's urgings. The book also evolved from a response to the personal frustration we have felt after attending a national conference or reading a published essay: How do *we* fit into this story? How do our histories as females moving through non–tenure-track or part-time positions, to full-time, yet untenured ones, holding administrative posts, teaching at non-research institutions compare with the history of someone who is male or tenured or teaching primarily graduate students?

With this collection of essays, we celebrate the true potential of our discipline's multivocal, heteroglossic, nonhierarchical nature. Our goal has been to create an occasion for teachers and researchers, like ourselves, who do not feel included in the story of our evolving discipline, to voice unheard perspectives—expressing views that are not represented in the prevailing central descriptions of the field, calling critical attention to issues that have been overlooked, writing in genres often deserted for the sake of academic discourse.

In our call for proposals, we intentionally identified no theme, no single story. Rather, we invited others to write from their own "unheard voices." Psychologists suggest that once you have been on the borders, you continue to carry that perspective with you, no matter the status or privilege you achieve. We suspected that inside many a composition specialist—even those who now seem comfortable in the professional arena—lives an ego who is always on the edge of the crowd, who does composition at the margins rather than at the center of the field.

In this way, unheard *voices* includes unheard *perspectives* as well as unheard *people*. Each of us is a composite of many voices, some more hushed than others, less encouraged by the louder voices around us. Certainly one might expect some individuals to embody an unheard voice more totally than others—part-timers, graduate students, people of color, women, teachers who have not had the time to publish or the financial support to attend conferences. But we all have unheard voices inside our heads. They express the chaos, the conflicts, the contradiction, the stories that are missing in the most familiar narratives of composition. As such, there is a certain amount of risk involved in raising them or in admitting their significance. One potential contributor seemed uneasy with the label: "What makes those you decide to include in your book [unheard] voices? Would all you do include agree with the terms of their positioning? I know I would like to know how I would be classified/characterized if I were to be selected." Another revealed an apparent prejudice against the value of such voices when he suggested that we rethink our title, believing it would undermine the voices to label them "unheard."[3]

But if composition is to make a reality out of its multivocal, nonhierarchical self-image, we must all be willing to take the risk inherent in speaking out, in speaking up. We must attend to our unheard voices— be willing to muffle the mainstream voice(s) long enough for the other(s) to respond or add to the story, to venture to be heard.

Answering the Call: Why or Why Not?

To invite the "unheard voices" of composition studies to speak out, then, we diligently tried to reach as many corners of the discipline as possible by announcing our plan in various publications and to different professional organizations; contacting writing program administrators, department chairs, and colleagues whom we suspected would understand our projects; following up on leads from those who mailed us proposals. Our attempts, though careful and spanning a little over six months, were undoubtedly incomplete. Admittedly, some publications we did not contact in time to meet deadlines, some we inadvertently overlooked, and others, we naively discovered, make editorial selections about which projects should be announced to the composition membership. All this considered, the proposals we received were telling both because of what voices *are* represented and what voices *are not*. Even with all the recent opportunities targeted directly for women to raise issues about gender and the academy, women responded in greater numbers than men to our call for unheard voices: forty-seven/twenty-two submitted; twenty-one/six accepted. We heard from only one composition teacher speaking as an ethnic minority. While race and ethnicity were underrepresented in the proposals we received, class was not: the respondents came from many different kinds of schools and taught many different kinds of students. Postsecondary teachers of writing from all ranks responded; four-year college faculty and graduate students in composition outnumbered two-year college faculty. And in spite of the support that the discipline has shown for employment parity and the value of teaching through the CCCC's *Statement of Principles and Standards for Postsecondary Teaching*, part-time and untenured faculty outnumbered the full-time and tenured faculty who answered the call. Clearly, something in our request for unheard voices and additions to the composition story caused women and part-time faculty especially to want to speak up for themselves rather than to let themselves continue to be spoken about. All those who accepted our invitation believed that they could make some revisions in the form and content of the most widely publicized narratives of composition. We were reassured that the intuitive sense of "unheardness" we had been struggling to articulate was being felt by many other composition professionals.

Still, since there are many voices we expected to hear that we did not, we find ourselves wondering why more two-year college faculty did not respond, why ethnic voices are so conspicuously absent. One potential contributor, an ethnic minority, told us that she didn't have much to say about basic writers; instead, she wanted to get back to more empowering concerns about African-

American writers and multicultural curricula. We refuse to believe, as suggested by one reviewer, that those who did not respond and thus who remain literally unheard, do so because they "lack . . . professional interest and/or savvy." Rather, we suspect that the powerlessness that comes with continually being unheard and uninvited has left them untrusting of our invitation or of their own voices. Maybe, like the graduate students who spoke out in the first "Burkean Parlor" in *Rhetoric Review*, they feel that insiders have silenced them once too often. Maybe they do indeed lack interest, not in the profession, but in entering a conversation that would require them to sacrifice so much of themselves.

In many of the proposals we received, the unheard voice is, most literally, someone who has not published in the most widely distributed professional journals or someone who represents the most silent ranks of the discipline—part-time faculty, two-year college faculty. On the other hand, we were surprised to receive proposals and inquiries from individual members of the discipline whom we imagined would feel included in the current stories of composition. For instance, after reading the prospectus, one well-known speaker in the field wrote to share his sense of being "disenfranchised or disconnected." We have come to realize that just because we speak at a conference or get something published in a journal does not mean we are heard. Some among us who have published feel we are unheard because what we have written does not seem to have changed anything in the discipline or because others have written about the same thing as if we never wrote about it or because we do not find our stories in those that the CCCC chairs and the most widely published writers in our field compose. Others who have published read in our call for proposals an opportunity to sound a voice or write in a form they had not felt welcome to submit to other publications. Apparently they too felt that, for whatever reason, there are voices inside of them that have not yet found a forum in which to speak.

The gains or losses that arise from considering oneself to be a "heard voice" or an "unheard voice" are not easy to figure out. Throughout the process of putting this collection together, we kept asking each other questions about the risks of being an "unheard voice," questions that we still are unable to answer: If you are "unheard" does that mean that you do not count as much as someone who considers themselves "heard"? If you are willing to sound an "unheard" voice does that mean that you do not care about status, that you believe it is more important to say what you think needs to be heard than to follow someone else's guidelines? What does it mean to want your piece to appear collected with others who identify themselves as "unheard"?

Positioning Voices, Telling Other Stories

We tried to respond to the proposals and drafts we received first from our own sense of being unheard, then as editors. But, mostly, our unheard voices were hopelessly intertwined with our editorial ones, making our responses both personal and professional. Indeed, one of our goals as editors was to invite writers to intertwine their own personal and professional voices. We encouraged them to experiment with discourse that is personal, revelatory; that mixes genres; that includes voices other than their own. For we believe, along with Peter Elbow, that "because personal writing invites feeling does not mean that it leaves out thinking. . . ." (Elbow, "Foreword" 10). Questioning the nature of critical discourse, Olivia Frey has wondered in *College English*—and we wonder with her—"What difference will it make if some of us . . . explore ideas without reaching any conclusions, or if we get personal in our essays. . . . [We] would like to think that such changes would stand knowledge on its head" (521–22). While we were responding to proposals and drafts, we sometimes recognized a mismatch between what writers propose to be willing to risk and their habit of succumbing to the pressures of academic writing for closure and a lack of voice, of concluding that "things aren't all that bad, are they?" It is a tall order to unlearn the survival strategies of the discourse that got us through graduate school, the kind, for instance, where we postpone taking a position by first developing a historical or a theoretical perspective. In many of the pieces in this collection, the authors have tried something different. Some have done so more obviously and self-consciously than others.

Unlike authors in thematic collections who share an interest in a subject, our contributors share a sense of absence. The unheard voices in this book attempt to shift our intellectual gaze from one set of events to another, widening that gaze to include what is absent in the already-talked-about events. But the pieces are not simply about new topics or about new interpretations of theories and research; they are not simply new arguments about already publicly acclaimed issues. Instead, underlying each piece is a personal story about, a sense of engagement with, or an outrage over the ways in which composition studies has become unmindful of its own margins. These writers take risks; they put on the table issues that are being avoided or talked around, concerns about the material conditions of doing composition that are usually discussed in small groups or private conversations, not in print. In these essays, writers are raising voices from within themselves that respond to the voices they have been hearing. Each one is speaking from a sense that the models put forth so far have not been adequate or appropriate. These models may be curricular, pedagogical, or administrative; they may be models of discourse or even models of professional development.

Once we had selected the proposals, we looked to them for the categories, for the absences felt by each contributor. In organizing essays generated from this sense, we were also organizing an alternate vision of the discipline, a vision that includes new focal points, new ways of listening to the voices among us. Although most of the pieces are by a single author, they often include many other voices of women, part-time faculty, graduate and undergraduate students. There is a kind of randomness or arbitrariness in our concatenation of the pieces in this collection. Others could reshuffle the cards and find other equally suitable patterns and connections, but this is the organization that crystallized for us. Rather than focusing on traditional or expected categories of pedagogy and research, theory and practice, autobiography and exposition, the sections of the book focus on the invisible pedagogue ("Lives Under Cover"), the model of power that dominates each layer of our discipline ("Seduction and Suspicion"), the ever-present, but seldom-included student voice ("'But You Never Asked!'"), and voices excluded from the professional development of composition ("Staking a Claim"). These sections are punctuated with four personal narrative pieces ("At the Risk of Being Personal . . .") in which the writers raise voices they may have seldom raised in public, sharing private moments from their own histories in the discipline.

There's No Guarantee

As we have said, this book intends to celebrate the dialogic potential of our discipline. But there will, by necessity, always be unheard voices in the dialogue, unmentioned perspectives, untapped resources. One colleague, grasping the gist of our project, suggested that a collection of "unheard voices" be published annually.

It is not uncommon for collections of essays to be preceded by a foreword written by a well-known person whose name alone sets up an approved context for the essays. We chose not to have such a foreword, wanting the pieces to create their own context. The fact that Kenney Withers and the reviewers for Southern Illinois University Press who understood the concept recommended that the collection be published brings visibility but not necessarily official sanction to these unheard voices. We do not want to give readers the impression that the voices need this validation in order to be worthy of being heard or that the goal of the book is to integrate ourselves into the presently unfolding story of the discipline rather than to cause, by our presence, changes in the way the story is unfolded. As Susan Miller reminds us: "Many . . . intellectual and 'practical' moves toward equality for composition reproduce the hegemonic superstructure by implying that bourgeois social climbing and successful competition for intellectual 'clout' are legitimate signs of improvement" (*Textual Carnivals* 51). Real changes in the way the story is unfolded, then, will not come from our simply being included or alluded to in the current narratives.

To become heard does not mean to become part of the center or to move away from the borders. Being published in this volume means that we—unheard voices and editors—have heard the unheard aspect of a contributor's voice and deemed that others should/will hear this aspect, too. Being published in this volume does not mean that the voice will ever be heard or need to be heard again. One publisher we discussed the project with was concerned about whether we and our contributors would ever publish anything elsewhere in the future. Unlike those in other collaborative tellings of the story of composition, the voices gathered together here may not be raised again next year in another collection. And then again some may be. As we write ourselves into the story of composition, our unheard voices will not necessarily become tomorrow's heard voices. There's no guarantee.

Notes

1. John Hollow's *CCC* review of *The English Coalition Conference* suggests that while he can understand the enthusiasm behind the story of

the discipline created at the conference, it doesn't ring true to him: "I am absolutely sure that, had I been there, I would have been happy to sign my name to all of [the claims]. Since I was not, however, and since my experience has been confined to reading this report, I have to say that much of what was concluded at the conference has for me the ring of overstatement" (474).

2. In his February 1992 "Editor's Column," Richard Gebhardt responds to charges that as editor of *CCC* he places "restrictions on acceptable forms of academic discourse" (7).

3. Similar feelings were expressed in *Rhetoric Review*'s first "Burkean Parlor," entitled "CCCC: Voices in the Parlor." In this opening exchange, journal readers had the opportunity to read a collaborative essay written by graduate students describing their feelings of exclusion from the discipline upon attending their first CCCC. This essay was followed by the reviews of blind referees from another journal to which the essay had been submitted. One reviewer commented that "one becomes an outsider [read: *unheard*] only if one allows that to happen" (210), that "you will only be outsiders as long as you define yourselves that way" (213). We feel, however, that this argument not only covers up a real prejudice against those who feel that their views or voices are unheard but also reveals a naive, Horatio Alger understanding of the profession.

Works Cited

Bartholomae, David. "Freshman English, Composition, and CCCC." *College Composition and Communication* 40 (1989): 38–50.

Beach, Richard, and Lillian Bridwell. *New Directions in Composition Research*. New York: Guilford, 1984.

Bullock, Richard, and John Trimbur, eds. *The Politics of Writing Instruction: Postsecondary*. Portsmouth, NH: Boynton, 1991. Gen. ed. Charles Schuster.

Burton, Robert S. "Response to Andrea A. Lunsford, 'Composing Ourselves: Politics, Commitment, and the Teaching of Writing.'" *College Composition and Communication* 41 (1990): 336–37.

"Call for Submissions." *College Composition and Communication* 41 (1990): 150.

"CCCC: Voices in the Parlor." *Rhetoric Review* 7 (1988): 198–213.

Conference on College Composition and Communication. *Statement of Principles and Standards for the Postsecondary Teaching of Writing*. Urbana, IL: NCTE, 1987.

Cooper, Charles R., and Lee Odell. *Research on Composing: Points of Departure*. Urbana, IL: NCTE, 1978.

Elbow, Peter. "Foreword: About Personal Expressive Academic Writing." *Pre/Text* 11 (1990): 7–20.

———. *What is English?* New York: MLA; Urbana, IL: NCTE, 1990.

Emig, Janet. "When Bad Things Happen to Good Ideas, III." NCTE Convention. Atlanta, 18 Nov. 1990.

Enos, Theresa. "Gender and Journals, Conservers or Innovators." *Pre/Text* 9 (1988): 209–14.

Frey, Olivia. "Beyond Literary Darwinism: Women's Voices and Critical Discourse." *College English* 52 (1990): 507–26.

Gebhardt, Richard C. "Editor's Column: Diversity in a Mainline Journal." *College Composition and Communication* 43 (1992): 7–10.

Hairston, Maxine. "Breaking Our Bonds and Reaffirming Our Connections." *College Composition and Communication* 36 (1985): 272–82.

Hillocks, George, Jr. *Research on Written Composition.* Urbana, IL: NCRE/ERIC Clearinghouse on Reading and Communication Skills, 1986.

Holbrook, Sue Ellen. "Women's Work: The Feminizing of Composition." *Rhetoric Review* 9 (1991): 201–29.

Hollow, John. Rev. of *The English Coalition Conference: Democracy Through Language*, ed. by Richard Lloyd-Jones and Andrew Lunsford. *College Composition and Communication* 41 (1990): 473–75.

"Information for *CCC* Authors." *College Composition and Communication* 42 (1991): 110–12.

Lauer, Janice M., and J. William Asher. *Composition Research: Empirical Designs.* New York: Oxford UP, 1988.

Lindemann, Erika, and Gary Tate, eds. *An Introduction to Composition Studies.* London: Oxford UP, 1991.

Lloyd-Jones, Richard, and Andrea Lunsford, eds. *The English Coalition Conference: Democracy Through Language.* Urbana, IL: NCTE; New York: MLA, 1989.

Lunsford, Andrea. "Composing Ourselves: Politics, Commitment, and the Teaching of Writing." *College Composition and Communication* 41 (1990): 71–82.

Lunsford, Andrea, Helene Moglen, and James F. Slevin, eds. *The Future of Doctoral Studies in English.* New York: MLA, 1989.

Miller, Susan. "The Feminization of Composition." *The Politics of Writing Instruction: Postsecondary.* Ed. Richard Bullock and John Trimbur. Portsmouth, NH: Boynton, 1991. 39–53. Gen. ed. Charles Schuster.

———. *Textual Carnivals: The Politics of Composition.* Carbondale: Southern Illinois UP, 1991.

North, Stephen. *The Making of Knowledge in Composition: Portrait of an Emerging Field.* Upper Montclair, NJ: Boynton, 1987.

Odell, Lee. "Diversity and Change: Toward a Maturing Discipline." *College Composition and Communication* 37 (1986): 395–401.

Ohmann, Richard. "Graduate Students, Professionals, Intellectuals." *College English* 52 (1990): 247–57.

Peterson, Jane E. "Valuing Teaching: Assumptions, Problems, and Possibilities." *College Composition and Communication* 42 (1991): 25–35.

Phelps, Louise Wetherbee. *Composition as a Human Science: Contributions to the Self-Understanding of a Discipline.* New York: Oxford UP, 1989.

Wallace, Elizabeth M., ed. *Part-time Academic Employment in the Humanities.* New York: MLA, 1984.

PART 1

LIVES UNDER COVER

The women who narrate the pieces in this section are "on the edge," leading professional "lives under cover," invisible to many in the field of composition. They are teachers not normally heard, working in classrooms and political situations not normally written about. Their voices take us to the margins of the discipline where we see them as outsiders looking in and as dedicated professionals getting by. Some of these writers help us to hear from others like them, composition professionals who share a sense of the creative power of a "life under cover." Despite the seemingly adverse political and material conditions they labor under, they are committed to teaching and to their students in ways as yet unaccounted for in the unfolding story of composition.

Still, the voices in this chapter are distinct and various. Some tell stories, others present the results of questionnaires and case studies, another writes an essay. And the quality of professional life they illustrate is not limited to part-time writing instructors. Indeed, many composition professionals practice to some degree at the margins of departments, colleges and universities, even the profession. From the stories these five writers tell, we learn attitudes and insights that can help us tap the creative potential of the "lives under cover" we all live.

Susan Pepper Robbins claims that her teaching friends rarely tell success stories but talk instead of how they are often overwhelmed by the lives of their students. Her short story describes an evening that begins in an inner-city English class and ends in an apartment in the projects, a time when the worlds of writing teacher and nontraditional student collide. Sarah Sloane's case studies reveal the strategies gay and lesbian students of English learn to make themselves both visible and invisible. The stories she has gathered show that gay and lesbian students often find they cannot talk from the full register of their experiences when teachers ask them to find their own voices. In a collage, Frances McConnel sets before us the powerfully charged language of the unfairly exploited—those "freeway flyers" who teach at more than one college at once—to give voice to their perspectives about their positions. In a reflective piece, Clare Frost, another part-time teacher, narrates her longing to be taken seriously as a professional and her attempts to join the "insiders," those full-fledged members of the composition community she sees surrounded by a high picket fence. Susan Hunter reads her experiences with freshman writing and writing across the curriculum against the grain of current narratives of composition to show how the pedagogy we prefer endangers our positions in the institutions and classrooms we practice in daily. She suggests that the tensions our different kind of pedagogy produces may force us to lead "lives under cover."

1

Tosca Was a Woman

Susan Pepper Robbins/*Hampden-Sydney College,*
Hampden-Sydney, Virginia

◆ ───────────────────────────────────────

   "Sharon's blood pressure's dropping caused her vascular dilation. That's why she's feeling some nausea, but the baby's just fine. There is no call for concern." Sharon came into Dr. Jones's office, leaned against the folding door and moaned "O God" in a West Indian accent. Her teeth looked too heavy for her body, maybe because the two eye teeth were gold. Her earrings ran in diminishing size and glitter up the arc of her ears, five in each ear. Chief and I both stood up to give her our chairs, but she waved us back.

   We were not a bad-looking couple, Chief Harris and I, sitting in Dr. Jones's office where we had rushed Sharon Palmer, crying and hanging pigeon-toed between us, from the community college where I teach and Chief Harris is "head honcho," he calls himself, of security. That is, we looked like we were from the same class, as my grandmother used to say. Only now, it's not a compliment like it used to be. Everyone wants to be beyond class, like rock stars. I know this from my sons.

Chief "Scooter" Harris is black or caramel colored, I am white or mushroom colored, and Dr. Jones, the OB-Gyn man, an acrylic black. Sharon has the complexion of an Alberta peach—she is a rosy orange when she is well, but she was sick and looked refrigerated.

I glued a look on the Chief's face to see how he was taking the news of "our" baby's condition. Except for our colors and city of origin—Richmond, still the capital of the Confederacy, black mayors to the contrary—we were looking and acting like concerned grandparents-to-be. Early forties, professionals. I had a new perm and blue poly-blend blazer, and Chief had his modified 'fro. We had both voted for Reagan two times; we cleared that up when we were carrying Sharon down in the elevator.

In the office, Chief and I both leaned forward to hear Dr. Jones. I nodded and then turned sideways to Sharon; at that point, I took in our—my and Chief's—failed efforts at style. Sharon's was on the money like students everywhere; ours was off-key like middle-aged people everywhere. It brought me closer to Chief Harris to see that he was—in spite of race—a failure at dressing. His club tie had sea horses on it, not all little ones, and looked ridiculous with his beige leisure suit. Under his white coat, Dr. Jones had on a blue oxford button-down. His stiff cuffs stuck out from the white coat. He was dressing Richmond. When he walked us to the door, I saw his khakis bussing his Weejuns. I felt my college days return. I was sad. Now I dressed the convenience-store style that all divorced women dress, the working ones.

Sharon moaned a West Indian "O God" again. She had on all natural fibers, like the doctor. Her pale blue dress was an icy polished cotton, expensive; a Laura Ashley I thought. I wished I could moan in a native tongue. White peole can't, among other things, moan. Sharon knew this and let go with one again. She was taking advantage of her minority status as usual. She was also happy to see that Dr. Jones had me beat at the education game. She knows my background from being in my classes two semesters: a terminal master's in higher ed.

She and the doctor dressed alike, but there the resemblance stopped. Sharon was looking for fun when she got pregnant, so her friends told me, and the doctor, sporting a big, gold wedding ring like Chief's, looked dead-dog serious, like Chief. Sharon could moan and weep, but she was not serious.

Sharon and I were menless; her "mon" had just given her up in my office when she called him to say she was "seek." Evidently, she woke him up. Drugs, I thought, because it was one-thirty. I'd been up since five grading papers. If I weren't a white middle-aged woman, I'd sell drugs and get to sleep late.

One "mon" left me by phone, too. Sharon and I had more in common than I had ever dreamed.

He hung up on her. The tears seeped out of her thick eyelashes and down on the blue dress. Chief by then had been summoned and took care of everything by saying, "Girl, forget him. Who's your doctor?" I was pressed into service by my division head, a woman who likes to help by assigning her faculty to do things her doctor won't let her do. So, Sharon between us, Chief and I left school.

It was pure fate that I had been teaching *Othello* at the time of the incident. Sharon is in my one o'clock class, sits in the back with her friends, the Roderigos of Richmond—plenty of money to put in their purses—thin-skinned mauve and pink leathers—which slap softly against them or hide in the folds of the new mini dresses. They grow their right little fingernails long and curved to scoop up toot. They explain freebasing to me the way I describe my latest cold pasta salad attempt in the faculty lounge.

I felt a teacherly pride that Sharon was using the same moan she had used when she read Cassio's "Reputation, I have lost my reputation." She hadn't had any sympathy for him and agreed with Iago's "pish." In fact, she got everyone in her claque to yell out "pish" whenever Cassio had anything to say. Her skills were transferring the way the workshop expert in learning strategies had said they must if we are really teaching.

When she got sick, Sharon had been reading Iago, and with her dark accent and better high school background she was the star of the crowd of wild girls, hissing "island" curses whenever Iago let fly about reputation or sex or money. Her sibilance added to the play, I had to admit.

I had just promised the class if they would try to appreciate Shakespeare's language, I would show *Citizen Kane* again. They seemed to agree and went on with the reading and forgot their weekly strategy of getting me started on my first days of teaching when students could read, not to mention write, when tokenism was the honored practice and black students were grateful if miserable to be in the white colleges. They like to hear my version of history; it's the music of nostalgia to them, like fifties songs and shoes.

My students are beyond the angst of segregation, and slavery is an exotica they memorize for history class. They feel free to pass judgments on Shakespeare that would stir up his dust. One student, Latonya, asked me if I had lived in the old days of separate water fountains and bathrooms. When I said yes, she said affably, her grandmother, who was in her forties, could remember all that too. She thought it would be nice if I got together with her grandmother to talk about those days. Was her grandmother bitter I asked. "No. Gumma is real sweet, a real sweet lady," she said.

I'm not a prize as a teacher as you can tell, or as a walk-on, stand-in grandmother to Sharon's baby. And I'm certainly not a consort Desdemona to Chief either. I was forty-two last year when I found out that Tosca was a woman, for instance, and I was shocked, having passed myself off in my family and classroom as the resident "culture vulture."

My talent as a teacher is pointing out to students that Shakespeare has some easy lines like "She is gone" or "Why did I marry?" They love that part of English 113. They like my addiction to audiovisual instruction too and beg to see *Citizen Kane*, which everyone knows I show in all classes every quarter.

I know all the tapes we have in the Learning Resource Center: Frost reading Frost; Eliot, Eliot; Lattimore, Homer. Our only opera in the LRC is *Madame Butterfly*, which I worked into a unit on "Man and Death" for freshman comp, English III. The cuts in budget kept our opera tape purchases down, so when I caught *Tosca* on "Live from the Met" this year, I was not prepared for her high bosom or murdering fury or suicide. I thought Tosca was a town.

When Sharon went down, swirling out of the orange desk, fluttering her hands on her stomach, her mascara dropping off her lashes in little dots on her cheeks, we called for Chief on the intercom. He came to class, and we dragged her out with her backpack and Toshiba music equipment. Gratifyingly, the class yelled after us, "She's gone." Chief stands six-feet-four and looks pregnant himself. His walkie-talkie clips on to all parts of his walrus self. He's Episcopalian. I'm Assembly of God and have adopted a Vietnamese boy. It's not going very well, but neither is my life with my biological child leftover from my divorce. Clifford is nineteen and has taken up a religion; except for that, I think that

I might have been a grandmother by now. Nyugen is fifteen and goes along with whatever Clifford says. They fellowship and share until I want to murder them. They hate Shakespeare, not that they know him, even the easy parts. I feel like I am living and cooking for Isaiah and his Oriental prayer-rug carrier. No, they do not have jobs—part- or full-time. No, they are not going to school because school "is of the world." " 'Nuf said," I yell back at them in my head using my old college lingo. I could use the language they gave up when they accepted Christ into their hearts. "Good shit," I believe it goes. Or, "pish."

As we drove up to the doctor's office, Chief turned the van's air conditioning up to full blast—pressing Sharon up against the door, while I braced myself in the back seat looking out between the two of them in the front. We had gunned across the Lee Bridge, Chief driving with his face turned to Sharon. I kept my eyes on the speedometer, which I hoped was broken.

The James River was black and glistening, and the rocks stuck out of it calmly as the foam flicked by. I stopped watching the speedometer and concentrated on the James.

After an hour with Dr. Jones, which included sitting in the waiting room watching a "soap" and conferencing with the nurse practitioner, it was time to take Sharon home.

Chief picked up Sharon under her arms and lifted her until her feet again hung pigeon-toed and swung her into the van. Then we backfired and roared into the Richmond no one admits is out there. Everyone I saw standing on the side of a boarded-up convenience store looked like he had just killed somebody to buy the Pepsi he was drinking.

Sharon's apartment was in the basement of a project. I had never been to one and don't want to visit one again. When the college van docked at the curb close to the building, I could see the expression on a pregnant woman's face when she yanked back her curtain. She looked bored and mad, like Tosca.

Still moaning, Sharon crawled on her sheetless bed behind the beaded curtain. Her two daughters would be home to fix supper, but I got out the last piece of white bread, to get Sharon to eat.

"How old are your daughters?" Chief was trying not to loom through the beads. "Seex and sev'n," she hissed. The cold white bread didn't blur the hiss at all. She looked at her digital clock radio and got a good station before we left. I heard Diana Ross singing to her old friend Marvin Gaye as we walked through the living room that had a collection of glass birds and silk ferns.

Aboard the van again, Chief and I blasted toward Western civilization, that is, the college. Used to Isaiah's rantings at home, I tuned in to Chief's cadences before we hit the line of traffic for Lee Bridge.

Passing Spring Street prison made him open up to full volume and lecture about Sharon. Rant and rave are not too strong to describe his delivery. He was staring at me, not at the streets flashing by.

The Richmond scenery kept improving as we got farther away from Sharon's, and that seemed to calm him down some.

"It's fungal spawn. That's what my father used to pound into my head. Fungal spawn. Here I have one child, a daughter, and I wouldn't think of having me more. With things like they are now, I'd have to be crazy. And I'm not talking money. I'm talking crime. And there's all kinds of crime. To me, having a baby and the father off and not thinking of coming back, married or in jail—I think Sharon's baby's daddy is married and told her it was her problem— now it would not surprise me one little bit if Sharon don't just kill him. I wouldn't blame her in a way; he couldn't be much. But like I say, it's a fungal spawn situation. Babies having babies. Them two little girls coming home to cook for their mama, her laying up in the bed that don't even have sheets. And what's in that place to cook? You can't cook sandwich meats, can you." Chief preached on, and when I gave him his cue for the finale—"What can we do, Chief?"— he screamed and started beating on the steering wheel so hard, I was afraid he might snap it off and send us airborne.

"She's gone, that one. There's not a bit of help you can give her. She'll have a baby next year. You should have heard her telling the doctor that she would take care of him if he tried anything funny. She meant a hysterectomy. I'm serious. She's into the so-called fast lane. Mark my words." I did, but I didn't know what to transfer them to.

2

Invisible Diversity: Gay and Lesbian Students Writing Our Way into the Academy

Sarah Sloane/*University of Puget Sound, Tacoma, Washington*

> The transformation of silence into language and action is an act of self-revelation, and that always seems fraught with danger.
> —Audre Lorde, "Breaking the Barriers of Silence"

Three years ago, I was sitting in a sunny classroom at Ohio State University taking my last course in rhetoric and composition before I would face the general exams that would admit me to candidacy for a Ph.D.[1] The course, "Gender and Writing," had been underway for about two weeks, and the teacher, Andrea Lunsford, had just asked each of us students to report to the class our plans for research that quarter. I was probably the only person in the room who knew it also happened to be National Coming Out Day, the day each October during which gays and lesbians are especially encouraged by their community to reveal their sexual orientation to friends, families, and coworkers. Although I knew many of the students in the room and felt relatively safe with them and my teacher, I still had to steel myself for what I was about to say. I was about to tell the class that I would be using the quarter to study how gay and lesbian student writers negotiate their evolving sense of personal identity within academic writing assignments, and within classroom contexts that often reflect the bigotry, ignorance, and fear of the larger communities that sometimes surround or comprise the academy. I knew my classmates would read my statement as indicating the possibility of my being lesbian. And I knew that that identification could be physically and psychically dangerous in the larger community in which we live. A few weeks before I had seen children throw eggs at a house rented by two gay men; marchers in a recent gay civil rights march in Columbus, Ohio, had been maced. I felt my heart rate pick up and my palms begin to sweat when it became my turn to speak. I counseled myself to talk loudly and clearly, and then I told my classmates about this project.

Because of this experience I was realizing yet again that visibility as a lesbian or gay person holds serious risk, even within an academy that is committed to nondiscrimination. However, telling the story of the outsider in the academy—outsider because of class, race, or sexual orientation, among other possibilities—is a powerful strategy of change. I view my collecting of stories of gay and lesbian academic writers here as an important project barely begun, as an important part of composing ourselves and fostering positive change. At the same time, I recognize that this evolving collection of stories is not comprised of definitive accounts. At this stage in the project, I intend only to report these stories and do not mean to imply representativeness or causality.

The gay and lesbian community in general comprises a unique minority because, to a large extent, members can choose whether or not to reveal their minority status to families, friends, coworkers, or in the case of those of us in higher education, to other members of the academic community. This characteristic of being able to reveal or deny membership within the lesbian or gay population clearly has huge ramifications for the ways this community defines and involves itself in the heterosexual majority culture. I hope to examine a small part of the dynamics of self-revelation and silencing that occur in the writing of lesbian and gay academic writers within the classroom community. In Lunsford's terms, I wish to examine how gay and lesbian student writers compose themselves.

The writing experiences of gay and lesbian students are complicated by their negotiating how visible to be. It is my sense, based on my own experience and on those reported to me by other gay and lesbian students, that the academic writing act in general can be complicated by questions of how much of self to reveal and that gay and lesbian students in particular learn to alter their discourse by omitting or transforming reports of personal experiences. All academic writing involves learning skills of selection, arrangement, and occasionally, concealment, but because of the larger context of bigotry often violently expressed against homosexuals, listening to how this invisible minority composes itself in the face of visible adversity may throw into relief some pressures in general under which academic writers compose.

It makes sense for gay and lesbian students to question the value of visibility. Stereotypes of gay and lesbian people are particularly vicious among college students (Page and Yee), and students who are aware of their gay identity learn quickly to hide it (D'emilio) or to pass as heterosexuals. On the other hand, enforced invisibility (related to what Adrienne Rich calls "compulsory heterosexuality") is profoundly unhealthy for gay and lesbian adolescents' process of developing identity and self-esteem. While strategies of *omission* (silencing those parts of our experience that are not safe to reveal) and *transformation* (such as "pronoun laundering") in the short run may comprise expedient strategies of staying safe, in the long run they may stunt the processes of students composing themselves as active participants in a community built on mutual trust and respect.

While scant research has been devoted to the processes of gay and lesbian identity formation (although many writers are quick to speculate about the essentialist or social-constructionist causes of homosexual identity), researchers agree that the development of adolescent gay or lesbian identity is a process fraught with difficulty. Parmeter and Reti document the high rates of suicide attempts among gay adolescents in California; a more recent study (*Ohio News*, August 1991) claims one-third of gay men between the ages of fourteen and twenty-one attempt to take their own lives. It is my own sense that a lack of role models, missing family support, and invisibility or negative stereotypes of gays and lesbians within the media coordinate to create a stifling climate of homophobic oppression in this country. Our gay and lesbian undergraduate students write against this climate and against the stereotypes believed by their peers (Page and Yee 115–16). Further, in their chosen careers following their university experience, gays and lesbians continue to learn strategies of omission and transformation, uses of language that Hall calls "balancing strategies" of denial, dissociation, and avoidance (73–74). If we understand our classroom context as directly related to the larger communities surrounding the academy, we can begin to understand the difficult rhetorical challenge posed to this invisible minority: Speak authentically and in your own voice, but don't reveal who you really are. Often it is far easier and safer to pass as heterosexual.

I report here on two students, one gay and one lesbian, and their experiences as writers within the academy. I plan to add to these reports over time in the hope of using this particular context to writers' experience as a site from which to examine the charged boundaries in general between speech and silence, visibility and invisibility, safety and risk in language practices.

I first attempted to contact undergraduate students through a local Gay and Lesbian Student Association (GALA). Identifying myself as a lesbian, I asked students who would be willing to discuss their experiences in writing courses at the university to call me at home. Students did call, and we made arrangements to meet in anonymous places: fast-food restaurants and coffee shops in the campus area. Some students showed up for these meetings; some did not. Perhaps my experience with Phil is representative. Phil made and canceled two appointments to meet at a local coffee shop and did not show up at the time of the third appointment we had made. Because he had asked me not to call him (he was concerned about his roommates learning he had agreed to be interviewed), I never learned why he failed to appear at any of the three appointments he made. Further, although six gay men initially contacted me via GALA, no lesbian contacted me. In the interest of presenting here the stories of both a gay man and a lesbian woman, I interviewed a woman in the English department whom I knew was a lesbian. Again, I want to emphasize that the following two descriptions of the academic writing experiences of Jeffrey and Jennifer are not meant to be representative or typical. Instead, I present the following two brief stories based on retrospective interviews and careful reading of extant drafts of class papers, as two stories of outsiders trying to balance their developing sense of identity as gay or lesbian within the demands of academic writing assignments and situations. I hope that in these stories you can see Jeffrey and Jennifer (not their real names, of course) weighing authenticity against safety, self-revelation against distortion or silence.

Jeffrey, a gay undergraduate communications major at a large midwestern university, had had a spotty academic career. He had flunked out of the university several years ago and had recently returned. We met in a local hamburger restaurant while he talked about his experiences as a gay man in his academic writing classes. In his freshman composition class, Jeffrey was required by his teacher to write an essay about a significant personal experience. He chose to write about a Boy Scout snorkeling trip to the Florida Keys. The paper began with the sentence, "She rocked me in her arms." The first paragraph continues in this vein, leading many readers to believe they are hearing a description of first sexual, and specifically heterosexual, encounter. At the end of the paragraph, however, Jeffrey "reveals" himself as a snorkeler, and reveals the "she" of the paragraph as the ocean. In his interview, Jeffrey said he began the paper with the metaphor of ocean as woman because he likes to find "an odd, creative, or different approach" to an assigned topic; he said he intended to mislead the reader in the first paragraph because it would be more "creative." I am not a psychologist. However, I suspect Jeffrey was being more than just creative. In this passage, I hear Jeffrey putting on a heterosexual mask and speaking in a heterosexual voice.

In the next writing class Jeffrey took, a sophomore-level "critical writing" course, Jeffrey was assigned to write an essay defining family. He chose to write about whale pods, or the dynamics within groups of whales, as an example of family. Jeffrey explained to me that this essay grew out of his own interest in animals and that he enjoyed developing his own "creative" definition of family. A family, as Jeffrey expressed it both in this paper and in an interview, is "made up of love," "encompasses experiences which members can look back on," and "does not necessarily include reproduction." He says love and bonding are two major ties within families, and his choice of topic was meant to reveal these ties operating in a "creative" context. In both his essays—his one about groups of whales existing as families and his earlier one about snorkeling in a womanly ocean—I hear Jeffrey laboring under a double burden of fulfilling an academic assignment and remaining true to his own authentic voice and vision. By choosing writing strategies he called "creative," Jeffrey was able to mask his homosexual identity and later to express obliquely his resistance to conventional, heterosexually based definitions of family.

The academic paper that Jeffrey had tried to write most recently when I spoke with him was written for a junior-level communications class three years earlier. Students in that class were asked to decide together what topic the class as a whole would write about. According to Jeffrey, the majority of the class wanted to write about the pros and cons of the forced quarantine of AIDS carriers. Jeffrey argued strenuously in the discussion before the class vote that he wanted to write instead about pit bulls—about "people's ostracism of the breed and prejudices and misconceptions about them." Jeffrey said he "fought tooth and nail" for that topic. Unfortunately for Jeffrey, the class voted to write about AIDS. Jeffrey said that as he walked home from school that day, he knew he was "never going to write that paper." During the same period, he was falling in love with a man he worked with; he said he was experiencing his first crush and that it was the first time he had openly acknowledged his gay feelings to himself. The assignment about AIDS took on a heightened significance for Jeffrey, and the rest of the quarter was traumatic for him. In his own words: "I disappeared. I went into my room and locked the door." Jeffrey eventually failed that communications class and dropped out of school. He says the required paper about AIDS in combination with his sense of his own emerging homosexual identity created such confusion in him that he was unable to write.

Currently Jeffrey is reenrolled at the university, an active member of the student Gay and Lesbian Association, and pursuing a career as a nonfiction writer with a special interest in writing about animal rights. Twenty-seven years old at the time of these interviews, Jeffrey hopes to finish his bachelor's degree within two years and to find employment as a feature writer for an environmental magazine. Outside of school, Jeffrey pursues a variety of writing projects for his own enjoyment: he writes science fiction and sometimes acts as a game master who writes scenes and descriptions for his friends who participate in role-playing games like "Dungeons and Dragons." Jeffrey has not felt blocked as a writer since he has returned to school, and he says he enjoys both his academic writing and his extracurricular stories and scripts. While I would like to claim that Jeffrey's current academic success is linked to his newly integrated gay identity, of course I cannot make that claim based on what he has told me. Therefore I report Jeffrey's story, as I report Jennifer's following story, simply to provide a limited and partial record of gay and lesbian undergraduate experience within the writing classroom.

I turn now to a second story of gay and lesbian writing in the academy. At the time of my interviews, Jennifer was a twenty-five-year-old woman finishing a master's degree in English at the same large midwestern university Jeffrey attended. Three years earlier, Jennifer had graduated from a small, private liberal arts college in the Midwest where she had completed a bachelor's degree in English. Because Jennifer saved copies of every academic assignment she had written since she was a freshman in college, I am able to report here how her teachers responded in their written comments to her emerging identity as a lesbian academic writer. Jennifer was not asked by her teachers to write personal experience narratives nor to address political issues as was Jeffrey; nonetheless, Jennifer's emerging sense of herself as a lesbian affected her choice of topic, her methods of analysis (and exercise of her skills as a feminist critic), some of her journal entries, and her extracurricular writing.

Jennifer shared with me thirty-one academic papers and several journals she wrote about English, American, and French literature between her freshman and senior years as an English major in college. In her papers, Jennifer increasingly refers to lesbian authors, feminist theory, and her own lesbian feelings and experiences. Her teachers respond in a variety of ways to Jennifer's experiments with the traditional form and content of an academic paper; Jennifer progressively reclaims and challenges the conventions of the academic literature paper, to varying degrees of receptiveness from her literature professors. I report here on Jennifer's academic papers chronologically, noting specifically those papers in which she wrote about lesbianism or sexuality in literature.

Jennifer's papers written during her freshman year for literature survey classes were short papers that looked at assigned texts thematically; she wrote one paper about ironic elements and another about character development within a novel. She received high grades on these papers, which were clear, intelligent analyses of particular texts without references to anything personal and certainly with no reference to homosexuality. (In fact, Jennifer managed to avoid using "I" in her papers for most of her first two years in college.) During her sophomore year, Jennifer made two direct references to sexuality within a text in two papers for a course on Shakespeare. In these two papers, one on Shakespeare's love sonnets and the second on disguises in *Twelfth Night*, neither reference to sexuality is commented on by the teacher. However, in a paper written about *Hamlet* for a class taken her junior year, a teacher corrects a particular line in Jennifer's writing for the first time. Jennifer had written about "the closet scene in Hamlet," saying, "He goes on and on, and is just about to rape his mother." The professor corrects the phrase "just about to rape" and suggests the alternative, "almost to the point of erotic engagement with . . . " Another of Jennifer's junior-year teachers comments appreciatively "Sock! Good rhythm!" when Jennifer describes Molly Bloom in Joyce's *Ulysses* as a woman who "simultaneously belies and affirms the traditional female stereotype." The content of Jennifer's papers begins to be informed by feminist literary theory in her junior year, and her literature professors begin to approach her papers' content by commenting on Jennifer's writing style.

For example, in a paper on "The Abuse of Ritual Structure in *King Lear*," Jennifer invokes Victor Turner and makes the large claim that rituals performed in "times of social and cultural crisis" are normally "therapeutic," but that Shakespearean tragedy inverts this relationship and rituals become poisonous or fatal instead. Her paper ends with the claim that "This [abuse of ritual] brings about the descent of the society and the tragic end for all." Jennifer's teacher edits stylistically several places in this three-page "B" essay, changing "descent of the society" into "near ruin," for example. In response to two paragraphs in which Jennifer questions *Lear*'s portrait of "the institution of marriage" and the play's portrayal of "the relation between parents and children," her teacher comments, "Big, undefined terms again obscure the argument, swimming around in the wild blue yonder." While in general no clear pattern of response emerges from the comments of Jennifer's teachers to her papers questioning marriage, family relationships, or sexuality of fictional characters, it is fair to say that at times her teachers wrote more numerous stylistic comments when the subject matter she approached was risky, provocative, or charged.

Not until Jennifer's senior year, and at first only in exchanges with a teacher who is an "out" lesbian, did Jennifer identify herself as a lesbian in one of her academic assignments. For example, in a course on French women writers, Jennifer wrote a journal entry that combined discussions of Colette's *The Pure and the Impure* with comments about her own joy in a new lesbian relationship. Jennifer writes, "I feel like I must be having this incredibly long dream." The professor writes in the margin, "Normal feeling." In papers for other classes that year, papers about works by Hellman, Morrison, and Colette, Jennifer analyzed relations among the women characters, discussed the possibility and promise of lesbian relationships in books, and connected these possibilities with her own life. In general, her teachers responded sympathetically to Jennifer's attempts to link her evolving sense of personal identity with the literary texts she read and analyzed.

Today, Jennifer says she writes about lesbian and gay people, ideas, and experiences in her letters and personal writing "for the visibility part of it. If I could, I would really want to be out [in my writing.] To get people to see that lesbians are in all facets of life. That they're not the deviant freaks that everyone is likely to think we are. That there are lots of us." She recently was granted a master's degree in English and is employed as a member of the communications staff at a large commercial bank.

My interviews with other lesbian and gay undergraduate student writers reveal that they feel alienated from the academy in a number of ways. One says, "I don't like academic writing. It's hard. I don't like doing it. I feel like the writing I'm doing is a waste. Someone's just going to grade it. My little five-to-seven page seminar paper is never going to matter to anything or anyone. I'm just going through the motions." Another says, "In this one class, I found the postmodern stuff really alienating because it was so much about heterosexuality. White boys. I was really tired of reading pompous white boys. I tried to write about that in my journal for the class." In my interviews with Jennifer and Jeffrey and other gay and lesbian students, comments about alienation from the texts, assignments, and discussions of writing classes were common. In many cases, however, gay and lesbian students were avid writers outside of the classroom, writing poems, short stories, or science fiction in journals or for their friends.

In an essay presented at CCCC in 1989, Sarah-Hope Parmeter ended her presentation about being silenced as an undergraduate writer and her current endeavor to allow divergent voices to speak in her own classroom with an exhortation not to silence those whose experience is different from the majority experience. She says such silencing encourages the separation of the heart from the university, and my discussions with Jeffrey and Jennifer, as well as my own experiences, certainly echo her findings. When we teach writing, we are teaching tools and systems of finding, defining, and conveying realities. Like Parmeter, I want to create a classroom context in which difference is respected, where self and voice are directly connected, and where all minority writers find safe places to speak in their own voices.

Even as I write this essay, in my mind I am imagining a parallel essay in which I say what I really think about the root causes of Jennifer's academic successes and Jeffrey's initial academic failure and I reveal my own rocky road to my present place as a faculty member at a small liberal arts school. Then I think of my own shaky status as a brand-new member of a small English department, and I wonder how that status will affect how I interact with my colleagues and what I will say. As a new faculty member, I have become a member of the academy with a new privilege and status; but my questions about how much of self I may safely reveal in my public writing, at conferences, and to my colleagues still need to be negotiated. This essay is already one answer to that wondering.

As a writing teacher, I am striving to create academic writing situations that allow students room to express experiences that dissent from the white, middle-class, heterosexual, and male experiences that are so often codified in our curriculum, assignments, and responses. "Personal experience" writing assignments in particular can require our gay and lesbian undergraduates to perform rhetorical tasks of double difficulty, tasks that require a balancing act between self-revelation and self-concealment. I imagine my students writing essays that do link the heart with words, that link private and public, home and school, and that allow true personal statement into academic writing. As I explore the experiences of gay and lesbian student writers in the academic classroom, I better understand my own academic experiences, and I feel better prepared to open my courses to the voices and experiences of all my students.

Acknowledgments

My friend and partner, Judy Doenges, helped a great deal in the early stages of this research, and I would like to acknowledge her indispensable aid, especially in conceiving of this project and in contacting some of these students.

Notes

1. I delivered talks based on a portion of the information contained in this essay at the 1990 Feminist Graduate Student Conference in Madison,

Wisconsin, and at the 1989 Conference on College Composition and Communication in Seattle, Washington.

Works Cited

Crew, Louie, and Karen Keener. "Homophobia in the Academy: A Report of the Committee on Gay/Lesbian Concerns." *College English* 43 (1981): 682–89.

Deisher, Robert W. "Adolescent Homosexuality: Preface." *Journal of Homosexuality* 17 (1989): 195–223.

D'emilio, John. "The Campus Environment for Gay and Lesbian Life." *Academic* 76 (1990): 16–19.

Gilligan, Carol. *In a Different Voice: Psychological Theory and Women's Development*. Cambridge: Harvard UP, 1982.

Hall, Marny. "The Lesbian Corporate Experience." *Journal of Homosexuality* 12 (1986): 60–75.

Kourany, Ronald F. C. "Suicide among Homosexual Adolescents." *Journal of Homosexuality* 13 (1987): 11–117.

Lorde, Audre. "Breaking the Barriers of Silence." Interview with Lauren Greene. *Woman of Power* 14 (1989): 39–45.

Lunsford, Andrea. "Composing Ourselves: Politics, Commitment, and the Teaching of Writing." *College Composition and Communication* 41 (1990): 71–82.

Ohio News. Aug. 1991: 41.

Page, Stewart, and Mary Yee. "Conception of Male and Female Homosexual Stereotypes among University Undergraduates." *Journal of Homosexuality* 12 (1985): 109–18.

Parmeter, Sarah-Hope. "Writing in the Real World: Homophobia vs. Community in the Composition Classroom." Conference on College Composition and Communication. Seattle, 17 Mar. 1989.

Parmeter, Sarah-Hope, and Irene Reti, eds. *The Lesbian in Front of the Classroom: Writings by Lesbian Teachers*. Santa Cruz, CA: HerBooks, 1988.

Pharr, Suzanne. *Homophobia: A Weapon of Sexism*. Little Rock: Chardon, 1988.

Rich, Adrienne. "Women and Honour: Some Notes on Lying." *On Lies, Secrets, and Silence, Selected Prose 1966–1978*. New York: Norton, 1986.

3

Freeway Flyers:
The Migrant Workers
of the Academy

Frances Ruhlen McConnel/University of California, Riverside

●◇ ───────────────────────────────────────

REBECCA: I did it because I needed a job and there were no full-time
jobs. I sent out twenty applications one year and got no
interviews. Started at one CC[1] where I took over after an
instructor got ill. Ended up teaching at four CCs and one
private college. Stopped because I finally got a full-time job. I
was ready to quit, so burned out. Every ten weeks you don't
know if you will be anywhere. I couldn't spend money because I couldn't automatically expect to get a job.

Rebecca, an A.B.D. in English, has just gotten a full-time job
at a community college. She was a lecturer at a UC campus from
1979 to 1983 and went on to work as a "freeway flyer" in Northern
California, teaching twenty-four classes a year at five campuses—
one was twenty-five miles south and one was twenty-five miles

north of the more central campuses. Rebecca says that meant "about twenty-two hours of teaching a week. Two hours a day, every day, prep and grading, about six hours a week commuting, two hours a week running off material. Two hours administrative. As an hourly I got paid anywhere from $24 an hour to $36—about $2,000 a month, including summers." She lives alone.

REBECCA: Of course, the schools knew you were teaching else-where. It was set up that way. You could only teach 8.99 classes in a district; you can't teach more than seven by five percent full-time or they would have to give you a contract (and benefits). (Union rule: this is how the union can work against hourlies. They do nothing to help hourlies.) You also have to watch how many *hours* you teach because this rule also applies to how many days a year you teach. This is why I taught Saturday classes that met only once a week. You have to watch out [for] yourself, because if you teach too many days, suddenly you'll discover they can't hire you the next quarter. You have to go out of the district.

Rebecca (not her real name—I am using pseudnonyms throughout) was a respondent to an open-answer questionnaire I created and distributed in 1989. Rebecca as well as my other respondents are known as "freeway flyers"—lecturers or part-timers or adjunct faculty members who teach at more than one institution at the same time. Freeway flyers are also called "gyp-sies," but this term is misleading. Like wildcats or grizzlies, they have a large range as their home territory, but they are not nomadic. Often, they are stuck where they are, being, often, women with families in permanent locations.

I developed my open-answer questionnaire on freeway flying as a result of my own experience beginning in the academic year of 1987–88, when I taught composition at the California State Poly-technic University, Pomona (in the CSU system), literary analysis (a thinly disguised freshman writing course) at Claremont McKen-na College (a private college in the Claremont consortium), and creative writing at the University of California, Riverside (in the UC system). In my conversations with other lecturers at these schools, I discovered, to my surprise, that quite a few of them also taught in more than one four-year college, that several also taught at two-year colleges, and that others had done so in the past. I wondered what had led other freeway flyers into such a life and what it was like for them. Since at that time I had read little about the experience of such teachers, I decided to find out about it directly, through the use of an open-answer questionnaire. I asked where my respondents taught and how they got into freeway flying; the differences in their students, their programs, their roles, their working conditions (including pay and benefits), their status, and their autonomy—or lack of it—at their different institutions; the advantages and disadvantages they saw in being freeway flyers; their preferences in teaching approaches; and their suggestions for improving the system. I also asked them to fill out a time-study table, including their course loads and hours spent teaching, grading and preparing, conferencing, running off materials, doing administrative work, and commuting.

I distributed my questionnaire on freeway flying to colleagues who taught writing (creative writing as well as freshman writing, and, in one case, speech) at my campuses and asked those colleagues to distribute it at their other campuses, including two-year colleges. I received approximately twenty responses—perhaps not a representative sample of California freeway flyers but a powerful group of individual voices telling stories that have rarely been publicly told.

What struck me most in going over the questionnaires was not the abstract conclusions I might draw from my survey nor the statistics I could put together but simply the power of these voices. In this essay I will do little in the way of filtering this material through the usual generalization process of such a study. Instead, I will present to you the words of eleven of the most articulate of my respondents, edited for brevity and in a few cases, for clarity.[2] I am doing this partly because it seems to me one of the things that most dehumanizes lecturers is the way they are often treated as bodies to fill slots, numbers to plug into an institution's statistical needs. (In many institutions, as compositionist Cynthia Tuell has pointed out, lecturers are not listed on college schedules by their own names but rather by section numbers, letters, or simply by a ditto mark under the name of the chair of the program.) What is needed is a stronger sense in the academic community of lecturers as dedicated and highly skilled individuals doing difficult jobs under trying circumstances—circumstances that could hardly be more trying than those of the teachers whose voices will be heard in this essay—freeway flyers.

This essay is organized according to the questions I asked, with time out along the way to introduce my respondents.

This Is Tuesday—It Must Be Irvine: Differences among Students

The most pressing of a freeway flyer's job is dealing with the differences in the students among the various schools. How do they see this instructor? How does the instructor see them? Is the lecturer, today, the only middle-class person in a classroom of well-off, blonde, California Anglos? And tomorrow, is she or he the only second-generation, college-educated person in a classroom of a variety of ethnic immigrants? What stands between this lecturer and the students, or these students and the task before them: boredom and complacency? lack of respect? desperation for future job security? poor preparation? first-language interference? exhaustion from work or partying? How can the freeway-flying lecturer provide this variety of students with what they need?

REBECCA: Some people can't do this job: they need more prep time. They get too rattled. There is a super problem teaching at a variety of campuses—all are different. You have to readjust your thinking. ("This is Tuesday; it must be Irvine.") A 1A class would have to be done differently on different campuses. One CC has underprepared minorities. But another has glib, adequate Anglo students. It takes an extra effort to adjust your teaching.

JOAN: The variety is enormous, even within the same system (CSU, for example). Some of the variety is in the ethnic or socioeconomic makeup. Some has to do with motivation of students, integration of minorities. Much has to do with whether the classes are day or evening. There are enormous differences in preparation, knowledge, motivation, time available, etc. Adult students have far different needs and should be handled quite differently from adolescents. Materials and methods have to be realistically geared to interests and experiences of the groups being taught. Sometimes this is not possible for a couple of reasons: (1) Materials are set by the department. (2) "Freeway Flyers" don't have the time to change materials to fit each class. Much as I hate admitting it, I have to say that teaching under those conditions means students do not get equal educational experiences. It is desirable, but not realistic.

Joan, my oldest respondent, has been a teacher for twenty years. She has taught at three CSU campuses, two private colleges, and four CCs.

JOAN: Typically, I taught sixteen courses per year—two semesters and the summer—averaging about $26,000 a year. I had no dependents at the time and I lived alone. At first it was with one college full-time, then at night while I held jobs in industry during the day. Most of these jobs were in mass media, both in writing and management positions. While I began teaching English classes because my degrees are in English, I eventually taught journalism and management classes as well because of my experience in the work force. This is what brought me to being a freeway flyer for the past four years. In a small private college in L.A. I began teaching ESL, as well as an incredible variety of other disciplines. Later, when an opportunity arose at a CC to teach ESL full-time, I applied, because I had found that particularly rewarding. That led to my teaching at my present CSU, which is now the only college I teach at. Frankly, I got incredibly burned out rushing from college to college, having to prepare anything up to five different courses per semester. I don't think I could handle more than two colleges at a time anymore.

DEBRA: Students at CPU are more pressured to live by the book (the syllabus) and to get good grades as quickly and as painlessly as possible, while the CC night students whom I teach already know the professional value in business dollars of "being an effective writer." Therefore, I find them much more willing to adopt long-term goals and to work harder for them. They also appear to feel less threatened by the instructor's authority or expertise, perhaps because training is a regular ongoing part of business life. CC students do not resent preparatory classes as much as four-year students, possibly because they receive college credit for their work. The resentments and hostility that four-year students bring to basic composition classes affect their attitudes and performance in reading and writing so seriously that an instructor often finds it necessary to deal with self-esteem problems in the first four weeks.

Debra has taught at two CSU colleges and one CC. Currently she teaches at one CSU and one CC.

DEBRA: I teach usually three courses a quarter but never in summer because I have two school-age children. We have a two-income household (thank goodness) because I bring in an unpredictable $10,000 to $15,000 a year. Secretaries make more than I do and don't take their jobs home.

GEORGE: CC students vary *widely*, but most are students from working-class backgrounds or ethnic minorities, in which education is marginalized. Many, however, as a consequence, view school as their economic salvation (though many regard it as an advanced high school also). The same is true of CSU students, to a lesser degree: a larger percentage are of the middle class; many are academically inclined; *most* are pre-professionals and regard school as a professional school. UC students—and private-school students—tend to come from higher-class backgrounds, to be the "good students"; and, unfortunately, to view writing as having nothing to do with them (they received "A"s in high school, so what is *your* problem?). I stereotype, of course.

George is a recent Ph.D. in English literature. He has taught at two CCs, at a small private college, at CSU and UC. At present he teaches about fifteen writing courses a year, spending about eighty hours a week at his work. He has a two-income household, with one dependent. He was one of the few people I interviewed who felt his schools did not know or approve of his teaching at more than one job.

GEORGE: The UC school where I teach did *not* know I was teaching at other schools. TAs at UCs are in a rather precarious position—not receiving enough money to live (at least in California), yet being expected to devote full-time to graduate work. Most schools view lecturers as second-class teachers and view lecturers (or TAs) who teach elsewhere as Judases who do not give full loyalty. Of course, the paradox is that the lecturers/part-time lecturer system (or TAship) positively *encourages* free-lancing, at least economically, because of lack of benefits and scheduling uncertainties.

UC instruction generally requires more assignments and more advanced assignments (i.e., analysis, literary analysis, research). CSU courses *tend* to be more basic, oftentimes either completely open or completely restricted, while courses assume a wide level of student skills. CC courses (at least in basic writing) assume minimal or *no* writing competence, for instance my schools don't require essays, only paragraphs from basic writing students—a real mistake. My private college, on the other hand, generally *assumes* writing competence of their students—even when it doesn't exist. But this puts the linquistic monkey on the student's back—a rather comfortable position for *faculty* at least.

It Varies from Gig to Gig: Differences in Policy

California freeway flyers have not only a specialized cross-cultural knowledge of students enrolled at different educational institutions but also of those institutions themselves. I have found that at different colleges the policies and expectations concerning lecturers and writing programs, while generally viewed by those colleges as the only rational policies and expectations, or even the only ones imaginable, actually exist as a result of historical and demographic accident, power struggles within the schools, personalities and ideologies of chairs and administrators, and other social circumstances. For instance, at one UC campus, writing lecturers teach seven courses a year, are expected to do research in composition theory, are paid competitive wages, are encouraged to choose their own texts, and are consulted on course and scheduling preferences. At another UC campus, writing lecturers teach nine courses a year, are defined as nonresearch employees, are paid the minimum the union allows, are required to use an assigned text, are treated cavalierly by secretaries, and can have their schedules and classes changed up through the second week of classes. The main reason for the differences between the two campuses seems to be that the writing program in the first school began with a powerful chair and backing from crucial administrators and the second school did not.

Freeway flyers can gain a special comparative knowledge of schools and school systems, a knowledge that could be valuable for their schools. But that knowledge instead tends to work against them, leading to frustration, and sometimes demoralization, since they are so seldom consulted on these matters.

Harriet is a fairly recent Ph.D. who has taught at two private colleges and one CC simultaneously. She teaches six to seven semester courses a year and makes from $15,000 to $20,000.

HARRIET: One private college where I taught was extremely professional—much freedom to design courses, very creative environment, excellent clerical support and equipment, good office space.

Another private college was very unprofessional—little to no clerical support, stinginess in terms of supplies and xeroxing, too much reliance on student evaluations (*only* criterion for judging teaching), grossly inadequate office space. My CC ranks between the above in all respects.

DEBRA: Good heavens. There is a Gulf of Mexico between CSU and my CC. The priority at my CC is not to give too many high grades and next, to submit a written "rationale" for how each grade is determined. CSU has a vaguer policy that one must acquire by osmosis. CSU seems to emphasize (more openly) teaching for critical thinking, clarity of expression, and uniqueness of viewpoint. Both schools send in a highly qualified observer when one is first hired; and the observer's reports (on myself, at least) are remarkably astute and fair.

KAREN: Private colleges expect more one-on-one work with students than does the UC or CSU (little is expected at CCs). Invitations to meetings and get-togethers are given at all institutions, but peer contact and support is minimal at most.

Karen has taught at UC, CSU, CC, and private colleges, sometimes simultaneously.

KAREN: I usually spend about forty-four hours a week at my six or seven courses a year. I make about $17,000 a year. Two incomes, one dependent. I got into this work while a graduate student, which I still am (in 1981 as an M.F.A. student at UCI, as a TA). I have taught only as a lecturer, and I also worked as a technical writer and administrative assistant while in graduate school. I have never received benefits; the best pay is at *some* private colleges and in the UC system.

CELIA: [What's expected of me] varies from gig to gig. However *all* the institutions in which I've taught expected a fairly constant and demanding involvement with students, and often they expected a good deal of "extracurricular" activity (serving on committees, advising students, judging contests, overseeing conferences and reading series, *ad infinitum*) for which I was [not]/have not been given recompense.

Celia is a published poet who has taught at two private colleges and two UC campuses. She teaches three to six creative writing courses per year, makes from $9,000 to $13,000 a year, has a two-income family with two children.

CELIA: During the last seven years I've taught on a temporary part-time basis at five different colleges and universities, usually simultaneously. Doing so was a problem in terms of energy and time expended in commuting from one campus to another. Before teaching at the college/university level, I taught in several preschools and substitute taught in elementary schools. (I was a student as well.) I no longer take on multiple teaching jobs because they seriously and adversely affect the quality of my life. However, I'm poorer for this choice.

I Believe in Freedom for the Teacher: Autonomy

The question of autonomy was probably the most exacerbating of my questions, since many of my respondents seem to have had some taste of the power and freedom of having autonomy over classes, and many found not having it an affront to their skill, knowledge, experience, and sense of themselves as professionals.

HARRIET: At my favorite private college, I have total freedom over the content and approach to my courses. This makes my teaching much more enjoyable because I choose materials which are exciting to me. Teaching there is an incredibly rewarding experience, so much so that it would hurt to give it up for a full-time position elsewhere (although I would have to take such an opportunity).

At my other private college, I have no freedom to design courses but a fair amount of freedom to choose texts. At my CC there is little opportunity to be creative—one gets the feeling that people there have been teaching the same courses the same way for thirty years.

JOAN: I prefer to choose my own texts once I have become familiar with the student body and the objectives of the institutions and departments. Frankly, I welcome using department materials the first couple of times I teach a course, but I would prefer total control. Some schools permit this completely; others allow no flexibility whatever. There seems to be no pattern in this: it doesn't matter whether it's public, private, within the same system. I cannot be as effective teaching from materials I feel are inadequate or which approach learning from a way I am not comfortable with. Sometimes I think student learning suffers enormously under authoritarian department rigidity.

REBECCA: I believe in freedom for the teacher. I don't want to use *your* book because I have to. And I hate grammar texts. But I think you should be able to explain why you are using a text. You need accountability. The funny thing at these schools is that you don't even get told what to teach. You have to seek out a course outline and go to the bookstore and check out what other people have used in a course.

At the CCs no one knows what's going on in the classes. Half of the hourlies didn't know what they were supposed to be teaching. They didn't know the level of the course. They got no guidance. Some of the courses are supposed to be transferable to state universities for credit, but if the full requirements aren't asked, the state universities won't accept the credit. I've read placement essays and I could see the instructors didn't know the difference between 201A and 201B.

There Must Be Something Wrong with You: Status

I did not begin this study with the idea that I would be exposing the miseries of an exploited class. I had no idea the answers to my question about status would be so painful to read. I was unhappy myself; I had gone from teaching literature and creative writing full-time on a tenure track, to not getting tenure, to taking time off teaching, to coming back as a lecturer teaching mostly composition. I felt then and still feel that teaching composition is as important as teaching my speciality—Shakespearean tragedy—but clearly the academy did not think so. Though I believed my feelings of rejection and failure were peculiar to my history, I found this was not the case.

EVELYN: UC looks at part-timers as outsiders, people who aren't good enough. At the CCs, they are often scared of us because many part-timers have more experience and are better trained than the full-timers. Lots of part-timers have Ph.D.s and are better qualified. At CSU, they are suspicious of people with full-time qualifications who have only part-time jobs. They figure there must something wrong with you.

Evelyn has taught at one UC campus, two CSU campuses, and one CC. She has a Ph.D. in linguistics and has taught languages as well. She began teaching in CCs in 1977. She teaches approximately four courses a quarter in three different schools. She has three dependents, one income.

EVELYN: Don't use my name. I'm not proud of living at the poverty level. I have some horror stories I could tell, but I don't want it known they happened to me. I'm saving them for my memoirs.

I have to take time off every once in a while, so I don't burn out. Teaching writing can burn you out. Sometimes it's just the summer. I did office work for six months once, where I could stop thinking and evaluating papers for a while. I can't escape them; I have file cabinets full of papers, a study full of them at home.

KAREN: Status is relatively low at all the institutions but particularly regarding the administration in the CSU; status tends to be relatively high with students at all the institutions, and relatively low with faculty, though somewhat higher in private colleges. I do not feel attached to any of these institutions, probably because I am never sure I will be working at any of them again and (I must) vacate my joint office after each term. I feel dedicated to the students, however, and hope to find a tenure-track position when I leave graduate school. My positions are more secure than I think, though, since I always am rehired.

JOAN: If you are made to feel a part of the group (which often means having a place that's yours), you feel committed to the institution. Some of this depends on administrative staff and personalities of colleagues. Generally, I felt like an outsider.

GEORGE: Generally, to be a lecturer *ipso facto* involves becoming an outsider, at least in terms of tenured faculty. This is to be expected: lecturers are the pedagogical "underclass" who "threaten" faculty and make them feel a bit guilty at the same time for their privileges. On the other hand, they've "earned it"—a tenure track. The relationship is that of Uriah Heep to David Copperfield: the underclass and the privileged at war for the same girl (tenure) who can save the hero. I think lecturers are to some degree blamed (blaming the victim of "administrative economy") as failed academics.

IRENE: Have I ever felt part of the academic mainstream? Never! I used to try, but the tenured people are so jealous of their territories, so afraid to discover that someone with only an M.A. (i.e., not the precious "terminal degree") might have equally good ideas and make equally valuable contributions, that it is not worth the effort. If things go well, they will take credit for your ideas. If they go poorly, you are there to blame. Alas!

Irene is a woman with an M.A. in linguistics. She has a B.A. in physics from Radcliffe, two years of scientific work at MIT, and is an active poet. She has been teaching since 1972 at CCs, UCs, CSUs, and private colleges.

IRENE: The poetry led to a job as a reader for the English department at a Los Angeles high school; this job introduced me to ESL, which I fell in love with. A friend mentioned a job in the Writing Lab at a local CSU campus and I applied there.

At the CSU where I formerly taught, I was valued until developmental teaching became "in." Then my brain was picked without credit at initial stages of developing the program, but later I and my colleague were excluded from the set-up process of a college-wide program with adjunct tutoring (despite our years of experience as tutors). Ultimately we were replaced by student tutors and when I got my M.A. there (4.0 G.P.A., honors, thesis), I was given classes to teach but offered pay four levels below what I had had before! I protested and saw my ten years of excellent evaluations drop to mediocre overnight.

They are nice to me at CSU and now I know the rules. Do your job. Don't volunteer. Don't interfere and don't expect the moon, i.e., don't cry when they [encourage you to] put in for a raise and the answer comes back you've reached the top for your degree already. Sorry, no raise after all!

REBECCA: The attitude is that you aren't as good as full-time. [But we're] not failures: it's just that our timing is off. The situation now is a result of budgetary problems in the state system and administrative carelessness—a lack of concern for the program. The CCs are just filling quotas according to ADA funding. Though there is a push to change that system. (An act has recently been passed in the California legislature that requires California CCs to hire at least seventy-five percent full-time employees.)

At one CC I know of, there were three full-time contracts dormant. One person had been teaching for three years in Berkeley as a high school coordinator. Instead of closing the contract and rehiring, they were hiring only part-time people instead. With no contract. If a class doesn't make, you are out. If a full-time teacher's class doesn't make, they bump a part-timer. The original idea of hourlies was that they would occur in emergency situations or if someone had a full-time job, someone with a certain expertise, that person would be hired to teach one class. It wasn't intended to fill full-time positions. I feel it has gotten worse over the last fifteen years, little by little, they've steadily increased the hourlies because it is "cost effective." [The year] 1975 was the last year a full-time person was hired at the CC where they hired me last year. There were hundreds of applications.

In general, hourlies are invisible. We have no office, we don't see or meet anybody. In order to get evaluated, I had to battle for it. You are supposed to be evaluated by the chair and another instructor. You had to fight to get this because no one wants to do it. You need it on your record.

EVELYN: There is no sense of a program where I am teaching. When I taught at Georgia State University in the writing program, they had a twenty-minute meeting every week. Someone would pass out an article from a writing journal and discuss it or discuss what he or she was doing. This wasn't done just to make us feel good—though it did accomplish that. There was a statewide composition exam graded by teachers in a different school, so you needed a sense of preparing all the students to succeed. But also the people who ran the program really cared.

DEBRA: At both places, I am an outsider in relationship to the administration and faculty. However, the students in both institutions give me a great deal of respect, saying that I "care" for them and have enlarged their vision—indeed, their dreams—of what they can accomplish through words; in short, they feel empowered. Unfortunately, although I am rewarded by the students' esteem, I feel undermined by the insecurity of my employment, a condition that cannot be ameliorated by my own dedication, expertise, or professionalism in attainments or attitude. I am annoyed by the knowledge that, unlike the university, business would double or quadruple my income, allow me to write my own job description, and, like my students, applaud my efforts. How long can I safely and sanely remain an insecure basement worker in the grand (and beloved) university? I don't know. Can I outstare the temptation to sell out to business? I don't know. I am dedicated to writing first, as a participant in creating meaning rather than in analyzing others' texts; and to teaching second, as an extension of the opportunity to create a receptive audience of people who *like* to read and write.

LOIS: The only time my "free-lance" status affects the classroom is when students complain about not being able to "get ahold of me." When they call the campus, especially at the CCs, they have a difficult time leaving a message. I've had students look at me strangely and say, "I tried to call but they didn't know who you were."

I Don't Need a Cake on My Birthday:
Advantages/Disadvantages

The longer you do this, the more the disadvantages outweigh the advantages. Since I initially did my study, I have settled down at one school, a pattern similar to many of my respondents. Lois was my respondent who remained the most enthusiastic about her work situation. She is the head of her household with two college-age dependents. She teaches speech at two CSUs and two CCs.

LOIS: I do think my status is one of an outsider but I see this as a plus. I like each of the institutions I work for and feel loyal to each—I have a mail slot and most in my department know my name—I don't need a cake on my birthday. I feel I have a career. I like *teaching*, I think I am good at it and I am doing it. Therefore I have a career I like!

Before teaching, I was a social service coordinator in a convalescent hospital and an adult education instructor (English as a second language). For two years I kept both jobs while teaching part-time. Then I decided I liked college teaching best, so I quit my secure jobs and became an insecure full-time part-timer. I find the part-time role to have many advantages. I like going to the different campuses. I like teaching both the CSU students and the CC students. I like not being required to attend meetings and to join in the politics of education. I make more money than many full-timers. One of the pluses of college teaching is the independence I feel.

The disadvantage, which does cause me real stress, is the lack of security—only one of the schools (a CSU) offers me a year contract. The others are strictly quarter/semester by quarter/semester. But so far this has been only in theory since I have had steady work for five years (knock on wood). But as one ages, this fear is increasing—can I go on like this for another twenty-two years (not that I'm counting). That's why I like the word "free-lance"; it connotes the sense of choice and creativity I feel rather than the stress and panic, which I also feel but wish not to concentrate on.

EVELYN: Part-time teaching is not seen as a career, but I see myself as a career teacher who hasn't been able to do it. If you want to write or have a family you need to be with, you can have the flexibility you don't get in a full-time job. You can turn down assignments. Of course you get stuck teaching remedial and basic classes. I have yet to teach a class in my specialty—linguistics. Also there is no chance for advancement, and part-timers are given no preference when there are full-time openings. Schools look with disfavor at people who are already there. They always want new blood. There are no affirmative action rules on part-timers.

REBECCA: If you knew there was an end in sight (a future full-time job), it's not a bad way to learn the business. This is the best apprenticeship you could have. You have to teach on your toes a wide variety of students, classes. For instance, I've taught ESL, "Basic Writing IA," 103, "Modern Fiction" (400 level), "American Dream" (300 level). You have to try out a variety of approaches. It gives you a great range, but you've got to make a commitment to find out about the system. You need to find a mentor to get you on committees, to find out how things are run. I took over a woman's class in reading and discovered how important that was. Now I teach reading in most of my courses. I get my students to read a little out loud. Six out of ten read word by word. These are kids raised on the media; they don't read and don't know how. If I hadn't taken over this woman's class, I wouldn't have learned these methods.

I Have No Health Insurance: Benefits

I myself get health benefits through my husband. This is true for many part-time lecturers. But, for others, this can be a serious problem. I interviewed Molly, a fiction writer in her twenties who was at the time pregnant with her first child. Molly's husband, unlike the husbands of many married freeway flyers, is not in a profession or business. He makes about $17,000 at his work and has no benefits. Molly taught at a local CC for four years; for one semester of that time she also taught full-time with the Job Corps. She now teaches two courses at her CC and two at a UC campus. She puts in about forty-five hours a week in preparation and makes about $16,500 a year.

MOLLY: At my CC I have no health insurance, no vacation time, no sick pay. No expenses are paid. I receive $28/hour *only* for class time. No pay for office hours, grading, or prep time. At UC the pay is much better, encompassing grading and conference time. I still have no benefits.

At my CC, part-timers make up a *large* majority of the faculty, and we're definitely on the fringe. This is the first semester we've had a representative in the faculty senate. We can be bumped out of class assignments anytime. Some have taught eight years part-time, never being hired full-time. For me, it's secondary to writing, so I don't mind part-time, but it's long hours for little pay, with no benefits.

EVELYN: Sometimes you can get into the system through the back door. I got retirement because once I took a job as a staff person at a CC full-time, and I'm still in the retirement system. But I want health benefits. I pay $258 a month for my family at Kaiser (HMO). How are we supposed to be teaching the value of education when most of us are making what our students get when they graduate?

My Wish List Could Go On:
Improving the System

Instead of offering a conclusion to this study—a conclusion that would probably be obvious—I would like instead to present some of my respondents' suggestions for improving the situation not just of freeway flyers, but of lecturers of writing in general.

Ben is a recent Ph.D. in literature who has taught at two private colleges and one CSU simultaneously, who teaches three quarter classes and five semester classes a year, makes about $18,000, and heads a one-income household with one dependent.

BEN: Institutions should not rely heavily on part-timers, as they now do; if a job needs to be done, it should be envisioned as a real job for real pay with real security. Part-timers, in order to gain pay increases, benefits, and recognition, should union-ize—an independent union, not linked to a public university system, is desirable. Part-timers should be invited to attend faculty meetings as nonvoting department members. Part-timers should be paid more—it galls me to think that I have several times taught more than a full load of classes (I once had five classes going at once), and yet I was paid about one-third as much as a full-timer would get.

KAREN: Planning an educational program, I would not admit more students than I felt could get tenure-track positions eventually; I would tell students about the job market and part-timing; I would offer courses in rhetoric, which make Ph.D.s more appealing in the job market. I would help students get published and help them through mock interviews, etc. (My graduate school falls short on most of these suggestions.)

GEORGE: The answer, of course, is full-time, guaranteed employment of qualified lecturers, inclusion in the academic community, appropriate pay scales and class loads that would *encourage* free-lancers to become academic members of a particular institution, and increased lecturer responsibilities. My wish list could go on—but since lecturers are an economic convenience of cost-cutting administrations, these remedies are largely fantastic, I think.

DEBRA: The instability of hiring is a blight on the reputation of universities who seek out a pool of highly qualified lecturers (only to exploit them) and who present themselves to the community as open-minded intellectuals, the thinkers, the cutting edge of policymakers, and the shapers of the future in our students.

To be specific in this suggestion, I think the universities across the country need to evaluate composition faculty by different criteria (performance in class, in the mass media culture, in composition textbooks) and empower sympathetic people to serve on hiring committees. The last item would begin to erode bias. Part of the perspective that I suggest includes viewing these composition professionals as artists-in-residence and making appropriate release time available. But this is too visionary as a beginning.

EVELYN: Get it to the public! Send it to the *New York Times* education section. There are presidential panels studying education. Change is not coming about *through* the institution. Changes come from outside.

Grapes of Wrath

Since Rebecca gave me the metaphor of *migrant worker* for freeway flyers and their situation, I have saved the last word for her.

REBECCA: I felt like the people in *Grapes of Wrath*, where the fruit companies distribute fifty thousand fliers for five thousand jobs. They say they are paying $1 a day, but when fifty thousand people show up, they pay them 30¢. When someone tries to get the people not to accept, this man says, "But my family has to eat." As an hourly, you know it's wrong and you are perpetuating the system, but your family's got to eat. You know you are being mistreated, but you are powerless. They don't have to hold on to you. You can't stop it. You forget you are as good as the full-timers. It leaves you without dignity.

Ultimately, they should make these jobs full-time; hourly positions should be minimal. I felt as an hourly I was being punished. Some hourlies are really disaffected and think, "What's the purpose of doing a good job?" Many resent it so much it comes out in their teaching. They take it out on the students. But most that I know don't. They care about the students and their teaching.

Notes

1. Throughout this essay, "UC" will be used for a college in the University of California system, "CC" for a college in the California Community College system, and "CSU" for a college in the California State University System.

2. I gave two very different presentations of the results of this study on panels at the Conference of College Composition and Communication in Seattle, Washington, in March 1989 and at the Young Rhetorician's Conference in Monterey, California, in June 1990.

4

Looking for a Gate in the Fence

Clare A. Frost/State University of New York at Stony Brook

I am a classic representative of the unheard voices of our discipline. I am female, part-time, and of course, untenured. Because so many teachers of composition fall into this category, I argue that the frustration I feel is not an aberration but commonplace and therefore needs to be heard by those central to our discipline. In this description of my continuing attempt to become a full-voiced member of the community of composition teachers, I speak for myself and for my colleagues who to date have had little choice but to remain "marginal and silent."

The depth of my longing to become more a part of the conversation is apparent in my reaction to receiving Sheryl Fontaine and Susan Hunter's prospectus for this book. I had spent that morning writing a proposal for the Conference on College Composition and Communication and the afternoon with my part-time colleagues, writing a draft to the dean requesting a salary increase. In my heart, I knew that neither enterprise had much chance for success. As I read the editors' invitation to submit a proposal for this book and saw that the topic of the book addressed my concerns, I started to cry.

I hate to admit it, but it's true. I was both startled and embarrassed by the level of emotion I felt, but I should not have been surprised, for over the years I have had a growing sense of my own frustration and alienation from the composition community.

It wasn't always so. My career in composition began nine years ago as a thirty-five-year-old graduate student in the M.A. program at State University of New York at Stony Brook. As part of my teaching fellowship, I enrolled in Peter Elbow and Pat Belanoff's course, "The Teaching of Composition." What I learned on Monday and Wednesday afternoons from Peter and Pat, I boldly proclaimed as gospel on Tuesday and Thursdays, in the one section of freshman composition assigned to me. Through this wonderful experience, my best ever as a student, I became a true believer in the process approach to the teaching of writing. I beamed when Peter complimented my "sure-fire" instincts as a teacher. My childhood dream of becoming a teacher was finally coming true.

A few months later the case study of Bob, the average American writer, that I had written for the practicum, was accepted by the Penn State Conference on Rhetoric and Composition. That hot July day in University Park, Pennsylvania, as I read my paper to a room full of attentive listeners that included my husband and children, I felt neither marginal nor unheard but very much a part of a wonderful profession. And when Peter Elbow hired me, the following fall to become one of his new "core" of writing teachers, I felt well on my way to becoming a full-voiced member of a wonderful profession. Peter envisioned a permanent team of teachers/writers who would give continuity and professional writing experience to a very large writing program of more than seventy sections a year, which up until that time had been taught almost exclusively by a new crop of graduate students each year. I was honored, in fact elated, to be part of this program.

Yes, the job was part-time, but at that time I did not realize how painful the word "adjunct" would become, nor did I know that torturous history of composition as the unwanted child of English departments more interested in belletristic literature than literacy. I only knew that I loved the frustration and the pleasure of seeing my own thoughts take shape through writing, and I enjoyed helping my students improve their own ability to express themselves through writing. I also expected to continue to write about my observations as a teacher, to grow more knowledgeable about theory, and to present papers at conferences as I had done as a graduate student.

As you've probably guessed, this is a "sadder-but-wiser" story, for the promise of the beginning of my career has not been fulfilled. By the time I received the editors' invitation to write this essay, eight years had gone by. Not only had I not presented a paper at CCCC or any other conference, I had not even *attended* a regional or national convention. Each year, Atlanta, St. Louis, Portland beckoned, but each year, the conferences came and went, leaving me feeling more and more left out.

The editors of this book picked "unheard, silent voices" as an image to describe and classify those of us who are not full participants in the conversation of our profession. Their metaphor certainly applies to me, but as I try to describe my alienation, I realize that when I think of myself in relation to the composition community, I am not only unheard but *unseen*.

The image I see is of a large, beautiful field, surrounded by a high, white fence. The full-time members of the composition community picnic happily within the enclosure, while I and others like me wander around and around outside the fence looking for the gate, the way in. Those of us outside are not only unheard but totally unpresent to those inside. On occasions (such as this) I manage to sneak a peek or catch a snatch of the conversation, but I am still isolated from the group.

Each spring the feelings of alienation are most intense. Just as I recover from the disappointment of not being able to attend one national convention, the invitation to submit proposals for the next year's meeting arrives. I drool over the description of the composition convention the way some yearn for chocolate mousse. I want so much to hear what others have to say about literacy, collaborative learning, basic writing, etc. I want to hear in person the voices I've heard in the journal *College Composition and Communication*.

Each year as I studied the invitation to submit a proposal, I vowed that the next year I *would* submit an idea. I *would* attend. Each year I had hope that next year would be different. I read and reread the opening address from the program chair, looking for the code words that identified the areas of particular interest for the upcoming conference. I saw the task of writing my paper as a classic writing dilemma—how to tailor what I wanted to say to an audience with specific needs. My experience as a newspaper reporter and interviewer made me confident that if I could determine the slant of the convention, I could shape my thoughts in that direction.

Almost from the beginning of my career as a writing teacher, I sensed that if I were going to be taken seriously by our profession, I had to do more than teach or talk about teaching practice. I knew my practitioner's knowledge had to be hinged to a theoretical model, and here was a major problem in my attempt to become part of the composition community—ignorance of theory.

For example, for the 1988 convention, the theme was "Language, Self, and Society." In my own living room, I had heard Peter Elbow and another faculty member discuss Bahktin's theories of language. It struck me that I could argue that one of my teaching practices—sharing my writing and writing processes with my students—could be linked to this discussion. I wondered: Wasn't I, by sharing my writing, serving as a model mediator of discourse communities, showing how my writing reflected the voices I had heard and the communities I was familiar with and how I adapted my writing to the needs of the various discourse communities, academic or otherwise, for which I wrote?

At this point in my academic career, I was surprised to learn that I did not have to have a paper written, or even started, to send in a proposal. I had thought my colleagues were sending in summaries of completed work. After all, this was the procedure I had followed for my presentation at Penn State. The whole process of being heard suddenly seemed easier. Now I merely had to learn how to sound like I knew what I was talking about. "My paper will examine Bahktin's theories as they relate to the classroom teacher who . . . " So I read a few articles about Bahktin in *College Composition and Communication* and wrote my abstract: "The Teacher As Potential Mediator of Discourse Communities."

My proposal wasnot accepted but I was invited to become a recorder for one of the sessions at the 1988 Conference on College Composition and Communication in St. Louis, Missouri. I had to ask someone in my department what a recorder was! But though I had gained an official role at the convention, I never did get to attend. My department only subsidized the trips of presenters and chairs, and I could not afford the more than $600 it would cost to attend the convention.

My inability and growing frustration to become part of the community is rooted in this example and what has followed. If I am to be honest about why I remain on the fringes of the profession, I must admit that there are personal as well as institutional reasons for my lack of success.

Earlier I used the phrase "I couldn't afford to go" to explain why I didn't attend the 1988 conference in St. Louis. This phrase is commonplace, but nonetheless, it needs examination. Whenever we say "can't afford," it means we value one "something" less than another "something." If my child needed an operation and a hospital in St. Louis was the best place for that surgery, I'd certainly be able to "afford" that trip. By saying I couldn't afford to attend the conference, I was really saying that I didn't think that the benefits of the conference for me would outweigh the cost of traveling expenses of almost ten percent of my gross salary for the semester to get there.

Perhaps, my decision not to spend that money says something about the priority my career has in my life. I have been happily married for twenty-three years and am the mother of three children. The role of wife and mother applies to many who teach composition part-time. For thirteen years I was a full-time homemaker and ever since I started to work eight years ago, I have juggled the competing forces of home and school. Well, fine, goody for me. Why should I now complain about my frustration? Staying at home was my choice, and I must accept some of the responsibility for my inability to achieve more success in my profession.

Obviously I have not devoted as much time to a career as I would have if I had been single, childless, or had different values. Time spent doing additional reading or writing in the field of composition means time I don't spend watching my son play basketball, attending a movie with my family, or helping my daughter look through college brochures. I already spend many hours and a great deal of energy being a good teacher—I feel very responsible for the fifty-five or sixty students who are put in my classes each semester. I give them as much attention as possible, read with full feedback a minimum of eight drafts per student each semester, see them individually in three conferences. It is the familiar litany of most composition professionals.

The truth is that after family responsibilities and more than thirty hours a week spent directly on the teaching of three sections of composition, I have to think carefully and pragmatically about how I'm going to spend the precious remaining time. Yes, I want to grow in and with the field. I hate my ignorance of theory and despise being "outside the fence." But if I'm to be honest I must admit that four years after I submitted the proposal to CCCC, I am only slightly more familiar with the important theorists in our field. This ignorance explains, in part, why I do not feel a complete member of the composition community.

But there are, in addition, to my own lack of drive and perseverance, institutional pressures that make it difficult for me to take myself seriously, and these exacerbate the effect of my personal choices. For the sad truth is that even if I become more knowledgeable—read theorists, attend conferences, present papers, take additional courses—I will receive *no additional institutional recognition of any sort*. I will not receive a penny more in remuneration for the courses I currently teach, nor will I become eligible for a full-time position or additional employee benefits. In fact no practical or professional benefit will result.

All the Dartmouth Conferences and Wyoming Resolutions in the world and all the good intentions of the composition community to improve the plight of the part-time composition teacher are not going to change these simple facts. Everything is upside down in higher education and everyone knows it. Higher education in this country does not place its value on what I value most: teaching. Research and publication are the twin gods of the academy. Teaching undergraduates, particularly the teaching of introductory courses, particularly the teaching of composition courses, especially at our large universities, is a low priority, a necessary evil.

In classic "catch-22" logic, the full-time faculty teach less than the part-time faculty. The five of us who comprise the permanent staff of the writing program at Stony Brook teach a total of twenty-six courses a year (some of us teach six, some elect to teach four). Yet, our combined salary for all twenty-six courses, is less than $100,000; less than the salary of some of the individual "big" names of our department.

I do not begrudge these individuals their salaries. They are eminently more talented and knowledgeable than I; but as I pointed out, how we spend our money reflects our priorities. It is clear from these salary disparities that the university places a much higher value on a well-published faculty who will attract quality graduate students and bring research money and prestige to the institution than it places on the teaching of basic literacy skills to beginning college students.

Here's a case in point: The group of five who are part-time at Stony Brook recently went to the dean for humanities and fine arts to ask for a raise. He was genuinely concerned with our plight and agreed that it was unfair that after eight years teaching at the university we still made less, per course, than first-year TAs. But he told us frankly that our best arguments were not the quantity and quality of our contact with students or the time we spent giving feedback on student writing but that we had also published, attended conferences, and served informally as mentors for new graduate students. Ironically, within the framework of what the university valued, and therefore funded, the duties we performed and valued the *least* (publishing and contact with graduate students) were what the university valued the *most*. I came away feeling that even though I had been hired by the university for a part-time, non-tenure-track teaching line, my position was now being evaluated retroactively by tenure-track standards. For less than $20,000 a year, with no hope for a full-time position, I was supposed to teach six courses, as well as publish scholarly articles, and offer assistance to new graduate students.

In a variety of ways, the English departments, which house most composition programs, and the larger institutions that surround these English departments (I don't think Stony Brook is unusual in this regard) let us know that the teaching of composition to undergraduates is not a priority. I know this, and my colleagues, part-time and full-time, know this.

Over the last eight years, I have learned that my job is a dead end, and this knowledge does influence how much time and effort I'm willing to spend to become a fuller participant in the composition community. I know that no matter how many composition theorists I read or courses I take, no matter how many students write glowing evaluations or how many colleagues recognize my abilities, I'm going *nowhere*. Why I haven't even been observed since I was a graduate student eight years ago! There's no reason to. My superiors have other ways of knowing that I am competent and conscientious. Because I am ineligible for any change in rank or promotion of any kind, formal evaluation is unnecessary.

Given the lack of status and money and recognition and hope for advancement, why would I or any other rational person continue in such a position?

Despite what I would call the misplaced priorities of the larger institution, teaching composition in the writing program at

Stony Brook has been a rewarding experience for me. The director has supported the efforts of her part-time staff to receive more money and status. In addition, she has initiated innovative placement and portfolio procedures and has encouraged my teaching experiments and efforts to become a more active member of the composition community.

And quite frankly, I am able to stay in this position because I am not the sole support of my family. Because my husband is a professor of economics, and my salary provides supplemental rather than essential income for our family, I have the luxury of choosing a position that gives me what economists call "psychic income," the nonmonetary reward of a given job.

I have remained in my position because of those psychic rewards I receive: I love the teaching of composition. I enjoy seeing my students use writing to tap into themselves, some for the first time in their lives. I glow when some of their final evaluations say that the course was better than they expected it or that their attitudes about writing have improved. For me, getting to know a new group of young people each semester and seeing what they can accomplish in a few short months is exhilarating. I don't find their writing boring, because I don't find them boring.

I may be a misfit in the academy but not in my classroom. For me it's not a job, it's a calling. The pain of being adjunct is not inflicted in the classroom, but in the hallowed halls of academe. My struggle to be seen and heard in this discipline is also a struggle to have faith in myself and what I'm doing. Quite frankly it's difficult not to feel like a second-class citizen when, in subtle and not so subtle ways, my colleagues and I are told we don't count. At Stony Brook, our offices are physically as far removed as possible from our full-time colleagues, our mailboxes do not cohabit with the full-time faculty, nor do our names appear on the list of English department faculty members published at the beginning of the year. These slights sound like petty complaints, but they are symbolic of a pervasive antipathy toward part-timers and teachers of composition in general by many of the full-time, mostly literature faculty, at many colleges and universities across our nation.

To a large extent my struggle to become a less marginal member of the composition community is tied to the struggle of composition studies to become more central in the Department of English. What I see and hear from my vantage point tells me that radical change must take place before the field of composition will ever achieve the same status as literary studies. Therefore, I agree with Maxine Hairston and others who argue that composition should break away from the English departments where they are located in most colleges and universities.

The only other hope I have is to find some way to educate the literature faculty, and the faculty of other disciplines, about what we teach in our composition classes. Some think: "All you do is that freewriting stuff." One faculty member was recently incensed at the inadequacies of our composition program because an English major in one of his classes wrote "might of" instead of "might have." Just as there are no institutional incentives for me to increase my knowledge in the field, there's no reason for our literature faculty to become more familiar with current composition pedagogy.

I also wish the composition community would encourage our universities to give teaching a higher value. Perhaps, if there were a two-track system whereby promotion and tenure were awarded for teaching skills as well as publishing credits, then what many part-time composition teachers do best and value most would become part of the reward structure. If what is done professionally in the classroom becomes half as important as what is done outside the classroom, then those of us who see teaching as our main priority might not feel quite so tangential, so unimportant to our profession.

Major institutional changes are, of course, easier to suggest than accomplish, but there are other, more easily implemented ways the Conference on College Composition and Communication might support those of us who are struggling in the trenches. For example, offering regional grants to help create local writing conferences, projects, and/or discussion groups would alleviate the isolation many of us feel. Recently one of my part-time colleagues, who coordinates the basic writing courses at Stony Brook, thought it would be interesting to network with our counterparts from other colleges in our area. The meeting was well attended and although it was originally scheduled for an hour and a half, it stretched to almost three hours as our colleagues, mostly full-time teachers from area community colleges, lingered long after the official meeting ended. They were even willing to brave the notorious Long Island Expressway at rush hour for a few more minutes of composition conversation!

In those few hours we had merely scratched the surface, asking and answering only the most basic procedural and structural questions: How many students do you have? Who teaches your introductory courses? What are your placement procedures? What's the percentage of basic or remedial or ESL students in your program? How do you judge the competency or the effectiveness of your programs? By the time we began to discuss the philosophies of our various programs, whether we tended to emphasize final products or process, grammar or voice, readers or journals, literary analysis or personal essays, the time was up.

The meeting was productive, interesting, and extremely frustrating; I felt like I was putting a good book down in the middle of the best chapter. But it is unlikely that a follow-up meeting will ever take place.

Except for the director and assistant director of the writing program, those of us who represented Stony Brook at this meeting were "part-time" composition teachers. Although my part-time colleagues and I talked a bit after the meeting about how we might organize a composition conference in the fall or try to establish an ongoing discussion group in our region, we realized that even a relatively simple undertaking like this would require many additional hours of unpaid labor and out-of-pocket expenses that we could not "afford" to spend. However such regional groups could become a reality if the Conference on College Composition and Communication offered grants or seed money for local efforts such as these. I know their existence would create an opportunity for professional growth that does not currently exist.

Those firmly established at the center of our discipline need to recognize the untapped potential of those of us on the margins of our profession. For me, just being asked to submit a proposal for this book has had an important ripple effect on my professional life. When I read the editors' invitation to submit a proposal, I felt emotionally overwhelmed but also quite flattered that established professionals in the discipline, all the way out on the West Coast, had thought that I might have something of value to say to the readers of this book. The editors' simple act of faith gave my morale a tremendous boost and made me more determined than ever that by hook or by crook, even at my own expense, I would get to the next CCCC. With their invitation, I felt included, or at least potentially part of the conversation.

Yes, I made it to Boston in 1991! Yes, it was wonderful. I heard Peter Elbow and David Bartholomae's "Dialogue on Academic Discourse" *in person*. I heard Nancy Sommers's eloquent "spicey" talk, "Creating Conversations Between Students and Their Sources," which was seasoned with insights about teaching and life. McQuade, Brannon, Hairston, and Heath were now authors with faces. I could now say that I literally had heard the sound of their voices, not just read their words in print.

And the positive "ripples" continue to widen. As a result of the presentations I heard at the various sessions I attended at the convention, I said to myself, "I can do this!" It gave me the courage to send a proposal to the State University of New York Writing Council Conference. That proposal was accepted, and a few months ago I read my paper "Teaching Without Assignments" and had the opportunity to hear and meet other New York State faculty members who are interested in composition. And there's more. As a result of those efforts, the director and assistant director of the writing programs at Stony Brook have asked me to be a member of their panel on the portfolio process that they've proposed for the next convention in Cincinnati in 1992.

This change in my spirit reminds me of the believing game we once played in Peter Elbow's "The Teaching of Writing" practicum that I took as a graduate student. Peter would give us a student paper and tell us to believe that it was a good paper. He would accept no negative comments at first. I was amazed how much there was to value even in a weak paper once I looked for the positives. The moral was: If you believe in a piece of writing, even though you might have to pretend at first, that piece tends to live up to your expectations of it.

I hope this essay proves that the believing game works for people as well as papers. If those central to our discipline believe that those of us on the fringes have something important to say, if they will only show us that *there is a gate in the fence*, namely, an interested audience and a future in this profession, I think they will be surprised how hard we'll work to become more knowledgeable and how much our presence will add to the character and quality of our profession.

5

The Dangers of
Teaching Differently

Susan Hunter/*Kennesaw State College, Marietta, Georgia*

Prefer to Teach Differently

As a compositionist, I teach differently from the ways many of my colleagues in other fields teach. Conferencing, responding, collaborative learning, peer review, portfolios, journals, dialectical notebooks, freewriting, writing to learn, workshops—what have become for me routine practices—distinguish me from a teacher of composition who lectures, a chemist or a mathematician who fills a chalkboard with proofs, a psychologist who gives multiple-choice tests, a literature professor who assigns term papers. Where lectures, recitations, and labs prepare students to solve quantitative problems or report back facts on a test, the currently preferred ways of teaching writing that I use enable my students to form a community of writers, collaborating to make knowledge. I like teaching differently; it feels "right" to me.

The articles and books I read from the most influential journals and presses in composition and the voices I hear at conferences support my instincts. These voices encourage me to take pride in my different ways, even to want to infuse them, as others are doing, throughout the curriculum. I consider, for example, how Richard Bullock, John Trimbur, and Charles Schuster can "unabashedly privilege certain practices in writing instruction over others . . . collaborative over atomized learning, critical and creative thinking over memorization and formulaic display, purposeful writing over exercises and drills" (xviii). Lisa Ede, too, implicitly privileges teaching differently when she sees "a substantial gap between what researchers and experienced practitioners in the field know about the teaching of writing and how writing is actually taught in many community colleges, colleges, and universities" (119). I note that the English Coalition Conference mandates a freshman English course not as a site where information is transmitted but as a setting for critical inquiry, collaboration, and reflection (Lloyd-Jones and Lunsford 28). I also read how my different pedagogy is embraced in writing-across-the-curriculum (WAC) programs that Toby Fulwiler and Art Young find working in colleges of many shapes and sizes (*Programs That Work*). Paul Connolly and Teresa Vilardi's book *Writing to Learn Mathematics and Science* reassures me that some teachers of introductory math and science are discovering that writing enables their students to learn concepts and theories, not just how to find the "right" answer.

I also read that today's process-oriented composition pedagogy is inherently liberatory and political. I find support for the political aspect of my different ways of teaching in James Berlin's claim: "Every pedagogy is imbricated in ideology, in a set of tacit assumptions about what is real, what is good, what is possible, and how power ought to be distributed" (492). My mission like Linda Brodkey's is "to instruct and support [my students] in a critique of received wisdom, which . . . means a sustained interrogation of the doxa out of which claims about reality arise and to which their claims and mine contribute" (600). Patricia Bizzell (672–73) and Dale Bauer urge me to claim "rhetorical authority" in the classroom and persuade my students to accept my political agenda.

Linda Shaw Finlay and Valerie Faith assure me that teaching differently can move my students toward Freire's "critical consciousness." Carolyn Ericksen Hill describes for me such transformative teaching and learning in *Writing from the Margins: Power and Pedagogy for Teachers of Composition*. Feminist composition teachers Elizabeth Flynn, Clara Juncker, Pamela Annas, and contributors to Cynthia Caywood and Gillian Overing's *Teaching Writing: Pedagogy, Gender, and Equity* associate the process pedagogy and social constructivism of my different ways with the feminist revision of cultural models and reevaluation of the experience of women. The connection between feminism and composition pedagogy may also arise from the fact that women are a majority in the part-time, full-time, and tenure-track ranks in composition (Holbrook), and some of us are feminists. Apparently, we keep choosing to teach English—still often denigrated as "women's work"—out of "the desire to reinvoke the transformational experience . . . for others," not as "an extension of the nonintellectual gifts of mothering transplanted to another, professional, scene, but something far more radical— . . . invoking change in others" (Aisenberg and Harrington 39). All of us who choose to teach differently—men, women, feminists, and nonfeminists—are trying to empower our students. So at the same time that undergraduates are being trained upon graduation to enter the professional worlds of the social, applied, and physical sciences, I, their feminist writing teacher with my different pedagogy, help them to come to know the power language gives them to shape and reshape those worlds.

Teaching Differently Matters

Not only do I *teach* differently, but I *value* pedagogy differently from the ways many academics do. I talk and write about teaching; faculty from a lot of other disciplines do not. Again I read that I am doing the "right" thing. As the "Statement of Principles and Standards for the Postsecondary Teaching of Writing" implies, it is difficult to judge composition professionals by traditional standards for promotion and tenure because we value teaching, curriculum development, and research differently from the way members of other disciplines, particularly those in literature, do (331–32). Questions posed in all kinds of composition scholarship are supposed to be grounded in the classroom. Janice Lauer and

Andrea Lunsford identify pedagogy as "the arena in which theory and research are enacted, tested, and refined; teaching becomes a field of symbolic action, a network of primary discourse acts, of layers of discourse about discourse" (110). David Bleich's "double perspective" claims "the political and social necessity of viewing the classroom as just as salient, vital, and important as the academy" (x). Stephen North defines "practitioners' lore" as a body of knowledge and practice as inquiry (19–55). The essays in Patricia Donahue and Ellen Quandahl's *Reclaiming Pedagogy: The Rhetoric of the Classroom* set out to "reclaim pedagogy as a theoretical field of study, a critical practice" (1). To Jane Peterson, 1990 CCCC Chair, teaching differently matters because "the teaching our current theories call us to is itself a mode of inquiry, a way of learning and knowing for us as teachers" (30). I could cite many more instances where composition scholars talk about valuing teaching, and they're usually talking about the value of teaching *differently*. The sheer number of articles and books focusing (for the most part in uncritical ways) on today's composition pedagogy must attest to the fact that what actually goes on in the writing classroom—ours and (I would hope) our students' perceptions of it—matters to us.

Warning: Teaching Differently Can Be Hazardous to Your Academic Health!

You will probably recognize the claims and observations I have cited as truisms in our field. What I miss in the narratives containing these is any hint of the complications truisms often conceal. In order to begin to fill in this blank in current stories, I will describe some dilemmas that my different pedagogy posed for me when I administered writing-across-the-curriculum and freshman programs at the small, private, liberal arts college of science and engineering where I once taught. There I encountered dangers in choosing to teach the way I want to teach, which is also, according to some of the most influential speakers in composition, the way I am supposed to teach. From these experiences, I have learned a fact that all of us teaching composition—graduate students, part-time, full-time temporary, and tenure-track faculty—need to acknowledge: the interactive, collaborative pedagogy I (we) prefer is not necessarily what our students expect or faculty in other disciplines deliver. Indeed, some students and faculty probably feel that teachers should transmit knowledge in the classroom rather than make it. Again, if I have read about these differences in the prevailing narratives of composition at all, I have found them recorded only partially or allusively. The actual political and cultural conditions we composition professionals practice in daily are rarely described. And so, I will also speculate as to why composition scholars usually remain silent about these persistent dangers, about why they may hesitate to grant such stories their places in the annals of our evolving discipline.

As an untenured assistant professor of English in a college where the physical sciences, engineering, and mathematics were the only majors, I faced the dangers of teaching differently at every turn. The dean of faculty's financial backing for writing across the curriculum, a freshman writing course, and a writing center made many of my colleagues in the humanities and social sciences department that housed these programs resentful. They felt that the dean was telling us what to teach and that offering writing courses made ours a service department. By starting a WAC program, administering the freshman writing course, and establishing a writing center, I had pledged my allegiance to the college and identified my profession as composition, forsaking my departmental "family" and the disciplinary niche of literature. In the freshman composition classroom, too, I was fighting a battle as a feminist teaching a required course that my talented, eighteen-year-old, mostly male students did not think they needed to take. They had to write and revise extensively for portfolio assessment, and they had to read a lot of writing by women. The faculty called the course "Humanities I: Rhetoric." The students had learned from their freshman orientation sponsors and the freshman *Look-book* to call it "Retch."

My colleagues were familiar with the idea of writing across the curriculum from a program that had been funded for a few years in the early 1980s. And lab reports, term papers, proposals, and engineering clinic reports were being assigned in many courses. But the students were doing all this writing with none of the support WAC pedagogy provides. The dean of faculty agreed to fund a renewed effort to make writing integral to learning. After an initial set of sparsely attended workshops led by writing faculty from another technological college along with scientists and engineers who were teaching writing-intensive courses there, some of the dilemmas of teaching differently began to surface. I found that

WAC workshops were viewed as "advice to teachers," as nonsubstantive, as not calling forth the mode of knowledge transmitted in the authoritative lecture model. Although I put before them interactive and collaborative methods of peer review, drafting, and responding, many faculty reverted to old habits and picked up their red pens to note on student papers "current-traditional" concerns. Many had great difficulty accepting the idea that writing could be used as a pedagogical tool. While WAC should thrive at this kind of undergraduate institution where effective teaching is supposed to be a priority, the pressures on faculty to do seminal research and to train their students to do likewise in the future fostered attitudes and practices antithetical to WAC. Many professors believed that WAC pedagogy emphasized the delivery system of education and would force them to neglect the quantifiable substance of what they had to teach. Many science and engineering professors claimed that asking their students to turn in drafts and do peer review would take time away from material that had to be covered and would add to their and their students' already overburdened workloads. Some humanities and social science professors believed opportunities for peer review and revision would make it difficult to evaluate a student's writing as the product of a single individual.

Despite the dangers this culture presented, those of us most at its margins—the untenured, the women, the semiretired, visitors hopeful of landing tenure-track positions—valued teaching differently. I consulted with three visiting professors—two computer scientists and a political scientist—about ways to encourage the *process* of writing in their classes. A semiretired professor who teaches mathematics as a humanistic discipline shared articles from *The Chronicle of Higher Education* with me about the problems with the ways math and science are taught in this country (e.g., Blum; Rigden and Tobias). After reading about James Reither and Douglas Vipond's model for collaboration in the classroom, a cognitive psychologist organized her freshman seminar so that students formed a research community. Her students coauthored papers and maintained a class archive in the library. A physicist developed ways for junior physics majors to use writing to learn the concepts of statistical mechanics. They read and wrote about articles that took them to what she called "the boundaries of their knowledge." When they put on a colloquium about writing across the curriculum publicized to the entire faculty, these faculty and some peer consultants from the Writing Center were the speakers and the audience.

The WAC program in the liberal arts college of science and engineering where I taught did not succeed as the ones at Michigan Technological University, St. Mary's College, Brown, or Rensselaer Polytechnic Institute had. Individual teacher's practices and attitudes changed, but institutional or cultural change did not happen, partly because the faculty who chose to become involved in the program were the transient ones, not those in the tenured ranks—not the engineers, for instance, who teach seventy-five percent of the majors in the school. (A few engineers did send their students to the Writing Center at the end of each semester for help "editing" their final project reports. Of course, the Writing Center consultants collaborated with the writers by talking and reading, not editing.) Maybe these faculty will go on to other institutions and carry that sense of cultural change with them as a personal mission. But if they hear that they spend too much time on their teaching, their efforts to use writing as a pedagogical tool in their classes will go "under cover" when they are reviewed for promotion or tenure.

In the freshman writing program I administered, recent Ph.D.s and A.B.D.s with part-time and full-time temporary appointments in literature taught—another marginal but enthusiastic group. These literary scholars came to believe that understanding how people compose texts is as important as understanding how they read texts. And our hallway talk turned to questions of response and revision, collaboration and evaluation. The eight of us collaborated successfully to develop a portfolio method of assessment. Our commitment to teaching differently worked to make us a community of teachers. We also saw the risks in teaching differently. Accustomed to viewing education as recording information conveyed in lectures, copying proofs from chalkboards, calculating answers to problems for homework, and memorizing facts and formulas for tests, our students did not see the point of the interactive, collaborative methods in their composition class. While we believed a portfolio system of assessment validates revision, in other courses our students continued to face harsh grading of their writing as final product rather than work in progress.

Many students preferred the highly structured, authoritarian lecture setting over the process-oriented, inductive, low structure of my composition class because the latter does not interact well with their cognitive or learning styles (Snow 22, 40). In a collaborative report about the underlife among freshmen at the University of Utah, Susan Miller concluded that neither the "content of [her expository writing course] nor the course conduct that contains it matches, in an *essential* way, the pedagogic/cultural values that shape and limit knowledge in other introductions to the academically literate workplace" (Anderson et al. 29). I observed a similar mismatch between the small-group discussions, freewriting, and revising the students were doing in my class and the lectures they listened to in their physics, chemistry, and math courses. I have since accepted a position in an English department at a state college where faculty and administrators claim to value effective teaching. But what about the place I left? Granted, the students there are so talented that it may not matter that they continue to write their five-page papers in two or three hours the night before they are due, caring about the grade not the comments professors write on their papers.

I could continue identifying dangers of teaching differently by relating many examples of how the members of my department implied or expressed their disdain for any course, program, or research associated with composition. Surely, the students perceived this elitism, as well. But finally, one of the most painful and telling dangers of teaching differently I remember from my freshman composition classes was at once political and personal. In raising questions about power and the status quo, in discussing exclusive language, gender and racial stereotypes, and writings by and about women, my feminist stance was apparent. And I felt alienated from the mostly male, eighteen-year-old students in my writing class. Especially when it had become part of the tradition of the school to call me and those women students who sympathized with my political agenda "femiNazis."

Why Didn't Someone Warn Me about the Dangers of Teaching Differently?

Had my reading about the value of teaching differently in our field been too selective? Is my viewpoint idiosyncratic, distorted, subjective? Had some warnings arrived too late for me to heed during the two years I was engaged in developing a campus-wide writing program? Trying to answer these questions, I find that the writers I read did and did not warn me about the dangers of teaching differently. More often than not, it was not their purpose to do so. The few warnings I was able glean did not speak to me or my situation directly enough for me to step back and take account of them. I discovered that the rhetorical purposes of academic writing and our field's move toward professionalization prevent composition scholars from writing directly about the dilemmas that teaching differently poses. And so, perhaps unwittingly, they downplay the actual experiences of real teachers, joining with the rest of the academy in causing us to lead "lives under cover." In what follows here, I do not discount the value of academic writing. I continue to learn a great deal from reading it and writing it. My point here is that the academic writing I read about composition pedagogy did not warn me about the dangers of teaching differently.

Part of the reason the warnings about the dangers of teaching differently were hard to spot is related to where they appear. Often, when the warnings are issued, they serve as "preface" or "afterword" to success stories. In Art Young and Toby Fulwiler's afterword to *Programs That Work*, "The Enemies of Writing Across the Curriculum," I recognized some of the "enemies" they identify: the unwillingness of a department to provide leadership for a campus-wide program as important to engineering and chemistry as it is to literature and history (289); the "traditional reward system" under which colleagues value referred publications more than undergraduate teaching (290); and the "entrenched attitudes" of students and faculty who believe that "the new writing pedagogy is 'soft' with its opportunities for collaboration and revision, not to mention its opportunities for reflection and sustained critical thinking, especially when compared to the rigors of the go-it-alone, one-time-only, machine-scored test" (293). That last "rigor"—the "go-it-alone" variety—turns up as well in the end-of-the-term paper in philosophy and the three-hour essay exam in literature. Ed White prefaces the WAC success story of his campus, California State University, San Bernardino, with two dangers I had encountered: (1) that WAC pedagogy opposes "the dominant mode of learning in most American higher education: the passive detached memorization of material from lectures and textbooks, evaluated by multiple-choice tests," and (2) that WAC pedagogy attracts those faculty who are "isolated and estranged [and] remain external to the ongoing life of the institution" (30). Since I read these essays after I had already witnessed the attitudes they describe, I cannot be sure that I would have recognized the warnings underlying these pieces had they been published while I was immersed in administering the writing program.

Other writers seem as if they will present a danger of teaching differently, only to overlook it in favor of a theoretical perspective or a large generalization about the value of composition pedagogy. For example, Dale Bauer begins her essay "The Other 'F' Word: The Feminist in the Classroom" with quotes from a feminist colleague's student evaluations that clearly showed the resistance of nonfeminist students to the teacher's feminism. The following comments sound like those my former students made: "I also think you shouldn't voice your 'feminist' views because we don't need to know that—it's something that should be left outside of class." "I found it very offensive that all of our readings focused on feminism" (385). When I read the opening of her essay, I thought Bauer would mention how such less-than-favorable evaluations adversely affected review for promotion or tenure. Instead, she presented a well-conceived theoretical argument for how a feminist teacher should go about establishing authority in her literature class. The danger of teaching differently as a feminist that I had perceived stayed "under cover." Jane Peterson recounts another experience many of us who teach differently are familiar with. As part of a formal evaluation procedure, the chair of her division came to observe her basic writing class when the students were working in small groups on drafts. After observing for a short time, she said: "This is all very interesting, Jane, but I'm going to leave now. Please come by the office to reschedule this visit for a day *when you're teaching*" (29–30; emphasis added). I thought Peterson would go on to warn her readers about the danger our teaching differently poses to our continued employment in an institution that interprets teaching as lecturing to transmit knowledge. Instead, she goes on to privilege teaching differently and exhorts us to value it when she concludes that "such stories illustrate how acting on our emerging theories has altered the shape of our work, i.e., changed our classroom practices. . . . We need to . . . consider the proposition that teaching today—the teaching that seeks to transform classes of students into communities of readers, writers, and learners—is itself a way of learning and knowing that has value for us as well as for students" (30). In "The Quiet and Insistent Revolution: Writing Across the Curriculum," Toby Fulwiler generalizes other dangers I had experienced:

"Professors in the quantitative disciplines often find qualitative written expressions difficult to evaluate; professors in the humanities commonly believe it their duty to critique and correct everything their students write; professors in the sciences sometimes see little value in the verbal written exploration and speculation of undergraduates." Fulwiler follows these conclusions with another general statement about the value of WAC: "A writing-across-the-curriculum program challenges all of these notions" (182). But he did not warn me that these disciplinary differences could undermine my efforts to set up a WAC program.

Also obscuring the dangers of teaching differently and pushing us farther away from the classroom is what Howard Tinberg and others in composition notice as our tendency to "rush to theory." Even essays that urge us to value teaching like Jane Peterson's 1990 CCCC address and Patricia Harkin's "Metacommentary on the Postdisciplinary Politics of Lore" authorize their discussions by connecting them to highly regarded theorists. For example, in a footnote Peterson labels composition teachers of the late 1960s and early 1970s "atheoretical" as a way of distinguishing them from the constructivist, Freireian teachers of the 1990s (33–34). Harkin sets out to theorize Steve North's concept of "lore" — the accumulated body of traditions, practices, and beliefs in terms of which Practitioners . . . understand how writing is done, learned and taught" (22). Harkin defines "teaching as a site or moment when we are free to bracket disciplinary procedures, *to do what needs to be done without worrying about meeting disciplinary standards of knowledge production*" (8; emphasis added). Unfortunately, she is unwilling to let teaching be what she defines it as. She implies that if we find a way to prove that teaching produces knowledge, then we can raise our prestige and gain esteem within the academy. To do so, Harkin proposes a conference where teachers work on a problem in the classroom and a panel of theorists comments on the implications of the teachers' practice ("Postdisciplinary Politics," 136–38). Yet if such a conference were staged within the composition community, it would not guarantee that either the teaching or this method of demonstrating its knowledge-producing qualities would be valued throughout the academy. Even within our field there are dangers associated with talking and writing about teaching unless we authorize it in relation to some mode of inquiry. North says we teachers need "to defend [our]selves — to argue for the values of what [we] know, and how [we] come to know it" (55). Such attempts to elevate pedagogy suggest that composition scholars have bought into the academy's denigration of it.

Writings about composition pedagogy allude to a tension between theory and research and practice that exists, then, not only within English departments and the academy but within the field of composition studies as well. That is, although we proclaim the importance of pedagogy as our discipline is being moved toward professionalization, we seem to be apologizing for our "classroom mentality" (Peterson 28). Our avowed concern with teaching contributes to our marginalization within English studies and within the academy. Now that we want to be "professionalized," we have to fight off that marginal position, so we cannot remain concerned with teaching with exactly the same fervor or commitment we have had in the past. Underlying the truisms that composition is a field in which teaching differently is preferred and valued is a mixed message: feeling the need to justify our concern with pedagogy, composition scholars, perhaps unwittingly, adopt the attitude so entrenched in the academy of privileging research over teaching. In *Rhetoric Review*'s first "Burkean Parlor," a graduate student noticed the devaluing of teaching: "Practice, as a body of knowledge, has gone underground at CCCC. . . . The outsiders, mostly practitioners and teacher-researchers, take to the hallways where, in groups of two or three, they struggle to maintain another community of knowledge (RKM)" (204). Howard Tinberg, a community college teacher, writes: "The low esteem with which classroom instruction is held among theorists and scholars in the field is the most serious problem confronting composition today" (38). We are told to teach, speak, and write as if pedagogy is more important to us than it is to many of the others who administer, teach, and learn in the institutions and classrooms we practice in. But when we write about it, we are supposed to distance ourselves from the actual experience of being in the classroom by assessing, theorizing, reflecting.

The pressures of academic writing to distance or conceal the particular and the personal may account for some of what I find misleading in the articles and books about composition pedagogy. In the field of composition, Peter Elbow questions the value of requiring freshmen writers to learn academic writing. Among literary critics, feminists Jane Tompkins and Olivia Frey question the value of adhering to the adversarial and distancing conven-

tions of academic discourse. It seems odd that composition pedagogy has much in common with feminism, but the discourse published—in our most widely circulated journals at least—is academic, making what Ursula LeGuin calls "the essential gesture of
the father tongue . . . distancing—making a gap, a space, between
the subject or self and the object or other." (qtd. in Tompkins 173).

We see this privileging of the academic and theoretical in the
kinds of papers our colleagues in composition present at the MLA
Convention in the "Division of Teaching Writing." At the three
conventions I have attended in the past four years, I heard James
Berlin, Susan Miller, and John Schilb give some excellent papers
about important historical and theoretical issues. But the papers
delivered under this rubric at MLA are rarely given by *teachers* of
writing about *teaching* writing. The only exception I have found is
a very important one. Richard Murphy's "On Stories and Scholarship," presented at the 1988 MLA Convention, which I did not
attend, fortunately for me appeared as an article in the "Staffroom
Interchange" section of *CCC* the next December. "Teacher knowledge," Murphy writes, "is represented . . . in one of its most important forms in the stories we tell ourselves and perhaps our
fellow teachers and students of moments of our teaching and
learning, moments in which we were thrilled or troubled or surprised by the most complicated joy" (469). But he shares with us
only some "fragments" of his stories of teaching. Like our colleagues in English departments, composition scholars rarely count
such stories of teaching. Murphy had to theorize about the value of
storytelling. The format of *CCC* required that his stories of teaching be surrounded by argument. In his award-winning book *Lives
on the Boundary*, Mike Rose could not just tell a story either; in
the preface he admits that his book is "both vignette and commentary, reflection and analysis. I didn't know how else to get it
right" (xii).

While theoretical perspectives, programmatic and disciplinary histories, and success stories are informative and necessary,
we also need to credit the personal histories of teachers, even if
they are less than encouraging about where the field of composition stands in relation to the center and the margins of the
academy. Their accounts can give us a localized perspective,
which we should value on a par with other kinds of perspectives
because they capture the reality of the composition classroom. I
know I would like to read what some of my freshman students

clamor for: stories written by better storytellers than I am with characters and situations I can "identify with."

Why Do I (We) Continue to Teach Differently?

How do we composition teachers who find our stories glossed over in current narratives of composition survive? We seek out places to tell our stories—hallways, parking lots, regional meetings, newsletters, a book like this one. We change jobs in hopes of finding a different story to tell and more sympathetic listeners to tell it to. Given all the dangers of teaching differently that I have noticed, you might ask why I persist in teaching differently or why I continue to make a living as a composition professional. Well, I have bought into a number of popular myths. Having been an academic all my adult life, I have been assured time and time again that I cannot do anything except teach. Besides, what I teach is socially responsible. And by participating in the system, maybe I will have a chance to subvert it. In reality, the voices of students call me back to the classroom: "I have learned more this past year than in all other years of school—especially in your classes and talking with you." The trouble is their voices get fainter every year, straining to be heard above the increasingly louder cries of "publish or perish," "this is just advice to teachers," "this lacks a theoretical perspective," or "I'll come back when you're teaching." Still, I do it anyway. I choose the dangers of teaching differently over the kinds of entitlement today's academy has to offer. A reader of an earlier version of this paper expressed the mixture of frustration and hope in a "life under cover" very well when he responded: "Oh my God, what should we do about this? There is no real answer right now. . . . is it just my discomfort at being presented with an apparently insoluable (for the time being) dilemma: I sure as hell am not giving up on my pedagogy, but I sure as hell might be doing myself in within the university system."

Works Cited

Aisenberg, Nadya, and Mona Harrington. *Women of Academe: Outsiders in the Sacred Grove*. Amherst: U of Massachusetts P, 1988.

Anderson, Worth, Cynthia Best, Alycia Black, John Hurst, Brandt Miller, and Susan Miller. "Cross-Curricular Underlife: A Collaborative Report on Ways with Academic Words." *College Composition and Communication* 41 (1990): 11–36.

Annas, Pamela J. "Style as Politics: A Feminist Approach to the Teaching of Writing." *College English* 47 (1985): 360–72.

Bauer, Dale M. "The Other 'F' Word: The Feminist in the Classroom." *College English* 52 (1990): 385–96.

Berlin, James A. "Rhetoric and Ideology in the Writing Class." *College English* 50 (1988): 477–94.

Bizzell, Patricia. "Beyond Anti-Foundationlism to Rhetorical Authority: Problems Defining 'Cultural Literacy.'" *College English* 52 (1990): 661–75.

Bleich, David. *The Double Perspective: Language, Literacy and Social Relations*. New York: Oxford UP, 1988.

Blum, Debra E. "Colleges Urged to Make Radical Changes to Deal with National Crisis in Mathematics Education." *Chronicle of Higher Education*, 17 Apr. 1991: A15–A16.

Brodkey, Linda. "Transvaluing Difference." *College English* 51 (1989): 597–601.

Bullock, Richard, John Trimbur, and Charles Schuster. Preface. *The Politics of Writing Instruction: Postsecondary*. Ed. Bullock and Trimbur. Portsmouth, NH: Boynton, 1991. xvii–xx. Gen. ed. Schuster.

Caywood, Cynthia L., and Gillian R. Overing, eds. *Teaching Writing: Pedagogy, Gender, and Equity*. Albany: State U of New York P, 1987. xi–xvi.

"CCCC: Voices in the Parlor." *Rhetoric Review* 7 (1988): 198–213.

Connolly, Paul, and Teresa Vilardi, eds. *Writing to Learn Mathematics and Science*. New York: Teachers College, 1989.

Donahue, Patricia, and Ellen Quandahl. "Reading the Classroom." *Reclaiming Pedagogy: The Rhetoric of the Classroom*. Ed. Donahue and Quandahl. Carbondale: Southern Illinois UP, 1989. 1–16.

Ede, Lisa. "Teaching Writing." *An Introduction to Composition Studies*. Ed. Erika Lindemann and Gary Tate. New York: Oxford UP, 1991. 118–34.

Elbow, Peter. "Reflections on Academic Discourse: How It Relates to Freshmen and Colleagues." *College English* 53 (1991): 135–55.

Finlay, Linda Shaw, and Valerie Faith. "Illiteracy and Alienation in American Colleges: Is Paulo Freire's Pedagogy Relevant?" *Freire for the Classroom: A Sourcebook for Liberatory Teaching*. Ed. Ira Shor. Portsmouth, NH: Boynton, 1987. 63–86.

Flynn, Elizabeth A. "Composing as a Woman." *College Composition and Communication* 39 (1988): 423–35.

Frey, Olivia. "Beyond Literary Darwinism: Women's Voices and Critical Discourse." *College English* 52 (1990): 507–26.

Fulwiler, Toby. "The Quiet and Insistent Revolution: Writing Across the Curriculum." *The Politics of Writing Instruction: Postsecondary*. Ed. Richard Bullock and John Trimbur. Portsmouth, NH: Boynton, 1991. 179–87. Gen ed. Charles Schuster.

Fulwiler, Toby, and Art Young, eds. *Programs That Work: Models and Methods for Writing Across the Curriculum*. Portsmouth, NH: Boynton, 1990.

Harkin, Patricia. "Metacommentary on the Postdisciplinary Politics of Lore." Paper presented at the CCCC Research Network. Chicago, 21 Mar. 1990.

———. "The Postdisciplinary Politics of Lore." *Contending with Words: Composition and Rhetoric in a Postmodern Age*. New York: MLA, 1991. 124–38.

Hill, Carolyn Ericksen. *Writing from the Margins: Power and Pedagogy for Teachers of Composition*. New York: Oxford UP, 1990.

Holbrook, Sue Ellen. "Women's Work: The Feminizing of Composition." *Rhetoric Review* 9 (1991): 201–29.

Juncker, Clara. "Writing (with) Cixous." *College English* 50 (1988): 424–36.

Lauer, Janice M., and Andrea Lunsford. "The Place of Rhetoric and Composition in Doctoral Studies." *The Future of Doctoral Studies in English*. Ed. Andrea Lunsford, Helene Moglen, and James F. Slevin. New York: MLA, 1989. 106–10.

Lloyd-Jones, Richard, and Andrea Lunsford, eds. *The English Coalition Conference: Democracy Through Language*. Urbana, IL: NCTE; New York: MLA, 1989.

Murphy, Richard J., Jr. "On Stories and Scholarship." *College Composition and Communication* 40 (1989): 466–72.

North, Stephen M. *The Making of Knowledge in Composition: Portrait of an Emerging Field*. Upper Montclair, NJ: Boynton, 1987.

Peterson, Jane E. "Valuing Teaching: Assumptions, Problems, and Possibilities." *College Composition and Communication* 42 (1991): 25–35.

Reither, James A., and Douglas Vipond. "Writing as Collaboration." *College English* 51 (1989): 855–67.

Rigden, John S., and Sheila Tobias. "Too Often, College-Level Science Is Dull as Well as Difficult." *Chronicle of Higher Education* 27 Mar. 1991: A52.

Rose, Mike. *Lives on the Boundary: A Moving Account of the Struggles and Achievements of America's Educational Underclass*. New York: Penguin, 1989.

Snow, Richard E. "Aptitude-Treatment Interaction as a Framework for Research on Individual Differences in Learning." *Learning and Individual Differences: Advances in Theory and Research*. Ed. Phillip L. Ackerman, Robert J. Sternberg, and Robert Glaser. New York: Freeman, 1989. 14–59.

"Statement of Principles and Standards for the Postsecondary Teaching of Writing." *College Composition and Communication* 40 (1989): 329–36.

Tinberg, Howard B. "'An Enlargement of Observation': More on Theory Building the Composition Classroom." *College Composition and Communication* 42 (1991): 36–44.

Tompkins, Jane. "Me and My Shadow." *New Literary History* 19 (1987): 169–78.

White, Edward M. "Shallow Roots or Taproots for Writing Across the Curriculum?" *ADE Bulletin* 98 (Spring 1991): 29–33.

Young, Art, and Toby Fulwiler. "Afterword: The Enemies of Writing Across the Curriculum." *Programs That Work: Models and Methods for Writing Across the Curriculum*. Ed. Fulwiler and Young. Portsmouth, NH: Boynton, 1990. 287–94.

AT THE RISK
OF BEING PERSONAL . . .

Hearing Our Own Voices: Life-saving Stories

Lynn Z. Bloom/University of Connecticut, Storrs

Prologue

"Should I have a baby?" young women ask me at professional conferences. Even women I've never met before ask this. Does gray hair automatically signal stretch marks? "How will motherhood affect my career? Can I get tenure if I have children? I can't decide, to save my life."

I am always surprised by the question, but there is only one answer I can give.

My Job as Ventriloquist's Dummy

Once upon a time, as a newly minted Ph.D. with a newly minted baby, I got the best part-time job I've ever had, a half-time assistant professorship at a distinguished midwestern university. Unusual for the early 1960s, and unique to that institution, my job was created in response to the dean's estimate of an impending shortage of faculty. "It's going to be hell on wheels faculty-wise around here for the next five years," he said. So I was hired for exactly half of a full-time job: half the teaching load, half the advising and committee work, half the regular benefits. Our second child was born, conveniently, during my second summer vacation. Though not on a tenure track, I did have a parking space; it seemed a fair exchange. I taught freshman composition, of course, and sometimes sophomore lit surveys. I even taught in a room that overlooked the playground of our children's nursery school.

During the whole five years I taught there, I never expressed an original opinion about literature, either in class or out. In the course of my very fine education at one of our nation's very finest universities, taught entirely by men except for women's "phys ed," where they allowed a woman to teach us how to develop graceful "posture, figure, and carriage," I learned, among other things, that only real professors had the right to say what they thought. Anyway, in the 1950s there were no concepts, no language to say what I, as a nascent feminist critic, wanted to say. I tried, in a fifteen-page, junior-year honors paper, "Milton's Eve did too have some redeeming virtues." The paper was returned, next day, in virgin condition, save a small mark in the margin on page 2 where the professor had apparently stopped reading, and a tiny scarlet "C" discreetly tatooed at the end. In shame and horror at getting less than my usual "A," I went to see the professor. "Why did I get a C?" I was near tears. "Because," he said in measured tones, drawing on his pipe, "you simply can't say that." End of discussion. I did not sin again.

I had majored in English because I loved to read and to write, and I continued to love reading and writing all the way through graduate school. But somewhere along the line, perhaps through the examples of my professors, measured, judicious, self-controlled, I had come to believe that my job as a teacher was to present the material in a neutral manner, evenhandedly citing a range of "Prominent Male Critics," and let the students make up their own minds. It would have been embarrassing, unprofessional even, to express the passion I felt, so I taught every class in my ventriloquist's dummy voice. Indifferent student evaluations reflected the disengagement this approach provoked—"although she's a nice lady," some students added.

Editing textbooks didn't count. Only the other women who taught freshman composition part-time took this work seriously. (Collectively we were known to the male full-time faculty as the "Heights Housewives," as we learned from the captions on the witchlike cartoons that would occasionally appear on the bulletin board in the English department office.) I had collaboratively edited a collection of critical essays on Faulkner intended for freshman writing courses, signing the book contract in the hospital the day after the birth of my first child. I was working on two other collaborative texts. The English department invited my Faulkner collaborator, a gracious scholar of international renown, to come to campus to lecture on the subject of our book, but they did not invite me to either the lecture or the dinner for him. The university's public relations spokesman nevertheless called and asked if I'd be willing to give a cocktail party for him, at my expense. That may have been the only time I ever said "no" during the whole five years I taught there.

Freshman composition didn't count. I was
so apprehensive about publishing original writing in my own name that when my husband,
Martin, a social psychologist, and I collaborated
on an article about a student's writing process, I
insisted that we submit it in Martin's name only.
Only real professors with full-time jobs could
publish academic articles, and I knew I wasn't
one. *College English* accepted it by return mail.
"Now do you want your name on it?" Martin
asked. "You should be first author." "Yes," I
said. "Yes."

My work in nonfiction didn't count. I proudly told the department chair that I was beginning research on a biography of Dr. Benjamin
Spock, soon to retire from his faculty position at
the same university. I had access to all the primary sources I needed, including Spock himself.
"Why don't you write a series of biographical
articles on major literary figures?" asked our
leader, whose customary advice to faculty requests for raises was "diversify your portfolio."
"Once you've established your reputation you
can afford to throw it away by writing about a
popular figure." I thanked him politely and continued my research, a logical extension of my dissertation study of biographical method. I could
learn a lot about how people wrote biographies, I
reasoned, if I wrote one myself. And because I
couldn't say to the children, "Go away, don't
bother me, I'm writing about Doctor Spock," I
learned to write with them in the room.

Ultimately, I didn't count either. A new department chairman arrived soon after I began
the biography. His first official act, prior to making a concerted but unsuccessful effort to abol-
ish freshman English, was to fire all the part-
time faculty, everyone (except TAs) who taught
the lowly subject. All women but one. He told
me privately, in person; a doctorate, after all, has
some privileges, though my office mate learned

of her status when the chairman showed a job candidate the office, announcing, "This will be vacant next year." He was kind enough to write me a letter of recommendation, a single sentence that said, "Mrs. Bloom would be a good teacher of freshman composition." I actually submitted that letter along with a job application. Once.

On the Floor with the Kitty Litter

One of the textbooks so scorned during my first part-time job actually got me my first full-time job, two years later. The department had adopted it for the freshman honors course, and the chair had written an enthusiastic review. Then, dear reader, he hired me! This welcoming work enabled me to find my voice. After ten years of part-time teaching, as bland as vanilla pudding, I felt free to spice up the menu. Being a full-time faculty member gave me the freedom to express my opinions about what we read and wrote and to argue and joke with my students. My classes became noisy, personal, and fun. I received tenure two years later, promotion, and an award for good teaching. But after four years in Indiana, my husband was offered a job in St. Louis too good to turn down. I resigned to move.

My voice was reduced to a whisper. I could find no full-time job in St. Louis in that inhospitable year of 1974 when there were several hundred applicants for every job. In hopes of ingratiating myself with one or another of the local universities, I taught part-time at three, marginal combinations of writing and women's studies. I taught early in the morning, in mid-afternoon, at night, coming and going under cover of lightness, and darkness. It didn't matter, for no one except my students knew I was there anyway. Department chairmen wouldn't see me; with insulated indifference, faculty—

even some I'd known in graduate school—walked past my invisible self in the halls. For administrative convenience, I was paid once a semester, after Thanksgiving, $400. Fringe benefits, retirement, the possibility of raises or continuity of employment were nonexistent. At none of the three schools did I have any stationery, mailing privileges, secretarial help, telephone, or other amenities—not even an ID or a library card. I was treated as an illegal alien.

Nowhere did I have an office, until I finally begged for one at the plushest school, frustrated and embarrassed at having to confer with my students in the halls on the run. After several weeks, the word trickled down that I could share space with a TA—and as it turned out, her cat, which she kept confined there. This office symbolized my status on all three jobs. It was in a building across campus from the English department, where no one could see us. It was under a stairwell, so we couldn't stand up. It had no windows, so we couldn't see out, but it did have a satanic poster on the wall—shades of the underworld. The TA had the desk, so I got to sit on the floor next to the kitty litter. I stayed there, in the redolent dark, for a full thirty seconds.

Then my voice returned, inside my head this time. Its message was powerful and clear, "If I ever do this again I deserve what I get." I did finish the semester. But I never went back to that office. And I never again took another job that supported such an exploitative system, even though that meant commuting 2,000 miles a week to my next job, a real job, in New Mexico. "Go for it," said Martin, and he took care of the children while I was away.

Poison in the Public Ivy

Four years later we moved again to eliminate my cross-country commute. Through research support, graduate teaching, directing a writing program, and supervising some sixty TAs and part-time faculty, my New Mexico job had given me a grown-up voice. I was beginning to talk to colleagues throughout the country, at meetings, through my own publications and those of my students, and I was looking forward to continuing the dialogue on the new job as associate professor and writing director at a southern, and therefore by definition gracious, "Public Ivy."

As I entered the mellowed, red-brick building on the first day of class, a colleague blocked the door. "We expected to get a beginning assistant professor and wash *him* out after three years," he sneered. "Instead, we got *you*, and *you'll* probably get tenure." I took a deep breath and replied in a firm voice, "You bet." "We" contains multitudes; one never knows at the outset how many. Although the delegated greeter never spoke to me again, it soon became clear that *we* meant a gang of four equal-opportunity harassers, all men, all tenured faculty of long-standing, all eager to stifle my voice. Their voices, loud and long, dominated all department and committee meetings and word had it, the weekly poker games where the decisions were really made. I could do no right. I was too nice to my students; everybody knows that undergraduates can't write. I was merely flattering the students by encouraging them to publish; that they did indeed publish showed they were pandering to the public. My writing project work with school teachers was (aha!) proof that I was more interested in teaching than in literary criticism; misplaced priorities. My own publications, ever increasing, were evidence of blatant careerism. I received a number of grants and fellowships; just a way to get out of teaching. The attendant newspaper publicity, though good for the school, reflected badly on my femininity.

Although I was heard in class, and increasingly, in the profession at large, I had no voice in the departmental power structure. The gang of four and by extrapolation, the rest of the faculty, already knew everything they needed to know about teaching writing; they'd learned it long ago as TAs. Faculty development workshops were a waste of time. The college didn't need a writing director anyway; the students all wrote well, the faculty all taught well, and Southern Public Ivy had gotten along for two hundred years without a writing director. Why start now? As a way to forestall my imminent tenure review, this hospitable group initiated a review of the position of writing director. If they could demonstrate that there was no need for the job, despite the thousand students enrolled every semester in required freshman English, not to mention the upper-division writing courses, oversubscribed and with waiting lists, and the initiative in other departments for a writing-across-the-curriculum program, I would not have the opportunity to come up for tenure. Because the review was, of course, of the job and not of the person in it, I, of course, could not be consulted; that would compromise the impartiality of the process. Nor could I discuss the ongoing review with colleagues; ditto. Or the department chair; ditto. Or the dean; ditto, ditto.

The review began in September of my second year. Nobody identified its criteria; nobody told me what it covered; I could not ask. Occasionally a friendly colleague would sneak into my office during that very long fall semester and tell me that he was so anguished by the proceedings he wanted to resign from the review committee; sotto voce I urged him to stay on it. A borrowed voice was better than none. Rumor had it, I heard, that I was talking to a lawyer. How unprofessional. Oh was I? I whispered. The campus AAUP president heard about the review; write me a letter, he said, outlining what's going on, and I'll send it to the national office. So I did. And he did.

Then, on a clear crisp evening in January, tenure became irrelevant. Our family dinner was interrupted by the phone call that every parent dreads. Come right away.

We saw the car, first, on a curve in the highway near the high school, crushed into a concrete telephone pole. Next was the rescue squad ambulance, lights revolving red and white, red and white, halted amidst shattered glass. Then the figure on the stretcher, only a familiar chin emerging from the bandages that swathed the head. "He was thrown out of the back seat. The hatchback door smashed his face as if he'd been hit with an axe," said the medic. "I'm fine," said our son, and we responded with terror's invariable lie, "You're going to be all right."

After six hours of ambiguous X rays, clear pictures finally emerged long after midnight, explaining why Laird's eyes were no longer parallel—one socket had simply been pulverized. The line of jagged-lightning stitches, sixty in all, that bolted across his face would be re-opened the next day for reconstructive surgery. "Don't go out in a full moon," sick-joked the doctor, howling like a banshee. "People will mistake you for a zombie."

Laird had to remain upright for a month so his head would drain, and our family spent every February evening on the couch in front of the wood stove, propping each other up. Every day the writing directorship review committee asked by memo for more information; every day I replied, automatically. I do not know, now, what they asked; I do not know, now, what I answered; or what I wrote on student papers; or what we ate or read or wrote checks for during that long month.

But I do know that in early March the AAUP's lawyer called me and his message was simple: "A university has every right to eliminate a position, or a program, if there is no academic need, if there are no students in it, for example. But it cannot eliminate a position just to get rid of the person holding the job. If Southern Ivy does this, they'll be blacklisted." He repeated this to the department chair; when the department voted, in its new wisdom, in late April to table the review of the writing directorship until after I had been reviewed for tenure, a friend, safely tenured, whispered to me, "You just got tenure." The thick copies of the committee's review were never distributed; I was awarded tenure the next year—and left immediately to become department chair at Urban State University, tenured, promoted to professor, with authority to have an emphatic voice. The review was never reinstated, says a faculty friend still at Southern Ivy; for six years the writing directorship went unfilled.

Escaping the Rapist

Life-saving stories embed life-saving lessons. We learn as we listen. We find our own voices gradually; we can lose them in the twinkling of an eye. When laryngitis strikes, we need others to speak on our behalf. But when we do have a voice, we need also to speak for others. Even more important, we need to use our new-found voices to enable the marginal, the isolated, minorities and women, men too, to speak for themselves. As administrators and as teachers, we fulfill roles that require voices, powerful and emphatic.

In fact, the best part of being department chair was helping others to find their own voices. Those who can speak for themselves, if they are of goodwill, can speak well for their university, their profession. It was fun, as chair of Urban State's large and diverse English department, to encourage a host of people to speak up for what they wanted, the very things for which I'd been silenced in the past. Of course you should write that article, that book. Don't worry about whether the subject is in or out of fashion, do it for its own sake, for your sake, for the fun of it. Query publishers; apply for grant support; there's nothing to lose. By all means, try that new course, new administrative role, new job entirely; the growth is worth the risk. You want a full-time job? Better plan to finish your Ph.D. Where do you want to go? Can we help you get some support? You're burned out, and here the dean is putting pressure on you to publish. Let's try to arrange a course schedule, a reduced load, a semester's leave to help you get a project underway. First, come up with a proposal. You're right, part-timers shouldn't have to confer with their students in the hallways. We'll find some space, even if we have to carve up the storage room. Your teaching evaluations reflect your own dissatisfaction with the course? Let's arrange for some conversations, and perhaps reciprocal class visits, with trusted colleagues whose teaching you like. Of course I'll write you a recommendation—for a teaching award, a grant, a fellowship, even for another job, if that's best for you.

Fortunately, even as department chair I could continue to teach, and I often taught "Women Writers." One day my class, not only writing-intensive but discussion-intensive, began arguing about the characters in Joyce Carol Oates's "Where Are You Going, Where Have You Been?" Some claimed that Arnold Friend, "thirty, maybe," who invades Connie's driveway in "an open jalopy, painted a bright gold," his eyes hidden behind mirrored, metallic sunglasses, is in love with the pubescent teenager about whom "everything has two sides to it, one for home and one for

anywhere that was not home." Others asserted
that from the moment they met, Arnold's " 'Gon-
na get you, baby,' " signaled the abduction with
which the story concludes, though he does not lay
a finger on his victim. After screaming for help
into a dead phone until she loses her breath,
Connie has no more voice and walks sacrificially
out into the sunlight and Friend's mockingly
waiting arms. As the love versus violence debate
continued, it seemed as if the class session would
end without closure.

I dediced to wrap it up with a life-saving
story of my own. "A decade earlier," I began,
"my husband, adolescent sons, and I were camp-
ing in Scandinavia. But it was a dark and stormy
night in Stockholm, so we decided to spend the
night in a university dorm converted to a youth
hostel for the summer. At 10 P.M., the boys
tucked in, Martin and I headed for the showers
down the hall. He dropped me off in front of the
door decorated with a large, hand-lettered sign,
"Damar. Women. Frauen. Dames." and went to
the men's shower at the other end of the long
corridor. As I groped for a light switch in the
pitch black room, it struck me as odd that the
lights were off at night in a public building. The
room was dead silent, not even a faucet drip-
ping. I walked past a row of sinks to the cur-
tained shower stall closest to the window, where
I could leave my clothes and towel on the sill.

"As I turned, naked, to step into the shower, a man wearing a bright-blue track suit and
blue running shoes shoved aside the curtain of a
shower stall across the aisle and headed toward
me. I began to scream in impeccable English,
'Get out! You're in the women's shower.' He
kept on coming. My voice had the wrong words,
the wrong language. I screamed again, now into
his face, looming over mine as he hit me on the
mouth. I screamed again, 'Get out!' as he hit me
on the cheek. My mouth was cut, I could taste

the salty blood as he hit me again in the head. I began to lose my balance. 'If he knocks me down on the tile,' I thought, 'he'll kill me.' Then I thought, still screaming, 'I don't want my children to hear this.'

"Then time slowed down, inside my head, the way it does just before you think your car is going to crash when it goes into a skid, and the voices, all mine, took over. One voice could say nothing at all for terror. I had never been hit before in my life. How could I know what to do? The man in blue, silent, continued to pummel my head, his face suffused with hatred, his eyes vacant. Another voice reasoned, 'I need to get my clothes and get out.' 'But to get my clothes I'll have to go past him twice.' 'I should just get out.' Still I couldn't move, the whirling blue arms continued to pound me, I was off balance now and afraid of falling. Then the angry message came, etched in adrenaline. 'I didn't ask for this, I don't deserve it, and I'm not going to take it.' I ran naked into the corridor."

The bell rang. "Oates's story is about violence, not love," I told the class. The students, whose effervescent conversation usually bubbled out into the corridor as they dispersed, filed out in silence.

That was on a Thursday. The following Tuesday, an hour before our next class meeting, a student, svelte and usually poised, came into my office, crying. "What's the matter?" I asked. "Saturday night," she said, "I was walking home alone—I live alone—and heard the phone ringing in my apartment. When I rushed in to answer it, I must have left the door open. Because after I'd hung up, when I went into the kitchen a man stepped out from behind the curtain, grabbed me from behind, and shoved a gasoline-soaked rag over my face. As he began to wrestle with me, he ripped my shirt trying to throw me down. Suddenly I heard your voice in my head, repeating the words you'd said in class, 'I didn't ask for this, I don't deserve it, and I'm not going to take it.' I ran, screaming, into the street and flagged a passing policeman. You saved my life."

"No," I said, "you saved your own life."

PART 2

SEDUCTION AND SUSPICION

The administration of our profession and our departments continues to be structured on a pyramid model that valorizes individual authority over collaboration and research over teaching. The authors in this section alert us to the ways in which we have been seduced by this model, reproducing its structure and accepting its value system. They encourage us to remain suspicious of its validity for the discipline.

Jeanne Gunner narrates the evolution of the "Statement of Principles and Standards for the Postsecondary Teaching of Writing" from its beginnings as the "Wyoming Resolution." This is the story of how disciplinary leaders can be so seduced by "MLA-like" power and status that they ultimately transform a document initially designed to protect the professionals whose identity "deviates from the traditional academic-scholarly mold," into a document which excludes these very people. Cynthia Tuell describes a second act of seduction, one in which composition teachers have willingly seen themselves through the eyes of "tenured superiors teaching literature." Condoning a perspective in which theirs is understood as "women's work," composition teachers have belittled their work and accepted their positions as subordinates.

Marcia Dickson challenges the viability of a WPA model that places the "power to command or legislate change" in the hands of the writing program administrator. She proposes a model of administration that eschews such power and desire for authority. In her feminist model, which reverses the value system of the authoritative WPA, the central administrative responsibilities include accessibility, communication, reading current literature, and training staff. Adding to the conversation about writing program administration, Michael Pemberton reveals the "tale too terrible to tell": Although most faculty appointments in composition include considerable administrative duties, our graduate programs, like the discipline, are suspiciously and harmfully silent about administration. For ideological, practical, and political reasons, graduate programs are leaving their students completely unknowing of the theoretical underpinnings of administrative duties and choices and consequently, unprepared for a significant portion of their professional future.

6

The Fate of the Wyoming Resolution: A History of Professional Seduction

Jeanne Gunner/*University of California, Los Angeles*

"Professional standards" means simply the standards of those
who have achieved prominence in the profession.
—Richard Ohmann, *English in America*

    The document that has come to be known as the Wyoming
Resolution is a statement against the exploitation of part-time and
temporary writing faculty. It is a simple document:

Wyoming Resolution
    WHEREAS, the salaries and working conditions of post-secondary
teachers with primary responsibility for the teaching of writing are
fundamentally unfair as judged by any reasonable professional standards (e.g., unfair in excessive teaching loads, unreasonably large
class sizes, salary inequities, lack of benefits and professional status,
and barriers to professional advancement) . . .
    AND WHEREAS, as a consequence of these unreasonable working
conditions, highly dedicated teachers are often frustrated in their
desire to provide students the time and attention which students
both deserve and need . . .

THEREFORE, BE IT RESOLVED that the Executive Committee of College Composition and Communication be charged with the following:

1. To formulate, after appropriate consultations with post-secondary teachers of writing, professional standards and expectations for salary levels and working conditions of post-secondary teachers of writing.

2. To establish a procedure for hearing grievances brought by post-secondary teachers of writing—whether singly or collectively—against apparent institutional non-compliance with these standards and expectations.

3. To establish a procedure for acting upon a finding of non-compliance; specifically, to issue a letter of censure to an individual institution's administration, Board of Regents or Trustees, State legislators (where pertinent), and to publicize the finding to the public-at-large, the educational community in general, and to our membership.

[Drafted June, 1986]

The chain of textual events leading from this document to the CCCC's "Statement of Principles and Standards for the Postsecondary Teaching of Writing" forms the focus of this essay. It is a study of when, how, and why a document that petitions for an end to the exploitation of writing teachers could have engendered an institutionally sponsored statement calling for the professional exclusion of many of these same individuals—more specifically, of those whose professional identity deviates from the traditional academic-scholarly mold. The history of the document and of the professional organization's responses to it reveals the mechanisms of professional power, an enactment of what Richard Ohmann has termed the "professionalization process." If we examine the changes in the substance of the Wyoming Resolution made over time in light of the steps in the professionalization process, what we see is a progressive silencing of the group that inspired the original document and their document itself transformed into a statement on academic privilege.

In this story of seduction, of organizational and disciplinary leaders blinded by the allures of what might be called "MLA-like" power and status, real people with real labor problems become abstractions and ultimately, the reification and symbol of the abuses they originally protested against. Their call for reform is redefined to satisfy the professional desires of leaders in the rhetoric/composition field: their document is used not to redress the problems cited by the resolution's original framers but to enhance the privilege of a small circle of the disciplinary elite.

The story begins with the original Wyoming Resolution. It develops through the opinion essay that formally presented the resolution to the CCCC membership in *College English*, the draft version of the "Statement of Principles and Standards," which is the first version of the official CCCC response, and the final version of the statement published in *College Composition and Communication*.

Textual History and Contrasting Rhetorics

The original Wyoming Resolution was composed and revised by participants at the 1986 Wyoming Conference on English, held in Laramie, Wyoming. In its revised form, the resolution was forwarded by its drafters to the profession's representative body, the CCCC, after the required signatures had been collected to establish it as a formal petition. The document became a CCCC initiative, to be voted upon at the 1987 CCCC.

Wyoming Conference attendees Linda Robertson, Sharon Crowley, and Frank Lentricchia published an opinion piece on the resolution in the March 1987 issue of *College English* ("The Wyoming Conference Resolution Opposing Unfair Salaries and Working Conditions for Post-Secondary Teachers of Writing"), in advance of the 1987 CCCC in Atlanta. At the conference, the membership endorsed the initiative, empowering the CCCC to take action on it. The task of translating the document into practical professional guidelines was handed to the newly created Wyoming Task Force, later the CCCC Committee on Professional Standards for Quality Education, and finally renamed the Professional Standards Committee.

The committee, chaired by James Slevin,[1] formulated its response and published the results in the February 1989 *CCC* ("CCCC Initiatives on the Wyoming Conference Resolution: A Draft Report"). The committee continued revising the draft in the wake of CCCC members' responses and discussions, particularly those held at the 1989 CCCC in Seattle.[2] In its final revised form, the document was approved by the CCCC Executive Committee and published in the October 1989 *CCC* ("Statement of Principles and Standards for the Postsecondary Teaching of Writing"). It was distributed to "over 8000 educators including high-level administrators and English Department chairs at all American postsecondary institutions" (*CCC* 40:61). It continues to be presented at professional meetings as the CCCC's "position on part-time and temporary faculty" (Peterson 3). This organizationally approved, final version of the statement, which is held to be the profession's response to the concerns of the Wyoming Resolution, proposes as a solution to the exploitation of writing teachers' labor a severe restriction on the use of part-time positions and the conversion of full-time temporary appointments to the tenure track.

Close examination of the relevant documents—the original Wyoming Resolution, the *College English* article presenting it to the CCCC membership, the draft and final versions of the CCCC statement—illuminates a continued undermining of the original goals of the Wyoming Resolution and a disturbing picture of the CCCC professional agenda. The three-page draft version of the statement reveals an already realized shift, in spirit and intent, from the original document. It is the first published evidence of what can be termed the betrayal of the Wyoming Resolution. The final version, the professional organization's official position paper, refines and finalizes the ideological shift from the establishment of fair working conditions to reinforcement of the traditional academic hierarchy.

The Wyoming Resolution protests the exploitation of postsecondary teachers of writing and outlines a path for addressing the problem of institutional abuse. In the document, the authors cite as their primary concerns salary inequities and detrimental working conditions. They assert that such conditions impinge upon the time and attention that highly dedicated teachers should and desire to give to their students. They call on the CCCC Executive Committee to do three things to ameliorate the poor working conditions that frustrate them:

1. formulate professional standards and expectations for salary levels and working conditions for postsecondary teachers of writing, after consulting with them;
2. establish a procedure for hearing teachers' grievances regarding institutional noncompliance; and
3. establish a procedure for acting upon a finding of noncompliance, specifically, a letter of censure and publication of the noncompliance finding.

In its rhetorical organization, the Wyoming Resolution exudes the spirit of historical imperative, calling to mind the Decla-

ration of Independence with its list of violations and the conse-
quential redress sought. The resolution is cast in the formal
language of legal petition tempered by multiple references to the
people whose petition it is—postsecondary teachers of writing. It
seeks to draw together, in action and identification, using the
collective term "postsecondary" in order to transcend the hierarchical divisions of graduate student, instructor, assistant/
associate/full professor. It employs human terms of "desire" and
"frustration"; it is replete with terms invoking ethical action,
referring to "responsibility," to practices that are "judged" "unfair," "unreasonable," "excessive," "inequitable," to needs that
"deserve" to be met. It devotes equal attention to salary levels,
working conditions, and grievance procedures. It ends with a call
for public involvement.

The opinion piece on the Wyoming Resolution published in
the March 1987 issue of *College English* has as one of its apparent
goals the encouragement of CCCC membership to vote on the
resolution at the yearly convention. The essay authors, Robertson,
Crowley, and Lentricchia, position themselves as the reporting
voice of the Wyoming Conference attendees and interpret for the
College English readership the conference events that led to the
drafting of the resolution.

The essay opens by reiterating the main points of the resolution: to establish a grievance procedure to redress unfair working
conditions and salaries (the order of concerns are transposed in the
College English essay—the original resolution cites salary levels
first, working conditions second). The essay acknowledges the
grievance issue as having central place in the authors' and document's intentions. The essay's authors write as their second sentence, "The resolution calls upon the Executive Committee to
establish grievance procedures for post-secondary writing teachers seeking to redress unfair working conditions and salaries"
(274). This fact is an important one in the textual chronology, as
subsequent analysis shows.

The authors of the opinion essay move on to describe the
context out of which the resolution developed: they emphasize the
conference theme—"Language and Social Context"—and how it
eventually turned into a discussion of the social context of writing
teachers. From teachers enabling students to "discover the freedom of self-expression" (274), the discussion, we are told, shifted
to a recognition that some teachers themselves "often feel unable

to speak freely about the fundamentally unfair conditions under which [they] labor" (274). At this point, it is reported, a kind of "share" session began. There were complaints about pay, course load, status, review—complaints, we learn, made by a range of people holding a range of positions: part-time, full-time, tenured.

The essay then takes up two topics raised at the conference by James Slevin: the underemployment of new English Ph.D.s and the threat to academic freedom posed by the use of part-time faculty. The unemployment plight has been caused in part, Slevin reportedly argued, by a trend to hire part-time faculty, who for the most part are assigned to writing courses. Together with this problem, the authors cite the second issue: the argument that "there are larger issues of academic freedom inherent in hiring policies which rely heavily on part-time or temporary positions" (275). These two concerns of the underemployment of new Ph.D.s and the issue of academic freedom later play a role—a devastating role—in the undermining of the Wyoming Resolution, forming the basis for its co-optation and reinterpreting the kind of change it seeks.

The focus of the opinion essay shifts attention from low salaries, poor working conditions, and the need for grievance procedures, which are the concerns of the resolution authors, to "the threats to academic freedom and the absence of job security faced by many teachers of writing" (276). In this revision of the document's main concerns, a critical transformation has taken place: instead of specific, material conditions—low pay, high course load, etc.—and a particular course of action—letters of censure—the issues have become abstractions: academic freedom and job security.

This shift in focus and values is radically extended in the *CCC* article, "CCCC Initiatives on the Wyoming Conference Resolution: A Draft Report." In its published draft form, the CCCC statement had already passed through the CCCC Executive Committee and been endorsed by it, though final approval was still pending. The resolution, as a petition, is an invitation to dialogue, the draft ostensibly a response: its title suggests that the CCCC statement is the professional and organizational reply to the Wyoming Resolution's concerns. The article, however, makes no reference to the resolution, thus distancing itself from it, with the effect of terminating the textual dialogue. The statement annexes and transforms the issues of the resolution. Two profound changes are particularly evident: the demise of the Wyoming Resolution's grievance articles and the rhetorical shift from its references to "teachers of writing" to the draft's references to "positions," a reformulation of real, working people into institutional units, into representations of institutional power expressed in terms of economics and social status.

The CCCC's response dismisses resolution items 2 and 3, which specifically address grievance procedures. The document opens with a three-item section devoted to "Tenure-Line Faculty." In item A, the "legitimate" scholarly base of the field of rhetoric and composition is asserted. From the start, then, this is a document that proposes and thenceforth assumes the traditional academic model, in its organizational and political aspects, as the one that should prevail in the composition field. Item B then appropriates teaching excellence to tenure-line faculty: "To provide the highest quality of instruction and research, departments offering composition or writing courses should rely on tenure-line faculty members with a demonstrated commitment to the teaching of writing" (62). The connection between tenure-line status and high-quality, committed instruction, as the CCCC sees this connection, is provided in the next sentence (emphasis added): "Evidence of this commitment [to the teaching of writing] can be found in *research and publication, participation in professional conferences*, and active involvement in curriculum development and design" (62).

One might make the obvious argument that commitment to the teaching of writing is amply displayed in years of teaching performed under unfair labor conditions and enormous salary inequities; surely this is one assumption behind the Wyoming Resolution. Just as surely, the CCCC redefines excellence and commitment, showing both derive not from the individual, but from the institutional: the traditional academic structure—the system of research, publication, and tenure.

Item B further interlaces composition teaching with the traditional structure by acknowledging the role mainstream English department faculty, i.e., literature faculty, should play in composition instruction. The effect is to form an alliance of composition/literature faculty, thus solidifying the composition/rhetoric faculty's position in the structure. The final line of the item—that faculty "professionally committed to rhetoric and composition" (62) should control composition programs—carves out and stakes a claim to the area of administrative power that a faculty so allied must seek to maintain for itself.

The final item in this first section reasserts a crucial assumption for the CCCC argument: Research is "fundamentally necessary to the quality of education at all levels" (62). With this assertion operating as a given, the statement goes on to outline its solution to the Wyoming Resolution concerns over salary and conditions by calling for the abolition of temporary or part-time positions and the establishment of tenure-track positions.

In the section entitled "Full-Time Temporary Faculty," we see the move from people to positions in order to eliminate the problem—the people themselves: "The use of [full-time temporary] positions to provide instruction . . . is exploitative. These positions are tolerable only as a stage in converting part-time positions into full-time tenure-track positions" (62). The term *positions* is used four times, *appointments* once, within the space of two sentences. The Wyoming Resolution's language, its repeated reference to "postsecondary teachers of writing," has been rejected, and the individuals ejected, to be supplanted by the abstractions "positions" and "appointments."

The Move to Professionalization

The motives implicit in the organization's stance can best be illustrated by comparing the rhetoric of the "Statement of Principles and Standards for the Postsecondary Teaching of Writing," the finalized, official CCCC statement on the Wyoming Resolution issues published in *CCC* in October 1989, with Richard Ohmann's analysis of what he calls the "professionalization process." He identifies six steps, each a historical stage in attaining the final goal of disciplinary control:

> Professions are socially made categories. . . . A group that is doing a particular kind of work [1] *organizes itself in a professional association*; [2] *appropriates, shares, and develops a body of knowledge*; [3] *discredits other practitioners performing similar work*; [4] *establishes definite routes of admission*, including but not limited to academic study; [5] *controls access*; and [6] *gets recognition as the only group allowed to perform that kind of work*, ideally with state power backing its monopoly. (250; emphasis and enumeration added)

In the case of the CCCC, step 1—professional organization— was established over forty years ago. This heritage is itself often invoked as the work of achieving step 2 goes on—the appropriation and development of a body of knowledge. We can see tangible evidence of the organization's enormous and laudable effort to consolidate the knowledge of the field in several early NCTE publications: Braddock, Lloyd-Jones, and Schoer's *Research in Written Composition* (1963), Cooper and Odell's *Research on Composing* (1974).[3]

Step 3—the discrediting of other practitioners performing similar work—is the step that describes what is happening on the immediate professional scene, though by examining the Wyoming Resolution and CCCC Statement, we can clearly see the beginnings of the final steps in the professionalization process as well—the establishment of the routes to admission, control of access, and the group's monopolization of the field.

Parts of the CCCC statement clearly demonstrate the attempt to discredit teachers of writing and to establish an exclusively scholarly model. As with the draft, the finalized document emphasizes that *positions* are to be converted to tenure track: "We offer guidelines as well for the professional recognition and treatment of part-time and temporary full-time faculty during the period when these positions are being transformed to the tenure track" (330). The poor working conditions cited in the Wyoming Resolution have been transformed in the CCCC Statement to mean temporary or part-time appointments. Again, real people's jobs are not to be upgraded, regardless of their rank or status; the change called for is the abolition of temporary and part-time positions in favor of tenure-track appointments.

An implicit assumption in this process of conversion to tenure track is that the new position will be occupied by someone other than the person who has been marginalized and exploited by poor working conditions: "The CCCC recognizes, with respect and gratitude, the extraordinary contributions that so many of these teachers have made to their students and schools. But it is evident that their working conditions undermine the capacities of teachers to teach and of students to learn" (330). Thus the statement seeks to solve the problem of poor working conditions by firing temporary or part-time writing teachers.

The statement does offer a rationale for this peculiar solution: "Quality in education is intimately linked to the quality of teachers" (329). "Higher education traditionally assures this quality by providing reasonable teaching loads, research support, and even-

tual tenure for those who meet rigorous professional standards"
(329). The logic here says that tenure assures educational quality
and that one cannot be a qualified teacher of writing if one is not on
the tenure track—if, in other words, one does not conform to the
traditional academic model. The statement goes on to reinforce
this view: "The excessive reliance on marginalized faculty dam-
ages the quality of education" (330); "assuring and sustaining
quality in education is incompatible with relying . . . on part-time
faculty appointments in rhetoric and composition" (333); "the
commitment to quality education requires that the number of part-
time writing teachers . . . be kept to a minimum" (333).

Having asserted the incompetence of compositionists who
are outside the traditional academic structure, the statement then
enacts what can be seen as step 3 of the professionalization
process—the discrediting of practitioners in order to assert the
group's power: "These guidelines are based on the assumption
that the responsibility for the academy's most serious mission,
helping students to develop their critical powers as readers and
writers, should be vested in tenure-line faculty" (330); "to provide
the highest quality of instruction, departments offering composition
and writing courses should rely on full-time tenured or tenure-track
faculty members who are both prepared for and committed to the
teaching of writing" (331); "whenever possible, faculty professionally committed to rhetoric and composition should coordinate and
supervise composition programs. *Evidence of this commitment can
be found in research and publication*" (331; emphasis added).

Thus professionalization steps 4 and 5—routes of admission
and control of access—have also come into play. All that remains is
to invoke the power of the state as a means of supporting one's
professional monopoly: "When institutions depend increasingly
on faculty whose positions are tenuous and whose rights and
privileges are unclear or non-existent, those freedoms established
as the right of full-time tenurable and tenured faculty are endan-
gered" (330). This leads us to the conclusion: "The quality, integrity, and continuity of instruction and the principle of academic
freedom are best ensured by a full-time tenured or tenure-track
faculty" (334). The foundation for a supply-and-demand staffing
procedure—graduate faculty in graduate programs producing
graduate students—has been laid.

This call for professionalization includes an increasingly
rigid view of writing program administration, as the statement

frames it: "Whenever possible, faculty professionally committed to rhetoric and composition should coordinate and supervise composition programs." Such faculty are to be defined by research, publication, and professional activity—in other words, they will come from the composition/rhetoric scholarly establishment, not from the ranks of the experienced but non-tenure-track individuals who have performed these functions in the past. In this and in articles such as Olson and Moxley's "Directing Freshman Composition: The Limits of Authority" (1989), it is difficult not to detect an attempt to assert professional control over what is apparently seen as a threatening subgroup. By removing the administrative power to an already-tenured faculty member, the hierarchy remains neatly in place, and the profession is able to deny the professional validity of what is in actuality a new class of practitioners—those whose expertise has developed outside the typical, traditional scholarly track.

The Wyoming Resolution is centrally about improving real people's working lives. The CCCC document is about standardizing the profession and improving the status of only certain composition/rhetoric professionals by encouraging the professionalization process. Its effect is to mandate a rigid professional track: To succeed in the profession—indeed, to be in the profession—one must be part of the profession as the CCCC has come to define it.

The formulators of the statement, even as they call for fully tenured or tenure-track composition programs, acknowledge that the document cannot be expected to lead to actual change. Thus behind the publicly asserted purpose of the document must lie some other motive. Some struggle is evident, some organizational crisis of identity, of divided loyalty. The organization seems to try to validate its chosen course of action through the self-deluding righteousness of the statement. In actuality, as composition programs and compositionists are institutionalized in the ways called for by the statement, they increasingly reflect the values of a larger professional community—values that we might ultimately associate with another, larger, stronger professional organization; with, in short, the MLA. This image, then, is the seducer, the Wyoming Resolution's rival for organizational favor. The CCCC has had two suitors, and it has shown in its statement, a sad and painful betrayal of the Wyoming Resolution, its final preference.

In its response to the Wyoming Resolution, the composition establishment, represented by the CCCC, shows its efforts to solidify its base in the academic hierarchy, particularly within the research university, and to extend its control over those aspects of the profession that formerly allowed alternative career paths to exist—careers that differed from the scholarly model. This professional agenda makes necessary the kind of rhetoric we heard in the chair's address at the 1989 CCCC in Seattle. In part it reads:

- We are strongly interdisciplinary . . .
- We are non-hierarchical and exploratory, intensely collaborative . . .
- We are dialogic, multi-voiced, heteroglossic . . .
- We are radically democratic . . .
- We are committed to maintaining the dynamic tension between *praxis* and *theoria*, between the political and the epistemological. . . . (Lunsford 76)

Ironically, later in this same speech, Lunsford praises Mike Rose's *Lives on the Boundary*, which is precisely the type of work that would be discouraged, perhaps made impossible, if the author were under the professional constraints of tenure and promotion considerations.[4] The book is not "scholarly" in the traditional sense. It is, in the most important way, personal; it does not reify people and social problems but works to reassert the faces of those who seek education—and who dare to see themselves as educators. In an instance such as this, one can argue that membership in the traditional profession is itself a major restriction on academic freedom because it rewards work that fits the mold and discourages work that fails to preserve the value of academic privilege and exclusivity.

The writer who deviates from the mold runs the professional risk of losing institutional approval. He or she may encounter professional silence or in notably unusual cases, direct reprimand, an example of which we can see in a series of notes in *Rhetoric Review*'s "Burkean Parlor." In this journal space, several anonymous conference attendees express their sense of alienation, anger, and disillusionment with the professional promise that seems to have been co-opted by the dominant forces of the profession. The choral voices speak their dissatisfaction with the professional hierarchy they see, with its impulse to make pronouncements about the profession rather than to address the concerns voiced by "the fringe, the margin, [which is the voice] of exigency, of need, of demands too troubling to be heard" ("CCCC: Voices"

198). The authors are identified by initials only. They are allowed to criticize the professional organization but in a manner that diminishes the professional authority of those views (unsigned journal articles); the *appearance* of tolerance and access, however, has been preserved. More ironically, the initials of the respondents belong to people whose names are nationally recognizable, and all of them are highly visible presences in the profession and professional organizations. The powerless remain nameless; the professional forces transcend the limitation, demonstrating their power.

Conclusion

Our primary professional organization has been less—much less—than a strong ally in writing teachers' effort to improve salaries, working conditions, and grievance procedures. The CCCC has been seduced by what might be called "MLA values," as the CCCC committee's recasting of the language and intentions of the Wyoming Resolution so painfully reveals. Those of us on the margins who have historically relied on the CCCC leadership to speak for us now find ourselves depicted as the source of the low status, less-than-professional standards and practices, and ethical problems of the profession. Blaming the victim is a too-familiar reaction to social problems that defy easy solutions and risk resulting in indictments of those in power. The CCCC, which has billed itself as "the learned society founded in 1949 to serve as the professional association for college teachers of writing" ("Statement" 329), has entered a new phase in its development. It has become institutionalized: it is run by a board of select men and women dedicated to the proposition of professionalism at any and all costs. As the defining power of our field, the CCCC has chosen a path that guarantees that stifling of diversity within the field of composition by forcing us into the traditional academic mold or out of the profession. Under CCCC leadership, we are moving inexorably closer to the elitist standards and values that have traditionally defined the larger field of English. The vision of a field unbound by the assumptions and presumptions of traditional academia has been eclipsed.

Certainly, the debate over these issues and the documents that they have produced continues. But we need ever remember the early phase of the debate as it is discussed here so that the will to professionalization, despite the human cost it incurs, does not become the exclusive guiding force of our professional leadership. If we accept the arguments put forth in the official CCCC statement, we endorse the professionalization process, enable it, collaborate with it, and continue it. Will I see you at the MLA?

Notes

1. The citation of colleagues' names in this essay, particularly that of James Slevin, is intended as part of the historical record and should in no way be construed as personal criticism. James Slevin and James Vincent have in particular and at various times made themselves available for extended discussion of the central issue of the essay, as have other members of the Professional Standards Committee.

2. Opposing the course of the profession as the CCCC committee appeared to be steering it, a group of composition professionals protested the new direction the committee had taken in the belief that the CCCC statement was an attempt to subvert the intentions of the Wyoming Resolution. In an open CCCC session, the protesting members of CCCC were accused of being racists, "scabs," and advocates of exploitation. The accusations came, ironically, from a member of the CCCC panel—the panel on professional standards. Opposition to the CCCC draft statement caused this emotional outburst.

A group of concerned, non-tenure-track faculty members gathered in a hotel room at the Seattle CCCC to discuss the implications of this statement and the committee's action. The following memo, the group's response to the committee, was submitted to the committee chair the same day:

> TO: Members of the Committee on Professional Standards for Quality Education
>
> In response to your request we are clarifying the concerns that we articulated at our meeting this afternoon on the Wyoming Resolution. Much of the commentary came out of the session entitled "The New Underclass: Nonregular/Nonpermanent Full-Time Composition Faculty." Similar concerns were voiced at the meeting by other part-time and full-time non-tenure-track faculty. The Wyoming Resolution, which is to be so widely distributed, will be taken as the official position of the CCCC. Because of this, we are concerned that it accurately reflect the interests of all those who teach composition. At this point we can articulate four concerns:
>
> (1) To make the Committee more representative, we believe that it should include part-time and full-time non-tenure-track faculty. Approximately ⅔ of the writing faculty in this country are non-tenure-track.
>
> (2) We also question the assumption implicit in the language of the document that the field is primarily defined by the research

university model. We believe that an equally important and more relevant standard in our field is teaching excellence. In the resolution ("Tenure-Line Faculty," Paragraph B), commitment to teaching is primarily defined in terms of research and publication.

(3) We object to Paragraph A under "Full-Time Temporary Faculty," which calls for the eventual elimination of full-time temporary positions in favor of tenure-track appointments. We, too, deplore the current exploitation of temporary faculty. However, given the criteria for tenure cited above, tenure would be available only to faculty who identify themselves primarily as researchers. Since many excellent members of our field define themselves primarily as teachers, they may not be tenurable.

(4) If tenure could be attained solely through excellent teaching, we would not object to conversions of non-tenure-track lines into tenure lines. We would like to see temporary positions become permanent, both full-time and part-time. We would also like to point out that establishing tenure-line positions may not be the sole solution to the problem of exploitation of writing faculty or the only way to ensure quality education.

[Signed by Susan Griffin, UCLA, Jeanne Gunner, UCLA, Cynthia Tuell, UC Riverside, and Lisa Gerrard, UCLA]

The CCCC statement in its revised form does not address these concerns. The research university model remains in its emphasis on publication and tenure. As of 1991, the committee does include members who are non-tenure track.

3. Several recent documents published by the NCTE and MLA further document step 2 in the professionalization process. We can note particularly James Slevin's article, "Conceptual Frameworks and Curricular Arrangements," in Lunsford, Moglen, and Slevin's *The Future of Doctoral Studies in English* (MLA, 1989). Slevin discusses the need for a course on the graduate curriculum so that graduate students will do right by "the profession we are eventually to entrust to their leadership" (38–39). In the Fall 1990 *WPA Newsletter*, WPA announced that its request for formal affiliation with the MLA had been granted.

4. Mike Rose, associate director of UCLA Writing Programs, holds an academic administrative appointment. As of this date, no composition professional holds a tenured or tenure-track position at UCLA.

Works Cited

"CCCC: Voices in the Parlor, and Responses." *Rhetoric Review* 7 (1988): 194–213.

"CCCC Initiatives on the Wyoming Conference Resolution: A Draft Report." *College Composition and Communication* 40 (1989): 61–72.

Lunsford, Andrea. "Composing Ourselves: Politics, Commitment, and the Teaching of Writing." *College Composition and Communication* 41 (1990): 71–82.

Lunsford, Andrea, Helene Moglen, and James F. Slevin, eds. *The Future of Doctoral Studies in English.* New York: MLA, 1989.

Ohmann, Richard. *English in America: A Radical View of the Profession.* New York: Oxford UP, 1976.

———. "Graduate Students, Professionals, Intellectuals." *College English* 52 (1990): 247–57.

Olson, Gary, and Joseph Moxley. "Directing Freshman Composition: The Limits of Authority." *College Composition and Communication* 40 (1989): 51–59.

Peterson, Jane. "A Letter to CCCC Members." NCTE, 1990.

Robertson, Linda, Sharon Crowley, and Frank Lentricchia. "The Wyoming Conference Resolution Opposing Unfair Salaries and Working Conditions for Post-Secondary Teachers of Writing." *College English* 49 (1987): 272–80.

Slevin, James F. "Conceptual Frameworks and Curricular Arrangements." Lunsford, Moglen, and Slevin. 30–39.

"Statement of Principles and Standards for the Postsecondary Teaching of Writing." *College Composition and Communication* 40 (1989): 329–36.

7

Composition Teaching as "Women's Work": Daughters, Handmaids, Whores, and Mothers

Cynthia Tuell/*University of California, Riverside*

When I began writing this paper, I talked about some of the issues I wanted to address with a colleague at my school, where we were both teaching composition on a part-time, temporary basis.[1] He said I was wrong to complain about our employment status since it serves the needs of the university, to which, of course, we must be sensitive. The university, he said, needs a flexible, expandable, expendable composition teaching staff, one that can adjust itself instantly to changes in enrollment and the supply of TAs. Though "regular faculty" at the school where we worked do teach occasional composition courses, my friend claimed that they shouldn't have to. "Why not?" I asked.

"Because they have to do research," he replied. "Composition takes too much time." He told me he didn't believe our non–senate faculty positions ought to be permanent or even long-term, not only because such a change would render us less flexible and expendable, but also because it would violate "the normal progression."

"What's 'normal'?" I asked. "What's 'progress'?" Well, my friend explained, the "normal progression" is to teach composition as a teaching assistant and, if need be, as a new Ph.D., until the right spot opens up on the tenure track in literature, a first-class research field. And then, one hopes, on up the ladder to glory.

In an earlier version of this essay, I went on to say that I found "a similar attitude everywhere when I talk to composition teachers." An anonymous reader claimed that my "everywhere" was unbelievable, that my everywhere was nowhere in his or her experience of listening to part-timers, who are "usually quite willing to complain." I grant that my part-timer friend's refusal to complain is highly unusual. Not so unusual, however, are the principles—and he *is* a principled man—on which he based his refusal. These principles I do find "everywhere" or "almost everywhere" or "often enough," even issuing from the mouths and pens of well-known composition specialists, who would surely disagree with my friend's implication that composition is a second-class research field.

For instance, Sharon Crowley's recent article, "Three Heroines: An Oral History," summarizes the careers of three "exemplary women in our profession" (202). All three of these "foremothers of courage and character" (206) began as part-time teachers, at jobs where they faced the part-timers' traditional sources of complaint—oddball offices, terrible pay, pervasive insecurity. "But," Crowley says, "none of these women was content to remain in untenured positions," then quotes one as saying, "I had to do what the big kids do—I know I wanted time to write, do research, get administrative experience, teach graduate students, live in an university climate. I knew if I kept at marginal jobs I deserved what I got." She calls the tenure-line position she soon acquired a "real job," at last (205).

This professional writing specialist and my part-timer colleague assume, in their admittedly off-the-cuff remarks, a similar developmental metaphor. If one follows the "normal progression," one gets to "do what the big kids do." Teaching composition— teaching *only* composition, only *teaching* composition—is not a real job, not a long-term, permanent job at the center of the university climate, in the eye of the storm. Doing it takes too much time away from the "real," "regular" university jobs: writing, research, teaching graduate students. If the university hires us to teach *only* composition, to only *teach* composition, our jobs are rightfully marginal, expandable, and expendable, what the university needs and we deserve.

I'm forty years old. I have taught composition passionately and with commitment for almost twenty years, sometimes part-time, usually full-time. Every year, I do it better. And yet I, too, sometimes joke that I still don't know what I want to be when I grow up. Famous, influential, glorified—I protest these patriarchal pipedreams in myself. I protest my own deep-seated doubt about the importance of the work I do, helping a few handfuls of freshmen to write just a little bit better, while the big, muscular world, oblivious to us, goes on about its epoch-building business, its significant strife and harrowing achievements. I protest in the memory of our billion dispossessed and forgotten foremothers, to whom I commit myself on feminine principle.

But, despite my principles, and like many of my similarly principled colleagues, not wanting to be dispossessed and forgotten myself, I sometimes feel like a failure, as though I'm not doing what I'm supposed to do, what I dreamed of doing, what my teachers so confidently expected me to do. No matter how we composition teachers may give ourselves to our jobs and believe that the work we do is worthy, we still often hope for a future in which we will at last "do what the big kids do," the "normal" thing: that is, what our forefathers have done. We feel this way because we are sensitive to, indeed we identify with, the institutions that exploit us. We are daughters and sons in whom the university strives to reproduce itself and most often succeeds. Given our long education and necessary string of "A"s in the cultural logic that grants us low status, we often wish to rescue our self-esteem by seeing ourselves, one day, in our fathers' shoes. Though we may wish to devour the father—to blow up the MLA convention-site hotel, as my friends and I in graduate school used to fantasize—we wish to devour him so we may take on his power, adopt his totems and taboos, and acquire his privileges, among them the right to the services of many women.

Though there is some demographic and much anecdotal evidence that women do indeed predominate in (though we don't dominate over) our profession (see Holbrook), I use the concept "women's work" as a metaphor. In a patriarchal culture, men's work is what the culture sees as the important, epoch-building work, while women's work is work that serves men. As Elizabeth Daumer and Sandra Runzo put it, "Reimbursed little or not at all, [women's] work hardly ever escapes, even when idealized, the connotations of 'preparation' or 'service' for a higher, presumably worthier entity or cause . . ." (45).

Composition is often named a "service course," that is, a service to the university: thus we are handmaids. The handmaid assists in the great educational enterprise by doing the dirty, tedious, but not very difficult work. We clean up the comma splices. We organize the discourse of our students as though straightening a closet. When it's straight, the "regular" professors teaching "regular" courses don't have to pick through the clutter and can quickly find the suit that suits them. When we can't manage to scrub them clean, we are called on to flunk out the great unwashed before they sully the orderly classrooms of the upper division. As handmaids, we are replaceable and interchangeable: "Anyone can do it," it's been said of teaching comp (Robertson, Crowley, and Lentricchia 276). As handmaids, we serve the needs of our masters, not the vision we may have of ourselves, of our work, or of our students.

At many universities, the preferred composition instructor— the first hired, last fired—is the graduate student of English. (Twice in my career, I have lost work to graduate students. One time, eleven of us, the entire professional basic writing faculty, were fired by our department in order to make room for the graduate program's expansion, to provide jobs for newly admitted TAs.) Why should this be so? Why should younger, usually apprentice, teachers enjoy this privileged employment status? I don't think it happens primarily because TAs always come cheaper. At my school, for instance, TAs are paid more per course than are lecturers. In addition, hiring TAs requires hiring graduate professors to attract, teach, and train the TAs. I don't mean to deny, however, that money is an issue in the question of our professional status or to deny that TAs are exploited even where they're preferred. For one thing, the universities can only sustain their exploitation of composition teachers in a job market flooded with former TAs. (Most of the graduate students who replaced me and my ten former basic writing colleagues have since gone on to become part-time and/or temporary lecturers like me.) But no, I think there is a deeper, structural reason: TAs are preferred because they confirm the "normal progression." In their position as appretice teachers and graduate students, they create the mastery of their masters. Though the title "teaching assistant" belies the actual responsibility that composition TAs assume, it nicely sums up the role the university conceives for the composition course and those who teach it.

Sometimes, though, there are not enough TAs to cover the necessary courses. Richard Lanham, for instance, cites a TA shortage as one reason for hiring visiting lecturers to teach in the UCLA Writing Programs (168). At schools without graduate programs, composition courses must be taught by other employees. Despite the overwhelming, continuing need for composition teachers at universities, colleges, and community colleges in my area, such employees are usually part-time and almost universally, temporary workers. When we are not handmaids, we are whores. Given the supposed literacy crisis, as whores we fulfill a temporarily necessary but embarrassing function. (Lanham cites the temporality of "the literacy crisis" as a second reason for hiring temporary lecturers [155].) As whores, we do it the way they like it, using their course structures, their textbooks, their syllabi; and we don't expect, because we will not get, commitments. In order to make a living, we may do it here and then do it again there and again somewhere else, freeway flying to wherever we may be called.

Why, despite the long history of the composition requirement in American colleges, should the people who teach writing so often be deemed temporary workers? Undoubtedly, money is a partial answer to this question, too, since temporary workers don't qualify for the retirement and other benefits career employees can claim. However, how we spend our money reveals what, and whom, we value. I think the notion of a "normal progression" can answer this deeper question, too. In *In A Different Voice*, Carol Gilligan argues that theories of "normal development" in psychology and education have been androcentric, or male-biased. In particular, she critiques Lawrence Kohlberg's developmental theory. Kohlberg derived his concept of normal development by studying white, middle-class, American males. When girls and women were measured against Kohlberg's "norm," they came up wanting. Similarly, the idea of a "normal progression" implies a norm of development. Measured against this norm, those of us who continue to teach *only* composition, to only *teach* composition, beyond our culturally allotted span come up wanting. We don't come up as composition professionals; we come up as failures. And no university wants to keep a failure (at least a nontenured failure) on staff forever.

Several articles on the state of our profession, written by people who firmly consider themselves compositionists, seem to assume a similar idea of a normal progression, one that belittles those of us who actually *teach* composition. In an article about writing program administration, Gary Olson and Joseph Moxley write, "Ostensibly, writing program administrators are their departments' specialists in rhetoric and composition—in many cases, their only specialists in this field" (56). But surely, any school where there is a "program" to administer must have a number of composition teachers. Are teachers not experts, too, even lacking a specialized Ph.D.? Dwight Purdy ties the "increasing professionalism" of our field to graduate programs in rhetoric (which create a need for graduate professors), TA training (which requires trainers), research, and writing program administration, about which he says, "What was a bad dream has become a profession" (794). Does he mean *the* profession? Does "the profession" mean being the masters?

Edward P. J. Corbett effuses too about the "enhanced professionalism of the composition teacher." Does he mean me? No. The "elevated status" he refers to belongs to new teachers, those who have been trained in the new graduate programs in composition and rhetoric, like the one Corbett directs. The "older" teachers, he says "are just serving out their time" (444). Presumably, without having once been students of the new graduate professors of composition theory, we cannot be professionals. At the end of his essay, Corbett admits that, despite the "exciting new developments in composition studies" he's outlined (444), he sometimes feels like a fraud as a composition teacher, because his students don't seem to become better writers (452). In her critique of this essay, Jeanne Gunner writes, "One's professional worth, then, can obviously be judged only by one's own writing." Those who teach *only* composition, who only *teach* composition, "must be judged by their students' writing, and will inevitably be revealed as frauds" (7).

I was surprised when I read these and other articles (see Irmscher) that, except for Corbett's despairing remarks, no one talks much about teaching. James Slevin, too, the chair of the

CCCC Committee on Professional Standards for Quality Education, like everybody else assumes that "professionalism" means
research, publication, upper-division and graduate teaching, and
administration. He says, with some irony, that because universities and English departments primarily identify "composition"
with the teaching of undergraduates, "[we] are therefore named as
basic, introductory, usually remedial, and generally any sort of
thing that someone with any self-respect would want to avoid"
(547).

Yes: composition is basic, introductory, remedial, and, where
it can be, avoided. Teaching graduate students is privileged over
teaching freshmen, even in "our" profession; administration and
research are valorized over teaching because administrators and
researchers at least hypothetically teach the teachers. Teaching
basic, introductory stuff—teaching children—is women's work.

The paradigm of women's work is motherhood, the most
fulfilling and the most accursed and compromised of all women's
roles. Though the nurture of children is often honored in words—
"M" is for the million things she gave me—it is not often honored
in deeds. Much has been written likening the role of the teacher to
that of the mother, mostly in praise of this metaphor (see Davis;
Daumer and Runzo; Emig; Flynn). I agree in seeing the metaphor
as apt; but I also think it explains our low status as professionals.
Nancy Chodorow and other Freudian feminists see women's exclusive mothering in a patriarchal culture as the source of all
misogyny, the source of women's disempowerment (see also Gilligan; Keller).

We fulfill a motherly role at the university because our
students are metaphorically young, often chronologically young
freshmen, and always considered developmentally young. (This is
why graduate students are deemed qualified to teach them, medi-
um-sized kids minding the little ones, looking up to the big ones.)
If our students were developmentally mature, according to the
mythos of the university, they would not need our courses. In 1892,
a committee at Harvard complained about how poorly freshmen
wrote and called on preparatory schools to do a better job (Berlin,
Writing Instruction 61). The call for better high school teaching in
order to ease the demand for college teaching has been a perennial
academic theme (see Berlin, *Rhetoric and Reality* and *Writing
Instruction*). At the University of California today, college credits
are not granted in "Subject A" (basic writing) courses because

such courses are considered "high school work" (this, even though as many as sixty percent of freshmen, supposedly the cream of the crop of California high schools, are required to take, and often retake, these "high school courses"). Thus those of us who teach them are seen as no "higher" than high school teachers. Very often, as with mothers, as with high school teachers, our intellectual powers and abilities are correlated with those of the students we teach. According to the university's hierarchical thought, the thought of the normal progression, we must be smarter than our students, else we would not be their teachers, but we must not be as smart as our masters, else they would not be our masters. We become, as Robert Mielke puts it, the "dark double" of the basic writers we often teach (175).

The metaphors of higher and lower are instructive. These metaphors are an example of an argument that Chaim Perelman calls a "symbolic liaison of coexistence," the idea that an attribute is superior that belongs to the superior being. "From the superiority of people over animals, of adults over chldren, we easily draw moral lessons" (103). Children are short and adults are tall; thus adult brains are higher from the ground. Adult brains can perform the "higher" cognitive functions such as abstraction, which I visualize as activity performed above matter, where the essences are extracted from the everyday flux of things and then enshrined in the floating palace of intellect, high in the sky. (Plato disliked the contingent, contextual nature of rhetoricians' thinking too, just as Lawrence Kohlberg found such modes of thought inferior, though functional, in women [Gilligan 18–20].) Men are, on average, taller than women, thus "higher." And women's work requires us to "lower" ourselves further, to bend and hunker down so we can hear and understand the words of those who are "lower" than we are, our children and our students. But, as Perelman notes, the argument from the higher and the lower only holds when we agree with the premised hierarchy (103).

The Freudian-feminist critique sheds light on this hierarchy. In Freud's "normal progression," the infant—implicitly male—ego grows from identification with and dependence on the mother through separation and individuation in the Oedipus complex, resulting in autonomy and what Freud called "the normal male contempt for women" (qtd. in Chodorow 144). Catherine Keller writes, "[The male] lust for power over the other . . . conceals an unconscious fear of the mother, in her monstrous ability to overpower the infant ego" (138). As the child grows into a man, fear and dependency are put away as childish things, locked in the closets of unconsciousness. The contempt he feels for his once and now-alienated childishness extends to a contempt for children and all basic, introductory, mother-ruled things.

Freud's argument in *Civilization and Its Discontents* and elsewhere that the development of the individual recapitulates the development of the race further illuminates the cultural contempt we feel for "lower" things. As the adult male ego "looks down on" and denies its earlier dependence on and merging with the mother, so the culture looks down on its own prehistory, with its roots in the mother religions (see Keller). As the adult ego seeks autonomy and freedom from the influences and demands of others—the goal of the never-give-an-inch, uncompromising, undying ideas of Platonic philosophy—so the university English department wishes to free itself from the socially contingent bases of its work. In *English in America*, Richard Ohmann contends that American English departments grew out of a historical and social base of freshman composition, a base which our literary critical elite now devalues and disparages. The work of teaching composition, he says, is "demeaning to professional egos" (229).

Several feminists have seen the process model of composition instruction as compatible with feminist theory (see Caywood and Overing). But though the university, in virtually every field of its discourse, increasingly holds to process philosophies, even feminist philosophies, it still sees products—patents, publications, research—as paramount. Though current theories may argue that publications are not final, autonomous products, but rather temporary statements whose meanings are always adrift in the flux of dialogic process, publications do have tangible substance; real ink on real paper in real books and journals, enjoying lifelong citation on curriculum vitae.

But such substantiality cannot be claimed for teaching. In *From a Broken Web*, Catherine Keller argues that in our culture the ultimate, and ultimately illusory, product is the finished, autonomous male ego. Janet Emig contends that masculine teaching is "a revelation, an expression of ego," while composition teaching requires letting ego stand aside ("Non-Magical Thinking" 132). Sara Ruddick argues that maternal thinking requires a capacity for attentive love, attention to the real child and not the fantasy child, a projection of our own ego (223). And in *Of Women Born*, Adrienne

Rich says, "The powerful person would seem to have a good deal at stake in suppressing or denying his awareness of the personal reality of others. . . . This quality has variously been described as 'detachment,' 'objectivity,' 'sanity'" (49–50). The products of "masculine" teaching can often be measured by an objective test, the name of which masks its source in the murky recesses of male ego. But composition teaching cannot be "objectively" measured, though plenty of people try to do so.

If our teaching must have products, and these products cannot be measured by objective tests, what can they be measured by? Patriarchal teaching often sees the student as its product. The word *fathering* implies a quick, decisive act that results in a physical product, a child. Just so, one of the criteria used at the University of California to evaluate the performance of teachers is "achievement of students in their field" (*Memorandum* 11). The achievement of the student is thus claimed an achievement of the teacher. In contrast, *mothering* implies an ongoing activity that helps to create the conditions in which someone else can grow and that, though the mother may die, always lives on in the child, along with countless contrary and enhancing influences, continually shaping growth. Teaching, especially composition teaching, like mothering, disappears into the one who is taught. Mothering addresses itself to the particular need of the particular child; thus a major achievement of a student in our field, an achievement in which we rejoice, may be simply that she passed. If motherly composition teaching does indeed help to create conditions for growth, and I believe it does, then all students who have taken composition might be seen, according to this logic, as "our" achievements. But they rarely are so seen; the student who achieves success in economics, chemistry, or literature is seen as a product of upper-division and graduate teaching. Such students are like Athena, who sprang fully achieved and achieving from her father's head, while her mother was denied her and denied by her. Composition teachers are like Metis, Athena's mother, and my symbol of motherhood, devoured by Zeus and laboring anonymously in the bowels of the university.

Why must mothers be swallowed by fathers, composition teachers by universities? Because mothers and teachers have real power, though such power may not be measured. As Geraldine Joncich Clifford notes, "Teaching, wherever performed, is a powerful molder of human beings; recognizing this, religious and political leaders have always tried to exercise control over those who teach the young" (176).

When a French woman saw Adrienne Rich with her three sons, she asked, *"Vous traivaillez pour l'armee, madame?"* (Do you work for the army?) (11). Sara Ruddick says maternal thinking often involves a willingness to "accept the uses to which others put one's children. . . ," to, in fact, train our children to find their suitable places in a man's world (220). In his chapter entitled "English 101 and the Military-Industrial Complex," Richard Ohmann says that "the attitudes we encourage students to have toward language—toward order, correctness, tone, dialect—have been and still mainly are an academic version of attitudes deeply held by those [businessmen, bureaucrats, advertisers] outside the academy" (94). Ohmann came to this conclusion by studying the neater pedagogy of composition textbooks, not the messier realities of composition classrooms, but I suspect that, despite the increasing predominance of the more liberatory process model of teaching since 1976, when *English in America* was published, and the current emphasis on collaborative learning, Ohmann would find even today, in many composition classrooms, a similar imperialist style being taught.

Why do we do it? First, because we have never lived in a democratic culture, it is hard to imagine exactly what, and to what purposes and what effects, we might do otherwise. Composition theory, scholarship, and research, our own and others', formal and informal, published and experiential, can be helpful to us in our imagining, though our imaginations, too, may be determined by what has always already been imagined. Even so, given the wealth of human imagining, democratic curricula and pedagogies, democratic parenthood, might be possible.

However, we are faced with a dilemma when we seek to implement a democratic vision. Do we teach toward the world that might be or toward the world that is? Though this dilemma may wrench us most painfully, we parents of real, beloved children have a lifetime of growth in which to provide models and advice, introductions to the complexities of what is and what might and what ought to be. As teachers of composition, we have ten or fifteen weeks with our students, who are always already grown. In the short time allotted to us, should we refuse, out of pedagogical theory or democratic principle, to teach our students the imperialist style the culture and the academy expect them to know?

Even if we can find our way out of this dilemma, and I believe it must be possible, we face another, fundamental obstacle. Because we are mothers under the power of the fathers, teachers under the power of our superiors, we do our work "according to the Law of the Symbolic Father and under His Watchful Eye, as well as, typically, according to the desires, even whims of the father's house" (Ruddick 222).

Adrienne Rich cites Bronson Alcott as a father enamored of a theory of childhood education, a theory whose "daily, hourly" practical application was left to the mother (222). Just so, at my school and many others, composition teachers are expected to apply the theories of their superiors. Just as a whole generation of Americans are sometimes dubbed "Dr. Spock's kids," and Dr. Spock is sometimes held responsible for our virtues and our vices, at my school and at UCLA the patrinomial tradition of authority rules. In the course catalogs, the teachers of composition classes are not listed by their names nor by the designation "staff." Instead, the name of the man in charge appears, the "teacher of record," the one who controls what's taught, how it's taught, and who teaches it. Even though such a man may be as good-naturedly democratic as Dr. Spock, it must boost his ego a bit to see his name in print hundreds of times over—the composition father of thousands; or mother of thousands, if the person "in charge" is a woman. This administrative solution to a practical problem—a problem that might not exist were composition teachers less expendable, replaceable, and interchangeable—symbolizes the university's attitude toward composition teaching. The person in charge, the one who has been granted authority, *names* who we are and what we do. (Often, writing program directors are not "authorities" in or teachers of composition, a related issue which aggravates our situation, but one I won't address here.)

This naming by authority comes from how the university views, including how it defines, the concept of authority and the role of teaching. Juanita Kreps, while calling for a revaluing of teaching within the academy, defines research as the "generation" and teaching as the "transmission" of knowledge (88). I find it hard to apply the "transmitting" metaphor to what I do as a composition teacher, since the "knowledge" I purvey, usually via textbook, seems a minor component of writing—how to punctuate, how to cite sources, for example. Instead, students learn through their experiences, and my role, like the midwife's, is to provide a generative atmosphere in which to assist and encourage them as they give birth to themselves as authors. While it seems to me this must be true to some extent of *all* teaching, I think Krep's metaphor is accurate in reflecting the university's hierarchy of values as well as its perception of teaching.

Geraldine Joncich Clifford quotes Grant Allen's remarks, published in 1889: "[Woman] is the sex specified to reproductive necessities. All that is distinctively human belongs to man—the field, the mine, the workshop; all that is truly woman is merely reproductive—the home, the nursery, the schoolroom" (170). Men produce; women merely reproduce. Scholars and researchers generate knowledge; teachers merely transmit, broadcasting, like animate radios, the programs others have produced.

Clifford's article outlines the recent history of teaching in the U.S. By 1859, teaching school was beginning to be seen as "women's work." By 1985, seventy-six percent of those receiving degrees in education were women. As school teaching became increasingly female-dominated, its status increasingly fell, so much so that Clifford cites a feminist who, in 1978, declined to call teaching a "profession" precisely because women primarily do it. What sort of feminist is it who devalues what women do? The hard-hitting kind, no doubt dressed in a "power suit," the kind who believes that women can and must do what men have always done, and that women who do what women have always done get only what they deserve. This brand of feminist told us in the 1970s and 1980s, and still tells us, "Don't be a nurse, but a doctor; don't be a social worker, but a lawyer; don't teach—publish." One effect of this rhetoric, as Clifford notes, has been to drive talented nurses, social workers, and teachers away from these essential jobs. In the past, teaching was marginalized because it suited patriarchal purposes to devalue women's work. Today, many women who call themselves feminists participate in their fathers' institutional logic.

In its recent attempts to escape from the institutional margins where patriarchy has thrust it, the field of composition studies has also adopted the logic of its oppressors. Stephen North argues that our increasingly professionalized field increasingly devalues teaching, not only in and of itself, as I've argued, but even as a mode of "generating" knowledge, knowledge not only constituted in students but among our professional community, the kind of knowledge the academy usually values. Composition, however, intertwines inquiry and practice in "an academically untraditional way," North claims. He says, "The spectacle of so many once and future Practitioners scrambling to find academic respectability by invoking the authority of any mode of inquiry *except* their own, *except* practice, can hardly be described as dignified" (374).

Why do the professional compositionists devalue teaching as a mode of inquiry? North claims that, in the practitioner community, most authority resides in private, experiential knowledge, unlike other academic communities where most authority is in public—i.e., published—knowledge (28). The "most authentic" way to disseminate practitioner knowledge is conversation, dialogue between practitioners and their experience, while "writing is, by definition, the medium least amenable to representing the results of Practitioner inquiry." Writing is "stylized monologue with a vengeance," which produces out of the "muddy uncertainty" of experience "a neater, more linear, more certain prescription," which falsifies practitioner knowledge (51–53). Since teachers contain their knowledge inside and among themselves, generating and applying it in the relative privacy of the classroom, teaching *only* composition, only *teaching* composition, will never make a practitioner publically influential.

In our culture, authority resides in the author. As long as composition teachers don't publish even their falsified knowledge, many in our field claim in effect that we get what we deserve. The CCCC's "Statement of Principles and Standards for the Postsecondary Teaching of Writing," sent in 1989 to administrative officers at every college and university in the U.S., calls for the conversion to tenure-line jobs of all but TA composition teaching positions. Though this is called for in the service of "the academy's most serious mission, helping students to develop their critical powers as readers and writers" (330), the "Statement" in no way questions the prevailing definitions of and criteria for tenure, which emphasize research and publication, most usually at the expense of teaching.

Quality teaching, like quality mothering, takes time. Formalized research and writing also take time. Do we have enough time to do both? In her article on women publishing in composition studies, Theresa Enos says, "We will somehow have to redefine or balance what we mean by the words *scholar* and *practitioner*. I would hope that it doesn't have to be either/or, that as women, especially, we can be considered as both scholars and teachers." But scholars are the ones, she implies, who really make a difference, who do the "groundbreaking" work. She says, "It is our particular burden as women that we have to do more and do it better to be agents of change" (214). Perhaps true heroines, mythical supermoms, *can* do it all. I worry, though, that the energy we put into producing the "neater, more linear, more certain" ideas that can be published, that can reach and speak to a national audience, is energy taken away from the experiential ideas we form and apply daily, hourly, in dialogue with our essential local audience, our students. If local and national, private and public, concerns coincide, perhaps we don't lose much time. But if they don't—and they very often don't, every student being a new creation—most of us will sensibly invest our time in the activities we will be rewarded for, here on earth.

I want to see *teaching* rewarded. I want more than our students' recognition that teachers *can* be "agents of change," more than that only they should rise up and call us blessed, though such rewards are powerful and provide for many of us the metaphorical food that sustains us. But such food can't be eaten for breakfast. When I compare my salary to those the "big kids" earn—tenured faculty, stockbrokers, CEOs—I'm outraged; but when I compare it to the salaries my children's preschool teachers earn—salaries I pay and could not afford to pay were they not very much lower than mine—I see that I am complicit, too, in the cultural crimes I protest. My family's middle-class income depends on the devalued services of women, services my culture tells me I have a right to claim because I can afford them. Nurturing and teaching children, even motherhood itself, has increasingly become a working-class job, part of the "service sector" of our economy, the lowest-paid and least-valued work, though it is— perhaps *because* it is—essential, essentially *adult*, work, on which the superstructure of our society entirely depends. To revalue it means nothing less than a paradigm shift of massive proportions, the realigning of the continental plates, the moving of mountains. We can begin the tectonic struggle by revaluing ourselves as well as repossessing and remembering our mothers who have gone before.

Notes

1. This essay was presented in another version at the 1989 annual meeting of the Conference on College Composition and Communication, 17 March 1989, Seattle, Washington.

Works Cited

Berlin James A. *Rhetoric and Realty: Writing Instruction in American Colleges, 1900–1945*. Carbondale: Southern Illinois UP, 1987.

———. *Writing Instruction in Nineteenth-Century American Colleges*. Carbondale: Southern Illinois UP, 1984.

Caywood, Cynthia L., and Gillian R. Overing, eds. *Teaching Writing: Pedagogy, Gender, and Equity*. Albany: State U of New York P, 1987.

Chodorow, Nancy. *The Reproduction of Mothering: Psychoanalysis and the Sociology of Gender.* Berkeley: U of California P, 1978.

Clifford, Geraldine Joncich. "Women's Liberation and Women's Professions: Reconsidering the Past, Present, and Future." *Women and Higher Education in American History*. Ed. John M. Faragher and Florence Howe. New York: Norton, 1988. 165–82.

Corbett, Edward P. J. "Teaching Composition: Where We've Been and Where We're Going." *College Composition and Communication* 38 (1987): 444–52.

Crowley, Sharon. "Three Heroines: An Oral History." *Pre/Text* 9 (1988): 202–6.

Daumer, Elizabeth, and Sandra Runzo. "Transforming the Composition Classroom." Caywood and Overing 45–62.

Davis, Barbara Hillyer. "Teaching the Feminist Minority." *Learning Our Own Way: Essays in Feminist Education*. Ed. Charlotte Bunch and Sandra Pollock. Trumansburg, NY: Crossing, 1983. 89–97.

Emig, Janet. "Non-Magical Thinking: Presenting Writing Developmentally in School." Gosawi and Butler 132–44.

———. "The Origins of Rhetoric: A Developmental View." Gosawi and Butler 54–60.

Enos, Theresa. "Gender and Journals, Conservers or Innovators." *Pre/Text* 9 (1988): 209–14.

Flynn, Elizabeth A. "Composing as a Woman." *College Composition and Communication* 39 (1988): 423–35.

Freud, Sigmund. *Civilization and Its Discontents*. Trans. James Strachey. London: Norton, 1961.

Gilligan, Carol. *In A Different Voice: Psychological Theory and Women's Development*. Cambridge: Harvard UP, 1982.

Gosawi, Dixie, and Maureen Butler, eds. *The Web of Meaning: Essays on Writing, Teaching, Learning, and Thinking*. Montclair, NJ: Boynton, 1983.

Gunner, Jeanne. "Caught in the Middle: The University, the Profession, and the Contradictions." Conference on College Composition and Communication. Seattle, 17 Mar. 1989.

Holbrook, Sue Ellen. "Women's Work: The Feminizing of Composition." Conference on College Composition and Communication. St. Louis, Mar. 1988.

Irmscher, William. "Finding a Comfortable Identity." *College Composition and Communication* 38 (1987): 81–87.

Keller, Catherine. *From a Broken Web: Separation, Sexism, and Self*. Boston: Beacon, 1986.

Kreps, Juanita M. "The Woman Professional in Higher Education." *Women in Higher Education*. Ed. Todd Furniss and Patricia Albjerg Graham. Washington, DC: American Council on Education, 1974. 75–94.

Lanham, Richard A. *Literacy and the Survival of Humanism*. New Haven: Yale UP, 1983.

Memorandum of Understanding. Contract. University of California and the University Council–American Federation of Teachers, Non-Senate Instructional Unit. Effective 1 July 1988–30 June 1990.

Mielke, Robert, "Revisionist Theory on Moral Development and Its Impact Upon Pedagogical and Departmental Practice." Caywood and Overing 171–78.

North, Stephen M. *The Making of Knowledge in Composition: Portrait of an Emerging Field*. Upper Montclair, NJ: Boynton 1987.

Ohmann, Richard. *English in America: A Radical View of the Profession*. New York: Oxford UP, 1976.

Olson, Gary and Joseph Moxley. "Directing Freshman Composition: The Limits of Authority." *College Composition and Communication* 40 (1989): 51–59.

Perelman, Chaim. *The Realm of Rhetoric*. Trans. William Kluback. Notre Dame, IN: U of Notre Dame P, 1982.

Purdy, Dwight. "A Polemical View of Freshman Composition in Our Time." *College English* 48 (1986): 791–96.

Rich, Adrienne. *Of Woman Born: Motherhood as Experience and Institution*. New York: Bantam, 1977.

Robertson, Linda, Sharon Crowley, and Frank Lentricchia. "The Wyoming Conference Resolution Opposing Unfair Salaries and Working Conditions for Post-Secondary Teachers of Writing." *College English* 49 (1987): 274–80.

Ruddick, Sara. "Maternal Thinking." *Mothering: Essays in Feminist Theory*. Ed. Joyce Trebilcot. Totowa, NJ: Rowman, 1984. 213–30. (Originally published in *Feminist Studies* 6 [Summer 1980].)

Slevin, James F. "Connecting English Studies." *College English* 48 (1986): 543–50.

"Statement of Principles and Standards for the Postsecondary Teaching of Writing." *College Composition and Communication* 40 (1989): 329–36.

8

Directing Without Power: Adventures in Constructing a Model of Feminist Writing Programs Administration

Marcia Dickson/*Ohio State University, Marion*

Don't look for my perfect model of feminist writing programs administration right away. There is none. This essay describes a three-year exploration of the problems of creating an ideal administrative structure, not a formula for ultimate administrative success. After spending three years working on various forms of this essay, I've been forced to conclude that there is no ideal model of writing program administration that a WPA can adopt in order to transform his or her writing program. In fact, I now believe that the only productive way to direct a writing program is to acknowledge that no one person can or should have ultimate control; faculties should collaboratively direct the writing program themselves.

This essay responds, in part, to Gary Olson and Joseph Moxley's "Directing Freshman Composition: The Limits of Authority," published in *College Composition and Communication* nearly three years ago. Concerned about the powerlessness that they, as WPAs, experienced daily, Olson and Moxley wanted to determine whether other WPAs also felt a lack of authority. Assuming that the chairs of English departments had ultimate responsibility and "administrative control over the entire department, including the writing program" (52), Olson and Moxley surveyed the chairs of 250 English departments in a range of colleges and universities across the United States. They sought to answer the following questions. Do directors create policy? select and train staff? promote curricular reform? Or do they serve primarily as coordinators?

Chairs were asked to rate twenty-one WPA tasks on a four-point scale from "essential" to "not important." The survey was designed to give a sense of the chairs' priorities, which would, in turn, indicate the relative level of authority that directors "enjoy" within the power structure of their departments. Chairs were also asked to respond to three brief-answer questions about their freshman English directors and policy for the writing programs.

The 136 (fifty-four percent) chairs who completed the questionnaire confirmed what Olson and Moxley suspected—WPAs have little administrative power (59). After completing the study, the authors determined that power to *command* or legislate changes in composition instruction can be invested in a sole person. Unfortunately, they lament, that person is usually the chair, not the WPA.

At first reading, the article validated my recent experience; I had just given up a job as a WPA, a position that represented a worst-case scenario. I was WPA, but I was also the only untenured faculty member in a department of people who wanted an educated administrative assistant rather than a composition reformer. When I decided to leave, one of my friends confessed that I had been hired "to do a job no one wanted done." She also told me I was starting to win.

I didn't want to "win." I wanted no part of a power struggle. But in the context of that department, I had no choice but to engage in the conflict. The department operated on bureaucratic concepts of rules, law, and order. Faculty members all knew *Robert's Rules of Order* and played strategic games with rules. In theory, everyone was equal. Even the chair could be defeated in any matter brought to a vote, and he frequently was.

This set of rules focused on individual power, creating an academic no-man's-land, where every man (and woman) *was* an island. And each would defend his or her sacred beaches to the death. Composition was taught by everyone, but many held the firm belief that it was a thankless course that should be taught by those who weren't fit for anything better. A common syllabus or a common book was out of the question. My job consisted of cleaning up the administrative messes that are inherent in an English department: conducting placement exams, working with the registrar, keeping an eye on the adjuncts, and serving on various committees that were vaguely connected to writing. Policy was up to the individual teacher, not an outsider. In other words, it was a typical English department.

As you might guess, as I read the Olson and Moxley article, I became hooked by the idea of having the authority to shape the composition program, but something bothered me. So I got on the phone with my former chair, a man who spent years dealing with the frustrations of being a WPA. From what he has seen and from conversations he has had with other chairs, he believes that the power available in English departments is, at best, limited, and, at most, an illusion.

He believes that chairs, as well as WPAs, lack the power to control every phase of program development. No chair or WPA makes autonomous policy determinations. Committees make most writing and literature program decisions, and committees are composed of faculty members—therein lies the problem. In most schools, each faculty member possesses the right to determine the way they conduct their classes, the manner in which they grade, and to a certain extent, the content of their courses. In short, they function under a sort of tribal anarchy.

To attempt to exert power over these anarchists is to court rejection and danger. If polite, they will simply ignore the WPA. If offended, or if they begin to suspect that he or she might actually make use of authority to intervene in their classroom, the WPA will be brought up on charges of violating academic freedom. While many departments are blessed with members who are more than willing to work with the chair and the WPA, this freedom to ignore and undermine authority is rampant. Although mostly the prerogative of senior, tenured faculty, such undermining activities are not unknown among junior, untenured faculty. The bottom line is this: neither chairs nor WPAs possess the absolute power to hire, fire, reward, or punish tenure-track faculty members who do not follow their administrative directives.

So much for full-time, tenure-track faculty. What about part-timers and power? After all, many writing programs rely on part-timers, and these members of the faculty surely depend upon the goodwill of the WPA. Not so. In remote areas, adjuncts are so scarce that the WPA has to court the part-time staff as well as the full-time faculty. And part-timers in both small and large schools are frequently the wives and (as now is becoming the case) husbands of the tenured faculty. Aware of academic freedom, and protected by their relationships with spouses or significant others, they need not fear a WPA.

Only graduate students, it would appear, come under the absolute control of the WPA. Except—graduate students tend to be mentored by faculty members, and when the advisors disagree with the pedagogical techniques recommended by the WPA, it's trouble for everyone. Several WPAs I know have been sabotaged by their colleagues. In one case, a literature faculty member advised practicum members that the WPA's methods were unsound. In another case, graduate students whom the WPA felt to be unqualified to teach were assigned teaching positions anyway because sympathetic literature faculty members wanted to keep the students in the graduate program.

No WPA can expect to have absolute power, but some are more vulnerable than others. Remember, most of the WPA positions advertised in the MLA and the CCCC job lists are for assistant (nontenured), not associate or full (tenured), professors. Many departments are not sure what to do with their WPA anyway, and—hiring and firing aside—no WPA can take action on political disputes when the administrator and the policy she or he tries to create are the focus of the dispute, especially when the administrator lacks the security of tenure.

Olson and Moxley ignore the reality of most WPA positions and envision an expert WPA, a reformer. However, a WPA who expects to reform the composition program is somewhat like the legendary, young West Point graduate who went from officer's training school at West Point straight to Tucson, carrying orders to reorganize and "shape up" seasoned sergeants and rowdy Indian-fighting troops. In the movies, these youngsters sometimes won the respect of the grizzled regulars. In real life, these educated lads often died because the regulars wouldn't cover their backs when the Indians showed up. Most WPAs don't die, but they do fail to get tenure.

After my conversation with my friend, the chair, and subsequent talk and rereading, I came to the conclusion that Olson and Moxley's hidden assumptions about the nature of power had skewed their interpretation of the results. They had already determined which tasks were "substantive" (indicative of power and authority) and which were "insubstantive" (not related to making and enforcing policy in the composition program).

They suggest that power in the writing programs is contingent upon the following "substantive" administrative duties (or privileges, depending upon how you look at it):

1. authority to hire, fire, and schedule composition instructors;
2. authority to determine and act upon serious political matters;
3. authority to create policy for composition classes. (52–53)

Olson and Moxley considered the following to be "insubstantive" duties:

1. remaining accessible throughout the semester;
2. communicating regularly with the chair;
3. possessing strong communication skills;
4. remaining current with developments in the discipline;
5. training inexperienced staff. (53)

For me, the Olson and Moxley model is a patriarchal/bureaucratic model because it emphasizes control rather than collaboration. Their assumptions about substantive and insubstantive duties of writing programs administrators were just the opposite of my assumptions, which I originally thought of as a *feminine* model, and now think of as a *feminist* model. My original megageneralization went something like this:

> Men try to legislate; rigid laws will not provide for human need.
> Women negotiate; recognition of others' needs will lead to strong groups and organizations.

My views were informed by two major feminist thinkers: Carol Gilligan and Sara Ruddick. Gilligan's *In a Different Voice* speaks about differences in male and female moral imperatives. Males, she argues, operate by an ethic that stresses responsibility and rights, females by an ethic of care that depends upon recognition of the needs of others (164). Ruddick, in "Maternal Thinking," attempts to reaffirm the positive aspects of what many people reject as the sentimental, illogical thinking of women. She presents an alternative philosophy for working out all sorts of problems—from domestic to worldwide—by focusing effort on ways to work with each other for the good of the children. "The children" become not only our own offspring but also the children of today's world and of future generations.

Truthfully, I'd just been battered by the ethic of rights in a department brought to an intellectual standstill by individual struggle for power. No wonder I thought that if a paternal model didn't make sense, that a maternal model would. The generalization possessed its own sort of reactionary logic. The WPA's job is not unlike maternal projects described by Ruddick, who asserts that benign maternal power promotes intellectual growth. The WPA could be said to nurture the writing program, carefully developing it in order to create the sort of intellectually sound program of which everyone can be proud. In my enthusiasm, I proposed a model of administration based on the principles expressed in "Maternal Thinking," arguing that Olson and Moxley's insubstantive items were feminine ways of administering and in fact, were the most substantive qualities of all. And I took my ideas to a WPA conference.

As you might guess, more than one person objected to the ideas that the feminine is necessarily the maternal and that the maternal is necessarily superior to the paternal, the matriarchal to the patriarchal. Responses went from smug, condescending smiles to the following sincere questions:

"What about women without children? Can they be maternal?"
"Can't men be good parents, too? Does gender determine everything?"
"Do we have to be parents to our students or to other faculty members?"

The objections were simple: The WPA is not the program's or the faculty's mother; the WPA deals with adults, not children.

I have no trouble believing that women who do not have, or who do not choose to have, children can govern by maternal principle and that even men can adopt, and have adopted, the sort of inclusive, supportive, personal administration that I call maternal—not matriarchal. My belief grows from that time in the seventies when feminists believed the maternal to be greatly underrated and sorely maligned. Yet over ten years after "Maternal Thinking" was published in *Feminist Studies*, and two years after the original presentation, nearly everyone who read the old presentation paper found a matriarchal hierarchy as problematic as I had found the patriarchal hierarchy. And as I examined their objections, I came to understand why, even if I didn't wholly agree.

In my zeal, I had ignored the fact that people would confuse the maternal with the matriarchal, failing to realize that there is a difference between maternal principles and a matriarchal administrative structure. The latter contains an inherent, potentially debilitating, hierarchy that is just as problematic as that found in patriarchal hierarchies. Both depend upon a model of power and control: Someone holds the power; others submit to it.

Adults frequently resist matriarchal power even more vehemently than patriarchal power. We reject the maternal in part because no one has the overwhelming power that mothers have; no one can produce crippling guilt like the women who raised us. A full century of psychoanalysts and prescriptive child-care psychologists have taught us to distrust and remove ourselves from matriarchal "control." Freud taught us to believe that boys can become men only by separating from their mothers and identifying with their fathers, that girls become women by transferring their love to their husbands, symbolically bearing children for their fathers. Our Freud (remember *Brave New World?*) says that Mom—the indulgent, the homebound, the destroyer of the progress of civilization (it's there—read *Civilization and Its Discontents*)—is only interested in protecting the small, domestic world that she rules. If we do not abandon her, we cannot grow; we cannot create strong and healthy worlds; we cannot make progress.

I am not, and will never be, prepared to accept this matriphobic model of the destructive mother, just as I will never fully accept the patriarch who is above reproach. For me, both the maternal and the paternal represent potential agency for encouraging growth. Their object is not the individual power and control implied in the terms matriarchal and patriarchal but the diffused strength that encourages collaborative and independent growth. This familial approach is more embedded in current feminist theory than in traditional patriarchal theories based on sets of rules and regulations. The democracy supposedly afforded by

Robert's Rules of Order and majority rule, both patriarchal constructs, seems limited and restrictive to me. I long for a simple, feminist conversation about the problems at hand.

Let's pause here a moment. I'll confess that there is a seduction at work when one is female in a predominantly male academy (or in any other male-dominated institution). As women without power or authority, we have a tendency to think that if we were queens of the forest, things would run better. The trouble with writing about the maternal and the paternal, the patriarchal and the matriarchal, is the ease with which writers can fall into what Jane Tompkins describes in "Fighting Words: Unlearning the Critical Essay": a male-model cowboy tradition—a fast-draw verbal contest to the death between scholars who represent the good guys and (in this case) the better girls.

This essay started out that way. But after working through several showdowns, I'll at last attempt to reconcile my desire to shoot down the theories of Gary Olson and Joseph Moxley with my desire to promote the primary principle I embrace: the only way to direct a program is to let the individual program shape itself according to the beliefs of the people who make it up and existing power structures of the institution in which it is located. For all I know, Olson and Moxley's type of administration might just work in their schools. Furthermore, given the way they think of authority, even if they adopted my maternal principles of administration, my policies would be transformed until one parental model of hierarchy replaced another. After all, many "collaborative" projects can be the results of one person putting pressure on a number of others to take part in programs they do not believe in or trust. No matter how often this group meets to discuss the theory behind the practice, if all the participants don't feel that they have the freedom to say, "This isn't working for me. What if we did this instead?" then the project will not encourage growth.

The power in both patriarchal and matriarchal administration rests in one ultimate authority. In the patriarchal administrative structure, the hierarchy is pyramid shaped—the closer one is to the top, the more power and control the person thinks she or he exerts. In the matriarchal administrative structure, the hierarchy is often envisioned as a circle of administrative groups radiating out from a controlling center—the closer the group to the center, the more powerful, because at the center is still an individual who makes the final decisions. Patriarchal and matriarchal academics appear to work by and insist upon this ultimate-authority formula—the authority figure makes a pronouncement and the underlings react. Academic administrators sit at the head of the banquet table; instructors sit down from them, or radiate out from them, in order of rank and indicators of importance.

A feminist model, at least in my mind, is more concerned with doing away with hierarchies than with perpetuating them. The feminist form of administration I envision allows for the blurring of the lines of authority and control. A feminist administrator becomes one of a group of instructors (not the *leader* of a group of instructors) that creates a collaborative program that considers human stories, issues, and abilities—before, during, and after creating departmental policy decisions. Such a WPA forgoes the illusion of control, sits neither at the top of the pyramid nor at the center of the circle and in effect, trusts the other members of the department enough to turn the asylum over to the inmates. Or if that sounds a bit irreverent—a feminist administrative structure is faculty-centered and privileges the personal. Dinner here resembles a family picnic with three adult generations and a whole mess of children. People sit where they want, and everyone is responsible for seeing that the family gets fed and the children don't drown in the lake. If everyone cooperates, the picnic is a success.

And how does this transformation from maternal to feminist affect "the limits of authority"? Let's look at Olson and Moxley's three substantive and five nonsubstantive tasks and responsibilities from a feminist perspective.

Substantive duties:
1. A WPA should have the authority to hire, fire, and schedule composition instructors.

Hiring and firing threatens everyone who might be hired and fired. That much should be obvious. What evidently isn't obvious to Olson and Moxley is that the very fact that one person can hold sway over so many people's lives creates a barrier between members of the program. Under a feminist administration, hiring and firing should be group decisions involving mentoring as well as evaluation. Such a system implies adequate conversation among colleagues, reasonable and unthreatening observation, and adequate access to pedagogical materials.

2. A WPA should have the authority to determine and act upon serious political matters.

3. A WPA should have the authority to create policy for composition classes.

I've lumped the last two items together because I feel that I have dealt with why they *do not* work—there is no real authority in an English department. However, one of the people who read this essay asked what happens to these duties under feminist administration? When wielded by a person who uses authority to threaten or control, we get a matriarchal model, fraught with all the problems of the patriarchy and the bureaucracy. If the WPA instead becomes a facilitator, a spokesperson for the faculty, the model becomes feminist and can be less threatening and more creative.

In my mind, in fact, the feminist WPA becomes a facilitator through the five duties that Olson and Moxley consider to be insubstantive.

Insubstantive duties:

1. A WPA should remain accessible throughout the semester.

2. A WPA should communicate regularly with the chair.

These two duties embody, in effect, opposite ends of the same issue. The WPA needs to be accessible to the faculty *and* the chair. This conduit position links the diverse members of the program. Being accessible means being ready to offer advice to those interested in developing new teaching techniques, being ready to discuss theory with those who need to understand how and why one assignment works and the other does not. Most of all, being accessible means being willing to talk about writing pedagogy without making the person you talk to feel threatened.

All this togetherness can be stressful, but the accessible WPA knows a program's weaknesses and strengths. She or he can draw in those who question new pedagogical techniques and those who look suspiciously at the classroom and assessment methods the administrator recommends. If a WPA is accessible, problems can be avoided or at least confronted before they become monumental.

3. A WPA should possess strong communication skills.

Olson and Moxley found this quality to be more window dressing than power producing, probably because it often hints of empty-headed salespeople or receptionists with more verbal verve than substantial knowledge.

Good communication skills do not have to be associated with salespeople and receptionists. A feminist WPA would possess the ability to listen, to ask the instructors for advice, and to let others talk out their reservations, their problems and their discoveries. These important communications skills, potentially more important than the ability to write memos and directives, will pick up on both stated and unstated needs and concerns. The feminist WPA does not speak as a superior being to a lesser being: "Tell me your problems and I'll work it out." In those cases the WPA, operating as Olson and Moxley suggest a director should, merely asks the faculty to "provide substantive input" rather than to become an active planning member of the program. Listening needs to involve reading subtexts and genuinely encouraging instructors to share in making policy. In the feminist context, the WPA creates dialogue: "Talk your way through this one; how can we make it work for all of us?"

4. A WPA should remain current with developments in the discipline.

Given the other demands of the WPA's job and the isolation he or she may feel if no one else in the department values composition, keeping current in the field is no simple task. Moreover, only through keeping track of the constant changes in composition can the WPA make suggestions that will appeal to those who are resistant and provide information to those who are ready to try a different approach to teaching composition. In a feminist department, the WPA would be given release time and a budget to allow her to keep current in the field. It would not be assumed that such duties should be performed on the WPA's own time.

5. A WPA should train inexperienced staff.

This last Olson and Moxley nonsubstantive duty is anything but a marginal administrative task. By introducing inexperienced staff and graduate students to the latest in composition pedagogy, WPAs not only create a cohesive program but also spread new ideas since these teachers usually find jobs at other schools. The authority that comes from being a teacher/mentor is far greater than the power inherent in being a legislator. The feminist WPA recognizes that part-timers and graduate students struggle with other worries — course work, dissertations, raising families. They need support as well as instruction, and being open to their needs will do more to influence them than anything else.

Catch your breath for a moment and allow me a narrative leap.

I taught Charlotte Perkins Gillman's *Herland* while I revised this article. Gillman's utopian female world reminds me of my original utopian feminine writing program. When Gillman formulated her utopia, she simply ignored or did not see certain inherent traits of human beings. In Herland, there was no war, no pollution, no unfair laws or politics, no overpopulation — but also no females who possessed innate sexual desires or competitive personalities. In my utopian model there was no unfair control, no competition, and no sacred intellectual territory — but I had assumed that no woman's actions were really governed by a need for personal control and that collaborative programs could easily resist outside influences.

That's the problem with utopias and models: they're like tests to find true princesses. In "Cinderella," for instance (not the Disney version, but the original gruesome version), the shoe fits only the woman it's designed for — no one else can wear it because the fairy godmother created it exclusively for Cinderella. The stepsisters (I was never convinced that they were particularly evil or ugly) had to make adjustments, cut off toes in one case and heels in the other in order to pass as a princess.

WPAs trying to fit utopian administrative models to real-world writing programs have the same problem, with repercussions that are just as serious. Programs, like women's feet, are different. To fit one program's administrative model to all English departments would require making adjustments in the personal pedagogical theories of the people who comprise the program. You can't go about lopping off pieces of people's pedagogies and expect to create a perfect writing program. Faculties will object; it could get bloody and messy; and you'll end up with the wrong princess to boot.

Models and utopias ignore the real-world restraints of individuals and their needs; they do not take into consideration either the nature of individual people within an institution or the internal structure of the institution itself. The WPA who applies her rigid model of administration to a writing program risks cutting off toes and heels of people. People who don't believe in process writing, for instance, shouldn't be penalized if they are using a different method of writing instruction but still doing a good job of getting students to employ the types of discourse that the department and the university declare exemplary. People who don't teach by models should not be denigrated by administrators who do. Policy on pedagogy should not be the prerogative of the WPA. Somehow the matter has to become a product of institutional agreement—a collaborative and complex plan for reaching collaborative goals.

I, therefore, will resist the temptation to propose a model of feminist writing programs administration. However, I will propose characteristics that feminist administrative structures might hold in common (which, I will note, are factors often cited as elements of successful business enterprise):

1. a willingness on the part of the WPA to relinquish control over the word—dictating official policy;
2. a heavy emphasis on collaboration;
3. an agreement to assign duties according to ability rather than according to title or rank—diversifying rather than delegating authority;
4. an ongoing conversation about the projects in which the faculty is engaged: teaching, research, and administration;
5. a workshop and a forum atmosphere that allows for experimentation in teaching and research;
6. a commitment to provide ample support and mentoring services for all levels of participants; and
7. a constant and steady system of rewarding excellence and effort.

These sorts of program characteristics can develop a sense of trust among members of the program, which is essential for a feminist approach to any collaborative effort. The WPA should not attempt to remove the cognitive/affective domain from the logical/rational enterprise of making a program work efficiently and cohesively. WPAs should realize that eventually administration becomes a matter of moral and ethical issues as well as of rational and logical issues. Intellectual growth depends upon having the freedom to act upon good ideas.

And one thing more (a feminist conversation never ends) . . . At the end of their survey, Olson and Moxley ask chairs to suggest additional qualities that a WPA should possess. I would suggest a sense of humor, flexibility, and what Ruddick calls "Maternal humility" — the knowledge that we are all severely limited as far as making our actions count for something and that it is practically impossible to predict the results of our work. (And yes, I've seen paters with these qualities, too.) It's not power a WPA needs to control a writing program; it's an ability to laugh when the program falls on its face or when the constant negative reactions to the perfect program that he or she constructed seem overpowering. Most of all, it's the ability to step back and let the program grow through the concerted efforts of the members of the community rather than by insisting that it conform to rigid and cripping policy.

Acknowledgments

I would like to thank Anne Bower, Deb Meem, Beverly Moss, Lynda Barry, and the editors of this book who all said, "Wait a minute, what about this?" enough times to make me think through my ideas.

Works Cited

Gilligan, Carol. *In a Different Voice: Psychological Theory and Women's Development*. Cambridge: Harvard UP, 1982.

Olson, Gary, and Joseph Moxley. "Directing Freshman Composition: The Limits of Authority." *College Composition and Communication* (1989): 51–60.

Ruddick, Sara. "Maternal Thinking." *Feminist Studies* 6 (1980): 70–96.

Tompkins, Jane. "Fighting Words: Unlearning to Write the Critical Essay." *Georgia Review* 42 (1988): 585–90.

9

Tales Too Terrible to Tell: Unstated Truths and Underpreparation in Graduate Composition Programs

Michael A. Pemberton/University of Illinois at Urbana-Champaign

Early in my career as a burgeoning writing scholar, I was given my first opportunity to work as a teaching assistant, beginning, as nearly all of us do, with a section of freshman composition. I received virtually no training to undertake this task and was given the distinct impression by other faculty members that no training was actually required. One week before classes began, I was handed a copy of the standard text (McCuen and Winkler's *Reading for Writers*), a few syllabi employed by previous TAs, and the directive, "Teach the book." That was it. No orientation, no discussions, no readings—just "teach the book." "OK," I thought, "how hard can it be?"

I soon found out how hard it could be, especially in an environment where there were few people willing to give me any guidance or advice about what I was supposed to be doing. As the quarter progressed, the other TAs and I were pretty much left on our own, somehow managing to stumble our way through interminable class periods filled with the wonders of comparison/contrast and process analysis essays. Lesson plans were made on the fly, and teaching days became a morass of anxiety, apprehension, and angst. Our insecurities and fears were only magnified by more "experienced" TAs who told us horror stories about throwing up before class meetings or breaking into tears in the middle of the night.

As I look back on this time, I must admit to some fond memories—mostly comradeships with the other graduate students who were sharing similar miseries—but I also feel a certain degree of resentment about the way I (and therefore my students) were taught to regard writing classes. My first experience teaching composition was, in most respects, a horrible introduction to the profession. I knew virtually nothing about composition theory, had no clue that there was such a thing as a "composing process," and did not do much good for my students other than being a sympathetic ear and a careful reader of their essays. (I sometimes wonder if it was only my own peculiar brand of masochism that caused me to choose composition studies as an area for graduate study.) Left to sink or swim in the treacherous waters of the classroom, I was fortunate enough to be one of the lucky ones, dog-paddling my way through narrative, descriptive, and classification essays, and figuring that mere survival could be counted a victory of sorts.

Today, some eight years and a Ph.D. in composition studies later, I once again find myself flailing in the academic deep end, dealing on a daily basis with problems and situations that my graduate coursework never prepared me for. To be sure, my years of graduate study were excellent preparation for continued academic success. My courses enabled me to talk coherently about cognitive processes, audience, speech acts, conversational analysis, discourse analysis, computational linguistics, and the merits of various composition pedagogies. I have learned about and am keeping up with the current journals in my profession (barely), I have attended most of the proper conferences and begun meeting the "right" people, I have learned the patois of my discourse community, and I am familiar enough with current research to be able to make contributions of my own. But all this academic and theoretical preparation has been of little help now that I am awash in a sea of administrative paperwork, faced with the task of helping to

create, implement, and shape a program for writing studies at a
large state university. Once again, I feel at times that I am struggling to keep my head above water, though I like to think that my
dog paddle is finally beginning to resemble something like an
Australian crawl.

After talking with numerous colleagues, sharing their impressions and experiences, and reviewing a number of relevant
documents (job lists and course catalogues), I am now convinced
that my situation and its accompanying anxieties/responsibilities
are quite common among recently placed Ph.D.s in composition
studies, and I am further convinced that our shared experience
points out a significant flaw in the design of most graduate programs in writing. To put the matter simply, the vast majority of
such programs actively conceal the "tale too terrible to tell": the
generally unstated, untaught, yet tacitly acknowledged fact that
composition specialists—including those fresh out of graduate
programs—will be expected to take on significant administrative
duties as a part of their regular assignments. These specialists will
almost routinely be asked to direct writing programs, supervise
large numbers of teaching assistants, establish writing-across-the-
curriculum courses, and play major advisory roles in shaping
university policies to accommodate growing demands for writing
curricula. New Ph.D.s enter into the field largely underprepared
for these responsibilities—often a significant proportion of their
job duties—and the scramble to develop the knowledge and skills
necessary to perform such duties is frequently a major obstacle in
their pressing need to publish and work towards tenure.

The reasons for this lack of training, I would like to argue,
draw from diverse origins, some ideological, some practical, and
some political. Like the "terrible truth" of administrative duties,
these reasons are themselves frequently left unstated—either
because they are unrecognized, ignored, or have been accepted as
common wisdom so long that they remain an unquestioned and
accepted part of the graduate studies landscape. In sum, they form
a ponderous, inertial mass that stubbornly resists any curricular
change that would move to correct or improve it. My purpose in
this chapter, then, is to identify and critique some of the rationales
often employed, consciously and subconsciously, to justify excluding administrative coursework in rhetoric and composition studies. I do this not merely as an exercise in faultfinding but to address
the crucial question of what graduate programs in composition

studies ought to be and how we can best prepare graduate students for the academic and institutional world in which they are likely to find themselves once they receive their terminal degrees.

The Inevitability of Administration

Trudelle Thomas, director of the writing program at Xavier, touches on the demand for administrators in a recent article in *Writing Program Administration:*

> Candidates entering the job market with Ph.D.s in Composition and Rhetoric quickly discover that they, more than other new instructors, must assume administrative responsibilities early in their careers. Many are hired immediately into positions as writing program administrators; others are hired with an eye toward moving into such positions within a few years. (41)

A brief review of the October MLA Job Information Lists over the past two years tends to support this assertion. Of the 177 placement ads for composition specialists, 87 (nearly fifty percent) were explicit about stating their needs: "Will serve as director of well-established Freshman Composition Program" (University of South Alabama); "must have experience and ability to direct writing programs" (California State University, Los Angeles); "specialist in rhetoric and composition to serve as Writing Across the Curriculum Coordinator" (University of Louisville); "potential to direct lab and comp program" (Creighton University), etc. Other job offerings were less forthright, advertising merely that the search committee sought a "composition specialist," but if my own experience interviewing for entry-level positions is any indication, I have few doubts that the subject of administration routinely came up in job interviews. In several of the interviews I had at the 1989 MLA, for example, I was told such things as "we expect that you will eventually take over the composition program," or "we won't burden you with administrative responsibilities for the first year or two, but after that . . ." Many of these statements came from colleges and universities that, at the time, had no other writing specialists on their faculty. At best, they had a professor or two with some training in linguistics or a collection of underpaid, overworked part-timers who had been teaching composition—and nothing but composition—for more than ten years. Many of these colleges had ambitious plans: they wanted to improve the quality of their writing courses; they wanted to begin writing-across-the-curriculum programs; they wanted to improve the quality of their writing teachers (ironic, in view of my own early experience); but most of all, they wanted someone who could show them how to accomplish all of these goals.

The push to place new assistant professors in administrative posts derives from two different but closely linked causes: the limited supply of PhDs in composition studies and the current demand for specialists in our field. Graduate programs in composition and rhetoric are starting to produce job candidates in significant numbers, but not, as yet, in sufficient quantities to meet the growing need. New graduates, as a result, tend to be "hot commodities," snapped up quickly by hungry English departments. My own recent experience on a search committee seems to confirm this state of affairs. Throughout the search process, our major concern was not so much *who* we would get as whether we would be able to get *anyone* for the position we had advertised. (As it turned out, in fact, our top two candidates took jobs elsewhere, and our search had to be cancelled.) The situation has become so competitive that some departments have taken to interviewing candidates and offering them jobs before the MLA conference takes place in December. The chair of one such departmental search committee was quite smug about this tactic when we talked about it at the CCCC. "I have no apologies," he said. "If we want to compete for these graduates with the big universities, then we have to be faster than they are. It's not our fault that they're so slow."

The scarcity of qualified graduates — and the limited budgets available in most institutions to hire new faculty — generally means that newly hired assistant professors will become the one and only acknowledged "expert" in writing and writing instruction in their home department. Their expertise will be consistently in demand, they will routinely be placed on a multitude of composition and curriculum committees, and they will generally be considered the "logical" person to administer and direct all sorts of writing programs. Before long, the new graduates will find themselves in largely administrative positions with little knowledge and less experience in performing all the job duties that are expected of them.[1]

Though this situation is occasionally addressed and briefly lamented in conference presentations or the journal *Writing Pro-*

gram Administration, it is virtually ignored in terms of any practical changes. Graduate courses rarely engage administrative issues or matters of university policy; neither do they place much emphasis on the "engineering" of composition scholarship, of moving from theoretical principles to the embodiment of those principles in well-defined program structures. The need for this sort of training seems obvious, but its realization in specific courses and syllabi seems conspicuously absent.

Lack of Course Offerings

As a part of our own research in trying to establish a new graduate studies program in rhetoric and composition, Gail Hawisher and I have determined that there are approximately twenty-five institutions in this country that have such programs in place at the present time,[2] and of these, I have examined the course catalogues of fifteen in detail, including those from institutions such as Purdue, Ohio State, the University of Texas at Austin, the University of Iowa, Carnegie Mellon University, the University of Southern California, and the University of California at San Diego. As might be expected, the course offerings are wide-ranging and diverse, indicative of the particular emphases and teaching philosophies of faculty members at the various institutions. Especially noteworthy are the many courses in writing pedagogy which are now being offered at several universities. According to a survey of writing programs undertaken by Carol Hartzog (1984), thirty-five of forty-two institutions (eighty-three percent) require some type of formal training for TAs who are to teach first-year composition. At some institutions such as Purdue and the University of Maryland, College Park, this training takes the form of a mentor program and weekly colloquia, but just as often this training is realized in formal course work (48–50). Ohio state, for example, in addition to its many courses in theory, style, and rhetoric, lists courses in "Teaching Freshman Composition," "Teaching Basic Writing," "Teaching College Composition in ESL," and "Teaching Business and Professional Writing" in its catalogue. The University of Iowa, similarly, offers a wide variety of pedagogical courses, a sampling of which includes "Approaches to the Teaching of High School Writing," "Methods in Teaching Freshman Composition," and "Teaching in a Writing Lab." Other institutions have similar, though less extensive, courses in writing pedagogy, courses which are no doubt taken by graduate students who will be working in these venues as a part of their teaching assistantships.

In none of these programs at any university of which I am aware, however, are courses offered whose subject matter is the management and administration of writing programs. No formal course work is available for those students who wish to learn techniques, strategies, and procedures for training teaching assistants, running a writing lab, supervising first-year or upper-division writing programs, proposing new courses, handling plagiarism cases, writing grant proposals, or becoming familiar with institutional hierarchies and chains-of-command—all of which will be essential in their later life in the university.

This is not to say, however, that formal, on-the-books course work is the only possible source of information about writing program administration for interested graduate students. Some few students may, as at USC, Purdue, and Illinois, serve a brief apprenticeship or internship as "Assistant to the Director of Writing Programs," where they will obtain some hands-on experience with the details of program management. Alternatively, many of the "facts" about the day-to-day operations of writing programs can be (and usually are) learned as the result of working as a TA within such a program. In the course of their own teaching experience, teaching assistants will likely become familiar with plagiarism procedures, tutor training, and the like. But rarely will these lessons about program administration be presented formally or explicitly; neither will they be offered to students in a structured or coherent manner. Instead, they will accumulate gradually as the result of circumstance or coincidence, existing only as a kind of pragmatic subtext that underlies the students' teaching strategies. As Susan Wolfson laments, "Most of the people in my generation foundered, or picked up advice randomly and anecdotally, and tried to gauge their circumstances through circuits of gossip about the fates of others" (62).

Steven North refers to this type of experience-based knowledge as *lore*, a cumulative assortment of anecdotal information about writing and writers which is passed from teacher to teacher on an ad hoc basis. Lore is the medium of "shared institutional experience" (28), a sort of "common wisdom" that is exchanged in coffee rooms, offices, informal gatherings, and hallways, not codified in the more structured and public venues of the classroom, the syllabus, or the course catalogue. It is knowledge gained in bits and pieces—often incomplete and frequently self-contradictory—but flexible enough to adapt to changing situations in the classroom.

North further observes that lore is a primary vehicle for knowledge transmission among composition's *practitioners.* Teachers talk informally about what works and what does not, how to handle a particular unit of instruction, what to do in class each day, and how to meet the needs of students who require special assistance. This sort of dialogue thrives among TAs, part-timers, professors, tutors, and anyone who teaches composition in a classroom or lab setting. But for graduate students in rhetoric and composition, this dialogue is now supplemented and contextualized by upper-division courses—usually required—in the methods, techniques, and strategies of writing instruction. Writing program administration, on the other hand, has no such supplemental courses and must, therefore, depend entirely upon lore for its transmission. Graduate students in composition tend to receive lore about program administration privately rather than publicly, in meetings with dissertation directors, in "tangential" discussions in other classes, and in preparation for interviewing at the MLA or CCCC:

> We all feel that we were given too little help in getting oriented to the facts of professional life. When I was a graduate student at Berkeley, formal and deliberate discussion of the business of the profession was considered by many faculty members to demean the mission of a PhD program: "we guarantee the quality of your degree and you figure out the rest" was the tacit assumption—so much so that even the existence of our placement committee was lamented by some faculty members for degrading vocation to business. (Wolfson 62)

Given that writing program administration is likely to be an important aspect of most job situations new rhetoric and composition graduates encounter and apply for, it seems crucial—if not mandatory—that we recognize this fact and provide students with the support and training they will need. We must remove administration from the domain of pure lore and make it a part of formal curricula in much the same way that training in writing pedagogy has been formalized in many programs. In order to do so, however, we must first confront the many obstacles that would work to restrict this necessary change in curricula. Interestingly, many of these obstacles are "lore-ish" in their own right, generally unstated except in informal situations but frequently the substance of coffeehouse conversation and informal dialogue.

Ideological Restrictions

Certainly no one would deny that composition's scholars and practitioners have been considered second-class citizens for most of their academic lives. Composition is generally looked upon as a service course at most universities: required, overenrolled, and staffed by an increasing number of graduate students and part-timers (Hartzog 63–64). Composition courses and writing programs are usually housed in English departments whose members believe that the pursuit and study of literature is what the department should really be about. Most full-time faculty members are reluctant to teach a first-year composition course, and many still have trouble recognizing that such a thing as "serious" scholarship exists in the field of composition. (Ironically, it is often these faculty members—specialists in literature—who are asked to review and assess the work of writing specialists in their departments. More than a few negative tenure decisions have been due, I suspect, to a committee's lack of familiarity with the journals and current work in composition.)

Understandably, most composition scholars take issue with these opinions and have been working assiduously for the last twenty years to prove that composition studies is a "legitimate" discipline with its own body of scholarship, research, and practices.[3] This strategy has become, of necessity, a largely defensive one. The position of most composition specialists in English departments is frequently tenuous, dependent upon the goodwill and respect of faculty members who do not always understand what writing studies are all about. In order to maintain this respect, however, we have often had to distance ourselves from the "service" function of composition and align ourselves with the "academic" function. One way of doing this has been to stress the empirical and theoretical aspects of composition research in our instruction and to offer courses that can pass the most stringent reviews of intellectual rigor. Courses in research methodology and design, rhetorical history, cognitive psychology, and discourse analysis are required of most majors, and the trend has been to deemphasize pedagogy and ignore administrative aspects of the composition field altogether.[4]

The difficulty this practice presents, of course, stems from composition's close ties with pedagogy (Lauer and Lunsford 110) and the practical matters of program management. The importance of pedagogy is evident in the amount of composition research that is classroom-based as well as the significant role that teacher/researchers have played in our profession. Even the most cursory review of journal articles in *CCC*, *Written Communication*, and *College English* will reveal the "trope" of "Pedagogical Implications" at the end of most articles. More to the point, however, most of the people in our field enjoy teaching, enjoy working with students, and like thinking of themselves as teachers. We learn about writing not only to understand how writing processes work, but how we can use our academic knowledge to further inform our teaching practices and improve the writing of our students. This emphasis clearly differentiates us from many other academics. It would be hard, for example, to maintain that scholars in English romanticism research Keats with the primary intention of informing the way in which they teach their survey of literature courses.

Composition's close ties to the classroom have, as I have shown, led to graduate composition programs with courses in pedagogy as well as theory. Most composition specialists welcome these courses as a healthy hybrid of the academic and the pedagogical. Nevertheless, some faculty members seem to view these courses with suspicion. At one time or another, in my experience, I have heard English department faculty express the opinion that these courses (a) are not academic; (b) should not be required for teaching assistants; or (c) should be given without credit. One literature professor of my acquaintance boasted that he had never taken a single English education course or any course that had pedagogy as its focus. He wore this lack of training as a badge of honor, testament to his "natural" skills as a teacher and to his belief that such courses were taken only by those who were pedagogically handicapped.

If this professor's opinion is representative of others in English departments, then it is no surprise that courses in writing program administration do not appear in course catalogues. Administration courses, at first glance, appear even further divorced from academics than do courses in pedagogy, which at least have academics for their subject matter. Program administration encompasses matters of budget, personnel, and interdepartmental relations. It is, in many respects, a function of the business environment that supports and subsidizes the university's academic pursuits and might, perhaps, be more "properly" envisioned as part of an M.B.A. curriculum than a degree program in rhetoric and composition. Writing program administration seems far too practical and attached to the real world for many in English studies to consider it a truly academic subject.

But this attitude is clearly a shortsighted view. Program administration can, in some respects, be viewed as the purest possible expression of theoretical principles in composition. As theory informs practice, program administrators are the primary agents of curricular and theoretical change. Part of the administrator's function is to apply theory to specific situations and contexts, to design curricula, policies, and standards that not only meet institutional needs but also embody the best and most current knowledge in the field. Such a practice is highly theoretical and often forces administrators to confront paradigmatic conflicts and oppositions head-on (Gale).

In addition, a graduate program that concerns itself solely with immersing students in the details of critical theory, social construction, cognitivism, and empirical research is fulfilling only a part of its educational mission. It should also be responsible for preparing its graduates to succeed in the jobs they enter after they graduate. Since program administration will undoubtedly comprise a part of their future job duties, courses in program administration should, logically, be an integral part of the major.

Practical Restrictions

Another argument against adding courses in program management to the rhetoric/composition curriculum is similar to the argument made by program directors in other fields, such as engineering: there is already too much material in the field for students to master to justify burdening them with additional requirements. Publications in composition studies have increased exponentially over the past ten years with new, important work appearing on a regular basis. Publishing houses such as Sage, Boynton/Cook, NCTE, Southern Illinois, and others have made firm commitments to scholarship in composition, and a proliferation of new journals has also multiplied the task of keeping up with current research. Where once there were only *College English*, *Research in the Teaching of English*, and *CCC*, there are now

Written Communication, Journal of Advanced Composition, Writing Instructor, Computers and Composition, Rhetoric Review, Visions and Revisions, Writing Center Newsletter, Writing Center Journal, Writing Program Administration, and a host of others. The hundreds of entries each year in the *CCCC Bibliography of Composition and Rhetoric* illustrate the increasing demands made on graduate programs to keep their students current in the literature of the field. The interdisciplinary nature of composition further complicates matters—especially for students whose interests and/or dissertations require reading in the specialized journals of other disciplines. My own graduate work in the study of writing-process models, for example, led me to investigate journals such as *Cognition, Cognitive Psychology, Synthese,* and the *Journal of Mind and Behavior.* Given the increasing amount of information and research that graduate students must assimilate in order to prepare themselves for future research and publication of their own, it is not surprising that there should be some resistance to courses in writing program administration, whose utility is rarely acknowledged in anything other than a covert fashion.

But this brand of resistance is clearly problematic and perhaps a bit naive. In essence, it seems based on two assumptions: first, that research focusing on program administration is less worthy of study than other types of composition research and second, that a course in program administration would detract from, rather than enhance, the quality of education given to graduate students. I have yet to see a convincing argument that either of these assumptions has merit. Any administrative course that operates under the assumption that practical writing programs are grounded in theory will demand that students in that course demonstrate the ability to incorporate theory into their program designs. They must be able to defend and critique writing programs from theoretical, epistemological, and pedagogical standpoints, and to do so they must draw from the most current and important work in the field. A course in program administration would not, therefore, deny them access to critical information. Quite the contrary, it would provide them with an important new arena for discovering new information and synthesizing it with the knowledge they have garnered from other courses.

A second practical argument against the inclusion of administrative course work looks beyond graduate school to the realities of assistant professorship: composition faculty and dissertation directors know that future tenure decisions will be based upon research, not teaching or success in running a program. Though administrative skills (and teaching excellence, for that matter) will unquestionably be important to composition specialists in their later jobs, it is generally felt that those skills will not be given much weight when tenure and promotion committees evaluate the progress and potential of assistant professors. This fact, accordingly, is used to argue against courses in writing program administration whose benefit to future tenure reviews is questionable at best.

Such an argument, however, ignores the fact that even though program administration skills—like teaching ability—may contribute little to favorable tenure decisions, demonstrably poor administrative skills can be used as reasons to deny tenure. Program administrators are expected to perform competently in all aspects of their jobs duties regardless of the weight (or lack of weight) such competence or management skills will be given in later promotion reviews. For purely pragmatic reasons, then, it is in the best interests of graduate students to gain experience in administration and in our best interests as educators to provide it.

Political Restrictions

But even if we agree that there is a need for some curricular support in writing program administration, the questions remain: What form should that support take, and how should it be implemented? There are no simple answers to these questions, in part because the answers depend upon institutional opportunities and constraints and in part because there are clear restrictions on what it is possible for significant numbers of graduate students to do at any one time. Writing program administration operates within an institutional hierarchy: a relatively small number of people are empowered to make program decisions and put them into effect. Consequently, there are few positions in any given college or university where graduate students can get hands-on practical experience in the details of running a writing program. Occasional positions as assistant to program directors or writing lab directors are available, as I mentioned earlier, but these positions are insufficient to meet the needs of the ten to fifteen (or more) graduate students who might enroll in a writing administration course each term.

Further, many institutions have clear and explicit rules that restrict the roles that graduate students (and even part-timers) can play in any sort of governance. Again, this varies from college to college and university to university. Some of the more progressive institutions allow graduate students active roles on faculty committees; others allow only advisory, nonvoting roles; and still others allow graduate students no role at all—not even the option of attending relevant committee meetings. Even in the most liberal institutions, the opportunity to serve on faculty committees is limited and frequently competitive. It would not be possible for an entire class of students to participate in writing program governance in this way. Other means to provide practical experience must be found, and specific course work focused on writing program administration seems to be the only reasonable solution. A portion of class time in each meeting could be spent reviewing and discussing the issues addressed in relevant committee meetings (this information being brought to class by the instructor or other representative). Besides giving students some "behind-the-scenes" exposure to program issues in their own institution, these discussions could also provide valuable insights or information that can be introduced at subsequent committee meetings. The class would thereby circumvent institutional restrictions on graduate student participation in governance, providing them a kind of representation by proxy.

Teaching Writing Program Administration

What form should a course in writing program administration take? Clearly, it should be a course that introduces students to the central aspects of program administration and allows them to confront some of the demands their future positions are likely to impose upon them. In the Appendix, I show what the syllabus for such a course might look like. As I envision it here, this course is divided into three major sections representing the three forms of writing administration composition specialists are likely to become involved with in their careers: first-year composition programs, writing centers, and WAC programs. Each of these sections begins with an historical/theoretical overview, focusing on the theoretical underpinnings and rationales for each type of program and reviewing the current research, which argues for their success or failure as models of writing instruction. These overviews are followed by discussions of the various instructional missions that the programs might be expected to serve: which segments of the student body the programs should be designed to reach; which of several distinct approaches can be used or have been used in the past; how different aspects of composition theory, genre theory, and pedagogical theory can influence the design of such programs; and so on. Lastly, each of the course's major sections treats the practical matters of administration: training TAs and faculty, managing resources, setting policies, handling budgets, supervising staff, and managing administrative duties so that they do not control the compositionist's life.

Certainly, many of the specific problems likely to be encountered by new directors in each of these areas will be idiosyncratic to particular institutions; WAC programs, for example, will take many different forms depending upon the size of the institution where they are located, the requirements for "writing-intensive" certification, and the attitudes of the faculty in various departments. But despite these differences, there are a number of commonalities that can be addressed in the classroom or a graduate seminar.

According to C. W. Griffin, for example, most successful WAC programs share three common features: faculty workshops, curricular changes, and facilities in writing centers for continuing faculty support (400–401). Training graduate students to direct a WAC program would therefore include training in how to prepare a WAC workshop (identifying interested faculty, getting inter-departmental support, scheduling the workshop, arranging for speakers, selecting readings, etc.); how to provide curricular change (reviewing college writing requirements, reviewing guidelines from individual departments and the faculty senate, working with faculty to modify existing courses into writing-intensive courses, and designing new courses for WAC certification); and how to provide support to WAC faculty (training TAs to evaluate discipline-specific writing, helping to design appropriate writing assignments, working with tutors in the writing center, etc.). The form such training would take would lie in the hands of individual instructors. Students might be encouraged to review and modify an existing WAC workshop syllabus or they could be asked to design one of their own—either individually or in small groups. Students could be asked to research the policies and procedures for proposing new writing-intensive courses at their own institution and then design a course that meets the needs of the college and an individual department. (Ideally, students could work with cooperative faculty in other departments to design these courses, learning a great deal about discipline-specific writing in the process.) A host of interesting, rewarding, practical, and academically challenging projects such as these might be envisioned and integrated into the existing curricula for graduate students in composition.

Theoretical issues would obviously be central to the design and implementation of a successful WAC program, and this course would stress the need to regard such issues carefully. Students who wished to construct or critique a WAC program would need to be familiar with current scholarship in social constructionism, discourse communities, and the disciplinary conventions that shape the representation of knowledge. Readings taken from the work of Charles Bazerman, David Bartholomae, Toby Fulwiler, Marilyn Cooper, and Art Young could be used to contextualize discussions of WAC as a program structure and help to give it shape within a particular institution.

I have long felt that one of composition studies' real strengths has been its fundamental grounding in real-world needs. We find writing interesting and important not solely for abstract, intellectual reasons but because it has clear, practical value as well. We believe that writing is a skill that our students will use for the rest of their lives, and I suspect that a large part of our satisfaction as composition teachers derives from our awareness that we prepare out students to face the demands of a society that requires increasing levels of literacy and communication skills from its college graduates. I think we should continue to apply this article of faith to ourselves and our graduate students. We need to prepare graduate students for the real-world situations they will find themselves in. If they are to take on positions of responsibility as the heads of writing programs, we should give them the same consideration we give our undergraduates, providing them with the training, experience, and guidance that will allow them to excel in the practical matters of administration as well as the more esoteric matters of research and scholarship.

Notes

1. Even in departments that have a sizeable contingent of tenure-track composition faculty, the likelihood of administrative work remains high. At

Purdue, for example, of the seven faculty listed in rhetoric and composition on a recent flyer, five are identified as directors of various writing units: the Writing Lab, Business Writing, Freshman Composition, Technical Writing, and the Graduate Program in Rhetoric and Composition.

2. The approximate nature of this number (twenty-five) should be readily apparent. Huber's 1986 survey indicates that forty-two programs offered Ph.D.s in rhetoric, writing, and composition (123), though the amalgamated nature of this classification made it less specific than we wished for the purposes of our own survey. Our number is composed of programs that offer degrees and/or specializations in composition studies alone.

3. The debate rages, even among writing specialists, over whether composition studies can actually be considered a discipline in its own right. Emig, Connors, and Hairston each address the issue from the perspective of Thomas Kuhn's notion of *paradigms*, while the writing directors quoted by Hartzog in her survey also reflect a deep philosophical split over composition's status: "Yes, [composition] is [a discipline]. . . . It's a discipline in search of recognition" (65). "No. The worst thing that has happened to composition is that it has begun to think of itself as an independent scholarly discipline" (67).

4. This is not to say that pedagogy is not considered an important part of graduate programs in writing and composition. Huber's survey of rhetoric programs indicated that a significant proportion (approximately twenty-five percent) considered pedagogy either their primary or secondary orientation (152). I would argue, however, that within English departments the tendency has been to stress composition as theory rather than composition as pedagogy.

Works Cited

Connors, Robert J. "Composition Studies and Science." *College English* 45 (1983): 1–20.

Emig, Janet. "Inquiry Paradigms and Writing." *College Composition and Communication* 33 (1982): 64–75.

Gale, Irene. "Conflicting Paradigms: Theoretical and Administrative Tensions in Writing Program Administration." *Writing Program Administration* 14 (Fall/Winter 1990): 41–50.

Griffin, C. W. "Programs for Writing Across the Curriculum: A Report." *College Composition and Communication* 36 (1985): 398–403.

Hairston, Maxine. "The Winds of Change: Thomas Kuhn and the Revolution in the Teaching of Writing." *College Composition and Communication* 33 (1982): 76–88.

Hartzog, Carol P. *Composition and the Academy: A Study of Writing Program Administration*. New York: MLA, 1986.

Huber, Bettina J. "A Report on the 1986 Survey of English Doctoral Programs in Writing and Literature." Lunsford, Moglen, and Slevin 121–75.

Job Information List: English Edition. New York: MLA, October 1989.

Job Information List: English Edition. New York: MLA, October 1990.

Lauer, Janice M., and Andrea Lunsford. "The Place of Rhetoric and Composition in Doctoral Studies." Lunsford, Moglen, and Slevin 106–10.

Lunsford, Andrea, Helene Moglen, and James F. Slevin, eds. *The Future of Doctoral Studies in English*. New York: MLA, 1989.

North, Stephen M. *The Making of Knowledge in Composition: Portrait of an Emerging Field*. Upper Montclair, NJ: Boynton, 1987.

Thomas, Trudelle. "The Graduate Student as Apprentice WPA: Experiencing the Future." *Writing Program Administration* 14 (Spring 1991): 41–51.

Wolfson, Susan. "The Informal Curriculum." Lunsford, Moglen, and Slevin 60–70.

Appendix:
Sample Syllabus for a Course in
Writing Program Administration

I. First-year composition programs
   A. Theoretical issues
      1. Rationale for a first-year composition program
      2. Relevant research
   B. Instructional mission
      1. Programs within the college
         a. Great-books approach
         b. Discipline-specific writing
         c. General freshman composition
         d. WAC
         e. Others
      2. Program philosophies
         a. Source-based writing
         b. Transactional writing
         c. Discourse sequencing
         d. Diverse genres
   C. Resources
      1. Demand for courses
      2. Available teaching assistantships
      3. Use of part-timers
      4. Scheduling and classroom space
      5. Budgetary issues
      6. Grants and external support
   D. Teaching assistants
      1. Training
         a. Scheduling
         b. Issues (process, conferencing, heuristics, etc.)
         c. Policies (plagiarism, late papers, grading)

       2. Supervision

       3. Hiring and firing

    E. Intra- and extradepartmental accountability

       1. Department meetings

       2. Committee meetings

       3. Faculty senate and curriculum committees

       4. ESL and "Second-dialect" responsibilities

       5. Department heads, deans, and chancellors

       6. Faculty complaints

II. Writing centers

    A. Theoretical issues

       1. Rationale

       2. Relevant research

    B. Instructional mission

       1. Student group (undergrads, grads, departments)

       2. Resources

         a. Computers

         b. Library/files

         c. Classroom facilities

    C. Staff

       1. Graduate students (schedules, stipends, training)

       2. Undergraduates (schedules, wages, training, problems)

       3. Support (secretary, receptionist, hourly workers)

    D. Tutor training

       1. Training before working as tutors

         a. A separate course

         b. Brief orientation

         c. Issues (problems, role-playing, procedures, etc.)

       2. Training while working as tutors

         a. Weekly meetings

         b. Tutor presentations

    E. Record keeping

       1. Student appointments

       2. Student data sheets

       3. Funding and budgetary issues

    F. Center activities and ongoing concerns

       1. Publicity

       2. Specialized workshops

       3. Guest speakers

       4. Hiring and firing

III. Writing-across-the-curriculum programs

    A. Theoretical issues: Purpose and justification

       1. Social constructionism

       2. Discourse communities

       3. Knowledge representation

    B. Faculty workshops

       1. Logistics (place, time, faculty members, etc.)

       2. Motivation

        a. Generating faculty interest
        b. Getting departmental support
        c. Rewards (stipend, recognition, other)
     3. Issues to be addressed
        a. Previous knowledge
        b. Support services
        c. Introduction to WAC
        d. Introduction to the writing process
        e. Assigning writing
        f. Evaluating writing
  C. Curriculum modification
     1. College policies and procedures
     2. Existing programs
     3. Institutional hierarchies and approval system
  D. Faculty support
     1. Personal contacts
     2. Writing-intensive syllabi
     3. TA training
     4. Working with the writing center
     5. Designing writing assignments
IV. Other issues
  A. Managing your time
  B. Continuing research and publishing
  C. Having a personal life

AT THE RISK
OF BEING PERSONAL . . .

Seeking Aunt Beast:
A Collage Essay

Jean Fairgrieve/*Walla Walla Community College, Walla Walla, Washington*

"Are you fighting the Black Thing?" Meg asked.

"Oh, yes," Aunt Beast replied. "In doing that we can never relax. . . . Of course, we have help, and without help it would be much more difficult."

"Who helps you?" Meg asked.

"Oh, dear, it is so difficult to explain things to you, small one. . . . Good helps us, the stars help us, perhaps what you would call light helps us, love helps us. . . . This is something you just have to know or not know."

— Madeleine L'Engle's *A Wrinkle in Time*

━━━━━━━━━━━━━━━━━━━━━━━━

Education. I've had so many different responses to that word all my life. When I was a child in the 1940s and 1950s, I hated school. I hated the building, the smell, the classroom, the desks in rows, the books, the coatroom with garlicky sandwiches and soggy galoshes.

Yes, in those days children wore galoshes over their shoes or they wore three-buckle arctics, those enormous rubber boots with the metal buckles and the gussets that leaked sometimes. Boots had to be huge so we could put them on over our genuine Buster Brown leather oxfords, the ones with the reinforced punched leather toes. Nikes and Reeboks hadn't been invented then. Tennis shoes were black, high-top Keds that we wore in summer, after the rains, or for gym class. One thing about the old Buster Browns — the uppers were stitched to the soles so they could be resoled. In those days, kids walked more than they do now, so the soles actually wore through.

My childhood was just prior to the days of the mother-cum-chauffeur. I can't say it was all bad. I think kids were less isolated from other people than they are now. Now middle-class kids, of which I was one — on the low side of middle — float around in their metal and plastic cocoons, and they often don't rub shoulders with people of other socioeconomic classes until they are teenagers.

I was shocked to find that one of my son's friends in the sixth grade had never used any form of public transportation, so we took him with us on the city bus one day. My, what an eye-opener that was for him. There he was, on the bus with all sorts of people, people with crooked teeth, retired loggers with missing fingers, schizophrenics from the local workshop who picked at nonexistent bugs, mothers on welfare, grannies on Social Security, and my son and me. That kid talked about his trip on the city bus for days, although he was probably glad to get back to his safe, clean car.

Looking back on my school years, I would say that I became literate despite the American public school system. All my life I have enjoyed learning immensely, but on my own terms, in my own way. As a child, I was always cooking up new learning projects. One particularly memorable project was that of nursing the neighbor's tomcat back to health.

I was ten years old, and I was determined that the cat (Duchess was his name — the neighbor had been reluctant to do the examination necessary to determine the cat's gender) was going to live. I went to the library and checked out as many books on nutrition and disease as I could carry in my bike basket and went home and read them. On the basis of my reading, I diagnosed Duchess's problem as malnutrition and designed a diet for him that I hoped would restore his health. It did. By the end of the first month of his diet, Duchess had become a magnificent specimen. His long fur was shiny and fluffy, his sores had healed, and he was fat. The neighbor gave him to me to keep after that.

That learning project had certainly paid off for both Duchess and me. The joy of knowing that my self-acquired knowledge and the application of that knowledge had helped Duchess recover his health reinforced what I knew innately—I was the one person best qualified to direct my own learning. Duchess was living proof of that!

Now, in my middle age, I am back in school—this time by choice. It was not easy for me to decide to return to school in 1987, for I had to fight all my old negative memories of previous experiences. This time, however, I had factors beyond my own selfish interests to consider. I knew that there was the possibility I might have to support my mentally handicapped daughter, and for that reason I could see the wisdom of earning a higher degree and improving my employment possibilities. Of even more importance to me was the feeling that I had been called to work with disadvantaged adults, that I was to use my talents to help adults improve the quality of their lives.

The turning point in my decision-making process came on a Sunday morning when I went up to the altar for Communion. I asked God if he would bless my decision to return to school, and I had the certain feeling that he did.

Graduate school has been a whole different educational experience for me. For the first time in my life, I have what Madeleine L'Engle was talking about in her book when Mrs. Whatsit compares life—or education—to the sonnet form: "'Yes.' Mrs. Whatsit said. 'You're given the form, but you have to write the sonnet yourself. What you say is completely up to you.'" That's what my experience of graduate school has been; I've been given the form in my classes, but what I have done within that form has been left to me. I see my instructors as peers who know a lot more about their subject areas than I do and who can help me learn what I want to learn. I am happy with my situation in graduate school. My only question is this: Why didn't the education programs in which I was involved as an undergraduate and as a public-school student offer me the same freedom to direct my own learning? I look back on the hours I spent in school watching the clock, waiting until the school day was over so I could get on with my own learning projects, and I think, "What a waste of my life!"

Today I finished Ursula Le Guin's *Wizard of Earthsea*. One problem I have when I read a book like that, full of fantasy and symbolism, is that I don't know how to take it. It's like seeing oil on water—I can make out all sorts of shapes and figures, but are they really there? Or is everything I see as ephemeral and as much an illusion as Ged's "changings"?

The book is about education, about living, and about power. I suppose that some modern educators would jump on the "empowerment" bandwagon and try to say that the book was the story of a person of low socioeconomic class who achieves success and fame because he gets an education. Of course, they could say that, but I think the book says a lot more than that.

I think the story is all about how young Ged, a person who is gifted, goes through life, meets temptations, succumbs to some temptations, abuses the power his gift gives him, and then finally learns to use his gift wisely, for the benefit of himself and other people. The hero could be anyone, though, not just a person with intellectual gifts. Interesting. Ged was a magician. At one point in the story there was mention of the word *magisteria*, at least that's what I think it was. What interested me was that when I took first-year Latin in 1953, I learned that the word for teacher was *magister*. The terms are pretty close, maybe so close that now I see the position of "teacher" in a slightly different light.

The village two days' walk from his village is a foreign land, and the island a day's sail from his island is a mere rumor, misty hills seen across the water, not solid ground like that he walks on.
— Ursula Le Guin, *Wizard of Earthsea*

This passage reminded me of the attitude I encountered when I visited a family in England. The family lived in Reading, about a half day's drive from Stonehenge, but they had never been to Stonehenge. I didn't let them know how astonished I was when they told me that.

One of the days I was their guest, they took me for a drive into the countryside. They seldom went for drives. I'm not sure why. Their car was small, and they could have afforded a drive once in a while, but they didn't seem interested.

About an hour away from their home was the White Horse of Uffington, a horse shape made on a chalk hill by Stone Age people. The people stripped the sod off the hillside to make the outline of a huge white horse, and then each summer they pulled the grass to retain the outline. Today, people still strip the sod from the outline, but their motives are twentieth-century motives—the White Horse brings tourist dollars to Uffington.

Near the horse shape were the Kennet barrows, huge mounds where long ago people buried their dead. And then we visited Avebury, a stone circle similar to Stonehenge. There I watched a thatcher at work on a village house. Each time we stopped in a little village, I looked into the church. Some of the churches I saw dated back to the days of the Norman Conquest.

All that, and my friends, people who had been born, raised, and married in Reading and whose children were repeating the process, didn't care to explore the realm beyond their city. Well, as I pondered that thought, I realized that my friends took very few risks in life. Maybe life was fraught with enough uncertainties for them without their deliberate seeking of uncertainties. Maybe that's why my ancestors left England and Scotland—they couldn't handle the certainty of life in their homelands. They liked a little spice in their lives, a little risk taking.

Thus, that which gives us the power to work magic, sets the limits of that power. A mage can control only what is near him, what he can name exactly and wholly. And this is well. If it were not so, the wickedness of the powerful or the folly of the wise would long ago have sought to change what cannot be changed, and Equilibrium would fail.
—Ursula Le Guin, *Wizard of Earthsea*

Lately I've been thinking about power, the power in my life and about my writing. Ten years ago, before my divorce, I felt I had no power, no control over my life. Now, however, I'm beginning to feel little green shoots, little buds of power. At the age of fifty-two, I'm a late bloomer, late to recognize and channel the forces that energize me. But what relationship does my writing have to the blossoming of my sense of power?

Until I was in my early forties, I wrote only documents necessary to daily life—personal correspondence, absence excuses for my children, notes to family members, and grocery lists. Oh, when I was in school, I ground out the required papers, and I received high scores on them, usually. My method for doing academic writing was to analyze the structure or pattern of a model paper acceptable to a particular teacher and construct my own paper accordingly. And I hated every minute of it. I felt the same way I did as a child in kindergarten when the teacher gave us pictures to color—I was angry because I had to stay in someone else's lines. I wanted to draw my own lines—why couldn't I draw my own lines? I didn't know the answer to that question; I felt that control over my writing, as with control over my life, belonged in the hands of others.

When I was forty-two, I experienced clinical depression and entered therapy. Because I didn't want to waste time in my sessions tracing the roots of my depression, I did that work at home. Some days I wrote four pages, and other days I wrote a dozen pages. I didn't know it then, but I was freewriting. As I wrote, I discovered pieces to the puzzle of my life that fit together, and by the end of two years, I had seven pounds of text to show for my efforts and had written myself out of the deepest part of my depression. Because that writing did not have the structure and form I associated with "worthwhile" writing, however, I assumed that it had no value and set it out with the trash one morning, hoping that the landfill scavengers couldn't read.

Sometimes when I think about my life, I chuckle at the ironies. About eight years after I pitched all that "worthless" writing, I found myself sitting in a college classroom being told to do freewriting, lots of it, in preparation for doing a collage essay. I was not to worry about being logical or organized; I was to write whatever came to mind in the order in which it came. Times and writing had certainly changed since I got my B.A. in 1961!

By the time I had to make my collage, I was ready for it. The choices, the choices! Not only did I wield my decision-making powers as I composed and revised my freewrites, but I made more choices and decisions as I arranged the individual pieces that comprised the collage. I, a person who for so many years had let others make most of my decisions for me, seized the power to make choices in my writing.

I have just finished reading Hermann Hesse's novel *Siddhartha*. Hesse talks about the path of life being a spiral. In my experience, that is the way it is. I've stopped worrying about not catching an insight the first time around. I know that if it is important, it will come around again and then I'll understand it a little bit more. Knowing that about my head saves me from expending energy on frustration. Sometimes an insight comes around many times before I really understand it clearly and see how it fits into my life. I've had to learn to be patient with myself.

I used to sit in school when I was a kid and think I was stupid because I couldn't seem to grab the brass ring the first try. I know better now; I know it will come around again and next spin around, I'll grab it . . . or the next spin around . . . But my question is: *Does it really matter?* Why can't we all just enjoy our rides? Siddhartha manages to come to that point near the end of his ride. So why can't the rest of us?

I remember learning to read when I was little. Learning to read was exciting; it was like being let in on a big secret, like becoming active in the world. The better I could read, the more independent I became, and the less I needed my parents — or anybody else.

My mother began teaching me to read when I was about two. I don't remember her teaching me then, but I remember her teaching my brother, and she claims that the method she used with me was the same. Each morning she wrote a new letter on the small blackboard in the kitchen. She taught me the name of the letter and the sound or sounds of the letter. The next day, she would review the letters I had learned and add another. By the time I was three, I could sound out words like *cup, cap,* and *pen*, simple, one-syllable words that followed the rules I had learned. *The* and *their* were still beyond me.

When I was four, I could read the basic readers my mother brought home whenever she substituted in elementary school. Reading the stories in those books gave me some satisfaction, but I was restless; I felt limited because there were so many words in the world that I could not sound out. I wanted to read the books that the "big people" read; if I could read those books, then I could be big like they were. And I needed to be big, so that nothing could hurt me, so big and so tough that nobody would dare to hurt me. The ability to read every word in the world would protect me, I thought.

I was four-and-a-half when I figured out how to read all the words the big people read. My father was a geography teacher, and we had a huge map of the world in our dining area. I could read "United States of America," "Canada," and the names of some other countries, but I could not decode "Pacific Ocean." Because my parents refused to read those two words to me, I became more determined to figure them out for myself, to show them that I didn't need their help. I remember how those words tossed and turned in my mind, and how their tossing and turning made me restless. They kept me awake at night, and they kept me wriggling and jittering during the day.

But I remember the exact moment when the code cracked wide open, the moment of ecstasy, the rush of adrenaline, and the feeling of power. My mother and I were in the Piggly Wiggly grocery store. She was down one of the aisles, filling her cart, and I was outside the entrance, leaning against the warm stucco wall and thinking. Those two words were tossing around in my mind like rocks in a tumbler. And then I remembered—I remembered that *c* didn't always sound like *k*, that sometimes it sounded like *s*, and so I tried it; I plugged that "s" sound into the two *c* slots in *Pacific*. No, that still wasn't right; I'd never heard the word *Pasifis*; I knew I had to try again. I tried plugging the "s" sound into the first *c*, and I knew I had the secret. Of course—*Pasifik*. I knew that word because I'd heard it so many times. And I knew that the Pacific Ocean was like a huge lake, a great, blue patch on the map. And then I knew that I could read any word in the world if I just stretched beyond the obvious and tried new approaches.

"Just stretch beyond the obvious." Now I am finishing work on my second master's degree, and I have kept those words from so long ago in mind. Oh, I don't know if my four-year-old mind thought of the concept in exactly those words; maybe I didn't even put words to the concept when I was four. But I've never forgotten the feeling, the stretching, the excitement of reaching beyond the obvious into the unknown, to find what I needed.

The kids who caught the brass rings when I was a kid were the ones who performed and conformed. I don't think that Siddhartha would have gotten "A"s in Rosella McCune's first-grade class in 1946. I didn't. She didn't like the way I read. I sounded my words out and refused to read from the big, Dick-and-Jane book that sat in the chalk trough. I refused to read the words that she touched with her pointer. Why should I? I already knew the damned things, had known them for several years. So I was put in the "dummy" group—until my mother found out and raised hell and put a plank under it. That gave me some satisfaction, helped make up for some of the pain that teacher inflicted on me. I wonder how Siddhartha would have done. Rosella probably would have put him in the dummy group, too.

The other day I reread the Gospel of Luke. I noticed that when Christ teaches by parable, he offers his audience the information they want and need, but he doesn't thrust it upon them. His listener is free to learn, to make the connections, or not to learn. This makes sense to me because it is consistent with what God said about free will and about justification by faith. God doesn't try to coerce people into believing in him; he leaves it up to the individual. That's scary! Freedom is usually more frightening than force. The ambiguity is what is frightening. The parables are ambiguous, for Christ doesn't always interpret them; he often seems to let people figure them out for themselves. And how do we know we have the "right answer"? Human beings tend to like "right answers."

Another feeling I had was that Christ was an intermediary of sorts when he taught, God's intermediary. Well, of course, he was that. But what I mean is that as I read Luke's Gospel, I could sense the power of God flowing through Christ to the people he was teaching. And that is possible, to some extent, for those of us who are less than Christs, too. When I taught in the Learning Center at Centralia College, one of my fellow staff members told me that whenever she faced a difficult student or a difficult day she prayed that some of God's strength would flow through her to the students.

I tried that, and it helped. Sometimes when I needed to help a student who smelled bad or who tried my patience, I would pray and I would also tell myself that the student might really be an angel, or the student might even be Christ. There were students I had to prepare for like that.

Just as Chris Zajac in Tracy Kidder's *Among Schoolchildren* had to learn to let go of Clarence, a very troubled young pupil, so have I had to learn to let go of students. When I taught grades six through twelve, that letting go was not so difficult as it was when I taught adults in a community college learning center. When I did classroom teaching, I didn't have the chance to know my students as I did in the one-on-one, learning center teaching.

Because I was the only staff member who had been through the divorce process, had lived on food stamps, was a single parent, and had used most community resources, my colleagues sent students to me to get help with their personal problems. I knew that I was inadequate as a counselor, that I was not qualified for the role into which I was thrust, but I knew, too, that none of the other staff members was any more qualified than I. So, I did the best I could.

I know something now that I wish I had known the first two years I taught adults: I cannot fix another human being. Yes, if I do my work well, I can help other people find the inner resources to fix or to heal themselves, but I cannot do the job for them. I accept my students for the people they are at any moment, and I help them grow, but I do not fix them.

Learning my limitations has lifted a boulder from my shoulders. I no longer feel entirely responsible for my students' failures—or for their successes. No longer do I ruminate on, "If I had just done . . . , then maybe he or she would have stayed in school," or "if I had spent more time with that person, maybe he or she would have studied harder for the test." I share their joy when they succeed, and I share their grief when they fail, but now I am able to separate myself from them, to distinguish where I end and they begin.

Peggy and I started at the Learning Center in 1983, she as a student and I as a teacher. When I first knew her she was about thirty-five years old, the mother of three children, newly divorced, and being supported by the state welfare system. Her elementary and junior high years had been spent in the public school system. When she was in the eighth grade, Peggy's parents enrolled her in a local Catholic girls' school because her epilepsy seizures had gotten worse. When Peggy had a seizure, she wet her pants. The humiliation she felt as a result caused her to refuse to attend public school where there were boys present, but she felt comfortable in the protected environment of the girls' school.

Unfortunately, Peggy's seizures also caused her to forget much of her learning. If she had progressed to learning the "sixes" in multiplication, for example, she would forget everything from the "threes" forward after a seizure. Learning for Peggy was a continuous process of making a little progress, having to backtrack and relearn, progressing forward a little, and then having to go backwards again and relearn. She did graduate from high school, but by the time she entered a vocational rehabilitation program, she had forgotten all her math back to adding and subtracting one-digit numbers, she could barely read a Harlequin romance, and she found writing absence excuses for her children difficult.

Peggy, however, was determined to become independent of the welfare system and to provide her children with what she considered a normal home life. She had very specific ideas as to the uses for her education—her education was to be a means to reaching her goal of providing her children and herself with the sort of life she wanted.

After Peggy had taken the learning-styles inventory required for all new students, I could understand why she had such a struggle with spelling and math. Peggy's test revealed that she was a strong auditory learner, but she did not learn efficiently when she was expected to learn visually. However, the philosophy of the learning center administrator was, "If it works, do it!" Peggy learned her times tables by taking home a cassette titled "The Singing Multiplication Tables." Each morning she did her exercises to that tape, and by the end of two weeks she had learned all the times tables. I recorded her spelling modules on cassette, and she learned them the same way.

Over a period of four years, I watched her progress from adding and subtracting to doing complex accounting problems, from reading simple stories to reading the texts in her freshman-level college classes, and from writing sentences and paragraphs to writing term papers. By the time I left the Learning Center to enter my graduate program, Peggy was taking secretarial and accounting courses, in an effort to get off welfare.

Last year, three years after I had left Peggy, I subscribed to my old hometown paper. I noticed one day that Peggy's home had been the site of a drug raid by the local narcotics squad. Peggy's children had been taken from her, and she was serving a jail sentence. I remembered how hard she had worked in school and how she had tried to give her children a good home, and I grieved for her. And then I let her go; I filled that imaginary, great blue balloon with "Peggy" on it full of air and watched it disappear above the trees.

I think of Peggy sometimes. I've even written her a letter, but I don't know if she got it. She's never answered. I just wanted her to know that I still care about her and that I hope she decides to finish her schooling someday. But I know that Peggy is Peggy and I am I, and I must follow my own path.

Anne was a woman in her early fifties who worked as a barmaid and lived with a man who beat her. Her overwhelming desire was to get a high school certificate so that she could get a job as a receptionist and move into an apartment of her own. She had the choice of taking the G.E.D. exam or of getting an adult high school diploma. She chose to earn the diploma because she thought that she would learn more. She also knew that her employment possibilities would be greater with a high school diploma, and she wanted to be able to say to herself that she really was a high school graduate.

Anne was a bright lady. She did well in courses that involved reading and writing. It was in math that she had her trouble. When we worked on math, she would become immobilized by anxiety. She confided in me that when she was a child, the nuns would throw erasers at her because she was slow. The other instructors and I spent hours each week with Anne, helping her over the rough spots. Other students helped her, too. She progressed slowly, but she did progress.

Eventually, however, she reached the section of the textbook that dealt with fractions. That was the point beyond which Anne could not go. I spent hours with her, patiently explaining various methods for finding the lowest common denominator, but Anne did not learn. The other instructors and I tried to figure out how we could work around fractions, but there was no way. One day, after a particularly stressful and frustrating session, Anne left early. That day I arrived home to find a pot of chrysanthemums and a thank-you note on my porch from Anne. Anne never returned to work on her diploma.

> And this goes on and hurries that it may end,
> and only circles and turns and has no goal.
> A red, a green, a gray being sent by,
> some little profile hardly yet begun.
> And occasionally a smile, turning this way,
> a happy one, tht dazzles and dissipates
> over this blind and breathless game.
> —Rainer Maria Rilke, "The Carousel"

PART 3

"BUT YOU NEVER ASKED!"

From freshman writing classes to graduate seminars in composition, students are the most visible members of the intellectual community we participate in. Yet there has been surprisingly little attention paid to what our students have to say about the teaching of writing as they experience it and as they prepare for a career doing it. The essays in this section reveal how our understanding of the writing classroom and the profession will be enlarged when we *ask* students how they feel and really *listen* to what they have to say.

Wendy Bishop begins this section by exploring the conditions of composition research that have led to an underrepresentation of the stories students are willing to tell about their own lives in supposedly prostudent research agendas. She warns us about the danger of using student-vacant research projects to inform instruction. Following Bishop's lead, Carol Lea Clark and Patricia Prandini Buckler, Kay Franklin, and Thomas Young seek out the stories, experiences, and feelings of freshman writing students. These teacher-researchers give us the opportunity to listen to those people who are most immediately and directly affected by the curriculum and pedagogy of freshman writing classes. Clark solicits stories from her freshman writing class and collaborates with her students to give voice to their perceptions of what it means to be a writer. Aware of the audience for this book, students are encouraged to say what they would like composition teachers who read this book to hear. Buckler, Franklin, and Young put before us the words and attitudes of some 270 students enrolled in writing classes and faced with disclosing personal information to their classmates. They found that students respond positively to writing personal experience essays significantly more often than they do to using classroom sharing procedures.

In the last essay in this section, Chris Anson asks questions about the ways in which the process of feeling a strong affiliation with composition has changed in the past twenty years. He lets us hear the voices of some graduate students in composition by weaving entries from journals—his own when he was a graduate student and those of graduate students he has taught—into a commentary on the ways in which the field encourages or presents obstacles to its potential members. Here again, as in the other pieces in this section, student voices resound with an authority they have rarely been granted.

10

Students' Stories
and the Variable Gaze
of Composition Research

Wendy Bishop/*Florida State University, Tallahassee*

Students' stories often confound, correct, explode, or refine writing theorists' constructs, researchers' findings, and teachers' assumptions. I intend to explore some of the conditions of composition research that have led to an underrepresentation of the student self-report in our research agendas, a result, perhaps, of the professionalization of our field. And I suggest there are dangers in using student-vacant research projects to inform instruction. In doing all this, I will argue that composition researchers, from the fully funded literacy expert to the beginning teacher-researcher, need to include students' voices in all discussions of student writing.

Finding Value in Students' Reports

For several years, I read and responded to composition research in graduate school. During the course of my studies, I
memorized the results of cognitive research projects and found
myself sketching the Flower and Hayes flowchart on cocktail
napkins or on exams. I knew what the state-of-the-art research in
the field *said could be said* about students' processes, that is, what
was scientific and therefore defensible, drawn from dependable,
controlled, and well-analyzed "data," for I was intent on becoming
a professional rhetorician after years spent as a writing teacher and
writer. When reading empirical reports in graduate school, I had
many questions, of course, about unsanctioned topics—what about
school pressures, home pressures, love pressures, life pressures?
What about writers as people, I had often wanted to ask? As a good
student, though, I mostly kept those questions to myself and
proceeded with my certification.

Not long after receiving my degree, I taught a class for junior
and senior English majors at my university titled "Theories of
Composition." The course offered my students information about
writers and writing, and they were interested, although often
asking why research reports had to be written in such a dry and
inaccessible manner. After training them as I had been trained, by
taking them on a tour of sections of famous research articles, I gave
them Kate Ronald and Jon Volkmer's research essay, "Another
Competing Theory of Process: The Student's." Their response
mirrored my own; when I first read Ronald and Volkmer I felt as if
those authors had gone ahead and asked the questions I had
pragmatically suppressed during graduate school.

Ronald and Volkmer claim our writing-process models seldom reflect our writing students' realities: students compose in
order to receive good grades and to please the teacher; they
procrastinate and draft under less-than-ideal conditions (at three
in the morning and so on); they suffer great anxiety; and they
evaluate their own work primarily on the basis of the grade they
hope or expect to receive.

My students valued this essay because it rang true to experience and to the discussions they had in groups on the first day of
class, concerning their own writing processes, discussions that
sounded like this:

The members of our group are surprisingly similar with respect to the way we write. Almost all of us do some form of formal categorizing. Some of us outline, some brainstorm, some write lists, and some of us just write. One thing remains constant among all six of us—we all procrastinate. I used to think I was a horrible individual for waiting until the last minute but now I realize that everyone procrastinates—maybe we do it to actually "psych" ourselves up. We all preferred to write straight through with breaks only for their nutritional value. Most of us need quiet in order to keep up our train of thought but one of us (surprisingly) preferred lots of loud music. With regard to writer's block we agreed that the only way to beat it is to keep working. We all seemed to have a lot in common—at least where writing is concerned.

These students compared their self-reports with Ronald and Volkmer's suggested, corrected view of the student composing process and found the previous research models and studies we had read strangely lacking. They resonated to Ronald and Volkmer's claim that more than texts are at stake in writing research. Students' habits, rituals, feelings, beliefs, institutional savvy, and so on are at issue because "student writers operate in very real, complicated rhetorical situations, ones that they know quite well how to manipulate, situations where plans, goals, and performance have different values from those outlined in published research" (93).

A research report based in student writers' experiences, which respected students' views, gave my students support for exploring their own writing. They felt that their dirty linen could finally be aired and that the generally not-talked-about-but-important aspects of writing, like procrastination or grades, could be raised. They were pleased to encounter a composition article that spoke to them and appeared to detail student writing experiences authentically.

After the response this essay received, I began looking for writing research studies that complicated my understanding of students' contexts and processes; I looked for discussions that emphasized students' voices, stories, reactions, corrections, and contributions to our field: student-present rather than student-vacant projects. While doing this, I found it essential to consider the development of composition research, asking why as researchers we had neglected to tap students' contributions, asking why they were not more fully in our professional gaze?

Professionalizing Composition—Some Gains, Some Losses

By all accounts, from the turn of the century to the early 1960s, composition was the least-valued strand of English Studies. If we read the institutional histories of Gerald Graff, Terry Eagleton, James Berlin, and Robert Connors, authors whose writings are informed by very different politics and beliefs, a great degree of consensus still exists. In the late 1800s, literary studies displaced an existing oratorical, classical college culture in America; members of developing English departments adopted the scientific educational model prevalent in German universities, annexing scientific prestige to their own work through a philological and linguistic emphasis, by "responding to the text as an historical artifact to be studied scientifically" (Berlin 191).

Graduate programs in English began in the late 1870s, and the new university offered education to anyone who could meet the entrance requirements, focusing attention on preparation for entrance exams. Entrance testing began in 1874 at Harvard, as did the freshman composition sequence. During the next seventy years, in overenrolled and often unrewarding undergraduate writing classrooms, the classical rhetorical aim of invention was overshadowed by a focus on arrangement and style and an unnatural emphasis on correctness. Writing was not subjective and student-oriented or student-directed. Writing was a scientific and objective skill that could be delivered through proper instructional strategies and copious instructor intervention; in essence, writing became what we now term "current-traditional."

In the 1960s, revolutions took place both outside and inside the writing classroom. Increasingly, current-traditional instructional methods were not preparing new open-admissions students to write with much success (see Shaughnessey), and writing was being viewed anew as a medium for self-knowledge and self-expression, as a way of thinking. The scientific-objective view of knowledge "out there" was being replaced with a subjective view of knowledge "in here." Expressivist views on writing instruction were popularized by several writing teachers-turned-expert-witnesses. Peter Elbow, Ken Macrorie, Donald Murray, and others started telling stories of what was working and was not working in the classroom, what worked and did not work for them *as writers*, and how well students responded to a different kind of teaching, essentially writing workshops.

Just at the time critical theorists were challenging and changing the larger edifice of English studies dominated by the study of literature, the writing classroom was also infused with energy: despair over conditions and excitement over possibilities. There were more and more students involved, creating *more and more teaching positions*. And, finally — if our field was to follow traditional academic models — there was a need to professionalize. Stephen North explains, "The freshman course was something nearly all of the rapidly increasing number of college students would take and represented in many cases the largest chunk of an English Department's budget" (14). He dates the birth of composition with a capital *C* from Albert Kitzhaber's address to the Conference on College Composition and Communication and publication of Kitzhaber's book-length study of college writing. In addition, the National Council of Teachers of English formed the ad hoc Committee on the State of Knowledge about Composition, which called for research, specifically scientific research — rigorous, controlled, repeatable. Writing research was generally conducted and answers offered within the social science tradition because writing teachers were being asked to "provide information about their activities and programs and about their students' performance and abilities to audiences . . . used to information being presented in the traditions of social science research" (Lauer and Asher vi).

Attempts to create composition as a profession, then, did not simply result in networking or calls for the development of new pedagogies. Professionalization requires and results from the credentialing of teachers, development of testing procedures, organization of graduate programs and their curriculums, and production of tenure-gaining publication through research: "Composition instructors in increasing numbers are being trained in rhetoric and composition Ph.D. programs, and are generating the necessary publication that will enable them to reap the same benefits as their colleagues elsewhere in the university" (Berkenkotter, "Paradigm" 155).

As did literary studies before it, composition annexed the scientific model of empirical research and publication. Still, thirty years after NCTE's call for improved and rigorous research, the scientific model is proving as problematic for composition studies as did the philological model for literary studies. At issue is the very definition of *human science* (Berkenkotter, "Paradigm" 152–53). The legacy of positivism in the human sciences is the decontextualized cognitive research that gained great visibility in composition from the early 1970s and retained that visibility through the late 1980s. Cognitive research is currently under some scrutiny though, primarily for what is seen as its practitioners' "reluctance to explore the ethical or political dimensions of writing in favor of the disinterested scientific stance [which] lends its conclusions about composing to indiscriminate application in the economic setting" (Berlin 218).[1]

Few in composition deny the usefulness of early cognitive research, but many question the valorization of the scientific method and its dominance in composition studies.[2] For instance, the scientific research report, which was so difficult for me to learn to write and my students to learn to read, often feels as if it distances us from the very students and classrooms we need to understand. The research report presents a stable, controlled environment very unlike the messy complicated and always changing writing classrooms most of us inhabit. The research report makes claims for objectivity, while masking a researcher's ideology and subjectivity through the use of author-vacant language, what William Firestone calls a "cool style." Cool style can be used to project a rhetorically convincing, impartial, and accurate "scientific" persona: "If one of the threats to the validity of a conclusion comes from the writer's own biases, as is considered to be the case in science, then any technique that projects a lack of emotion has considerable persuasive power" (17).

According to the researcher's training and community, the report he or she writes will be intensely rhetorical, adhering to the conventions of the community. This is so because research is not only a method for making knowledge, it is a means of professionalization, for initiating the novice researcher into the research community he or she hopes to join. Stylized research reports, then, provide the research community with this researcher's "new" information, showcased in a sanctioned, and therefore, safe format: "Thus what is original (and potentially threatening) in the study is neutralized through its being contextualized into the community's existing knowledge" (Berkenkotter, "Legacy" 76).[3]

In choosing writing research methods, then, much more is at stake than simply choosing the best tool for answering the research question at hand. Research initiates the novice and increases field membership; usually it maintains rather than challenges community consensus. All research follows this path, but not all researchers have been able to admit this self-serving and subjective view of knowledge making. Particularly, a subjective view contradicts key tenants of the positivistic epistemology.

Lately, in composition, there has been some questioning of the prevailing research tradition—and our acceptance of the positivistic research paradigm—and that is not surprising for, currently, "science" is under review in many branches of academic study. As researchers in our own and in other fields have become alert to their own rhetoric (their ways of reporting their research and advancing their own and their communities' claims), many, as I have, have increasingly questioned the choice of those in composition studies who borrow the scientific model as the most appropriate one for studying spoken and written discourse and for validating the results of research to others within the academy.

Self-analysis is not easy; it is not surprising that composition, as a field, has not looked at the ramifications of its belated but rapid professionalization process and its choice of research paradigms. It is surprising to me, however, that we have so often ignored our own strengths. We are humans studying humans—as they write. In order to suit the parameters of any research model, such a field should not, as Lad Tobin claims we tend to do, deny the value of the subjects who are being studied, student writers:

> That most student conceptions of their own composing process have been overlooked is not surprising: there exists a deep-rooted distrust of all retrospective student accounts. See, for example, Barbara Tomlinson ("Talking"), Linda Flower and John R. Hayes ("Images"), and Louis Rubin. The basic argument in each case is that student writers lack the experience, perspective, metacognitive sophistication, and technical language to describe accurately and fully their own composing processes. However, although all of these authors warn against uncritical acceptance of student retrospective accounts, they also admit that such accounts can be valuable in certain ways for student and teachers. ("Bridging" 456)[4]

However, by ignoring students' voices, we emphasize the need for our professional intervention and do this at the risk of obliterating any notion of student expertise.

Thomas Newkirk makes the argument that most educational research, including empirical research in composition, develops its claims by "establishing the inadequacy of the more traditional sources of knowledge. . . . custom, ritual, 'common sense,' and personal experience" (122). Thus, researcher knowledge is more valuable than teacher's experience (see North). In a similar way, we are at risk of seeing researchers' and then teachers' knowledge as always more valuable than students' knowledge and experiences. In a *required* first-year writing class (where enrollment has been mandated by knowing "authorities" — whether institutional, local or state), students' views, opinions, and experiences are easily suppressed. The implied illogic seems to run something like this: If they had any say in the matter, we know most would not be in these classes; if they are in these classes, therefore, they must not have anything valuable to say about the matter.

Let me share a literacy story, told to me by a friend. Before she entered first grade, my friend's daughter could already read entire beginner's books by herself. The first week of school she was given a reading-readiness test, which she failed. She was sent home with a note telling her parents she would only be allowed to work on some basic exercises for the first few months of the year until she was ready to undertake more demanding tasks, all aimed at preparing her for reading. At that point, her father went to see the teacher and said: "Would you just ask her if she can read?"

As researchers considering student writers, we need more often just to ask. That is what my students felt when they read empirical research reports followed by the research essay by Kate Ronald and Jon Volkmer. Essentially, they were telling me, "If researchers had just asked us, we could have told them that we procrastinate, that we avoid writing, that we care a great deal about grades."

Convention-Making and Convention-Breaking Research

Experimental research studies serve our professionalization process too well when they "verify" the obvious and the commonsensical or when they exclusively serve community interests, asking questions about writing or writing students in a manner that supports the research community's agenda. Additionally, such studies may exclude conflicting, complicated, or ambiguous research directions since empirical research seldom focuses on questions of gender, race, and class, nor does it challenge current structures of institutional power. Such moves may be part of a traditional academic strategy that discredits personal experience, especially the experiences of disenfranchised individuals; consid-

er the large number of women who form the majority of composition teachers and the students whom they teach, students who
actually "experience" the results of research through curriculum
mandates and pedagogical experimentation (sentence-combining,
computer-aided instruction, WAC, process workshops, competency-
based education, and minimum competency testing) (see Newkirk).

When subjectivity, context, and human roles are bounded in,
writing research changes. Then, what we might label experimental shades quickly to quasi-experimental, a positivistic qualitative
study may be reconsidered as a phenomenological qualitative
study and clinical case studies are sometimes better understood as
teacher-researchers' reports and stories. The few guides to research available to our field still group all "valid" qualitative
studies under the umbrella of scientific, empirical study; but the
fit is becoming uncomfortable as ethnographic writing researchers
become more insistent that they are working in different ways and
with different ideological intentions, that they are working within
a different epistemology.

Analysts of research paradigms have always had trouble
bracketing and confining qualitative research. Stephen North
finds that ethnography does not fit well where he places it, under
the general category of "researcher," which includes experimen-
talists, formalists, and clinicians (136–40). And Janice Lauer and
William Asher and Carol Berkenkotter ("Paradigm") separately
define qualitative methodology as research grounded in the rigors
of the scientific method, including controlled data collection,
coding, analysis, triangulation, and reporting. However, those very
invocations to rigor may be protecting the scientific status quo and
keeping a diverging strand of thought and research safely contained under the umbrella of empirical academic research.

I know that the "fit" is problematic, for I completed an
ethnographic dissertation that was grounded with positivistic war-
rants ("A Microenthography"), and then I began to understand
that work from a more phenomenological perspective, as constructed narrative (*Something Old*). Linda Brodkey suggests that
qualitative research can be critical, and I am not the first to discuss
the way storytelling works in research (Bishop "I-witnessing";
Murphy). My views derive from postmodernist discussions within
anthropology (see Geertz; Clifford); for some anthropologists storytelling is an adequate—perhaps the only possible—reporting
strategy, a strategy that accentuates a researcher's situatedness

and subjects' voices. This is necessary since we all carry a certain amount of our professional baggage along with us at all times. Still, I believe qualitative, ethnographic, phenomenologically grounded research in context offers composition researchers an exciting and productive way of knowing that can accommodate and validate students' stories about their own writing.

While qualitative research seems a useful way to afford such accommodation and validation, it is not the only way. In composition, more projects are slowly appearing that use a variety of methodologies yet take into account students' perspectives and contexts. For instance, Susan Wyche-Smith has investigated students' writing rituals and compared students to each other (those whose habits aided their own composing and those whose habits hindered their own composing). By doing this, her study is unlike early cognitive or clinical reports that often compared student writers to expert writers, with students always in the implied "deficient" position. And, like Ronald and Volkmer, Wyche-Smith found student writing activities were embedded in demanding life scripts where teachers, classrooms, and writing itself vied for student attention and often lost: "College is hard. It's a big change for me. The very first week of this semester I was out of it, totally out of it. But now I'm trying to get back on the ball. But I messed up, I'll probably have to take some classes over" (4), says one of her students. Through questionnaires and interviews, Wyche-Smith found students spent less than ten hours per week on homework for fifteen unit loads and double that amount of hours at jobs (8). Why aren't students drafting better papers? In part, because they are working too much.

When I say research methods, questions, and contexts are changing, I do not mean to imply that there is no need for further change. In my opinion, far too few reports like Ronald and Volkmer's and Wyche-Smith's are published, and they receive far too little attention. Scientific research is still dominant and that type of research, by definition, narrows the focus of the researcher's lens to a point so small that—theoretically—no explanation can be missed because no variable is unaccounted for. However, context-intensive researchers, their work derived from a phenomenological epistemology, insist that by reducing the lens size to such a small point, explanatory power is actually lost. Humans cannot be understood out of context. With small lenses, we may become "blind to the logic of a students' interpretation and the ways that interpretation might be sensibly influenced by the students' history" (Hull and Rose 287). With small lenses, we may focus on parts of a process or piece together a grand model, but we do so at the risk of missing students' stories and sidestepping their realities.

Myopia, blindness, the bracketed view of scientific research have led many researchers to design less focused-down, more context-based research projects, even within the positivistic tradition. For instance, Jennie Nelson looks at the ways students *and* teachers view assignments, whereas ten years ago such research might have investigated a much smaller aspect of assignment making. Nelson asked students and their teachers about assignments and discovered they held entirely different perspectives on the same activity ("This assignment should be challenging," claims a teacher; but "this was an easy assignment," claims one of that teacher's students). Nelson finds that "the special nature of school settings, with their emphasis on rewards for products, may have an important impact on the way students define and approach writing tasks" (392). I find it heartening that she has taken care in her study to include student perspectives and voices and to consider context, something that early cognitive writing research did not manage to do and that practitioners are now considering or advocating (see Berkenkotter's "Paradigm"; Flower).

In addition, there are both formal and informal research reports available that accept and acknowledge students as knowing contributors to research. Finding his own and his students' metaphors for composing at a variance, much like the teachers' and students' whose assumptions Jennie Nelson studied, Lad Tobin began informally to listen to, collect, and study those metaphors, discovering

> not only that Michael and I had very different models of composing, but also (and more importantly) that metaphor offers student and teachers a significant (but little used) means of communication . . . . there is still a disturbing failure of communications about composing—between students and teachers and between students' conscious knowledge and vocabulary and unconscious attitudes and strategies. ("Bridging" 445)

Tobin's observations suggest that teaching students the most productive habits of expert writers may not be a useful classroom strategy if we fail when doing so to acknowledge the conditions under which student writers compose:

> Much of these student writers' dissatisfaction is with the process itself, the inevitable frustration of trying to translate thoughts into written language,but even more of it seems a result of the scene or situation in which they find themselves—of being forced to write on demand, to write in a way that makes them feel powerless, to write for a grade. (Tobin, "Bridging" 450)

And despite our good intentions, we in composition may have been ignoring students' contexts in our enthusiasm to share our research-informed expertise, wanting students to tell us what they have learned—about what we have learned—about the writing process. We may offer them "new" information but neglect to ask them what they already know.

To start research where students are, rather than to suit our own or our graduate program agenda, we need to acknowledge students' as legitimate contributors and to study their emotions and feelings. Since the study of feeling and affect requires a wide lens and a wide gaze, these areas have not seemed very amenable to empirical study or popular among scientific researchers. Alice Brand reminds us that: "It should come as no surprise that any movement to examine the emotions of writers is without members and that emotions theory is without place in contemporary writing research" ("Hot Cognition" 7); in a more recent article, she notes several important moves in the direction of investigating writers' emotions:

> We know that affective traits and personality overlap conceptually and empirically (Plutchik and Kellerman). We are just now recognizing that personality may govern discursive style (Jensen and DiTiberio; Selzer), just as discursive style has an impact on personality (Brand, *Therapy*; Denman). In fact, how personality influences the way writers function is the direction I think composition research is ultimately headed. ("The Why" 441)

I agree with Brand, for I see this movement in the work of Robert Brooke and John Hendricks, whose ethnographic study was galvanized when students did not respond as well as expected to Brooke's writing instruction. Students' unexpected responses led Brooke and Hendricks to investigate the role of personality in writing. And Brooke's most recent study of writing workshops focuses almost exclusively on the way identity formation drives the responses and realities of writing students in those classes; along the way, he develops an impressive theory after the fact for a model of writing instruction that has been used for many years.

Today, then, some researchers are entering landscapes that were formerly off limits because of our profession's intentionally limited experimental gaze. Ethnographers (who are often also teacher-researchers) are studying student affect and emotions and considering writing motivation, and some of these individuals have gone one step further and set up research teams that include and rely on students. While studying academic writing, Susan Miller and five student researchers found more than they were looking for. Miller claims she

> originally thought we would be discovering how many and what kind of writing assignments and evaluations students encounter, and perhaps connecting this information to teaching practices in other disciplines. But I increasingly became aware that as a particular kind of teacher, I was facing delicate questions about my own course content and disciplinary identity . . . . increasingly [research] made me self-conscious about my own version of academic literacy. (Anderson et al. 27)

Like the work of Tobin and Ronald and Volkmer, this study of writing in institutional contexts did not focus on a limited picture. Instead, a team of students as researchers entered several academic classrooms to observe, question, discuss, and report; these researchers looked for patterns and told stories; they explored ways that the institution drove the students and the students agreed to be driven:

> I consequently also need to reconsider the students' repeatedly documented isolation, even from their classmates, and the distancing strategies, humor, and anger they found to naturalize it. It took no special training in psychology to realize that our frequent group discussions of how often each one fell asleep in class and while studying, Alycia's legalistic view of attendance, Worth's calculated visits to professors, and John's assessment of what he pays professors to do were all expressions of admittedly WASP students, stinging and stung by a system they fully expect to join. (Anderson et al. 31)

These researchers asked difficult, complex questions about writing, writers, and writing in context. In their work, the dream of positivistic unity is abandoned. Their research asks questions about individuals in contexts more than it attempts to discover large-scale explanations for the big questions that might reside out there in the universe of composition studies—a universe that they experience in myriad and often conflicting ways.

This kind of research will change composition studies. When teachers become researchers and students' stories, interpretations, and contributions count, then knowledge making and professionalization come into better balance. I have seen this happen, as over the last ten years, I have been tracing the trajectory through many of the positions I have described here—student writer, writing teacher, aspiring professional researcher, teacher-researcher. And I am inclined by these experiences to fight the negative effects of my own professionalization by attempting always to bring my work back to the classroom, sharing it with writing students and new teachers of writers. In this, my suggestions for reform are something like the suggestions of the middle-class recycler that I am also. Yes, I still buy too many canned, bottled, and packaged foods, but I also try to recycle and compost and do my part. Yes, my own research is situated, and yes, my own discussions of writing teachers and students work to advance my professional career, but they can also advance the success of the writing classes I teach to the extent that I focus my research there and to the extent that I help students and new teachers join in the previously closed conversations of my profession.

Because my gaze is determined, subjective, situated, I am inclined in the direction of context-based research, although I know it is not the only way to solve the problems I have raised. A context-rich methodology, however, lets me make my subjective, situated, and ideological claims through interrogation of my subjectivity, situatedness, and ideology; when I research, I am learning as much about myself—my group, my norms, my profession—as about the students I study. And I do not believe a research methodology is useful unless it allows for some degree of this type of self-critique, unless it encourages and achieves some degree of methodological metaknowledge. Without such self-knowledge, something gets lost.

Too often in the past, what got lost was the student, the student writer who inspires a large portion of our work. (I am aware of those who argue that not all research has to return us to the classroom; but a great deal of it already does.) Therefore, we must challenge prevailing paradigms. And our gaze must be wide since our methods address a writing classroom that is conflictual, interactive, dynamic. In her research analysis, which borrows from Bahktinian critical theory, Joy Ritchie says:

> The experiences of this teacher and these students suggest that we cannot describe the process of learning to write as a tidy, predictable process. . . . We must resist reductive descriptions of our students' development as writers. Each student comes to our class with a unique history, with different assumptions about writing, and different needs. So we should expect that each writing workshop will compose a different "polyphony" of disparate elements which each student will appropriate and reshape in different configurations. The process does not end with the writing class, and it may not appear to have the same characteristics in any two students. (171)

Challenges to positivist research come from these polyphonic classrooms. Reliability is not at issue here; writers as humans are as complex as the communities they form and can never be studied the same way twice, exactly. Validity is not at issue here; we do not always study what we thought we were setting out to study, but we are still learning from reflective practice.

We need to realize that composition came out of eclipse and moved toward academic professionalization within a very short time span, and while such changes have been taking place, the gaze of composition research, like the gaze of any community, has been variable—looking at what is profitable, convenient, safe, and sure. But our profession, I am proud to say, is quite a bit more ornery than that. I think the most promising studies are those that challenge the conventions even as we try to set them up. If qualitative studies are increasing, it is because they offer if not perfect vision then an engaging type of double vision: a way to look at the researcher, who is often a teacher, as well as a way to look at those researched, often that researcher's own students. In my own projects, I try to listen to the stories of the students I work with, as well as to those of my colleagues, and I always find I learn by considering cases and stories, by attending to metaphors and sketching out analogies. I also learn somewhat by reading scientific research.

And, I try to avoid the hubris of feeling that my gaze is the best gaze or only gaze, by taking any knowledge gained back with me to the writing classroom. When I share writing research about students, *with students*, they are sure to respond with the story of what it really is like for them; and my job is to listen. Mike Rose suggests:

> We need an orientation to instruction that provides guidance on how to determine and honor the beliefs and stories, enthusiasms, and

apprehensions that students reveal. How to build on them, and when they clash with our curriculum—as I saw so often in the Tutorial Center at UCLA—where they clash, how to encourage a discussion that will lead to reflection on what students bring and what they're currently confronting. (236)

Equally, we need approaches to research that honor "the beliefs and stories, enthusiasms, and apprehensions that students reveal" (Rose 236). Listening to students' stories helps me to remember that we occupy only a small portion of their lives, while they loom large in ours. How students are included in composition research is for me a continuing issue.

Notes

1. For a published conversation of sorts on this topic, see also Berkenkotter, John Clifford, Flower, Foster, Reynolds, Schilb.

2. See Reynolds, however, for a counterclaim that experimental studies are not dominant.

3. This essay, for instance, demonstrates the problems of academic writing style; as I compose, my practitioner (teacher's) anecdotes vie for a place within my traditional essay, containing a literature review and heavily cited discussion. And I develop an important (to me) "argument" without myself believing in or feeling comfortable with traditional, argumentative essay conventions.

4. This important claim is found in a footnote, not in the body of Tobin's essay.

Works Cited

Anderson, Worth, Cynthia Best, Alycia Black, John Hurst, Brandt Miller, and Susan Miller. "Cross-Curricular Underlife: A Collaborative Report on Ways with Academic Words." *College Composition and Communication* 41 (1990): 11–36.

Berkenkotter, Carol. "The Legacy of Positivism in Empirical Composition Research." *Journal of Advanced Composition* 9 (1989): 69–82.

———. "Paradigm Debates, Turf Wars, and the Conduct of Sociocognitive Inquiry in Composition." *College Composition and Communication* 42 (1991): 151–69.

Berkenkotter, Carol, Thomas Huckin, and John Ackerman. "Conventions, Conversations, and the Writer: Case Study of a Student in a Rhetoric Ph.D. Program." *Research in the Teaching of English* 22 (1988): 9–44.

Berlin, James A. "Writing Instruction in School and College English, 1890–1985." *A Short History of Writing Instruction: From Ancient Greece to Twentieth-Century America.* Ed. James J. Murphy. Davis, CA: Hermagoras. 183–220.

Bishop, Wendy. "I-Witnessing in Composition: Turning Ethnographic Data into Narratives." *Rhetoric Review*, forthcoming.

———. "A Microethnography with Case Studies of Teacher Development Through a Graduate Training Course in Teaching Writing." Diss. Indiana U of Pennsylvania, Indiana, PA, 1988.

———. *Something Old, Something New: College Writing Teachers and Classroom Change.* Carbondale, IL: CCCC/Southern Illinois UP, 1990.

Brand, Alice G. "Hot Cognition: Emotions and Writing Behavior." *Journal of Advanced Composition* 6 (1985–86): 1–15.

———. "The Why of Cognition: Emotion and the Writing Process." *College Composition and Communication* 38 (1987): 436–43.

Brodkey, Linda. "Writing Critical Ethnographic Narratives." *Anthropology and Education Quarterly* 18 (1987): 67–76.

Brooke, Robert. "Modeling a Writer's Identity." *College Composition and Communication* 39 (1988): 23–41.

———. *Writing and Sense of Self: Identity Negotiation in Writing Workshops.* Urbana, IL: NCTE, 1991.

Brooke, Robert, and John Hendricks. *Audience Expectations and Teacher Demands.* Carbondale, IL: CCCC/Southern Illinois UP, 1989.

"CCCC: Voices in the Parlor." *Rhetoric Review* 7 (1988): 194–213.

Clifford, James. "On Ethnographic Authority." *The Predicament of Culture: Twentieth-Century Ethnography, Literature, and Art.* Cambridge, MA: Harvard UP, 1988. 21–54.

———. "On Ethnographic Self-Fashioning." *The Predicament of Culture: Twentieth-Century Ethnography, Literature, and Art.* Cambridge, MA: Harvard UP, 1988. 92–113.

Eagleton, Terry. *Literary Theory: An Introduction.* Minneapolis: U of Minnesota P, 1983.

Firestone, William A. "Meaning in Method: The Rhetoric of Quantitative and Qualitative Research." *Educational Researcher* 16 (Oct. 1987): 16–21.

Flower, Linda. "Cognition, Context, and Theory Building." *College Composition and Communication* 40 (1989): 282–311.

Flower, Linda, and John R. Hayes. "A Cognitive Process Theory of Writing." *College Composition and Communication* 32 (1981): 365–87.

Foster, David. "Hurling Epithets at the Devils You Know: A Response to Carol Berkenkotter." *Journal of Advanced Composition* 10 (1990): 149–52.

———. "What Are We Talking About When We Talk About Composition?" *Journal of Advanced Composition* 8 (1989): 30–40.

Geertz, Clifford. *Works and Lives: The Anthropologist as Author.* Stanford, CA: Stanford UP, 1988.

Graff, Gerald. *Profession Literature: An Institutional History.* Chicago: U of Chicago P, 1987.

Hull, Glenda, and Mike Rose. "'This Wooden Shack Place': The Logic of an Unconventional Reading." *College Composition and Communication* 41 (1990): 287–98.

Lauer, Janice M., and J. William Asher. *Composition Research: Empirical Designs.* New York: Oxford UP, 1988.

Murphy, Richard J. "On Stories and Scholarship." *College Composition and Communication* 40 (1989): 466–71.

Nelson, Jennie. "This Was an Easy Assignment: Examining How Students Interpret Academic Writing Tasks." *Research in the Teaching of English* 24 (1990): 362–96.

Newkirk, Thomas. "The Politics of Composition Research: The Conspiracy Against Experience." *The Politics of Writing Instruction: Postsecondary*. Ed. Richard Bullock and John Trimbur. Portsmouth, NH: Boynton, 1991. 119–36. Gen. ed. Charles Schuster.

North, Stephen. *The Making of Knowledge in Composition: Portrait of an Emerging Field*. Upper Montclair, NJ: Boynton, 1987.

Reynolds, John F. "Motives, Metaphors, and Messages in Critical Receptions of Experimental Research: A Comment with Postscript. *Journal of Advanced Composition* 10 (1990): 110–16.

Ritchie, Joy S. "Beginning Writers: Diverse Voices and Individual Identity." *College Composition and Communication* 40 (1989): 152–74.

Ronald, Kate, and Jon Volkmer. "Another Competing Theory of Process: The Student's." *Journal of Advanced Composition* 9 (1989): 81–96.

Rose, Mike. *Lives on the Boundary: A Moving Account of the Struggles and Achievements of America's Educational Underclass*. New York: Free, 1989.

Schilb, John. "Ideology and Composition Scholarship." *Journal of Advanced Composition* 8 (1988): 22–29.

———. "The Ideology of 'Epistemological Ecumenicalism': A Response to Carol Berkenkotter." *Journal of Advanced Composition* 10 (1990): 153–56.

Shaughnessy, Mina P. *Errors and Expectations: A Guide for the Teacher of Basic Writing*. New York: Oxford UP, 1977.

Tobin, Lad. "Bridging Gaps: Analyzing Our Students' Metaphors for Composing." *College Composition and Communication* 40 (1989): 444–58.

———. "Reading Students, Reading Ourselves: Revising the Teacher's Role in the Writing Class." *College English* 43 (1991): 333–48.

Wyche-Smith, Susan. "Time, Tools, and Talismans." *The Subject Is Writing: Essays by Teachers and Students on Writing*. Ed. Wendy Bishop. Portsmouth, NH: Boynton, forthcoming.

11

Student Voices:
How Students Define
Themselves as Writers

Carol Lea Clark and Students of English 1803/
Texas Christian University, Fort Worth

"When I found this class was straight writing, I almost died because I knew I had to take it to graduate," one of my students wrote during an essay the first day of freshman composition class. Another contributed, "If I had to rate myself as a writer, I would put myself below average. I have a hard time putting my ideas and thoughts down on a blank piece of paper."

What is it about the act of writing, and writing in composition class in particular, that inspires such fear in some students and such a sense of inferiority in others? Perhaps it has something to do with how the students define words or concepts such as *writer*, *writing*, and *freshman composition*. In this essay I will let the students of my spring semester freshman composition class at Texas Christian University, in their own words, explain why. The quotes that follow are from those students. They were generated in a series of informal writings (e.g., "spend five minutes defining the word *writing*"), which the students knew would be used for this essay. Some also chose to write one of their graded essays in the class about the purpose and value of freshman composition. We also talked in group and individual conferences about what I should include in this essay. Moreover, students wrote in-class essays on the first and last days of class on "how I see myself as a writer." (Note: At the students' request, I am using initials instead of names to attribute quotes.)

Initially, the students were puzzled by the suggestion that their comments about freshman composition would be of interest to anyone. I wondered why they should be puzzled. No one, they explained, had asked them in high school or the first semester of freshman year in college what they thought about having to take a certain course or what they thought about how a course should be taught. No one was asking that kind of question in any of their current courses. In general, they said, they do what they are asked to do in a course; that is part of being a student. A. P. explained that in the majority of courses students are expected only to receive, memorize, and store information. She described one professor: "For three days each week he would lecture straight from the book; on the fourth we would watch a film, and on the fifth he would give us a test. This way of teaching didn't encourage me to be creative or stimulate my critical thinking skills." And even when a student's creativity is challenged, it often is not by choice. K. F. remembers:

> We came into English class [in high school] and found a sheet of paper on each desk. It was a poem with the instructions, "Explicate the following poem line by line in the space below." I became very upset because I didn't know how to do it—nobody did. Or so we thought. We all looked at her with tears in our eyes because we knew this was for a grade and no one likes to turn in an empty test paper. She simply said, "Write exactly what you think that the author is saying, that's all."

K. F. got her paper back with an "A." She had done her best and learned, if somewhat painfully, the teacher's point that she could indeed explicate a poem. Neither K. F.'s teacher or A. P.'s teacher asked what their students thought of their assignments.

But this time these students were being asked to analyze a course in more depth than what is required for an end-of-class evaluation, and by the middle of the semester, they seemed to take seriously the idea that their comments might be considered thoughtfully by other instructors. But to be honest, the questions they answered and the discussions we had about this essay had to be fitted in around the main agenda of the course, which was to develop and improve their ability to write on a variety of subjects. We did not discuss this essay everyday, but we did so at frequent intervals during the semester.

We, students and instructor, also agreed from the beginning that their experiences would not necessarily be representative of all freshman English students. Students at Texas Christian University, a private, mid-sized university in the sunbelt are, admittedly, on the conservative side. But their comments are well considered, well intentioned and, hopefully, revealing.

Why are these student voices important? In other words, why should we ask students what they think about a class the university requires them to take, which we call "freshman composition"? We instructors are, or should be, market researchers. Just as manufacturers of automobiles test-market a new color or perfume companies a new fragrance, we should be interested in how our public *responds* to what we are selling. On a deeper level, are we not also scientific researchers, wanting to know what effect what we do to our clients, or subjects, has upon them? Of course, we can do quantitative pre- and posttest studies. But can we not also just *ask* our students for their opinions? Can we not learn from what they have to tell us—something that might make us more effective teachers? Their comments may not be considered scientific research results; but they may be clues toward future research, and they may be cause for contemplative consideration.

What Is a Writer?

At the beginning of the semester I asked all the students in my class, "Are you writers?" The overwhelming answer was "No." They wrote, of course, personal letters and class assignments, and most expect to write as part of their postcollege careers. But they are not writers, or so they believed. S. M. writes, "I do not really see myself as a writer. I am not too fond of writing formal papers or research papers. It seems that I write only when it is necessary."

Asked "What is a writer?" A. J. replies, "I think of famous-name novelists such as Ernest Hemingway or Jack London." L. P. decides, "A writer, in my opinion, is a newspaper columnist or a novelist, not someone who writes as part of school work." Another,

S. M., contributes, "A writer is someone who is able to put his or her ideas in print." And a third, J. K., more eloquently, decides, "A writer creates life in what are simple letters and words." Another, B. J., though, labels himself a writer, but only when the idea is suggested to him. "Yes, it's true. I am a writer. It was not until just a few minutes ago that I realized it, but I am. . . . Many times when I have a problem, I like to write in a journal. . . . I ask myself questions and then attempt to supply some suggestions or possible solutions."

According to Michel Foucault in his essay "What Is an Author?" certain texts have authors whose names remain integral to the text and whose presence establishes relationships with other texts. A novel by Ernest Hemingway may be scrutinized for themes that are present in his other novels. *Catch 22* may be analyzed in the context of Joseph Heller's own military experiences in World War II. Other texts, such as private letters and contracts, have anonymous writers; they do not have authors.

Perhaps my freshman students, because they lack the experience of having their words inscribed and valorized, see themselves as lacking a sense of public ownership of their texts. They are not authors, or so they believe.

Mimi Schwartz, editor of *Writer's Craft, Teacher's Art*, believes that students *should* see themselves as writers, and twenty-five teachers in a seminar she led on the writing process agreed with her that students "did need to *feel* like writers in order to write well" (ix). Interestingly, she asked the teacher-participants in her seminar, "How many of you consider yourself writers?" Only two hands went up. Somewhat surprised, she asks why the rest did not think they were writers. After all, they had been writing all their lives. They responded: "'We're not good enough . . . famous enough . . . creative enough. . . . What we write—memos, letters, articles, reports, diaries, grants—that doesn't count,' said the Noes. (The Yesses, who hadn't published much more, felt, as [Schwartz] did, that it did count)" (ix). For these teachers, as for my students, self-identification as writers did not depend on the amount written or published but on some subjective self-evaluation of whether or not public ownership of the text was warranted.

What Is Writing?

What is writing, according to these freshman students who see themselves as anonymous producers of text rather than authors? Some, such as A. K., define it as communication. "Writing is communicating your thoughts, ideas, and opinions on paper for others to read." "It is a way of expressing yourself," says J. P. Another, T. J., considers form: "It can be in letters, songs, books, notes, etc." D. M. comments about audience, "It is a means by which a person can influence another through well-formed thought-provoking statements, articles, and essays." A. J. addresses a more complex issue: "The difficulty in defining 'writing' overwhelms me. . . . I mean writing can be simply defined as what I'm doing at the moment as the ink flows from my pen to the paper. However, this definition isn't acceptable; writing also conveys the thoughts that feed the pen."

Writing frequently does not come easily. C. B. says he does not write much because he has a hard time putting down his thoughts on paper. "When I do get something written down, it never comes out the way that I wanted it to." The only times he writes by choice are when he writes letters to family and friends. He admits that he is sometimes jealous of others who seem to write more easily. M. B. says he can better express himself orally than in the written word. "If someone were to sew my mouth shut, then I would wither away. They say that the pen is mightier than the sword, but to me, a pen is only a piece of plastic with ink."

For others, the words flow more easily. S. J. found writing difficult until a friend made the suggestion that she not worry so much about the first draft but just let her ideas and feelings come out; she could edit later. Now the words flow more easily and enjoyably, and she even plays with different writing styles. D. C. explains why she thinks many do not like writing. "I really believe that most students who dread writing papers only think that way because they have not figured out what method of time management works for them." She herself manages the writing so that she does not "stress-out" about papers. For some, like S. B., the ideas come more quickly than they can be written. "I can create the perfect images, the perfect words in my mind, but then my brain works so fast that if I slow down, I lose that perfect thought." She has found that using a tape recorder and a word processor helps her deal with the flow of words. Sometimes patience works. J. G. writes,

> The pressure to create hovers over me like a dark cloud. Even in the best circumstances I can't force the writing. I can't say to myself,

'Okay, ideas, come out,' and have it happen. My most creative ideas seem to come when I'm not concentrating. It is almost as if somewhere in another part of my mind the story originates and then is revealed to me.

Beginning a composition is usually the worst part. Several students report that inspiration follows only after a painful period of writing. I. M., a student who brought in draft after draft until she finally succeeded in achieving "A" papers, writes, "Writing eloquently does not come easy for me. Sometimes, I must sit for hours, days and brainstorm on a single topic." D. M. agrees, remembering

> many a day of sitting and staring at that cold, blank terminal. The hands stood cocked and ready to go at the spark of an idea. Questions wandered freely in a mind empty of answers. Sometimes the agony would stretch for hours and days, maybe even weeks. I would aimlessly participate in trivial activities just to get away from that brooding, death-like assignment of writing a paper. And then, amidst all the pain and suffering, like a glorious revolt against tyranny, the idea would come! This idea would start the clock ticking on how to answer the many questions of what's going into the paper.

S. M., in contrast, does not believe in waiting: "Instead of staring into space waiting for a thesis to come to me, I now just force myself to start writing anything to get the process started. Sure, writing is hard at the beginning, but it gets easier after I get past those first few words."

This intense struggle at the beginning of a composition, a period most of the students seem to face, sometimes results in an emotion that could be described as dislike or, less politely, as hatred. N. B. explains, "If I am totally honest, I will have to admit that I hate writing as a rule. I think this stems from the struggle I face each time a writing assignment is given." E. J. agrees:

> I always have a terrible time starting a paper. I just can't face it. I find ways to occupy my mind with other things when I know I should be working on my paper. For example, I would listen to the radio or talk on the phone, and I know darn well that I shouldn't be doing that, but I can't help it. Starting is hell.

What about "Freshman Composition" Specifically?

A. J. writes, "When people used to say the words 'freshman composition' to me, it would send chills down my spine. The thought of having to write so many papers on 'the college level' just scared the daylights out of me." But after writing a few papers, he is more confident of his writing ability. Several other students mentioned they had avoided freshman composition the first semester in college because it was "dreaded," but they took it the second semester because the course is required to graduate. The reason for avoiding the course, for one student, was that in other subjects the answers are right or wrong, black or white, but in composition, evaluation is up to the instructor's discretion or personal judgment. Fear of a critical audience was also a concern. T. J. explains, "Although I write many letters to friends and such with no problem, I get uncomfortable at the thought of someone reading my ideas and then judging them and how they are stated." T. C. reports, "I was scared to death that what I had to say in my papers would be completely off base from what my professor was expecting. What I wrote down on paper could be right or wrong and could throw my entire grade point average up or down." M. B. mentioned the syllabus, "yellow paper totaling five pages . . . 'read this,' 'respond to this,' 'draft due' and 'paper due,'" and thought to herself with resignation, "Well, I have to take this class sometime."

But how do these students define freshman composition? S. B. says, "Writing a response to a reading, open discussion, writing and peer editing—these are the usual day-to-day activities." "It's a class that forces students to use their minds creatively," writes A. K. "We are allowed and encouraged to express our thoughts and opinions on various subjects as compared to our other classes where we usually just sit and write notes." Peer editing is a new experience for many, and after trying it, most find it helpful. E. J. writes,

> I came into the class thinking that other students couldn't possibly help me. Then I got a "D" on the first assignment. I was quite upset and didn't want to tell anyone about that. But I started listening to what the instructor was telling me about how peer editing groups could help. Now, my papers wouldn't be complete without someone giving me ideas or ways to expand and upgrade my paper. Peer groups help you to express yourself to the reader because they will tell you when you are vague and when you need to expand on something.

Freshman composition is different from high school where English meant, according to S. B., "an endless line of Shakespeare [plays], and occasionally your teacher would assign you to write a five-hundred-word essay on why Romeo liked Juliet so much." L. P. remembers, "I did not enjoy writing in high school at all. I thought of it as a burden instead of something that I could enjoy. . . . we were asked to write about things that I was not at all interested in. I also found it hard to write about a book that I hadn't even read." B. R. agrees, "I wasn't really able to invest myself in my high school writing. I would just write the paper once and could find no way to improve it. I was having the same problem with my first paper this semester. It was dull; I hated it." But then B. R. put it away for a couple of days and came back to it. "Suddenly," he continued, "I saw the topic from a different angle, and I completely rewrote the paper. In high school I didn't, or couldn't, take the time to do that."

Others find the relaxed, small-class atmosphere of freshman composition similar to high school English class. D. M. contributed, "In senior English we had readings and discussion, just like this class." Most, like L. P., found the length and the level of sophistication expected for college composition essays to be a surprise. "I was shocked to learn that a five-hundred-word essay was an 'easy' assignment." "In high school," wrote C. F., "students usually waited until the night before to do their schoolwork. We can't do that in freshman composition because of the deadline for a rough draft to be peer edited."

How Bad Is It Really?

During the course we studied what other writers such as Ernest Hemingway, Annie Dillard, and Calvin Trillin had written (or said in interviews) about the writing process they used. Students wrote, sometimes in the first person, about topics they chose, as well as about topics dictated by the instructor. By the middle of the semester, the reaction from most students seemed to be that freshman composition was not as "bad" as they expected. C. C. reports,

> At the beginning of the semester the stark white pages seem to develop eyes and stare back at me. I searched them for ideas, yet they seem to exist for the sole purpose of intimidation. I think I stopped fearing the white page so much after we studied what published writers have written about writing. I learned that people who write for a living have some of the same fears that I have.

J. M. says, "When I registered for this class, I just knew it was going to be the most useless class I'd ever take in college." She already knew how to write, she thought. But, after a few weeks she realized that college instructors expect a more sophisticated style of writing than she employed. In high school, "if you had five paragraphs, including an intro, three body paragraphs and a conclusion, you would probably receive an 'A.'" Those standards didn't "cut it" in college. Still, "it takes too much of my [the student's] time." A few students actually admitted that they enjoyed the course. D. M. says, "I can write about the way I feel, the way I want others to feel. And through constructive criticism, I receive the feedback necessary toward developing into a mature, adept writer." Or, if not enjoyable, students considered the course at least useful. According to N. B., "This class has made me learn how to write about things that don't particularly interest me. I had to learn that there are many perspectives from which essays can be written and that I could find a perspective of my own which *did* interest me." A. C. says freshman composition allowed him some freedom to try new ways of expressing himself:

> This is the first time I have been able to write in the first person or to write essays that weren't research projects. In this class I had to write about what *I* thought, about my opinions, and I had to take responsibility for those opinions. Although it was extremely difficult at first, I found it to be a helpful growing process.

T. T. seems to agree, saying the course has expanded her perception of what makes a good topic:

> I've found that my own life is worth writing about. I live in a house now with two dogs and two roommates—all of the opposite sex. Our experiences often seem similar to those in the old comedy series *Three's Company*. I can't resist writing about the time someone washed the dog with human shampoo and bubbles flooded the yard. Or the night when two people suddenly need the bathroom at 3 A.M., and they actually resort to a coin toss. Not all our experiences are so lighthearted, but all are my *real life*, and I want to write about them.

This "freedom" of expression does not come without effort, according to M. B.: "Before, I would write one version of my paper, and that would be it. Now, no matter how well the paper is originally written, I do not feel good about it unless I have read it over many times and have made changes."

Some students find that the skills they develop in freshman composition help in other classes. K. C. says,

> For my last assignment in Spanish class I wrote an essay in Spanish on travel and tourism in Mexico. I was incorporating my writing technique and literary devices from English grammar and translating them into the Spanish language. Without becoming aware of my writing in English this semester, my essay in Spanish wouldn't have been as easy for me.

J. P. decided, "As a communications major my first choice would always be public speaking. But I realize now that writing is a way to accomplish the same goals, and, in some ways, is a better way. During a speech I cannot take my words out of the air once I have spoken them."

What Did They Learn?

L. M. writes, "The most important things I have learned [are] that I know how I write, where I do my best writing, and that I have a better paper when I plan ahead and plan my time." E. J. says, "One deep lesson that I learned in college [composition class] was expressing myself to the reader so that he or she can understand. I seem to have a habit of writing fragmented and incomplete sentences that make sense to me and not to the reader." And A. D. decides,

> Because of freshman composition I have grown as a writer. My style and ideas have remained much the same, but I have become more open about expressing them. This I can credit to being forced to read [my papers] aloud and to having my words read by others. In the beginning of the semester, I found it very difficult to 'expose' myself to others through my writing. I can't say that freshman composition has completely changed the way I see myself as a writer, or that I'm happy with the way I write now, but it has made me more comfortable with sharing my ideas. I'm not so afraid of writing something wrong or different from what everyone else is writing.

By the end of the semester, a few more of the students were willing to define themselves as writers. K. B. says, "A writer is someone who is successful at conveying his or her thoughts on paper, and one who is able to create images in the mind of the reader. By using this definition I think I am very close to a 'writer.'" T. C. decides, "Everyone is a writer. People do not have to be publishing books to be writers. If you have written something down on paper—a note to a friend in class, a letter to a relative, or even a phone message, that is writing." S. E. says,

> Reaffirming my statement earlier this semester, I *am* a writer. Although I do not plan to make writing my career, it will always be a valuable part of my day-to-day life. Once I graduate from college (if that ever happens), I plan to be a teacher of the deaf. Because of their limited means of communication, both sign language and written English have become more important to me. My letter writing is also important to me because I often find it easier to express myself in the written word rather than orally. So, I write when I need to apologize to someone; I write when I want to tell someone that they are special to me; I write to stay in touch with close friends who have moved away.

But L. P. was one of the ones who had not changed her mind, "I do not consider myself a writer because I do not feel I have a set writing style or an organized way [in] which I write every time."

Do composition courses such as mine, thus, reinforce some students' lack of self-identification as authors or writers? Peter Elbow writes, "Students must write 'up' to teachers who have authority over them" (139). And he points to Sara Freedman's study of teachers' response to what they thought were student essays but which had been written by other teachers. The teachers' evaluators did not think these "student" essays were sufficiently deferential. In freshman composition, students are not asked to write peer to peer but student to teacher. Their texts generally are not published. Perhaps if we instructors treated students like part of the community of writers, students would be more likely to identify themselves as writers.

But perhaps the issue is not only how we treat students (as anonymous writers, not authors), but the essential definition of the word *writer*. Students are not writers (or authors) if the connotative definition of the word is so restrictive that it creates a perceived reality that students, though they write, are not part of the community of writers.

But does it *really* matter whether students identify themselves as writers? I think it does. My freshmen students' lack of immediate self-identification as writers was a stark contrast to the group of third grade students I visited recently as part of the Fort Worth Public School District's Keystone Project. This award-winning program focuses on training teachers as change agents in the use of current process-oriented composition theory and pedagogy in elementary school classrooms. The third graders I visited have all "published" books; that is, they have written books that they illustrated, bound, and exchanged with other students. Many had been among the six hundred students of the school district who attended a "Young Author's Conference," where they affixed gold seals to the books they so proudly read to other "authors."

I was in the third grade classroom to share some of my own experiences as a writer, but first I wanted to know about their experiences. "Raise your hands if you are a writer," I said to them. All hands were raised. We decided together that what I have done in publishing a book is not so different from what they have done. They struggle through rough drafts, revise, edit, and publish their work. They are "pros" at the process, and their achievements are remarkable. After seeing the gleeful faces and the excited waving hands as third graders identified themselves as "writers" and hearing the spirited talk about future books they will "publish," I think that it does matter. Humans have a deep need to express themselves, to make sense of their world through representation such as writing or art. Lucy Calkins, whose landmark work with school children inspired the Keystone Project, writes: "By articulating experience, we reclaim it for ourselves. Writing allows us to turn the chaos into something beautiful, to frame selected moments in our lives, to uncover and to celebrate the organizing patterns of our existence" (3). In countless schoolrooms somewhere along the way, most young people lose the excitement of expressing themselves in writing, and they lose any identity they may have of themselves as writers. They have experienced too many red-marked "awks" and "frags" on their heartfelt stories. They have been asked to combine too many sentences written by someone else and to complete too many assignments that had nothing to do with their lives. Richard Marius points out that composition teachers often react to student writing, especially to what they perceive as poor student writing, with hostility: "Teachers respond as if the student has walked across a deadline, ignoring the 'danger of death' signs. The teacher draws a red pen and shoots to kill" (83). No wonder students hesitate when faced with freshman composition, which they perceive as yet another writing-on-command situation whose ante has been raised to college standards.

Recommendations

I am conscious of a colleague's comment that she is not sure who is the author here—Carol Lea Clark *and* her students or just Carol Lea Clark. In effect, I have appropriated my students' words, editing them and rearranging them for my own purposes. Yet, on another level, I, as a teacher and as a writer, have been changed by my students' words and by the interaction between their words and mine. In this sense, I think it is accurate to attribute authorship of this essay to myself and my students jointly. And this brings me to my (our) first recommendation for other instructors of freshman composition:

1. Listen to your students. Yes, I know this sounds patronizing, but from listening to my students, I have learned that they do not think instructors *do* listen. Do not just discuss their essays or even just the current issues of the day. Discuss how they *think* and *feel* about the assignments they are given. Students have valid and well-considered comments, if they are but asked to contribute them. If enough instructors, before the end-of-term evaluations, ask, "What do you think about freshman composition, 'American Novel I,' or 'History after 1900'?" and if instructors make some adaptations in their course expectations based on student responses, students will feel that they have a say in their own educations.

2. Be a writer yourself. Schwartz writes that a teacher who does not consider him- or herself a writer cannot effectively encourage students to be writers. "Like the mother who doesn't swim, trying to coax her child into the water—it won't work" (ix). Students agree. D. M. said, "Most English instructors don't write. They just assign writing. I liked the fact that we had a chance to read and even criticize my instructor's writing. I liked hearing about her struggles to get words in a row on a computer screen."

3. Treat your students as writers. After listening closely to my students this semester as they described their writing experiences in freshman composition, I have become profoundly aware that these students experience all the "hell" of the solitary writing experience that "real" writers face—the fear of the blank page, the inability to get the ideas in the mind to translate into words on a page. But only rarely do they experience the benefits of being a writer. Their words are not valued, as are the words of "real" writers or even the third graders mentioned above who have had

their words "published." And knowing that their words will be evaluated by a critical pen—of whatever color—rather than valued, it is hard for students to have a pride of ownership in their work.

I am impressed, after reading innumerable student essays and comments about their writing, with the essential willingness of most students to accept criticism and to struggle bit by painful bit toward improvement. In their final essays, written about their experiences in freshman composition, almost all could write metacognitively about why one paper "worked" and another did not. They had considered each essay carefully. They *remembered* what they had written and why. B. T., for example, explains,

> My last paper, the one on poverty, was the hardest to write but perhaps the most rewarding. I tried writing about articles that other people had written but the story just wasn't there for me. I must have tried ten different approaches. Then I decided to use personal experiences of my summer construction jobs with a missionary group in inner cities, and, suddenly, it was a paper. I truly think that this was the best paper I have ever written.

B. T. and most of the other students *do* have pride of ownership in their essays. They feel pain when one paper fails and pride when another succeeds. Whether these students know it or not, or whether anyone else recognizes it or not, that pride in their words *does* make them writers.

Works Cited

Calkins, Lucy McCormick. *The Art of Teaching Writing*. Portsmouth, NH: Heinemann, 1986.

Elbow, Peter. "Reflections on Academic Discourse: How It Relates to Freshmen and Colleagues." *College English* 53 (1991): 135–55.

Foucault, Michel. "What Is an Author?" *Critical Theory since 1965*. Ed. Hazard Adams and LeRoy Searle. Tallahassee: Florida State UP, 1986. 138–48.

Marius, Richard. "Writing and Teaching Writing." *Writer's Craft, Teacher's Art*. Ed. Mimi Schwartz. Portsmouth, NH: Boynton, 1991. 81–90.

Schwartz, Mimi. Introduction. *Writer's Craft, Teacher's Art*. Ed. Schwartz. Portsmouth, NH: Boynton, 1991. ix–xii.

12

Privacy, Peers, and Process: Conflicts in the Composition Classroom

Patricia Prandini Buckler/Purdue University North Central
Kay Franklin/Purdue University North Central
Thomas E. Young/Purdue University North Central,
Westville, Indiana

"Write about what you know" is a basic tenet of writers and composition teachers. The examination of the self and reflection on personal experience are staples of the writing class.

Since the Dartmouth Conference in 1966, the personal experience essay or autobiographical essay—"autobiographical writing that emphasizes personal revelation and reflection" (Peterson 170)—has been widely incorporated into the American composition curriculum. Derived from the British "expressive" model of composition pedagogy, this approach treats writing as a natural extension of an individual's experience (Gere 41–42).

Following the early lead of James Britton and Janet Emig, American composition has come to "focus on the personal . . . to explore what goes on in the individual writer's head" (Bizzell 55–56). For example, our own first-year writing assignments ask students to "use your own personal experience and observations as the basis of your essay"; to "explain some component of your own personality or identity in terms of earlier life experience"; to "analyze an event in your life that caused you to change your mind."

Many writing teachers believe that through such essays a student learns to objectify personal experience, to integrate that experience with new knowledge, to analyze the self, to find a voice, and to gain confidence as a writer. The self-disclosure concomitant to such personal experience writing is considered healthy, even therapeutic, and is often taken for granted by writing instructors (Tobin 339–40).

Yet recent research and practice in the teaching of composition also stress the social experience of the writing class. The students routinely brainstorm in groups, read drafts out loud in class or have them read by the teacher, read and critique each other's writing, have their essays duplicated for large-group consideration, or at the very least, share their writing with a classmate/proofreader.

By "publishing" their writing in this way, students get the benefit of a genuine audience's response and avoid the circumscription of writing exclusively for an audience of one teacher while they emulate the writing situation of professional authors.

The collaborative method or writing workshop pedagogy resembles the "personal-style classroom in procedure," and the two approaches are often combined. Virtually all the essays in Charles Bridges's *Training the New Teacher of College Composition* advocate personal experience writing and some kind of group work on student texts. When these approaches to teaching writing converge, however, we encourage students to disclose their thoughts and feelings in a personal experience essay that is then "published" in the writing class.

Although every writing teacher can attest to the surprising willingness of certain students to reveal extremely personal information, other students clearly have reservations about exposing their personal thoughts and feelings to scrutiny. Such students may be reluctant to object to required personal experience essays, especially since this type of assignment is so common.

They may protect their feelings or their privacy in different ways—by self-censorship, by fictionalizing their accounts, or by limiting themselves to the most superficial and uncommitted exploration of the experiences they are conveying. In other words, their discomfort within the writing class can impede their development as writers.

Our suspicions that some students disliked this fairly typical combination of personal experience writing and classroom sharing were based primarily on anecdotal evidence until vigorous comments by some students at the Westville Correctional Center impelled us toward a fuller investigation. (The correctional center is a medium-security state institution for men where Purdue University North Central offers a credit program.) When we decided to follow up on the reservations articulated by these students, and inferred from our campus students, we found no published material on this particular issue of privacy in the writing class; therefore, we stopped taking student complicity or neutrality in this circumstance for granted and decided to find out what our students really thought.

Following the recommendations of Lauer and Asher in *Composition Research*, we devised a thirty-question survey geared to find out quantitatively how large numbers of composition students viewed the mixing of personal experience essays with classroom collaborations. The questionnaire included some background questions to differentiate among such subgroups as Westville Correctional Center inmates, older students, younger or more traditional students, males, females, and so forth.

The second part of the survey asked for short, essay-type answers to two questions. One invited students to discuss their attitudes toward personal experience writing; the second encouraged them to comment on the practice of sharing their writing in class.

Some 270 Purdue North Central students enrolled in writing classes participated in the study, including 19 students in the college program at the Westville Correctional Center. While we had expected that various subgroups would show dissimilar responses, the results were in fact remarkably similar for all subgroups. Statistics from the questionnaire, confirmed rather eloquently by the short essays, showed that students have strong positive or negative reactions to the personal essay and collaborative classroom arrangements; that they respond positively to writing personal experience essays significantly more often than to using classroom sharing procedures; and that a significant, persistent minority are particularly concerned about reading their papers aloud, revealing too much about themselves, or being judged by other students.

Results of the Empirical Study

All the students surveyed were taking "English 101, English Composition I," the first-semester freshman writing course at Purdue North Central, during the 1988–89 or 1989–90 academic years.

The characteristics of the students who responded to the questionnaire matched those of students throughout the institution as a whole with respect to age and sex—as if the study had been a deliberate sample of all students at Purdue North Central. However, since most students take English Composition I in their first year, the freshman class was significantly overrepresented in the survey. But, not only were the students surveyed representative of the Purdue North Central freshman class, they responded willingly; so there does not appear to be any problem with nonrepresentativeness due to self-selection.

With its distribution of nontraditional, non-degree-seeking, and associate degree students (including offenders at the Westville Correctional Center), Purdue North Central cannot be considered representative of the four-year, undergraduate institution in America—our student population profile more closely resembles that of the typical community college. And while we had significant numbers of students participating, the study did not look at a variety of institutions, so we are leery about carrying its generalizations too far.

Nevertheless, our study shows a clear need at our institution, and possibly at others like it, to reconsider the responses of students to the prevalent pedagogy of the personal experience essay and the collaborative classroom.

Figure 12-1 uses a sample copy of the "Composition Student Attitude Survey" to which 271 students responded. For the first twenty questions, the students could choose from five possible responses: (1) strongly agree; (2) agree; (3) no opinion; (4) disagree; (5) strongly disagree.

The right-hand column displays the combined percentages of the students who answered *agree* or *strongly agree* to a given statement, so the right side provides a general numerical index of agreement and the relative intensity of agreement.

Figure 12-1. Degrees of Agreement with Specific Statements from the Composition Student Attitude Survey
Composition Student Attitude Survey (Revised Form 9/90)

+ = agree ? = disputed − = disagree	Directions: Use a pencil to answer the following questions by filling the correct block on the computer card.	Entire data set percent agree or strongly agree
+	1. I enjoy writing about my personal experiences. (1) strongly agree (2) agree (3) no opinion (4) disagree (5) strongly disagree	80.8
+	2. Critiquing my classmates' writing helps me improve my own writing. (1) strongly agree (2) agree (3) no opinion (4) disagree (5) strongly disagree	55.7
+	3. I enjoy reading about my classmates' personal experiences. (1) strongly agree (2) agree (3) no opinion (4) disagree (5) strongly disagree	66.8
+	4. I don't mind exchanging papers in small groups, but I am embarrassed to read my paper aloud to the whole class. (1) strongly agree (2) agree (3) no opinion (4) disagree (5) strongly disagree	55.4
?	5. If I were called upon to read my paper to the class, I would leave out some parts of it. (1) strongly agree (2) agree (3) no opinion (4) disagree (5) strongly disagree	35.8
+	6. I would not want to read my paper aloud, but I would not mind if the teacher read it without using my name. (1) strongly agree (2) agree (3) no opinion (4) disagree (5) strongly disagree	53.1
+	7. Having my classmates comment on my essays helps me improve them. (1) strongly agree (2) agree (3) no opinion (4) disagree (5) strongly disagree	64.6
−	8. I worry about criticism from my classmates during critiquing sessions. (1) strongly agree (2) agree (3) no opinion (4) disagree (5) strongly disagree	26.2

Figure 12-1. (continued)

+ = agree ? = disputed − = disagree		Entire data set percent agree or strongly agree
−	9. I find it embarrassing to write about my personal thoughts and feelings for English class. (1) strongly agree (2) agree (3) no opinion (4) disagree (5) strongly disagree	13.7
?	10. Only the teacher should critique my essays. (1) strongly agree (2) agree (3) no opinion (4) disagree (5) strongly disagree	32.1
−	11. I look forward to having my personal experience essays critiqued in class. (1) strongly agree (2) agree (3) no opinion (4) disagree (5) strongly disagree	14.1
?	12. I look forward to having my other (non–personal experience essays) essays critiqued in class. (1) strongly agree (2) agree (3) no opinion (4) disagree (5) strongly disagree	26.9
+	13. I write better papers when I include my own view. (1) strongly agree (2) agree (3) no opinion (4) disagree (5) strongly disagree	82.7
−	14. I am concerned that what I say may be used against me. (1) strongly agree (2) agree (3) no opinion (4) disagree (5) strongly disagree	20.7
+	15. I find my own personal experience a good source of ideas for my writing. (1) strongly agree (2) agree (3) no opinion (4) disagree (5) strongly disagree	80.8
?	16. When I write about personal experiences, I am careful not to reveal too much about myself. (1) strongly agree (2) agree (3) no opinion (4) disagree (5) strongly disagree	36.2
+	17. I don't want other students to judge me on the basis of what I have written in my paper. (1) strongly agree (2) agree (3) no opinion (4) disagree (5) strongly disagree	60.1

Figure 12-1. (continued)

+ = agree	Entire data set
? = disputed	percent agree or
− = disagree	strongly agree

−   18. The other students have no right
to see anything I have written.   21.8
(1) strongly agree (2) agree (3) no opinion
(4) disagree   (5) strongly disagree

−   19. I resent being asked to show my
papers to other students.   19.6
(1) strongly agree (2) agree (3) no opinion
(4) disagree   (5) strongly disagree

+   20. My personal life is no one else's
business.   43.2
(1) strongly agree (2) agree (3) no opinion
(4) disagree   (5) strongly disagree

Background Information Questions

21. Sex (1) male   (2) female

22. Age (1) 18–24 (2) 25–31 (3) 32–38   (4) 39–45
     (5) 46–52 (6) 53–59 (7) 60 or older

23. High school education (1) high school graduate   (2) G.E.D.

24. Post-secondary education
(1) This is my first college semester;
(2) I am a freshman, but past my first semester;
(3) I am a sophomore;
(4) I am a junior;
(5) I am a senior;
(6) I already have an Associate Degree.

25. College writing classes successfully completed (not counting current enrollment).
(1) one   (2) two   (3) three   (4) four   (5) five

26. I attend college
(1) full-time (12 hours or more)   (2) part-time (under 12 hours)

27. I take my classes
(1) on campus   (4) at New Prairie High School
(2) at Portage High School   (5) at more than one location
(3) at North Judson High School (6) at Westville Correctional
                              Center
If you answer (6) above in question 27, *continue.*
If you did *not* answer (6) to question 27, *stop here.*

Figure 12-1. (continued)

For Westville Correctional Center Students Only:

28. Time spent in W.C.C.:
    (1) 1–2 years   (5) 9–10 years
    (2) 3–4 years   (6) 11–12 years
    (3) 5–6 years   (7) 13 years or more
    (4) 7–8 years

29. Time spent in other correctional institutions:
    (1) 1–2 years   (5) 9–10 years
    (2) 3–4 years   (6) 11–12 years
    (3) 5–6 years   (7) 13 years or more
    (4) 7–8 years

30. How many courses have you taken so far in the Purdue program at
    the Westville Correctional Center? Include classes you are taking
    here at present as well as correspondence courses.
    (1) 1–4   (4) 13–16
    (2) 5–8   (5) 17–20
    (3) 9–12   (6) more than 20

Note: 271 respondents; not all responded to all statements.

On the left, a plus sign indicates general agreement by the respondents, the minus sign disagreement with a particular statement, and the question mark uncertainty—no clear agreement or disagreement. More specifically, *agreement* was arbitrarily defined to mean that the combined *strongly agree* and *agree* responses had a percentage total that exceeded the combined *disagree* and *strongly disagree* responses by at least fifteen percentage points. *Disagreement* was defined as just the reverse. The uncertain, disputed cases resulted when the percentage totals of the combined *agree* responses and those of the combined *disagree* responses were within fifteen percentage points of each other.

It should be noted that the minus signs indicating disagreement usually appeared when statements contained negative terms (item 8, *worry*; item 9, *embarrassing*; item 14, *concerned*; item 18, *no right*; item 19, *resent*). To rephrase item 8, for example, we could say that the students largely agreed with the statement, "I do *not* worry about criticism from my classmates during critiquing sessions." Minus signs—and the corresponding low percentages on the right—are thus generally endorsements of the public revelation of private experience just as much as the plus signs and the high percentages are.

We do not mean to suggest, however, that the students had no qualms about writing and talking openly. The negative sign by item 11 and the very low percent on the right mean the students are saying, "I don't look forward to having my personal experience essays critiqued in class." And there are several question marks. In item 5, students are saying that they would leave out parts of their papers if they had to read those papers aloud to the class; in item 12, they do not particularly look forward to having essays critiqued in class (item 12, incidentally, had the highest *no opinion* response of any item); from item 16 it is clear that some students are careful not to reveal too much about themselves. And in item 20 especially, a number of students are saying, "Mind your own business."

Still, some overall patterns are obvious. The highest combined *agree* percentages—80.8 for items 1 and 15, 82.7 for item 13 (item 15 had the highest *strongly agree* response of any item)—these percentages involved items concerned with personal experience in writing: I enjoy writing about my personal experiences; they are a good source for ideas; I write better papers when I include them. Personal experience considered relatively abstractly—students like that. But when, as in item 16, "revealing" is involved, or as in item 20, "personal life," then the students are less enthusiastic. It seems that writing about oneself is fine when the student has control and can set the limits. They seem to be saying, "Sure, I like writing about myself, but *this* is off limits, not open to public view. No trespassing."

When the items deal more specifically with classroom sharing than with writing about oneself, the agreement percentages drop off—not necessarily to the outright rejection of the idea of sharing but to a noticeably lower level of endorsement. Item 2— critiquing my classmates' writing improves my own—55.7 percent; item 7—having my classmates comment on my essays helps me improve them—64.6 percent. These are not insignificant percentages, but they are not 80 + percent, either. And, with items 11 and 12, there is clearly no real enthusiasm for classroom critiques. Items 4 and 6, which deal very specifically with techniques of classroom sharing, can teach us something: most students do not mind a small public and do not mind anonymity but are embarrassed to read their work aloud to a whole class. In general we find ambivalence. Students say they do not worry about criticism from classmates (item 8), but they do not want to be judged by other students based on their writing (item 17).

Another worthwhile overall pattern should be mentioned: nearly all these items indicate a persistent minority of nay-sayers for whom the whole business of writing about personal matters and collaborating with classmates is "bad news."

Computer tabulation of the various subgroups of respondents showed that for no subgroup was there any major variation from the percentages given previously. Female, male, freshmen, sophomores, on-campus students, students in the Westville Correctional Center—all were in substantial agreement with these figures.

This is not to say that percentages did not vary by as much as 20 percentage points in some instances, or that the columns of pluses, minuses, and question marks would be identical for all of the groups. But, overall, what has been said for the total set of respondents could be said for each subgroup: writing about personal experiences is more strongly endorsed than is classroom sharing.

The smallest subgroup (nineteen respondents) and the one that deviated most significantly from the whole group of respondents consisted of the students at the correctional center. Of course, there is the statistical problem of small groups wherein a few individuals can mean big percentage changes. Yet, if the left-hand, plus/minus column of this group were placed next to the plus/minus column for the whole group, only two items would not match: items 4 and 5. In each case, the shift would be of only one category: for item 4, a shift from *agree* for the whole group to *disputed*; for item 5, from *disputed* to *disagree*.

Even comparing the percentages of agreement columns of the correctional center group and the whole set of respondents, differences between the responses of the two groups equal or exceed 20 percentage points in only two instances: items 4 and 20. In item 4, the difference is essentially a shift of Westville Correctional Center opinion of 20+ percentage points from the *agree* column over to the *no opinion* column. (The correctional center group is less enthusiastic about reading papers aloud in class.) In item 20—"my personal life is no one else's business"—the difference is a shift of correctional center opinion to the *agree* column. Correctional center students want their privacy in this instance.

Figures for the essay questions are of a different sort (see figure 12-2). The same students who completed the questionnaire responded to two elaborately prompted essay questions—the first on writing about personal experience and the second on sharing writing in class.

Figure 12-2. Ratings of Responses to the Essay Questions of the Composition Student Attitude Survey

Composition Student Attitude Survey Essay Questions

Directions: On the paper attached, write answers to the two essay questions below. Try to write at least a page for each answer, but not more than two.

1. Writing teachers often make assignments that require students to write about their personal experiences, feelings, and thoughts. (We're going to do so now, too.) Explain how you feel about personal experience essays. Describe how you plan your essay when you're asked to include personal information. How do you feel when you're asked to write about yourself? In what ways should personal experience be used as part of composition classes? How can personal experience be used best to help students improve writing skills?

2. Students in writing classes are usually expected to share their writing in class. How do you feel about this? In what ways do you think class or small-group discussions about your own texts help you improve your writing or the writing of others? What do you learn from working on other people's papers? How would you benefit by working exclusively on your own papers? How would you change editing and revising workshops so students can benefit most? What do you see as the advantages or disadvantages of sharing student writing in class?

Essay 1 Personal Experience Writing			Essay 2 Sharing Writing in Class		
PERCENTAGE OF ESSAYS RATED			PERCENTAGE OF ESSAYS RATED		
1	(positive)	34.3	1	(positive)	18.4
			55.1			38.2
2		20.8	2		19.8
3		8.9	3		7.3
			14.9			14.6
4		6.0	4		7.3
5		5.8	5		5.4
	(neutral)		9.4	(neutral)		9.2
6		3.6	6		3.8
7		1.5	7		5.0
			4.7			13.1
8		3.2	8		8.1
9		7.4	9		11.5
			15.9			24.9
10	(negative)	8.5	10	(negative)	13.4
		100.0	100.0		100.0	100.0

Note: 270 respondents; not all responded to both questions.

Each essay was read by two independent readers trained for this project. (Besides the authors, these readers were Michal Mitol and Beth Rudnick.) These readers rated each essay response on a one-to-ten scale, with one indicating the most positive response, ten the most negative, and five or six a balanced or neutral response. The analysis of the essay responses yielded results that closely correlated with those of the empirical survey.

Figure 12-2 shows that 70 percent of the respondents to essay question 1, "personal experience writing," generally regard personal experience essay writing as valuable, with about one-third saying that they feel extremely positive about it. Over 20 percent of the responses were rated as negative, and about one respondent in six felt very negative (nine or ten) about such writing.

On the other hand, responses to essay question 2, "sharing writing in class," fall into a different pattern. While the weight of responses to this question is positive, just over 50 percent of the responses are rated in the positive category; the negative responses reach nearly 40 percent of the total. Thus the positive to negative ratio shifts from roughly 70/20 for essay question 1 to closer to 50/40 for essay question 2.

Very few responses to either essay question fall into the neutral category—about 9 percent in each case. (For comparison, the no opinion response of the empirical survey averaged a bit above 20 percent.) The net effect is that the percentages for essay question 2 fall into an inverted bell curve with the more extreme attitudes well represented and the neutral middle more lightly represented. This table presents considerable negative response to the idea of sharing writing in class, while it demonstrates the strong reactions—positive or negative—students can have toward collaborative activities in the composition class.

These numerical results permit a few general conclusions. Current pedagogy implies that using personal experience and collaborative writing techniques benefits student writers. It certainly may benefit them—but these numbers show that the students say "yes" to personal experience essays significantly more often than to certain sharing procedures. A significant, persistent minority of nay-sayers are particularly concerned about having to read their papers aloud, to reveal too much about themselves, or to be judged by classmates. The numbers further indicate that reactions to the personal essay and public critiques are based on individual or personality differences among students and are not predictable on the basis of sex, age, grade level, or other identifiable group traits.

Interpretation of Subjective Responses

The underlying philosophy of the experience/collaboration method assumes a neutral attitude on the part of the students. For the system to succeed, they must willingly incorporate personal material in their writing; they must share the product with peers, if not comfortably, at least without crippling concern. Since our study found relatively few neutral feelings, reflecting on what the students had to say is enlightening.

First for the good news. Students who feel comfortable about writing personal experience essays seem to have a positive self-image and a willingness to trust (or at least not distrust) their teachers and the educational system: One said, "Teachers are not in the habit of asking for essays that reveal more than a student should want to share." Another wrote, "I am a person of deep confidence and self-esteem, therefore I feel free in sharing my personal experiences."

Positively inclined students recognize and accept that personal experience essays make their writing easier and more fluent because they provide practice, help the paper to flow, and build confidence. Because the writer already has the information, he or she finds more to say. The knowledge that no one can tell the authors of personal experience papers that they are wrong helps take off writing pressure. Moreover, this type of assignment helps the teacher to know the student better and makes the papers more interesting to read.

Many respondents appreciate the therapeutic value of personal writing. Self-examination and self-revelation are an unexpected bonus: "I worked through some personal problems." "It [personal writing] helps me to understand myself."

Students at the Westville Correctional Center articulate this process particularly well: "I believe looking at oneself is a valuable learning experience that is worth the pain." "This process has actually helped me to reappraise my personal values and started me questioning the motives of my past actions."

With regard to sharing their writing, several students are enthusiastic: "I feel that people want to learn about me as a person." "I don't mind letting other people read what I write. Isn't that the whole purpose of writing?"

Many, however, insist: "I want only the teacher to criticize my papers." "I think I might have been more open if the teacher was the only other person reading them."

Others grit their teeth and suffer, acknowledging that sharing with peers, though difficult, has benefits: "Revising is a good thing; I need feedback; it should be good for you but it makes me uncomfortable."

Still others recognize that they can grow with the process: "The first time I had to share I was a little nervous, but once I thought about the input someone else could give me, I relaxed." "I have no trouble sharing my writing in class now as I did before. I was always afraid someone would think what I had written was stupid and that I was a terrible writer. Now sharing my essays in groups helps improve my writing and by reading other students' essays, I can learn things from them." "The best thing that comes out of discussing papers is that most people make different mistakes." A correctional center student observes, "I can take criticism and must risk negative feedback if I am to go to the limits that I have set for myself."

And now for the bad news. The on-campus students who view personal experience essays negatively see them primarily as a tiresome intrusion: "I get tired of talking about myself; no one else wants to hear my life story; personally, I feel that the teacher just wants to be nosey."

The Westville Correctional Center students express a darker, more cynical view: "There are things about me that I wish not to be known, intimate things which I would not want my classmates to know and others I would not want even the instructor to know." "Prisoners have no privacy save thoughts and dreams. . . . personal experience essays take away the last things we possess as human beings: our privacy." This writer considers it an indication of how much the inmates value education that "we wrote what was required, in spite of our feelings."

In their negative feelings about sharing work, the students are brutally direct. Their responses contain the kind of strong, descriptive language and specific support their teachers always hope to see in classroom assignments.

The least negative comments express doubts about the competency of peers to evaluate: "Students teaching students can be the blind leading the blind; students are here to learn not teach; five minutes between professor and student will do more good than hours of group discussion."

At worst, the idea of sharing evokes deep fears and anxieties. The following comments represent ideas repeated over and over again in the responses: "I'm afraid to be laughed at or cut down; I get anxious; I hate it; I abhor the idea of my papers being passed around to students; it's embarrassing and unnecessary; it's humiliating."

Understandably, the correctional center students voice even more serious concerns, including fear of retribution: "In a prison setting, sharing private stories is not a good idea. . . . Students tend to carry what is said in classrooms back to the dorms. This, of course, results in private matters being made public and could lead to trouble."

In order to avoid exposure before peers, students devise a variety of strategies to protect their privacy, ranging from prudent selection of ideas to out-and-out fabrication. Some cope by using the writer's prerogative to choose: "Personally, I tailor personal experience essays to be nonrevealing." "I select only good experience." "I don't have to write about an embarrassing time. I can choose what I want to write about." "I usually have to sit down and think, 'how personal do I want to make this.'" "I . . . determine what I want known and what I don't want known." "There is an imaginary boundary line that I will not cross." It is difficult to tell from these essays where selection ends and censorship begins.

Some other reported strategies for self-concealment are easier to evaluate: "I don't write about myself; I write fiction." "I just tell what really happened, unless, of course, there were circumstances that would be better altered from the real truth." "Here at Westville there is daily competition for survival, acceptance, and peace of mind. To share your inner thoughts with another inmate is unwise. So when asked to write a personal experience that I have had, I lie."

What, then, to make of these findings? What implications do they have for using experience/collaboration in the writing class?

First of all, further study is warranted. Purdue North Central is an all-commuter, public institution with a broad mix of ethnic backgrounds, educational preparations, and life-styles. Perhaps a residential, private college with homogeneous students, or even a large public, residential institution like Purdue's main campus would show different results.

Assuming that our results are transferable, however, we must recognize that two-thirds of our students have strong feelings, some very negative, about experience/collaboration practice, which they may voice only under cover of anonymity. We should be aware that they feel especially vulnerable when sharing with peers and given that they manage to share their work despite their distaste for so doing, may also harbor feelings of coercion by their teachers. In short, we must acknowledge that these problems exist and adjust our methods accordingly.

Perhaps we can spend more time talking with students about the methods we use and providing more opportunities for anonymous feedback. We must create that neutrality of feeling, which allows students to expend their energy on learning to write rather than protecting their privacy.

None of us should be surprised that students hesitate to trust new teachers and unfamiliar peers with personal information. That so many are willing at least to trust teachers gives us a foundation on which to build further confidence.

It seems essential to address the issue from the first day of class. We may need to spend more time discussing our practices and airing students' feelings about them. Allowing students to have a say in the procedures may alleviate some of their anxiety. While they must not decide the "if," they surely can help to determine the "how" of classroom techniques. Frequent opportunities for anonymous feedback will provide an index of student comfort and might constitute the basis for making changes.

Furthermore, we should clarify what we mean by "personal experience." Students need to understand that asking them to support an idea from their own experience does not require them to tell about their breast reduction surgery, abusive spouses, or incapacitating addictions. They must be convinced that as writers, they are masters of the ideas and words they produce, and that the process of choosing, evaluating, discarding, and substituting material, including experiential material, is integral to all writing and essential to good writing; students are not cheating when they elect not to write about something too private to share.

Finally, we should take a hard look at assignments to make sure they are not "loaded" and that they invite a range of experiences acceptable to write about.

Trust results from an accumulation of positive experiences. From the number of respondents who realize that they can survive and learn from the experience/collaboration method, we know that it is possible to provide a positive learning situation for many student writers. With informed preparation, it may be possible to include more of them.

Because writing is ipso facto a personal act, the circumstances in which students learn to write are emotionally charged. Their feelings about the class and their level of comfort with the type of subjects assigned are critical to their growth or lack of it as thinkers and writers. If, after adjusting our methodology, students still are secretly miserable or embarrassed in class, and if they consequently produce less committed work, then we must, despite its virtues, seriously and directly challenge the pedagogy that combines personal writing and class collaboration.

Works Cited

Bizzell, Patricia. "Composing Processes: An Overview." Petrosky and Bartholomae 49–70.

Bridges, Charles W., ed. *Training the New Teacher of College Composition*. Urbana, IL: NCTE, 1986.

Gere, Anne Ruggles. "Teaching Writing: The Major Theories." Petrosky and Bartholomae 30–48.

Hairston, Maxine. "The Winds of Change: Thomas Kuhn and the Revolution in the Teaching of Writing." *College Composition and Communication* 33 (1982): 76–87.

Lauer, Janice M., and J. William Asher. *Composition Research: Empirical Designs*. New York: Oxford UP, 1988.

Peterson, Linda. "Gender and the Autobiographical Essay: Research Perspectives, Pedagogical Practices." *College Composition and Communication* 42 (1991): 170–83.

Petrosky, Anthony R., and David Bartholomae, eds. *The Teaching of Writing*. Yearbook of the National Society for the Study of Education, 85, Part 2. Chicago: U of Chicago P, 1986.

Tobin, Lad. "Reading Students, Reading Ourselves: Revising the Teacher's Role in the Writing Class." *College English* 53 (1991): 333–48.

13

Rites of Passage: Reflections on Disciplinary Enculturation in Composition

***Chris M. Anson**/University of Minnesota at Minneapolis–St. Paul*

The field of composition, as Alice might have put it, grows "curiouser and curiouser." Emerging in the 1960s from the shadow of English studies, composition found itself at the mercy of large-scale political, institutional, and ideological changes already taking place in higher education. Unable to build a coherent foundation from the rubble of its rejected traditions, it collected a hodgepodge of often conflicting philosophies, approaches, and methodologies from an array of language-oriented disciplines. The resulting lack of disciplinary single-mindedness was soon reflected in a continuing series of introspective accounts of the field and its goals (Burhans 1983; Connors 1983; Emig 1980, 1982; Hairston 1982, 1985; Lauer 1984; North 1988; Phelps 1988).

In the past dozen or so years, the field has, as it predicted of itself, been growing up. It may still be searching for some grand

Kuhnian paradigm, but many more colleges and universities at least recognize the importance and legitimacy of its scholarship. The number of journals publishing works in composition continues to grow. Half a dozen academic and university presses have added new book series to their lists. Fledgling organizations begun five to ten years ago, such as the National Testing Network in Writing, are flourishing. Locally sponsored annual meetings such as the Wyoming Conference, the Penn State Conference, and the biannual New Hampshire conference are holding their own or expanding. Graduate programs continue to add composition-related courses to their curricula. And, by all counts, the number of tenure-track positions with a dominant focus in composition remains steadily high. Many inequities still exist, of course, as Sharon Crowley points out in her report on the CCCC Committee on Professional Standards for the Teaching of Writing. But the evidence strongly shows that in the past fifteen years composition has very much come of age.

Changes like these are bound to affect the field's disciplinary persona—how it represents itself, how its culture behaves, how its aspiring members feel about being drawn into the community. But instead of attracting scores of future composition scholars, the development of the field has ironically made it seem more difficult to embark on the intellectual journeys that lead to a strong affiliation with our community. In my many conversations with graduate students in composition, I have sensed a new apprehension, a skepticism about the sort of "knowledge" produced in the field. For many students, the commitment to a life of inquiry into the nature of writing seems harder to form or takes longer to develop. The gulf between novices and experts seems wider to them than it did a dozen years ago. The prospect of research and publication is not quite as alluring, in spite of—or perhaps because of—the need to prepare themselves more ambitiously than their predecessors for tenure-track jobs in composition. It is enough for them to stick closely to the major works in composition, leaving most other related disciplines (with the exception of feminist scholarship) alone. Something faintly cynical hangs in the air.

When I first wondered whether it is becoming more difficult to gain membership in the field of composition studies, I chided myself for being so naive. Was entering the field of composition really so enjoyable a dozen or so years ago, and did people really feel so quickly affiliated? Is that process really more difficult now, or do my impressions come from the usual tendency to idealize the past and create golden years out of ordinary times?

Interested in this problem, I asked a group of new graduate students in composition to write and talk informally in our seminar about their sense of membership in the field, how they feel about what they are learning, and what they think the future holds for them. Twelve years ago, I had myself reflected on many of the same issues in a series of journal entries in several early graduate courses in composition at Indiana University. As I reread those old notes, recalling the impressions I shared with other "second-generation" composition specialists, I immediately felt the contrasts with the experiences of new graduate students interested in entering the field today.

This chapter is my attempt to come to terms with those contrasts. As such, it represents a significant risk: nothing of what I am finding in my ongoing discussions about this issue with colleagues and students has been empirically verified among a larger population or can be generalized to other people in other places. This is not a study nor pretends to be. In fact, to vigorously defend its methods, findings, "sample size," and the like, would demonstrate exactly the sort of empirical paranoia that has already become a mark of tension in the field.

Instead, I would rather propose a series of questions to foreground my reflections. As the field develops self-esteem, have we become more divisive? Or is that simply a product of being located in a more general academic culture that itself grows ever more competitive? Should the mere existence of perceived barriers to affiliation in our field suggest that a problem exists? Should we care enough to intervene, or is that simply encouraging more useless self-absorption? Is the field becoming more coherent and unified, or will it remain simply a loose confederation of people from a mixture of disciplines representing widely different intellectual views? Why do new students of composition theory and research *expect* coherence and then become disillusioned by diversity, instead of finding a voice for themselves amid the buzz of productivity?

On Affiliation: Teacher or Scholar?

As North (1988) shows at length, composition defines itself in terms of its twin roles of scholarship and teaching. In many other fields, especially at large universities, research bears almost no relationship to instruction; the former gets nurtured and rewarded while the latter stagnates from neglect. I have rather proudly talked with faculty members in other fields about the close connection between what we in composition do professionally and what we do in the classroom. In contrast to many other less pedagogically oriented fields, the tensions that exist in composition between teaching and research often arise largely *because* so much scholarship seems to depend on application, and vice versa.

In the early years, when scholarship in composition was just starting to take itself seriously and ask for legitimacy, the interdisciplinary potential of research in the field was electrifying. By the late 1970s and early 1980s, when I first became interested in composition as a field, a sense of intellectual excitement surrounded and energized everything from the most local chitchat with fellow teaching assistants to the most important scholarly meetings. Nothing escaped scrutiny. Nothing seemed too unimportant to consider or reconsider. And nothing, not even what had emerged in the work of Britton, Emig, or Perl, was really *known* about writing. Not even the most distant and threatening territories were left unscouted. I remember a time in graduate school when some of my friends and I read everything we could get our hands on in the area of artificial intelligence to see what implications it had for composition. For several weeks, we handed around slim, alien-looking books from the computer science library. Most were almost unreadable, but we thrashed ahead. We were spellbound by anything in the study of language and linguistics that promised something new—the psychology of reading, computational semantics, speech communication, learning theory, transformational grammar, sociolinguistics, rhetoric. We could hardly get our fill. Listening to myself a dozen years ago, I can still feel the excitement:

> Someone, I'm not sure if he's a faculty member or research assistant in psychology, joined us outside the bookstore when we were leaving this afternoon. Jeff showed him what he'd bought, a used copy of Chomsky's *Aspects*, and we began talking about how Chomsky has influenced language study in psychology. This guy does stuff mainly with reading, and he was rattling on about some equipment that measures eye movements and how you can develop a model of reading from what happens to the eyes (Jeff took a course with a professor named Pisoni over there and said it was great.) Then we got on to writing and he started some wild speculations about neurology.

Could you measure brain wave patterns during the act of writing. Couldn't that tell you something about what's happening at certain junctures, and so on. For example, the early stages vs. the later stages. After he left, Jeff and I walked back to Ballantine just going crazy over the possibilities, and we began to wonder whether the School of Medicine would let us do some sort of encephelograms, and what that would involve, and what else you'd need to know about neurology (I suspect quite a bit). Then we laughed about how we're just trying to get through Jackindoff's stuff on semantics, never mind brain studies! Still, I'd like to learn more.

While this passage reflects a kind of youthful faith in the potential for scholarship to provide most of the answers about writing, it was also, I suspect, the faith of the field. When someone recommended the work of William Perry and Lawrence Kohlberg to me, I soon found that established composition scholars were exploring the applications of learning theory to the processes of writing. When I read about saccades and regressions in the reading process, someone, somewhere, was reflecting on the psycholinguistic intersections of reading and writing. And so it went—trying on new ideas, watching as composition explored ethnomethodology, psychology, anthropology, reader-response theory. Eager to work this new material into our teaching, my close graduate-student friends and I indulged in a kind of pedagogical mania, daily typing up all sorts of handouts based on schema theory, the Myers-Briggs Type Indicator, hemisphericity. The whole enterprise was like a busy public studio littered with artwork at various stages of completion— messy, to be sure, but exciting, energized in its chaos. The classroom provided a fascinating scene for writing, and contributed in obvious and compelling ways to our thinking. And beneath it all lay research. It was the scholarly side, the *investigative* side, that made teaching so rich.

Most of the problems that beseige the pedagogical side of the field were even more obvious then. Composition drew little or no respect from the rest of the liberal arts (for that matter, from almost anywhere else with the exception of the school of education). It was even tougher to talk anyone out of equating writing with grammar, much less convince them that composition was a scholarly field. Conditions of employment for composition teachers were at best unglamorous, at worst reprehensible. Every university I visited housed composition TAs in the same rotting, barracklike structures, the most worthless properties on campus. We felt alternately marginalized and trivialized, a kind of sanitation department necessary for the linguistic cleanliness of the intellectual environment, where "real" disciplines carried on their important work.

But we also felt great hope. The process approach had come with such religious force that we could hardly control its implications for research and teaching. It was as if we had stumbled on the "One True Way," released into a kind of instructional nirvana of process over product, response over evaluation, compassion for struggling writers over contempt for their ineptitude. There was a cause, of sorts, that drove us forward to find the evidence (empirical and otherwise) for our convictions.

Now, after two decades of voluminous scholarship in composition, new tensions between teaching and research seem to be developing. Many of my students find it difficult to embrace research but want strongly, almost passionately, to teach. There is the sense that scholarship—even under the auspices of "teacher research"—really doesn't have much to *say* about teaching, that the living, breathing world of the classroom or the writing lab holds the greatest promise for a sense of self-definition, a career, a goal. The same rejection of tradition in composition is there, but some of the spirit of scholarly inquiry, the sense of possibility, is gone. After studying composition long and hard, examining its various traditions, research methods, findings, and future prospects, Jim, a graduate student writing in 1991, wraps up his affiliation with composition this way:

> How do I feel about myself relative to the field of composition? Well, let me see now. I see myself right now in the fringe of the field. I don't have a full-time teaching job, and it looks to me as if such jobs are pretty hard to come by. I am interested in continuing to teach writing, but I'm a little less certain how interested I am in producing scholarship or research. Teaching, for me at least, needs to come first. Even if I do succeed in securing a teaching position that continues over a number of years (or even quarters!), I still may not be interested in becoming a scholar or researcher. I certainly understand why others would, but my reading of the field is that it is fraught with inconclusiveness: it seems to be what in business is called a mouse-milking operation—a lot of effort for very little return. Maybe Barry Kroll is right, that composition is still in a preparadigmatic state. If and when a paradigm becomes established, perhaps research will become more fruitful. On the other hand, perhaps teaching writing really is a craft that can't be analyzed scientifically.

Jim expects a coherent body of research and finds instead what I have always felt to be a healthy eclecticism, newly reflected in books such as Janice Lauer and J. William Asher's *Composition Research: Empirical Designs* and reinforced by constant debates in the field for or against experimental studies, naturalistic inquiry and ethnography, teacher-based research, historical studies, metanalysis, and the like. It is not so much the presence of diversity that seems to alienate him (it has been there all along), but something almost exclusionary about the various factions that diversity represents ("number-crunchers need not apply"; "oh, God, another loosy-goosy ethnographer"). Early in a recent advanced graduate seminar, I reminded the group that some compositionists find it perfectly acceptable to mix research paradigms in a single study, blending quantitative analysis with naturalistic techniques, for example. The class accepted this pronouncement jubilantly and came instantly to life. But why? The assertion seems no more enlightening than any other typical remark in a graduate class. After experiencing adversity between different research camps, maybe the mere thought of scholarly unity and intellectual compromise moved them. I'm not sure. But it may be worth considering just what effect our representations of this or that "group" or "camp" or "subfield" have on the way our students construct the field for themselves.

The lack of clear boundaries around the discipline, as Andrea Lunsford has pointed out, is nothing new:

> Our history as a profession—certainly in the span of CCCC's life—is not easily perceived as proceeding in an ordinary and traditional academic way—a clear setting out of boundaries, hedging certain subjects and people in, keeping others out. Instead, our field has seemed more heterogenous, more expansive and inclusive, gaining, in Kenneth Burke's words, "perspectives by incongruity" rather than following some linear path to academic disciplinarity. (72)

If a field is *insecure* about its heterogenity, however, it may tacitly try to create sometimes artificial boundaries around itself: us and them, acceptable and unacceptable, old-fashioned and hip. While students like Jim may be comforted by a veneer of coherence, perhaps because it helps to organize their learning, that veneer can also solidify into a stronger and less easily penetrated barrier to membership. As Elaine explains in her reflections, such an apparently healthy evolution toward unity and focus could do away with the inclusiveness Lunsford rightly recognizes in the field:

Moving in the direction of tightening up the boundaries and thus, potentially eliminating or reducing the chaos of the field, would be one way to approach the problem [of the field's lack of coherence]. The question remains whether this would then help or hinder entrance into the field for newcomers. It would certainly be a move to define the field more clearly and that potential tangibility would both help one to see the nature and limits of the field but would also probably keep many out who would not, or could not, fit into the designated parameters.

As Elaine insightfully suggests, professional affiliation can be thwarted when an aspiring member who seeks the safety of a coherent mission and the presence of well-defined intellectual boundaries must float, like Perry's relativists, in a sea of cross-disciplinary indeterminacy. Burton Clark, commenting on the nature of the professoriate in higher education, points out that this "dual commitment" (to the one discipline and to the many) is often necessary to avoid isolation and fragmentation:

> In the language of sociology, there is a role enlargement or role elaboration in which the individual moves in a seamless blend from one posture, one set of demands and expectations, to another. But these multiple memberships are also a fundamental source of *integration—the* way by which the system "naturally" combats the fragmentation of specialization. Absolute isolation is reduced; individuals are caught up in two or more perspectives. (117)

Instead of providing integration, however, the multiple memberships that combat the natural fragmentation of composition (back?) into its various epistemelogical and disciplinary components become, for Elaine, the source of tension and the struggle for power:

> I do know that since I've been back here in school I haven't seen an enormous difference in the way the field of composition treats its incoming members than literature studies or education or any other fields do. It is all so territorial. That is what I don't want. That is what I have struggled against. The reason I am in composition studies is that it is the one place where I thought I would be able to somewhat erase the boundaries between the fields of study and move back and forth sharing what I have in more than one area, letting more than one area inform what I already know.

What Elaine seeks is what Clark calls role elaboration—a sense of belonging to a cohesive community that allows for multiple affiliations. Claudia Greenwood clearly documented this problem in a study of returning women students in composition, in which most of her subjects had great difficulty becoming fully integrated into the field even on a purely scholarly, rather than social, level; "there was simply not enough time to accommodate all of the roles reentry women must play" (134–35). What we must understand more fully are the reasons why the multiple memberships that have so positively defined the roles of composition scholars (and made working in the field so fascinating) are now presenting greater problems to those entering the field.

Initiation

Rites of passage in academia are psychologically constructed from a general but fairly tacit social agreement about initation imposed collectively by the scholarly community. When composition was first discovering its potential as a research field, that community seemed relatively nonthreatening and noncompetitive (feisty though it was in defending itself against the attacks of outsiders). Initiation, if there was any, pretty much meant talking the talk. Anyone could come in, within reason, and from any level of experience. And although there were (and probably always will be) the usual philosophical camps, each armed for its own intellectual battle with the others, it felt more like a game than real warfare.

As a new student of composition, I had already constructed academia as somewhat competitive, but there was something especially warm to me about the people in the field. I recall a series of debates between Janice Lauer and Ann Berthoff about cognition in writing, originally published as comments and responses in *College Composition and Communication* and then reissued in W. Ross Winterowd's collection of essays on composition theory, *Contemporary Rhetoric* (1975). The usual scholarly warfare was present in these well-known theorists' banter, but I recall a professor talking about how much they respected each other, how committed they both were (and I might add, still are) to reforming the teaching of writing in the United States. Debates like theirs were exciting to me, but there was something more, a sense of collegiality, that made their discussion seem like an animated conversation between two friends rather than a bitter intellectual feud. And then there were many others who seemed almost incapable of feuding in any form, the Donald Murrays and Andrea Lunsfords of the field.

This "field warmth" came through especially strongly during my first attendance at a CCCC conference:

> Well, the conference is over. I had so much just to hear that I hardly wrote anything down! Diane couldn't show up on our panel, so Pat did a paper instead of chairing the session. Then I did a response to the panel. I guess I must have taken the job seriously or something, because someone, I think it was Michael, remarked that I was furiously writing down notes during the whole session. I couldn't really see what tied together the papers, since they'd all interpreted the word "models" differently—as literal (literary?) models, like essays by E. B. White, as "theories" (models of writing), and so on. So I think the response seemed a little garbled, but Michael said it went fine. What really amazed me about the whole conference was how there didn't seem to be any sense of status. Imtiaz tells me that it's hard to get on an MLA panel if you're a graduate student and when you are, there's a sort of understanding that you're just shit. But no one seemed to care at the conference. I felt sort of naive telling this to the other students there, but they said they experienced exactly the same thing: when Michael introduced us to certain biggies we'd read, they asked us what we were doing, and seemed to take an interest in what we thought. We weren't just "students." We met all sorts of people, Corbett, Troyka, O'Hare. It was like being at an all-stars game. I think I went to fifteen sessions in all; I took the most notes at one on writing anxiety, with a guy named Daly. It was great to meet so many people and talk about their work with them, in the flesh.

Now listen to John, a graduate student who, in 1991, is just beginning to take a major interest in composition as a field:

> Concerning membership in the community I would have to say that I don't really feel like a true, voting, card-carrying, numbers-and-theory-toting member of this particular discourse community, or academy within the academy. I would only be deceiving myself if I thought that kind Mr. Hillocks or fair Ms. Emig would look at me like anything other than the imposter I would be if I pulled up a chair next to one of them at the next CCCC convention and started in with some airy, knowing persiflage about the most significant composition theory. It seems to me that some right of passage, or some sort of dues paying, is in order before one can truly claim to be a member of the composition research community. The short of it is, one must first do some research. Real investigation; involving, perhaps, various tangible, three-dimensional instruments, and with real subjects; i.e., warm-blooded, squirming, sometimes indifferent and ill-tempered bodies that are live students.

John's construction of the field gives great value to empirical research. But the consequence of this is to prefigure himself as alienated from the field until he can produce an acceptable study— a rite of passage. It is simply not enough to be, in North's term, a practitioner, to read avidly in the field, take a keen interest in its principles, critique its theories, or even try to apply those theories to teaching; to be a "composition person" requires some sort of credit rating, which, like getting one's first American Express card, has the requisite of its own attainment.

To some extent, I also assumed (until I found otherwise) that the experts in the field would think me a novice unworthy of even casual talk; that tendency may be natural and universal. In the intervening years, however, it is likely that the sheer quantity of research and scholarship on writing has worsened the perceived chasm between experts and novices, between members and those who aspire to belong. Composition now has a tradition of research too voluminous even for the Ph.D. booklist to subsume (note the advent of ever-fattening yearly sourcebooks such as the *Longman Bibliography of Composition and Rhetoric*). The discourse has grown up and become more sophisticated, requiring more prior knowledge, and that must carry with it the potential for alienation. From the perspective of the aspiring composition scholar like John, the belief that membership in the field requires doing research (and ideally, getting it published) becomes a major source of frustration when considered next to the parallel and more manageable goal of teaching. And although his entry buys into the notion that one must be literally indoctrinated into the field, a bit later he questions the very process of this sort of "dues paying":

> How should composition change in respect to the way people become encultured in the field? I think the sometimes seemingly low student more or less must dictate or be allowed to dictate the levels of discourse in composition research. By this I mean that if too many teachers are "excluded" from the community, or otherwise disenfranchised, by discourse that is too abstruse and irrelevant, and as a result potentially valuable pedagogies never even make it into the classroom, then perhaps the theoretical dialogue needs to change—change to accommodate the practical, day-to-day needs and concerns of the teacher and students. . . . Composition researchers need to take the time to honestly investigate just how much impact research and theory is having in the classroom. Not merely how much it *should* have, but how much does it have, and can have. Janet Emig's opinions as to the relations between the layers of the neocortex and the stages of cognitive

maturation may have their place (I believe they do have a place in composition research), they may also be, nevertheless, nothing but the strangest caviar to the general composition populace.

The tension at work here—the usefulness of research and scholarship for the daily work of literacy instruction—has the effect of debilitating the aspiration to "investigate" writing rather than to simply make it improve, as Susan comments in her reflection when she says that

> the division implied between "professionals" (what we aspire to be) and "novices" misleads us into thinking that what we do in composition is not quite related to what we do as teachers. I, for one, always want to keep my feet on the ground, looking at research from the perspective of one who teaches writing.

Yet the preponderance of "pure" research in composition eventually wins out. Like most of her peers, Monica first expresses uncertainty about empirical research designs but then, with a rhetorical sigh, resigns herself to the hurdle she has constructed for her own membership:

> The various forms of research still seem to overlap and mix together (I guess that's what they are supposed to do). . . . The main problem I have with composition research is the statistical aspect. I have a vague notion of what chi squares are used for, but I have no idea how they are calculated. Somewhere there has to be a table or short booklet which explains the necessary statistics in layman's terms. As with most academic disciplines, it seems that the one sure way to become part of the field of composition research is to go out, do a study, and get it published. If you use the proper discourse and quote from, or at least mention, the "giants" of the field, then you've met the minimum requirements for a composition researcher.

Again, the pessimism is clear. But what has led to this ambivalence? What may be causing this simultaneous skepticism and exasperated admiration for the inquiry that so attracted me to composition and still serves as the driving force in my (and so many of my peers') professional lives?

In "Love and Hate in the Academy," Peter Loewenburg (1985) describes the tendency for academics to rid themselves of feelings of worthlessness and inferiority by "projecting" them outward, usually on others. Projection, as Loewenburg describes it, "is often a form of manipulation which is a defense against anxiety, that is, against the fantasied dangers of the inner world" (68). Projection is almost always discussed in terms of individual behavior; for example, authoritarian people who cannot tolerate it when their subordinates in scholarly rank do not capitulate to authority are said to be filled with envy for the "virility they do not share" (71); their authoritarianism is the product of having cowed before authority in their own past.

To my knowledge, no one has considered ways that a discipline might "project" through its available scholarly and intellectual channels, evaluation procedures, and so on. In such a scenario, it might be possible for the constituency of a field (that is, what we call *"the field"*) to experience such anxiety over its perceived inadequacies, lack of power, or lack of disciplinary coherence that it projects those feelings on to its own aspiring members. As a field *becomes* a field, in other words, it can also develop strategies that work against its own best interests by alienating or excluding the very people it would hope to draw in and support. What some graduate students may be experiencing in their wry comments about membership are the effects of "field projection," a sense (conveyed by the habits of the profession) that good ideas and some energy are no longer entirely adequate to belong. In part, those habits are reflected in the nature of the field's oral and written discourse, the media that give it life.

On Scholarly Discourse

John's reflections focused on the nature of discourse in the field of composition—a source of great concern among graduate students today. In my own early years studying composition theory, the strongly interdisciplinary nature of the field practically required one to "code-shift" (often quickly and effortlessly) from one sort of discourse to another as we lurched from Grice and Searle to Goodman and Smith, from Shank and Abelson to Fish and Riffatterre. And our writing also required these multiple intelligences: most composition scholars have simultaneously worked on two entirely unrelated projects written in different styles (and sometimes even invoking different assumptions and epistemologies). Interestingly, the fact that composition opened its doors to the study and legitimizing of *all* professional and academic discourse may have lent itself to a less critical view of such discursive schizophrenia.

But listen to Dana, whose reflection so fully captures some of the frustrations I hear from new members of the field:

> I'm amazed at how "researchy" [composition] seems. . . . I think there are a whole lot of other ideas about writing that are more useful and tangible than the scientific stuff. And, of course, the scientific writing. I'm very against it. If institutions like universities are ever going to exist as a progressive social force in American culture, the writing and studying that goes on here has to be clear and tangible so that the ideas can reach the more popular culture. Now, I sound like a really crazy person, so idealistic, but it is how I feel. Academics is making me crazy. I feel there are good possibilities for schools, and the abstraction and formality of academic writing is not helping. . . . And if I haven't made that point clear enough, I'll stop and take this in a new direction. I think it's obvious that I think the "enculturation" into this field and into most higher-level academic fields is not a positive thing. I think it is fairly laughable, yet I can't laugh because here I am at the keyboard hoping to get a degree so I can teach, which will demand that I publish, which will demand academic discourse, which I hate. So, I'm not really laughing.

As Dana's comment suggests, much writing in the field of composition tries desperately to sound scholarly. Because the field maintains so many bonds to other disciplines, we end up wearing discursive hats, now the de Mannian poststructuralist, now the nominalized, passivized reporter of statistical significance, at one moment the generative linguist and at the next a cultural critic spouting off about problematics and signifiers. The more insecure we feel, the more we gravitate toward discourse that alienates in order to seem inclusive, that invites people to understand itself while closing the door on those who do not already belong. Scholarly discourse *is* often unapproachable. The reason for this, as Brown and Herndl (1986) point out in their study of corporate writers with job insecurity, is closely tied to competition and apprehension about membership. People write to sound important, to give themselves legitimacy. Ironically, the frustration of potential new members reading unnecessarily complex or academic discourse may well have its source in the anxieties of the writers themselves who, a bit farther along, still feel less than affiliated. Even the most optimistic of the students I have talked to are not unaffected. An eager reader of research, Michael, for one, decides that he has "tempered some of [his] original enthusiasm for 'hard' research, realizing that some of that stuff is so technical that it might even be characterized as stifling, or at least highly exclusionary."

The sanctioned and, to use Mary Louise Pratt's (1977) term, "pre-selected" discourse in the field is not the only potential problem for new members. Barbara Tomlinson, in a perceptive essay about the nature of composition's "discourse communities" (1989), comments on what may be reflected in professional (usually anonymous) reviews in the field:

> I do not think that such a widespread phenomenon [that reviewers are frequently willing to be rude in their reviews] should be taken for granted, however: If nothing else, it implies that reviewers, at least momentarily, believe that authors either (1) have *consciously* violated widely circulated and agreed-upon research standards and deserve to be punished, or (2) are too dumb to be considered members of the discourse community and need to be "insulted out," so to speak. Issues of courtesy aside, I do not think that in composition studies we currently have the kind of consensus that might justify such behavior; instead, I think that it is an index of the degree to which composition participates in a number of overlapping and conflicting discourse communities. (91)

Now, for myself and for a good many colleagues, the often bitterly critical discourse Tomlinson deconstructs seems to be emerging as a common practice (recently cautioned, in fact, in at least one set of instructions to reviewers of manuscripts submitted to an NCTE journal). Increasingly, we seem to be using our words in hostile, combative ways, as Mike Rose (1992) notes in his response to what he perceives to be another compositionist's unnecessarily caustic and personal attack on one of his books: "Recent essays in *College English* and elsewhere by Olivia Frey and Jane Tompkins are asking us to reconsider the adversarial ways we academics establish our authority. Our discussions seem to be getting increasingly nasty, with people attributing all sorts of muddle-headedness and nefarious motives to each other, and I don't see—never did see— how this kind of tack advances our thinking about complex issues" (83). Some might say "welcome to the real world." But we might wonder whether it is the kind of world, at least for composition, that we want to build. Established compositionists can scoff at unjustifiably negative reviews, toss them into a drawer, and go on with their work. Those aspiring to join us, however, may not respond with such self-assurance.

We must begin to take more seriously students' responses to discourse in the field; they provide a kind of litmus test, not even gained completely from as candid a work as North's reflective account, in which he still cannot avoid situating himself in his book or being situated by its readers. In contrast, our new students' perceptions represent some of the purest that we can find, at once involved enough to know the field and detached enough to speak, if not without great emotion, at least without great risk. At some point, we must squarely face those perceptions as legitimate and often critical positions about who and what we are.

The Caution of Context

Nothing of what we can conclude about the ways people become members of our field can be understood outside the specific institutional context where that membership, in large part, takes place. Frustration, depression, lack of a career goal, disciplinary confusion—all of these negative aspects of academia may reflect inadequacies of particular departments or programs characterized by hostile or unhelpful faculty, negligible support, a stormy or downright dull intellectual climate.

Composition at my own institution—especially the part that hires and trains graduate students to teach writing—gets consistently glowing evaluations from exiting graduate students for its accommodation, humaneness, and guidance. Students write about teaching as the "real entry point" for affiliation, giving them the "human reasons why composition theory and research matter." Course work, too, helps to provide students with "an excellent initiation . . . into the realm of composition studies" (Kim), giving "new considerations to more traditional pedagogy, opening up more ideas, or at least shaking up the denizens of the ivory tower" (Jeff). "With the new knowledge I now have of the landscape of composition," Mike writes, "I feel I know some more about why and how I fit in." Elaine finds that "in the midst of all that goes on at the university, our composition community here, at least, [is] a beacon in a sometimes very tangled, disconnected place to be." What, then, of the perceived barriers to affiliation?

The answer might well be found in the sort of community where affiliation takes place. Local communities are much easier to create and maintain, through teacher-support groups, research networks, dissertation help sessions, even the social ties of graduate seminars. The frustrations I hear from students of composition research have less to do with becoming affiliated with the local community as with that more nebulous and threatening body, "the field" at large (and *as* large as it has become). Where once the annual meeting of the CCCC provided a sense of community and collaboration, now students return from it a bit bewildered. In the past two or three years, that bewilderment seems related to the increasingly political and politicizing nature of our discourse. The smaller, more intimate conferences seem to do more to welcome in new members, as Lida discovered when a few months after attending the CCCC convention she went to Wyoming: "Bringing my project to the Wyoming Conference last June solidified that 'real-world' experience [in composition] as positive. In the relaxed atmosphere of this conference, I received lots of encouragement and support from experienced researchers and teachers who took the time to express interest in a newcomer. I came away from this conference feeling that making a place for myself in the field would be possible." Increasingly, composition seems to be relying on subgroups, smaller memberships, to replace the sense of community once provided by the field as a whole. Perhaps this is inevitable. As Loewenburg points out, the structure of all institutions of higher education (and their disciplines) is status-oriented, hierarchical, and competitive. Perhaps by consciously reflecting on the conflicts between our inner and outer worlds, we can more effectively draw graduate students into a system that might otherwise exclude them or lead to the cyclic rehearsals of exclusionary behavior. It is when, Loewenburg contends, "a group has developed insight and skill in recognizing forces of envy, status, security, authority, suspicion, 'territory,' hostility, and the memories of past events, [that] these forces can no longer be as powerful in distorting discussion and impeding decisions" (79).

Finally, we must realize that nothing can stop intellectual and disciplinary fissures in the field. Nor should they be stopped. Complacency spells the demise of inquiry; tension gives it life. But composition experts must become more aware of how they represent those tensions. Displaying the sort of divisiveness that increasingly characterizes our scholarly "arguments," reviews, and interaction at conferences does little but alienate new members and silence their voices. In digging up old notes and journals from the dusty boxes in my attic for this chapter, I was humbled to read some of my own mistaken assertions about writing in a few of my seminar papers. But I was also surprised and delighted to reread the comments of my teachers, who cautioned while they gave hope, and made it seem as if, despite the many contradictions and disagreements, we were all of a mind, trying to know more and do better as the people most empowered to develop advanced literacy in our culture.

Coda

At best, my presentation of membership in composition here must remain hopelessly problematic, as if I were portraying freshman attitudes toward writing by quoting a few students enrolled at one school. The very act of appropriating the unheard voices of young (and not-so-young) graduate students struggling to find their identities in a field still uneasy with its own role, direction, and place in the academy is suspect on several grounds. Some might even call into question the ethics of doing so. Why not let them speak for themselves?

The fact remains that most of the students who are playing a role in my thinking about enculturation and membership in composition are still voiceless in our field. Some, unless as a community we invite them in, may remain so. In presenting some of their struggles to be heard (and to decide whether they want to be heard), it is my hope that those of us who feel relatively comfortable in our discipline—who define our professional lives in terms of our membership in it—can keep alive the welcoming spirit and the sense of professional excitement that has characterized the field from its early years.

Acknowledgments

Thanks to the many colleagues and students, especially Elaine Pilon, Lida Strot, and Robin Brown, who shared their views with me about the subject of enculturation in composition and responded to drafts of this essay. Thanks especially to the members of English 8810, "Introduction to Composition Research," whose collective voices provided the impetus and much of the material for this essay: Jon Ballingrud, Joyce Banghart, Johan Christopherson, Mike Condon, Kim Donehower, Monica Eden, Laurie Kienberger, Dana Lundell, Elaine Pilon, Kara Provost, Jeff Radford, Maggie Reed, Jim Runnels, and Lida Strot.

Works Cited

Brown, Robert, L., Jr., and Carl Herndl. "An Ethnographic Study of Corporate Writing: Job Status as Reflected in Written Text." *Functional Approaches to Writing*. Ed. Barbara Couture. Norwood, NJ: Ablex, 1986. 11–28.

Burhans, Clinton, S., Jr. "The Teaching of Writing and the Knowledge Gap." *College English* 45 (1983): 639–56.

Clark, Burton R. "The Professoriate." *The Future of State Universities: Issues in Teaching, Research and Public Service*. Ed. Leslie W. Thompson and David A. Wilson. New Brunswick, NJ: Rutgers UP, 1985. 115–27.

Connors, Robert J. "Composition Studies and Science." *College English* 45 (1983): 1–20.

Crowley, Sharon. "A Progress Report on the Wyoming Resolution by the Committee on Professional Standards." *College Composition and Communication* 42 (1991): 330–44.

Emig, Janet. "Inquiry Paradigms and Writing." *College Composition and Communication* 33 (1982): 64–75.

———. "The Tacit Tradition: The Inevitability of a Multi-Disciplinary Approach to Writing Research." *Reinventing the Rhetorical Tradition*. Ed. Aviva Freedman and Ian Pringle. Conway, AK: L & S, 1980. 9–18.

Greenwood, Claudia M. "'It's Scary at First': Reentry Women in College Composition Classes." *Teaching English in the Two-Year College* 17 (1990): 133–41.

Hairston, Maxine. "Breaking Our Bonds and Reaffirming Our Connections." *College Composition and Communication* 36 (1985): 272–82.

———. "The Winds of Change: Thomas Kuhn and the Revolution in the Teaching of Writing." *College Composition and Communication* 33 (1982): 76–88.

Lauer, Janice. "Composition Studies: Dappled Discipline." *Rhetoric Review* (1984): 20–29.

Lauer, Janice M., and William J. Asher. *Composition Research: Empirical Designs*. New York: Oxford UP, 1988.

Loewenburg, Peter. "Love and Hate in the Academy." *Decoding the Past: The Psychohistorical Approach*. Berkeley: U of California P, 1985.

Lunsford, Andrea A. "Composing Ourselves: Politics, Commitment, and the Teaching of Writing." *College Composition and Communication* 41 (1990): 71–82.

North, Stephen M. *The Making of Knowledge in Composition: Portrait of an Emerging Field*. Upper Montclair, NJ: Boynton, 1988.

Phelps, Louise Wetherbee. *Composition as a Human Science: Contributions to the Self-Understanding of a Discipline*. New York: Oxford UP, 1988.

Pratt, Mary Louise. *Toward a Speech-Act Theory of Literary Discourse*. Bloomington, IN: Indiana UP, 1977.

Rose, Mike. "A Comment on 'On Literacy Anthologies and Adult Education: A Critical Perspective.'" *College English* 54 (1992): 81–83.

Tomlinson, Barbara. "Ong May be Wrong: Negotiating with Nonfictional Readers." *A Sense of Audience in Written Communication*. Ed. Gesa Kirsch and Duane H. Roen. Newbury Park, CA: Sage, 1990. 85–98.

Winterowd, W. Ross. *Contemporary Rhetoric: A Conceptual Background with Readings*. New York: Harcourt, 1975.

AT THE RISK
OF BEING PERSONAL . . .

Appearance as Shield: Reflections about Middle-Class Lives on the Boundary

Irene Papoulis

•◇ ————————————————————————

    I began reading Mike Rose's *Lives on the Boundary* with the assumption that the book would engage me in my capacity as a college teacher who had worked with Equal Opportunity Program students. However, by chapter 2, when Rose began describing his own life as a disadvantaged student, I realized to my surprise that I was identifying with his story not primarily as a teacher, but as the high school and college student I myself had been. "But how can you possibly identify with Rose?" I asked myself. "You had a privileged education!"

    It's true. According to Rose's sense that students with a solid intellectual background do

well in school, I should have been a sparkling
and productive student all my life, since I was
one of the "smart" ones. My father has a Ph.D.
and writes books, and my mother had a B.A.; my
parents always took an active interest in what I
was doing in school; it never occurred to me or
to any of my four siblings that we would not go to
college. In spite of the fact that I was good at
intellectual work and surrounded by models of
engaged and active students, I perceived myself
as being on the periphery throughout most of
my schooling. Rose's description of himself as a
listless high school and beginning college student—"I did what I had to do to get by, and I did
it with half a mind" (27); "what a disengaged,
half-awake time it really was" (42)—reminded
me deeply of my own feelings and attitudes in
high school and college.

Rose's boundary status had to do with the
fact that he was not adequately introduced to, or
comfortable with, the world of scholarship. For
me, the sense of alienation had causes that were
psychological and social, and it manifested itself most tangibly in my confusion about the
way I looked. Throughout high school I dressed
in strange, "hippie" clothes—wooden beads; a
shiny purple vest; bright, clashing colors—in a
school where girls wore plaid skirts with matching sweaters and knee socks. As I got dressed in
the morning I often wondered why I felt so compelled to look unusual, and I could not give myself
a satisfactory answer. I had only a very nebulous
sense of what I now see as the paradox that was
stifling me: on the one hand I wanted desperately
to be noticed and heard, and on the other I felt a
deep, irrational fear of being exposed.

My senior English teacher was a loud-
voiced and thoughtful man named Mr. Grossman, whose AP class was legendary in our
school for its challenging nature. He taught
Giles Goat Boy, Portrait of the Artist as a Young

Man, and *The Crying of Lot 49,* books which fascinated me, as did Mr. Grossman's exhortations about them. He added to my growing sense of what literature was, and even as I focused my energy on preventing Mr. Grossman from calling on me to speak, I had plenty of confidence in my own ability to study and assimilate literary ideas. It was painful: though I knew I wanted to be heard, I remained silent, deeply afraid of voicing my own opinions, while other, mostly male, students raised their hands and plunged in. Mr. Grossman was aware of me, I could tell, as my teachers often were; he would see that I paid attention, and would look at me with approval and attempted encouragement. I knew he wanted me to talk and be a part of things, and his silent appeals comforted me in one sense—they made me feel noticed—but in another sense they always made me feel worse, too, because I felt I was letting him down with my refusal to speak and thus become a real part of the class. One day Mr. Grossman saw me walking alone in the hall. "Why don't you say something in class?" he asked me. "You know you have plenty to say, probably more than most of those other people who voice their opinions freely. Just cut loose!" I remember staring at him, flattered and excited, and resolving to be a completely different student, if only so that he would be proud of me. The next day in class, though, the fear was still there, and Mr. Grossman didn't do anything differently to help me change; nothing happened, except that I agonized inside myself because I had let my teacher down. In spite of the fact that I was intellectually competent in the subject matter, my confusion about my physical presence in the classroom gave me a sense of alienation and lassitude that had striking parallels with the young Rose's feeling that school was not a place where he could become fully engaged.

It is useful to notice that Mr. Grossman's methods corresponded to what our culture sees as male behavior. Unlike the female English teachers at my high school, he seemed to pride himself on being rough and confrontational. He was result-oriented, wanting us to come up quickly with answers, and if we did not, he gave us pointed advice. I know he wanted to teach all of us to think and read better; I imagine that it never occurred to him that the girls in our class might feel a disturbing and inarticulated confusion in their attempts to identify with, say, Stephen Dedalus. In introducing students to challenging books, Mr. Grossman probably did not think of considering either the gender of his students, or their response to the fact that virtually all the protagonists we read about were male. Furthermore, in spite of his obvious concern for students, many of my classmates, especially girls, were afraid of him. In my burgeoning fascination with volatile male intellectuals, I did not think of myself as afraid. In fact, I deeply admired him for challenging us. I fantasized about being able to talk freely—even very loudly—in class, to be, perhaps, a young version of Mr. Grossman. Yet something stopped me, something kept me mute, awkward, and ineffectual. I could not understand what it was that held me back, and I was annoyed at my own frustrating inability to cut loose in the way Mr. Grossman had advised me to. It was only many years later that I realized the nebulous thing that stopped me was, most likely, my femaleness, which did not have an articulated position in Mr. Grossman's classroom.

I think Mr. Grossman had closer relations with the boys in our class than he did with the girls. Though I do not know for sure, I suspect that he connected with them in the way that Jack MacFarland connected with Rose and his friends: a man initiating young men into the exciting world of male intellectual pursuits. When I read Rose's descriptions of his experiences with MacFarland, I felt jealous. As I analyze my jealousy I see that it is twofold—most obviously it grows out of the fact that I never had a teacher in those years who took much of an interest in me, but it is also a result of the sense that even if I had been in MacFarland's class with Rose I would not have been able to become an equal participant in the discussions, especially those that occurred outside of school. Evoking Woolf's sister of Shakespeare, I imagine myself as Mike's imaginary sister: If she sat in on those exciting discussions at MacFarland's house, Mike's sister would have wondered how she looked sitting on the couch. Were her legs close enough together? She would have imagined that Mike's friends, even MacFarland himself, looked at her in a judging way, assessing her appeal. When someone brought up a joke about women, she would laugh awkwardly, wanting desperately to be one of the crowd but feeling embarrassed in spite of herself. She would notice that women writers were rarely part of the discussion. Seeing that to Rose "knowledge [was] a bonding agent" (37), she would wonder at her own inability to feel deep bonds after an intense discussion of, say, *Heart of Darkness*. She would come to doubt her own capacity for intellectual work, feeling that her presence was an irritant to the men who were so singularly interested in "knowledge."

When I was in college, at a smaller, East Coast version of UCLA, I continued to feel marginalized for reasons similar to Mike's imaginary sister's, in spite of the fact that I was probably as prepared intellectually as Rose would have wished himself to be. In spite of my dream that once out of high school I would finally be able to express my own ideas loudly in groups, I retained the pathological fear I'd had in high school of opening my mouth in class. While I found some lectures and texts fascinating, my lack of engagement in class discussions made me take in much of my course material without much excitement or focus. I received very little academic guidance, and for reasons quite different from Rose's, my relationship to college was like his in his first year at Loyola—I felt that I was on the boundary.

At the same time, I remained obsessed with my appearance. I worried for hours about what I would wear, and then searched the faces of people walking by me on campus to see if they approved or disapproved of the way I looked. I continued the practice I had begun in high school of conceiving of my physical appearance as an elaborate edifice I needed to create in order to make myself appear to be an interesting person. That edifice was a shield against my doubts about my own worth. The painful paradox that had begun in high school continued: I tried to dress in a way that would seem eminently noticeable, and at the same time, I shrank from expressing my ideas in all but the most private discussions. My college appearance began to differ from my high school one, however. Instead of wanting to look simply unusual, I now wanted to look sexually attractive. If men were drawn to me, I reasoned subconsciously, I would be legitimate.

Though I wanted to encourage erotic responses, however, my own sexuality had little or nothing to do with it. My fear of speaking in class was the result of a paranoid feeling that anything I said would somehow reflect my deepest sexual identity and thus display me naked in front of everyone. I did not think of my ideas about academic subjects as mere rational opinions, I saw them instead as the potential expressions of a deep secret about myself that I did not want to tell. So I created what I saw as a socially acceptable sexual persona, paradoxically, to hide what I felt was my more latent, and private, sexual self.

My senior advisor was the first teacher who took a serious interest in my work. Though I felt that he admired me as a woman, his apparent fascination with my writing made me trust that his interest in my ideas was genuine. He encouraged me to stop by during office hours, and he asked me many questions about my views on a wide range of topics. He complimented my writing; he understood it; he offered feedback I could use. I was thrilled and felt that finally I was being genuinely understood and acknowledged by a teacher I deeply admired. His attention made me feel especially intelligent and charming, and I was delighted that my own unique ideas were capable of exhilarating someone so venerable. Soon, though, my professor began to close the door of his office when I came in, to open the bottom drawer of his filing cabinet and pull out his gallon-sized bottle of sherry, to serve me glass after glass, to move to sit next to me on his couch, and to kiss me and tell me I could understand him like no one else could. Even in my innocence I knew he was deceiving me with such a statement, but I secretly agreed that I was special, and in my quest for adventure I decided I was having an important mentor/student relationship with him. I still did not talk in class, and when he got tired of my expressions of self-doubt and began leaving his office door open again, I was too embarrassed to ask for more help with my writing or reading.

While at the time I felt singled out in a very special way because of that interaction, and rarely spoke of it for years, I realize now that attempted seductions by teachers are extremely common. While they can seem like mutually exciting and harmless adventures, they can do great damage when the student—usually a woman—comes to conclude that her ideas only have value when they are coupled with flirtation and sexual attractiveness. My experience confirmed the knowledge I had acquired, somehow, subconsciously, of how to encourage erotic responses in male teachers and how to seek out the kind of men who would act on those responses. Such knowledge comes relatively easy to most college-aged women, and while it may be wonderful in some contexts, it can do profound harm when it is used to cover the one thing that needs to be uncovered in the classroom in order for learning to occur. That one thing is the honest self, the fund of unique opinions, responses, and questions that make up a particular individual.

One of my first opportunities to gain access to that fund in myself occurred in graduate school in English, when I took a seminar with Sallie Sears, one of the few female professors I had ever encountered. Professor Sears had a welcoming classroom manner that, in its correspondence to culturally female behavior, was different from any I had seen before. She did "call on" members of the class, but not in the humiliating way I had become used to, where a teacher would call my name, wait impatiently for me to blush and stammer, then move on, exasperated, to the next person. Professor Sears waited for me to speak, and even if I was clearly uncomfortable, she would repeat and give a thoughtful response to what I had said. In her office, sometimes, she told me about her own nervousness speaking in front of groups; I felt that she understood my reticence and did not consider me a failure because of it. She got me to feel, somehow, that she wanted to hear what I had to say, not so that she could judge me but because she might herself be interested in my different viewpoint. I spoke a few times in class and finally began to appreciate the excitement that can result from sharing one's ideas in a complex and vibrant class discussion.

Though Professor Sears was erudite, she did not impose her knowledge on us. Instead, she would present a tantalizing question and then retreat for a while, listening to us dissect it. Her manner was gentle and noninvasive. She was very comfortable waiting. While she freely shared her own knowledge and concerns with us, she often refused to say anything that was "the answer" about the complicated material we were struggling with; she enjoyed ending her classes on a questioning note, encouraging us to come back the next time having thought and written more about the topic. I did not become a completely different student in her class, but I began to be consciously aware of—and thus able to begin to control—the incredibly potent censor I had in myself, which had prevented me for so many years from speaking up.

In trying to define exactly what it was that enabled that Professor Sears to encourage me to speak, I return to Rose's comments about what his students need. "The more I come to understand about education, the more I've come to believe in the power of invitation" (132). Professor Sears found a way to get me to understand that she was genuinely inviting me to express my ideas, with no strings attached, and under her welcoming gaze, I could blossom. Granted, I had prepared myself psychologically for a teacher like her through self-analysis and the desire to change, but her attitude toward me was different from any I had experienced before from a teacher. My life in large public universities had prevented me, as it continues to prevent countless students, from getting the kind of help from teachers that Rose rightly points to as crucial, especially for a student who feels, for

whatever reason, that he or she is on the boundary. Without consciously following a fixed pedagogical strategy, I think, Professor Sears acted
as the "midwife teacher" that Belenky et al.
describe in *Women's Ways of Knowing*: she
made a space that was inviting and then waited
for her students' own truths to emerge. "Midwife-teachers focus not on their own knowledge
(as the lecturer does) but on the students'
knowledge. They contribute when needed, but
it is always clear that the baby is not theirs but
the student's" (218).

When I became a teacher myself, I tried to
utilize what Professor Sears had implicitly
taught me about working with students. I found
that both composition, with its process orientation, and feminist theory, with its analysis of
women's particular experience, had laid theoretical foundations that could help me with the
kinds of students, women in particular, who
were handicapped, as I had been, by a fear of
being exposed in the classroom.

Two of my freshman composition students
at the University of California, Santa Barbara,
jump into my memory here. One is Darla, an
EOP student. She had waist-length, thick, curly
hair, and she clearly spent a long time spraying
it each morning. I never felt I saw her real face
because she had an artificial mask of foundation covering it at all times, along with heavy
mascara, deep eyeshadow, bright rouge, and
shiny red lipstick that never wore off or
smudged. She sat in the back of the classroom
on the first day of class and tried to keep her
mouth shut. When I addressed a direct question
to her, she looked at me with a fixed smile and
shook her head, remaining silent. She was the
kind of student Rose encountered in the Tutorial Center at UCLA, a young woman who had
been a star in her inner-city high school but who
was frightened by college, scrambling to find a

way to discover and perform what was expected of her. Darla's makeup and her tense smile seemed to be an elaborate disguise, a sad distortion of the idea of being "dressed up for school," an attempt to hide the pain of not knowing how to play the game. Her writing was tortured and convoluted, and it worked as a smoke screen against anything that she personally might have to say. She always came to my office when I asked her to, but *only* then, and she would do her best there to resist my attempts to find out more about the interesting hints of her ideas that had gotten through her self-censoring mechanisms. "What am I supposed to write in my journal?" was one of her favorite questions. However, the answer, "what you think of the material, what strikes you, what questions you have," as well as my handout that suggested all kinds of response prompts and techniques, left her confused. She wanted an assignment that had an answer she could look up in a book.

As I got to know Darla I was stuck over and over again by her self-effacing nature when it came to schoolwork. She was very attentive but always shrouded when the class discussed theoretical issues, and she told me privately that she was sure she had nothing to add. Yet if the conversation turned to nonacademic subjects, even in the classroom, she would relax and speak freely. She was not afraid to assert herself in general; it was theoretical matters that intimidated her. I felt that her physical appearance was a subconscious attempt to keep those matters at bay as she went through her days at school. By making up her face much more than necessary, she seemed, unconsciously, to be creating a literal mask that would hide a self she perceived as nonacademic. I imagined her moving from classroom to library to lab, going through the motions of scholarly life but always remaining disconnected from that life by her frozen smile and her very tangible facial shield.

With my feminist orientation, I did my best to be like Professor Sears and help Darla write what she thought, not what she imagined she was supposed to think. I like to believe that my trust in the importance and value of her own ideas got through to her. Yet even as she began to express those ideas, she seemed unwilling to let go of the belief that she existed on the boundary of a world—academia—that she would never really enter. Her hope was that she would intersect with that world satisfactorily enough so that she would get a college degree, but no more. I tried to show her that by responding in her own terms to academic material, she would "enter the conversation" with just as many rights as any other speaker, but her doubts about that possibility went very, very deep.

Kelly, a middle-class student, ostensibly had no doubts at all about school. She stared at me on the first day of class as I was not used to being stared at by college students: her high school–style expression said, "You are the enemy." She wore provocative clothes—miniskirts and off-the-shoulder blouses, for example—and was rather disruptive in class, clearly used to being simultaneously a "bad girl" and able to figure out what a teacher wanted. She flirted continually with the boys in class, often encouraging them to talk to her and answer her written notes instead of participating in discussion. I got the impression that her flirtatiousness with the other students was her way of distancing herself from engaging in the intellectual work of the class.

Kelly's journal was the thinnest in the class, filled primarily either with intriguing but undeveloped insights, or with statements like "I don't have much of a reaction," or "this story was boring," subterfuges designed to keep her own opinions at bay. Though she was intelligent and had a general sense of how to play the academic game, Kelly seemed to be choosing sexuality over scholarship. I often asked her to come talk to me, and she usually broke the appointments she made. When we did talk, I tried to look past her self-deprecation and focus on her ideas, eliciting and responding to her point of view. Her fear of expressing herself seemed to be quite deep: her impulse was always to doubt and mock her own ideas. I shudder to think about what would happen to her in the hands of a teacher like my senior advisor; her feelings about school, I imagine, would fluctuate wildly, according to his feelings about her, and she would end up hurt.

The confusion about who one is as a woman often gets connected, much more strongly than the question of who one is as a man, with the sense of who one is as a student. Too often women are afraid of pursuing their scholarly ideas because of an underlying sense that those ideas *in themselves* are not worthwhile. Like Darla, Kelly, and me, many young women, even those who have the skill Rose describes as the ability to "weave [their] knowledge into coherent patterns" (8), isolate themselves from the academic conversation because of their fear of not being legitimate theorizers. Actively, albeit unconsciously, those women censor themselves, retreating behind the shield of their physical appearances. Some students create other sorts of physical shields. Being overweight, for example, or worrying desperately that if one gains a pound one is hopelessly fat, can also form a shield. Because they can seem trivial, all such visual shields lend themselves to misinterpretation. Teachers can easily see them as petty obsessions, unrelated to schoolwork, which should simply be dismissed or looked disparagingly upon. Other teachers, like my senior advisor, can do greater damage by taking advantage of the apparent meaning of pseudosexual shields.

The result of such responses from teachers is that many middle-class students can experience a sense of alienation and lassitude that has clear parallels with that of the economically or educationally disadvantaged students Rose chronicles. Rose indicates that a sense of alienation from school is a result of the fact that, for whatever reason, one does not feel one has the status of a bona fide student. The status certainly seems unattainable when one is ignorant, as underprivileged students often are, of disciplinary structures, but it also seems out of reach when one has concluded, rightly or wrongly, for whatever reason, that one's opinions are not in themselves welcome in the classroom. As women often do, Darla, Kelly, and I each felt we *needed* to construct an elaborate persona that would hide our opinions from the outside world. Such a need grows to some extent out of the personal experiences of individual women, but it is also a socialized response to that fact that most public school classrooms in the United States, from kindergarten through university, still tend to be oriented around male experience.

The fear of exposing one's ideas transcends economic and educational status, as does a sense of marginalization. As I reflect on what happens to alienated women students, I am pushed to reconsider Rose's sense of a "boundary." He implies that the academic world is an edifice of sorts, filled with people who can play by the rules. His "lives on the boundary" are those of the students who have not been initiated into the ways of thinking that are acceptable within that edifice. When faced with the impersonal, seething presence of large universities, students on the boundary feel personally inadequate, replacing the fact that they simply have not received the right kind of training with the belief that they are somehow not good enough, not in the right league, not the kind of people who could possibly succeed in such an environment. I see such a feeling often in my EOP students, but since I have also seen it in myself and other middle-class students, my first response to Rose is that he should enlarge his sense of boundary to include well-prepared but psychologically alienated students like me.

Yet as I think further about this, I begin to question the notion of boundary altogether, to reject Rose's apparent sense that the academic world is in many ways a fixed system. If I subtract myself and other middle-class students from the mainstream, I notice that the "boundary" is getting awfully big. How many students are completely apart from it? If we consider all the people who exist as teachers or students in colleges and universities, we would probably find that those supposedly on the boundary greater outnumber those in the mainstream. For that matter, is anyone, even a full professor, perfectly assimilated into the realm of academic pursuit? Some people certainly seem to be. Since they do not seem to form anywhere near a majority of the academic community, though, maybe there is a problem with the very notion of a "boundary," which implies something merely on the edge of a fixed entity.

Rose himself seems quite ambivalent about the notion of a boundary. In spite of his obvious sympathy for people who are excluded from the academic mainstream, his narrative, and even the title of his book, indicate that he believes, on some level, that the academic world is a place with strict, exclusionary conventions, and that his initiation into it, as well as that of his students, involved learning to abide by those conventions. After all, it was his gradual coming to terms with Western intellectual history that made him feel that he was getting *off* the boundary. Along with this implication, though, Rose has a strong theoretical objection to the idea of a fixed tradition. In the conclusion to his book he discusses the danger of the "canonical orientation": "It simplifies the dynamic tension between student and text and reduces the psychological and social dimensions of instruction. The student's personal history recedes as the what of the classroom is valorized over the how" (235). He goes on to say that the teachers who were most important to him were those who "knew there was more to their work than their mastery of a tradition" (235) and acted most powerfully in their capacity as guides and mentors, not transmitters of explicit facts. So, though Rose has implied earlier in his book that boundaries are fixed, he contradicts that implication in this concluding argument. That contradiction, I would venture to say, is a function of his own ambivalence about the nature of the academic enterprise, an ambivalence shared by many academics. Moving away from the canonical orientation, as Rose advocates here, requires that we reconceive, or even abandon, our notion of a fixed academia, surrounded by a distinct boundary.

In abandoning that notion, Rose implies, teachers need to consider much more than raw subject matter: "To understand the nature and development of literacy we need to consider the social context in which it occurs—the political, economic, and cultural forces that encourage or inhibit it. The canonical orientation discourages deep analysis of the way these forces may be affecting performance" (237). I want to insist on adding "psychological forces" and "gender-role expectations" to the list of influences on literacy. Though we are becoming more aware of those influences, confusions about gender and physical appearance remain entrenched in

much of the academic world, as does the notion
of mainstream and boundary. The way a person
looks, for example, can still determine whether
or not he or she is to be viewed as an acceptable
academic. In addition to students, many female
professors themselves feel compelled to use
their physical appearance as a shield. In contrast to the Darlas and Kellys, who unconsciously use exaggerated sexuality and other
visual means to *mask* their ideas, professors
often make a conscious decision to use a non-
sexual physical appearance to shield their sexuality. Valerie Steele, in a recent article in *Lingua
Franca*, describes women academics' choice of
clothing as follows: "Certainly, femininity is
out. So is anything too conspicuous or body-
revealing . . . the majority of women in academia tend to minimize any sartorial eroticism"
(18). That minimization is not due to carelessness about one's image and certainly is not the
result of a lack of actual eroticism. It has to do
with the awareness that academic culture often
does not welcome or reward women who are
clearly both sexual *and* intellectual. Because
academic women are so invested in being the
latter, they purposefully might wear "frumpy"
clothes in the workplace as a way to get their
ideas respected. If so, they would be doing the
opposite of what the students I described do, for
a reason that is actually quite similar to that of
"sexy" students—they feel they must act as
though whatever they see as their actual identity does not belong in the world of ideas. They do
not feel, in other words, that they can "be themselves" and be academics at the same time.

Rose makes his belief very clear that we
need structures that will help students with
their most important need: "to gain confidence
in themselves as systematic inquirers" (141; emphasis added); professors, too, need such confidence. By examining their own ways of con-

structing physical and other shields, teachers can sometimes become more capable of working effectively with self-doubting students than teachers who are inveterately sure of their own ideas. Mr. Grossman's invitation to me to "just cut loose," though heartfelt, did not achieve its purpose, perhaps because Mr. Grossman took his own self-confidence as a matter of course and thus had great difficulty understanding my inability to speak. Professor Sears's impulse to wait and listen grew, perhaps, out of her own identification with my shyness. Though both teachers' invitations had the same general purpose—to get me to voice my own responses—the latter was more effective because it gave me explicit room to be awkward and uncomfortable if I needed to. Mr. Grossman would most certainly have welcomed my awkwardness if it led to more talking and thinking, but he did not manage to help me realize that; because he seemed stumped in the face of my silence, I was too. I do not at all want to imply that one must be shy oneself to understand shyness; however, it is important to realize that shyness cannot usually be dealt with by a simple admonition to speak. Professor Sears's own experience led her to see that by refusing to expect fixed, concrete answers she could, like a midwife-teacher, help me move most effectively toward answers of my own.

"Midwife-teaching" is one name for a framework that is built on ideals—nurturing, attention to the other sometimes more than oneself, acceptance of multiple viewpoints, preoccupation with process more than product—that are associated in our culture with female experience. It is a kind of teaching that is coming to be more accepted in academia, and though it can be seen as "female" or even "feminist," it is not at all dependent on the gender of teachers or students. In fact, in spite of any implications to the contrary, Rose himself often seems to act as a midwife-teacher in the classroom scenes he describes. He clearly has a profound desire to nurture the thoughts of his students and to avoid imposing a rigid structure of ideas on them. Furthermore, he has something else in common with Belenky et al. and other feminists in his insistence that social relationships are absolutely essential to learning. As he points out, the notion of self-reliance is "serious nonsense" (47); students always need encouragement, support, and frequent interaction with others in order to become fully engaged in their schoolwork. He recognizes implicitly, I think, that constructing any kind of shield against such things is inevitably self-destructive.

If I had had more "midwife-teachers," I probably would have had a very different experience of school. While at the time I thought my own psychological problems were the sole reasons for my inability to become fully engaged in classrooms, I see now that the methods my teachers used played a central role in my educational experience. I never once was required to participate in a small group in a classroom, for example. If I had been, I may well have found the courage to speak up, especially if, for example, the teacher invited the group to share the opinions of all members. I also desperately needed a teacher who would gently but relentlessly force me to articulate my own responses; like all shy students, I had plenty of things to say, and I suffered because no one in school seemed patient enough to find out what they were.

The perception that one is on the boundary, then, transcends economic and cultural status. Students who feel alienated in the classroom, for whatever reason, tend to construct shields to hide their own ideas. Teachers at all levels will do well to remember that learning occurs only when students can find a safe way to lower their shields.

Works Cited

Belenky, Mary Field, Blythe McVicker Clinchy, Nancy Rule Goldberger, and Jill Mattuck Tarule. *Women's Ways of Knowing*. New York: Basic, 1986.

Rose, Mike. *Lives on the Boundary: A Moving Account of the Struggles and Achievements of America's Educational Underclass*. New York: Penguin, 1989.

Steele, Valerie. "The F Word." *Lingua Franca* Apr. 1991: 17–20.

PART 4

STAKING A CLAIM

The four pieces in this section identify issues of research, pedagogy, and the profession that have been consistently ignored or excluded from our disciplinary discussions. Each author or group of authors seek to enlarge the purview of composition, staking a claim for new or "renewed" attention to perspectives that have been too easily dismissed and voices that have been too often unsolicited.

Helon Raines and Elizabeth Nist insist that "reforms in the profession and advancements in the teaching of composition" must include the participation of community college faculty. Based on interviews with community college teachers about professional issues identified by their colleagues and responses from well-known individuals in the profession, Raines and Nist invite the reader into a dramatic exchange of multiple voices. Sheryl Fontaine identifies what she feels are the tacit assumptions underlying our discipline's complete lack of attention to M.A. studies in composition. She claims that unless we reconceptualize the function of the master's degree in relation to the overall professional development of our graduate students, we will continue to promote an intellectually unhelpful degree, one which is, indeed, "terminal." Gary Hatch and Margaret Walters revive the work of Robert Zoellner's "talk-write" pedagogy. They explain what is mistaken about the various criticisms held against his work and argue that Zoellner offers one of the few real alternatives to the mentalistic pedagogy currently dominating the teaching of writing.

Nancy McCracken, Lois Green, and Claudia Greenwood criticize themselves and other researchers for having invariably overlooked the role of the teacher's gender in student-teacher interactions. Urging researchers to face the obstacles that have prevented attention to this concern, the authors reexamine their own research with this in mind.

14

Writing in the Margins: A Search for Community College Voices

Elizabeth A. Nist/Anoka-Ramsey Community College,
Coon Rapids, Minnesota
Helon Howell Raines/Casper College, Casper, Wyoming

◆● ───

Characters

Community College Voices

ANN ANONYMOUS	A colleague who does not wish to respond to the search questions as presented and who does not wish to be identified.
PAUL BODMER	Chair, English department, Bismarck State College, Bismarck, N. Dak.; past chair, Midwest Regional Conference on English.
JO ELLEN COPPERSMITH	English faculty, Utah Valley Community College, Orem, Utah.

Louise Deutsch	Chair, English department, Cape Cod Community College, West Barnstable, Mass.
Dan Jones	Chair, Division of Business, Humanities, and Social Sciences, Wytheville Community College, Wytheville, Va.; treasurer, Southeastern Conference on English in the Two-Year College.
Michael Kowalski	English/philosophy faculty, Snow College, Ephraim, Utah.
Keith Kroll	English teacher and researcher, Kalamazoo Valley Community College, Kalamazoo, Mich.
Katy Kysar	Part-time English instructor, Anoka-Ramsey Community College, Coon Rapids, Minn.
Barbara Lewis-Jensen	Part-time English instructor and full-time instructional assistant, Writing Center, Modesto Junior College, Modesto, Calif.
Karen Love	Teacher/newspaper columnist, Western Wyoming College, Rock Springs, Wyo.
Patricia Malinowski	Chair, Department of Developmental Studies, Community College of the Finger Lakes, Canandaigua, N.Y.; Coeditor, *Research & Teaching in Developmental Education.*
Mark Reynolds	Past chair, Southeastern Conference of Two-Year Colleges; editor of a forthcoming NCTE book on English in the two-year college; Jefferson Davis Junior College, Brewton, Ala.
Larry Roderer	Professor of English, J. Sargeant Reynolds Community College, Richmond, Va.
Toni Rowitz	Professor of Communications, Oakton Community College, Des Plaines, Ill.
Charles Taylor	Instructor of English and literature, Illinois Valley Community College, Oglesby, Ill.

Respondent Voices

CHARLES ANNAL	Division chair, Division of Arts and Sciences, New Hampshire Technical Institute, Concord, N.H.; past chair, National Two-Year College Council.
LYNN BLOOM	Aetna Chair of Writing, Department of English, University of Connecticut, Storrs, Conn.
RICK GEBHARDT	English chair, Bowling Green State University, Bowling Green, Ohio; editor, *College Composition and Communication.*
JANE PETERSON	Communications faculty, Richland College of the Dallas County Community College District, Dallas, Tex.; past chair of CCCC.
MARY SAVAGE	Consultant in multicultural education; storyteller/writer/teacher, Albertus Magnus College, New Haven, Conn.; actively works with secondary and college teachers of English.
RON SEVERSON	Writing 101 coordinator, University of Utah; on leave from directing the writing program at Salt Lake Community College; chair of the Western States Two-Year College Conference.

Chorus (Questioner voices, all participants in the pilot study)

BETH CAMP	Chair, English department, Lenn-Benton Community College, Albany, Oreg.
LYNN DUNLAP	Instructor of composition and literature, Skagit Valley College, Mount Vernon, Wash.
DALE EDMONDS	Dean, Division of English and Modern Languages, Portland Community College, Portland, Oreg.
NANCY FISHER	Professor of English and WAC director, Roane State Community College, Harriman, Tenn.
TOM FLYNN	Associate professor of English, Ohio University at Belmont, St. Clairsville, Ohio.

TAHITA FULKERSON	Chair, English department, Tarrant County Junior College, Fort Worth, Tex.
ARNOLD LAHREN	English faculty, Bismarck State College, Bismarck, N. Dak.
BILL LAMB	Program director of writing, Johnson County Community College, Overland Park, Kans.
HARRIETT LEITHISER	Assistant professor of English, Germanna Community College, Locust Grove, Va.
FAYE LENARCIC	Professor of English and dirctor of Writing-to-Learn program, Herkimer County Community College, Herkimer, N.Y.
JOE LOSTRACCO	Chair, Department of Humanities, Rio Grande Campus, Austin Community College, Austin, Tex.
DOLLY MALEY-TARVER	Head of English and acting coordinator for the Writing Center, Virginia Highlands Community College, Abingdon, Va.
JAMES O'NEILL	Chair, Department of English, Umpqua Community College, Roseburg, Oreg.
TERRY SHELLENBERGER	Writing Program Coordinator, Utah Valley Community College, Orem, Utah.
BARBARA UNGER	Writer and teacher of creative writing, Rockland Community College, Suffern, N.Y.

Investigators

ELIZABETH NIST	Teacher/writer, Anoka-Ramsey Community College, Coon Rapids, Minn.
HELON RAINES	Teacher/story-teller, Casper College, Casper, Wyo.

Reader

Setting

The time is now.

The place is here, on the page. You, reader, are a member of the play, so we hope you will write, too.

In our college classes our students begin by writing in the margins of the texts they read. Eventually, they write their own papers;

then we, their teachers, write in the margins of their work. Sometimes the voice in the margin isn't heard; at other times, the voice in the margin overpowers the voice in the center of the page. This play is an experiment. We invite you to join the conversation that follows. Please write in the text and in the margins.

ACT I

SCENE 1

Kathy Kysar, a "part-time" community college teacher, sits at a desk in the front of the room. On the top of the desk are eight piles of papers: four piles of thirty blue books and four piles of thirty research papers. It is the end of the term.

KATY KYSAR: I went to a national conference to satisfy the cerebral craving I experience at the end of every quarter, but I only wandered from panel to presentation to discussion. Sometimes I felt locked out by the rhetoric and jargon; occasionally I waded through the words to the concepts and enlightenment.

At a cocktail party, I finally found some "colleagues" (other single people of my generation). In a taxi on the way to a disco, we introduced ourselves. They were from Ivy league schools, teaching at Rutgers, Yale, and Cornell; I wasn't. They had Ph.D.s; I didn't. They had tenure; I didn't. They were critical scholars; I wasn't. There was a silent judgment of me: measured against these "good" (read the subtext) things, I was "not good." After that taxi ride, I learned to keep my mouth shut and tell everyone that I had taught in China last year, my only arresting accomplishment.

The next day I went to my appointment with a career counselor. I was essentially told that my M.F.A. was worthless in the job market and that she couldn't help me until I received a Ph.D. The assumption here was that a community college was not a desirable place to be and that I should get a Ph.D. and get a "real" job.

On the last day in an obscure hotel apart from the center of the convention action was the two-hour community college panel discussion. I took with me the anger that had built up for the whole conference, hoping to find my peers at last, hoping to leave the critical jargon behind and engage in energetic conversations about pedagogical topics. What I was greeted with instead was a small group of community college instructors whose presentations held no theoretical substance. They mostly complained about budgets and traded lesson plans. I spoke to the head of the committee for the following year and suggested some more challenging topics. He lifted his head slowly, a tired Eeyore, and looked at me with disdain.

Late that afternoon I was sitting in the Amtrak smoking section with an unemployed Ph.D. drinking Bloody Marys and deconstructing *Pretty Woman* on the television screen. I had finally found a place where I was wanted. Here amongst the cigarette butts in the basement of the dining car, I was an intellectual, free to play with critical theory and treated with respect.

I returned not refreshed and invigorated, but feeling depressed, cynical, and marginalized.

[She looks grimly at the piles of papers in front of her]

Four classes, thirty students each. My students need a lot of mentoring and encouragement. I feel I am wilting.

I'm tired of a system that dictates a hierarchy: tenured professors who teach critical theory are at the top; nontenured M.A.s who teach composition are in the basement; the college literature professors tenured at small four-year colleges are stuck somewhere in the elevator around the fifth floor.

It may be time for us to make some trouble, to join together in the basements of academe and despite our work loads, demanding students, and incompetent administrations, create a place where we are valued. We may be in the basement, but we're also closest to the ground.

SCENE 2

Helon Raines, from Casper College in Wyoming, and Liz Nist, from Anoka-Ramsey Community College in Minnesota, decide to draft a proposal for this study of community college voices.

LIZ NIST: By compiling average figures from information about faculty gathered in a national survey of 236 community colleges, we are able to construct a profile of the average community college writing teacher. This person is white, female, has a master's degree plus fifteen to thirty hours, and has taught between eleven and twenty years in a department of ten people. She is between forty and fifty and has a thirty-five percent chance of retiring in the next ten years. More of her students are women than men with their average age between twenty-six and thirty and increasing. Most of them are not English majors, so she does little advising.

HELON RAINES: Unless she is the exceptional one or two people in the department, she does not publish books, although she may publish a few articles or poems each year. She is more active in professional organizations than in publishing and will attend one or two conferences per year. Occasionally she gives a paper; more often she is involved in community service and departmental service. For these extra activities, she is likely to receive a pat on the back rather than any financial reward.[1]

LIZ NIST: Other than the fact that she may go blind from reading untutored writing that would be the equivalent of 2,500 pages of print per semester, she thinks she has a good life. She believes that "writing is a worthwhile human activity as well as a lifelong process," so she is dedicated to improving writing, and she is sustained by the belief that writing can be taught.

HELON RAINES: We believe that reforms in the profession and advancements in the teaching of composition will ring hollow without the participation of community college faculty. Sheer numbers of students who take composition in community colleges mean the voices of those who teach these classes need to be included in the central narrative of composition studies. Without our stories, the text of teaching writing is incomplete.

LIZ NIST: Our chapter develops anecdotally issues of composition in community colleges using multiple voices to identify those issues and multiple responses to extend the dialogue. In this way, we have intentionally generated a text of polyphonic voices, a text that does not insist on consensus. This project does not attempt to find solutions to issues raised but rather to privilege the dialogue of community college faculty.

HELON RAINES: In designing this project, we developed a four-phase plan for gathering information and synthesizing materials. The first phase was the pilot study to focus the issues. We taped nonstructured telephone interviews of community college colleagues to explore how they describe their academic discipline and their roles as professionals.

LIZ NIST: From these initial interview responses we identified four promising issues for phase 2. Originally, we had planned to conduct group interviews at national conferences as well as at community colleges across the country. However, for many reasons, we substituted a written survey sent to community college colleagues who, we hoped, could relate to us their specific experiences with these issues. We planned then to use their stories to describe the culture.

HELEN RAINES: In phase 3 we asked community college administrators, university faculty, and well-known voices in the profession to respond to the "central" narratives we collected. We mailed these "leaders" the draft of the text from the pilot questions and stories about those issues and asked them to record their responses, comments, questions both in the text and in the margins.

LIZ NIST: Phase 4 was the compilation and organization of their responses into the interactive play presented here.

We believe this project is a positive step in gaining more visibility for community college faculty. We also believe the published text indicates how important it is for these voices, previously underrepresented in the literature of the profession, to participate fully in the construction of the story.

HELON RAINES AND LIZ NIST: In this investigation then, we invoke a conversation. The participants respond with enthusiasm, commitment, and sensitive reflection, and they verify an eagerness for "talk" among those who teach and administer writing programs. Together their voices generate a polyphonic discourse in which dissonance challenges consensus.[2]

SCENE 3

CHORUS: (*a collage of voices, from telephone interviews*):

The four-year universities lack understanding or appreciation of the contribution we make. . . .

They don't do research on their undergraduate population to know enough about the kinds of students coming to them from community colleges. . . .

They don't seem concerned about this population in spite of its size. . . .

Articulation is also an issue. . . .

But the top issue is the number of part-time and adjuncts. . . .

Administrators in general, nationwide, have moved to part-timers—not for their expertise, but for economic reasons. . . .

. . . violates the mission . . .

. . . integrity of the teaching program. . . .

National mission of community college—who's looking at this and what are we finding?

And what about the relationship of community colleges to other entities in higher education?

. . . tensions

Address the difficulty of maintaining dialogue with teachers in the high schools. . . . How do we share our successful writing?

How can we get student work published?

Teacher burnout is another burning issue. . . . I went to a conference on women's studies held on a four-year college campus. The conference leader wanted to know what I was doing teaching at a community college.

Halfway through a patronizing presentation to community college writing faculty from across the state, a university writing program director suddenly paused . . . said he was so used to talking to TAs at his university that he just realized, midway through his "lecture," that we were all *the* "professionals". . . .

. . . extremely diverse philosophies. . . .

[The voices of the chorus come together in unison on four questions]

CHORUS: A philosophical question: how do we define ourselves and what we do? In other words, how would we describe ourselves as writing teachers if we were to be the subjects of our own histories?

A narrative question: how do we tell our stories and the stories of our students?

An information question: how does funding affect any or all of these areas in your college or in your professional experience?

A speculative question: if you could plan the future of community colleges, what would you want to occur?

ACT II

Community college teachers write responses to the survey questions gener-ated by the chorus (voices from the pilot-study telephone interviews). The respondent voices of community college leaders and university faculty also enter the play. We hope, reader, that you are here too—writing in the text and in the margins.

SCENE 1

CHORUS: How do we define ourselves and what we do? (Theorists or practitioners, science or art, classicists, cognitivists, epis-temic rhetoricians, other?) In other words, how would we describe ourselves as writing teachers if we were to be the subjects of our own histories?

BARBARA LEWIS-JENSEN: If I had to label myself as a teacher, I suppose I would say I'm a collaborator in a writing commu-nity. I discuss everything with my students from the creation of our course to the creation of the texts we read and write. When my students read, I read. When my students write, I write. We focus on all processes, all participants, and all discoveries in our community.

MICHAEL KOWALSKI: I would describe myself as a *craftsman*, one who teaches the basic craft of writing. In teaching a craft, one emphasizes doing it and redoing it.

JO ELLEN COPPERSMITH: I believe community college teachers must be practitioners but with an awareness of the theorist directing our work. As we strive for progressive new ways to excel in our work with students, often it seems necessary to become a defender of classicism as we link older knowledge into a greater understanding of the new.

PATRICIA MALINOWSKI: The description, I believe, that would de-scribe us best is "idealists who are forced to be practitioners." I offer this description because the needs of the students who are often the mission of the community college necessitate that we become very practical. Often students desire a "quick fix" to writing problems, which will allow them to survive in an increasingly complex world.

PAUL BODMER: The intended result is to help the student become a more reflective thinker and writer. I have defined my course as a course in thinking as well as communicating.

CHUCK ANNAL: I think that finally our goal is to make them indepen-dent of us, get them to the point where they don't need us.

CHARLES TAYLOR: I am a theorist and practitioner, so that makes me a generalist. My emphasis is on student-centered learning. I chose to teach in the community college rather than to teach in the four-year institutions. I am committed to good teaching, and community college teaching is where I find that good teaching takes place.

RON SEVERSON: As Charles says, we are practitioners and theorists, but my experience of teaching in a community college challenges the separation between practice and theory, teaching and research. While some academics theorize multiculturalism, for example, or seek it mainly in texts, community college teachers live it with their students, daily. Community college classrooms, in my experience, tend to be more pluralistic than university classrooms. One cannot confront the conflicts and possibilities in this pluralism without constant reflection. The theory/practice split makes no sense in such an environment. Perhaps pragmatism does. You teach, you learn, you teach better.

RICK GEBHARDT: I'm impressed—but not surprised—by the commitment you two-year college teachers have to teaching and by the sense of pride you take in the strength and successes of two-year college teachers. This pride and esprit de corps is justifiable, but does it also imply something of an us/them tendency to valorize two-year college teaching and underappreciate the teaching going on in four-year colleges and universities?

For example, Charles, if you taught in a liberal arts college, I think you'd say the same thing because student-centeredness and close faculty relationships with students are at least as central to the mission of that kind of institution as they are to two-year colleges and work loads usually are more conducive to them. Even if you taught in a large university, as Ron is doing right now, you would have found many classes and teachers that meet your idea of student-centeredness and concern.

LOUISE DEUTSCH: But back to this question, were we to be the subject of our own histories (or herstories), I fear we would most likely fall into the chasm of defining ourselves and what we do in preconceived academic categories. I think that just as women and other marginalized groups need to develop linguistic expression that more accurately reflects themselves and their mission, so do writing teachers in the community colleges. Until such time, even professional journals such as *College Composition and Communication* and *Teaching English in the Two-Year College* will remain inadequate and we will use our professional development dollars to attend four-year college conferences!

MARY SAVAGE: I've been thinking about this question and the responses, and this particular question strikes me as an odd start to discussion. I agree with Louise and Barbara's resistance to thinking of their work against already-made categories. Now I know we are always thinking in already-made words, but this start I'm afraid is likely to foreclose people thinking about ourselves narratively, as subjects.

KAREN LOVE: I agree. As I discussed these questions with other people in my department, our first response to such pondering as "how do we define ourselves" was flippant. "The emperor has no clothes!" (We get that way in the late spring when pressure builds.) But in our response, we saw that we are indeed, perhaps by necessity and perhaps by inclination, extremely practical. And we know we are doing a much better job than the universities in teaching writing because we have accumulated experience, years of positive interaction and sharing of ideas, opportunity for professional development (sabbaticals and travel money), and our college takes our work seriously, instead of handing it to inexperienced graduate students or part-timers.

LYNN BLOOM: Karen may well be right, that community colleges do a better job of teaching writing than the universities. Around the country, the trend in universities is to have freshman English taught either by TAs or adjuncts. Even those full-timers who want to teach freshman English can't because, with swelling enrollments, they have to teach upper-division courses. Universities entrust our most innocent students to our most innocent teachers. There are some advantages in this, but they aren't likely to outweigh the virtues of experienced teachers teaching (and teaching a lot more than writing) novice undergraduates, whatever their age and stage in life.

RICH GEBHARDT: But I believe the key factors here—taking writing seriously and having faculty members teach writing—are as true at many liberal arts colleges and smaller universities as at community colleges, and the availability of funds and time for faculty development are probably more ample at colleges and universities. Part-time teaching, of course, isn't strictly a four-year school phenomenon and at institutions of all types, the part-time cadre includes some very experienced and committed teachers. The grad-student writing teacher *is* particular to graduate institutions and as a person who worked in a small college for years before moving to a doctoral department, I appreciate Karen's reservations about them. Still, it's not true that all graduate fellows are inexperienced teachers.

TONI ROWITZ: I'm inclined to agree with Rick. Writing teachers at the community college level aren't any different from any other writing teachers. I see all of us faced with commensurate tasks, the shapes of which are altered by the ages and abilities of our students. I see the two-year college teacher as a practical, artistic, thought-provoking, challenging, evaluating nag, whose underlying love of the language gets him/her over the daily humps of apathy, lack of learning, distorted learning, negative attitude, and terror of the page/pen, typewriter, or word processor, exhibited by students. We must not only prepare students for transfer or career; we need to create a nurturing yet realistic environment that encourages risk taking and mistake making; and finally, we need to role-model writers, adults, failures, and success stories.

RICH GEBHARDT: I appreciate your sentiments, Toni. Clearly there are differences to be found—in students, work load, faculty expectations, etc.—among the thousands of postsecondary writing programs in the country. But my contacts with hundreds of high school and college writing teachers make me more comfortable looking for similarities—for allies in a tough fight.

KEITH KROLL: Well, in my opinion, we really need to overcome the false dichotomy of teaching and research that pervades community colleges and define ourselves as teacher-researchers. It is through teacher research that we can begin to empower ourselves in the classroom, the college, and the profession. The classroom of a teacher-researcher also works toward empowering students by encouraging cooperative and collaborative learning.

MARY SAVAGE: That phrase "teacher-researcher" is one that strikes me because it crosses education and composition. I wonder how it works in practice. People who talk about "writing process" frequently also think about "teacher research" (since much of that theory originally came from research). What I'd like to know is how often do college composition teachers do research as a routine way of setting goals and evaluating classes?

CHUCK ANNAL: I suspect that time is an issue for many. Trying to organize and disseminate research findings while teaching may simply be too demanding. What do you think, Jane?

JANE PETERSON: I find the range of responses here predictable, partly because the parenthetical prompt to this question implied various contexts that necessarily affect responses and partly because we do vary. Two-year college composition teachers are not homogeneous. Some of us *chose* to teach in community colleges instead of four-year colleges or universities; some moved to community colleges from high schools; and some ended up in community colleges because four-year or university jobs were not available but have stayed by choice, while others stay because they have no options and consider their positions undesirable.

What I find most compelling in the responses is the resistance to the assigned task in general (only a few of you even attempted philosophical responses) and to the prompts, which were largely ignored or politely disparaged. This resistance signifies to me both our greatest strength and greatest weakness as college writing faculty. When it emerges from an awareness of what is going on in our field (as comments from Louise, Mary, and Keith suggest), it marks our creativity, vision, or belief that what is possible for students and for us transcends established boundaries. But when it stems from embraced ignorance that is "justified" by our working conditions, it reveals an insularity I consider a weakness but which is probably more common in our community than this conversation suggests.

The central role that *students* play in our definitions of who we are and what we do seems to be to be the factor which sets us apart—for better and for worse—from our colleagues in universities. The "for better" relates to our being, for the most part, genuine synthesizers—those who live the interplay of theory and practice, who do not separate what we do from students, those for whom and with whom we work and learn. The "for worse" relates to the common misinterpretation of that synthesis, the belief among many of our four-year colleagues that we are incapable of such separation, a belief unfortunately promoted by a vocal segment of two-year teachers who disparage all theory and research as irrelevant to classroom teachers.

READER:

SCENE 2

CHORUS: How do we tell our stories and the stories of our students? (Think about Mike Rose's *Lives on the Boundary*.)

KAREN LOVE: This question demonstrates how an assignment, although given in all good faith, can fall short. The people in my department did not understand the assigned question. It seems like a prime example of writers misjudging their audience. This is some "in-crowd" language, the meaning of which we are not aware.

PAUL BODMER: Well, I'm not completely sure what the question means either, but I'll take a chance. I think we tell our stories and the stories of our students as we look closely at the process of writing. All writing must ultimately have a narrative line. And when we try to discuss how the creating process works, we do so by telling the stories of our experiences and our students' experiences. I am limited here in that I have not had the chance to read Mike Rose's book.

BARBARA LEWIS-JENSEN: Me either; Rose's book is one of my summer projects.

LOUISE DEUTSCH: Add Heilbrun's *Writing a Woman's Life* and M. C. Bateson's autobiographical volume. We need to "break the silences" to illustrate clearly and vigorously the kinds of "boundaries" that we have already broken through as well as those that continue to confine us. In fact, we're only just beginning to tell our students' stories of success through nontraditional means.

CHARLES TAYLOR: I'm actually interested in this question as an opportunity to tell stories about our students and/or about our programs. For instance, I recall Mildred, who entered the school wanting to become a nurse; she also had to take my beginning composition class. Over time, she did not succeed at the nursing program, but I worked with her as she wrote expressive essays about her chronically ill mother. Because of a lot of effort, Mildred earned a "B" in the class but soon returned to her job in the factory. Two years after the class I received a letter from her explaining that her mother had passed away, but that she had those class writing assignments that marked her relationship with her mother. Mildred felt that college had been worth it—she would return soon.

RON SEVERSON: I think *stories* are important, but I do question our reliance on expressive writing for its own purposes: developmental, creative, therapeutic, emancipatory, or otherwise. Theories of developmental psychology made claims about the development of children's abilities. It may be true that a child needs to write in an expressive mode before she or he can handle academic or professional writing, but I mainly teach adults who are fully developed cognitively. We need to help these students engage in the sort of writing that may help them gain the advancement they desire . . . and deserve. If Mildred wants to get out of the factory and become a nurse, she needs the opportunity to study the sort of reading and writing that goes on in science classes and in the medical industry.

PATRICIA MALINOWSKI: We "tell" our stories by passing on our success stories to our students while sharing our failures with our colleagues.

MICHAEL KOWALSKI: I believe we tell our stories in the lives of our students. A twenty-year-old college dropout (stop-out?) was waiting on me at a local video store. She said, "You know that research paper class was one of the best experiences I ever had in school." She had gained confidence and self-esteem from becoming a miniexpert on one topic.

LARRY RODERER: One of my most unforgettable students was a young man in the maximum security unit at Powhatan in Virginia. He received parole recently and now pursues a two-year degree in paralegal studies at the community college. He might have a future in journalism because he's such a good writer. He took several courses from me by correspondence but was difficult to work with at first as one who felt extra sensitive about any form of criticism. When he gained trust in me and in the college program, he never faltered. I don't know whether I helped him much, but I appreciated being witness to his progress.

TONI ROWITZ: We tell our stories orally to our colleagues, friends, families, and students as anecdotes, examples, warnings, or fables. Mostly, we *live* them in the way that we teach. Writing well and teaching others to do so is living or creating the stories of ourselves; what happens in the class—and outside of it—are the stories of our students.

JANE PETERSON: I like Toni's description, and the three stories told by Charles, Larry, and Michael typify our storytelling tradition as two-year college teachers: we usually tell stories that highlight positive effects on students and only occasionally mention the effects on us. We seldom speak in detail of students who have had an impact on us. The type of storytelling that Paul suggests (through examining texts) represents a more traditional form of research or scholarship fairly well accepted within the profession even when it comes from a two-year college teacher, as the response to Shaughnessy's *Errors and Expectations* demonstrated.

MARY SAVAGE: This past year I have been collecting stories from mothers of elementary school children on the Lower East Side of New York City. This has been powerful stuff. The struggle of ordinary people to live life well! Now the stories of people teaching in community college has to be powerful stuff as well. We just need more scope and time and a gentler occasion than these directed questions and answers.

RON SEVERSON: I haven't heard any stories today about the student who didn't much need us but who used the knowledge and credit earned in our class to graduate and get a better job or go on to a university. We tend to forget these students. Only our students can tell these histories.

CHUCK ANNAL: I'm surprised that no one's brought up the issue of talking about one's own successes and failures as a writer. I write along with students and tell "stories": about what happens along the way as I go through successive drafts, about my joys and frustrations. My hope is that these "stories" reveal me not as an authority on writing but as a person, like my students, struggling with the dynamics of written expression.

JANE PETERSON: I think we need to build on our tradition: continuing to tell stories but to more audiences, specifically students' stories to faculty in other disciplines, who do not often create opportunities to learn about students' lives, and to administrators, who have little contact with students and seem to forget they are people, not just numbers. And we need to write our stories, tailoring them to specific audiences for specific purposes: to future community college teachers (especially when we address high school and community college students of color) to illustrate the challenges and rewards of our work; to those within the profession to raise new issues and questions about theory or practice or offer support for existing ideas; to administrators to improve attitudes about our professionalism, illustrate problems of working conditions, and increase their sense of students as people; to legislators to educate them about what constitutes literacy as well as for the reasons cited for administrators; and to the public for two purposes—to gain their support in changing public education, which we are a part of, and to illustrate the value of higher education (recruit students and teachers).

READER:

SCENE 3

CHORUS: According to many, the most serious problems for community colleges have to do with funding and low budgets as these impact program development, faculty development, salaries and benefits (including professional development), teaching loads, and the employment of part-timers and paraprofessionals. Please comment on how funding affects any or all of these areas in your college or in your professional experience.

CHARLES TAYLOR: The most serious problem facing the community college is part-time instruction. I believe this exploitation is the future of the community college, and our only defense is unionization and professional organization of faculties.

CHUCK ANNAL: Unfortunately, Charles, you are right. More serious is the administrative philosophy that creates the problem in the first place.

Ron Severson: I agree. Seventy-seven percent of the writing courses at my [community] college are taught by part-time faculty who earn $780 per course. Some are qualified to teach; some are not. No writing class at my college has ever been cancelled for lack of a qualified teacher.

There is progress. Loads for full-time faculty, three or four courses per term, are reasonable. We have hired five new, full-time writing faculty in the past two years, in addition to a writing program coordinator. Given an incredible growth rate, however, this has only reduced our overall dependence on part-time faculty from eighty-five percent to seventy-seven percent.

Barbara Lewis-Jensen: Actually, funding has not posed as many problems at Modesto Junior College as it has at some state universities.

Mark Reynolds: I am not so sure that the funding problem is not more an administrative problem at my college and often at others. Administrators' priorities do not always put instruction, students, and faculty first. These areas often suffer because administrators apply available funds elsewhere. Part-time faculty are hired to make more money available elsewhere. Fewer full-time faculty mean increased class loads and larger classes, causing instruction, students, and faculty to suffer. Tight money means little or no money for travel or professional development, but often administrators misapply . . .

Chuck Annal: Administrators . . . who are these guys? But don't forget, there's also often serious infighting. Sad, but true.

Mark Reynolds: But often administrators *do* misapply what is available when they do not value instruction, students, or faculty as highly as they value physical plants, self-promotion, or large administrative staffs.

Rick Gebhardt: I could swear I've heard the same message — delivered in similar language — from department colleagues at a four-year college and at a doctoral institution. I don't deny that two-year colleges face special problems. But if the issue is support for first-year composition teaching, then all of us have a lot in common. One of the most common problems I'm hearing here is reliance on and exploitation of part-time teachers. Significantly, no one had any solutions to this problem; finding them is, I think, one of the key items on the common agenda of college composition.

RON SEVERSON: I for one don't believe a community college's reliance on part-time faculty to teach writing differs much from a university's reliance on graduate students to teach writing. An equal number of qualified and unqualified people teach writing in both arenas. Often, part-time writing faculty at community colleges want to make composition studies their vocation. On the other hand, many graduate students want to qualify themselves in other areas so they can some-day turn the teaching of composition over to their graduate students.

PAUL BODMER: Funding, or the inadequacy of it, affects all areas. First, salary funding in our state has been very stagnant with the result that faculty feel trapped and unable to see a very positive future. The low salary also encourages faculty to teach overload schedules to try to keep pace with inflation. The complete lack of funds for general faculty development accelerates the problem mentioned above because there is no chance to escape and meet with colleagues from across the region and country. While this is not just a problem with community colleges, it becomes intensified because community colleges do not enjoy the traditional reverence of their position in higher education nor society's value of their mission as universities do—nor do they have the foundation dollars and alumni associations to lobby for them with governmental agencies.

KEITH KROLL: In all honesty I have to admit that in my five years at Kalamazoo Valley Community College, the administration has never denied my funding requests for attending conferences—MLA (2), CCCC (4), MRC (2), etc.—particularly when I have presented a paper. In addition, they accepted my "Professional Development Plan," which awards academic credit for professional publications.

PATRICIA MALINOWSKI: For us, funding does severely limit the development of creative and innovative programs such as paired courses, i.e., reading/writing. Present funding also necessitates that we depend upon dedicated part-time faculty who often are difficult to find.

LARRY RODERER: One of the most stark experiences we had here with the budget occurred in 1985. I received an assignment at the prisons to compensate for not having sufficient seniority to stay at the main campus. The trade-off was to still have a job, and since then—now that the budget has improved—I've enjoyed full teaching loads. Tight constraints remain problems for us all and reflect themselves in our treatment of adjunct teachers, if not of full-time researchers and administrators.

KAREN LOVE: I guess our story is a bit more promising. We have a brand-new facility, our numbers are up, but we are holding the line on class size. We are making every effort to protect part-timers, and we continue to work toward implementing the standards of the Wyoming Conference on class size, faculty load, and part-time faculty. We see improvement on almost all fronts. Salaries are up a little, and we have a steady supply of professional development money ($400 per year each). We have been able to cut our class size to a maximum of seventeen for basic English and twenty-two for freshman comp. We have added the option of a one semester sabbatical at full pay, which made it possible to reduce our faculty load from twenty-eight to thirty-two down to twenty-seven to thirty semester hours per year. We are in a pretty good situation here.

TONI ROWITZ: In all but two areas, I'm also fortunate to work in a school that has sufficient funds, although work loads need improving, and we still do not pay part-timers enough.

LOUISE DEUTSCH: It's really easy to use dollars as a "rock in the road," but there will *never be* enough money to meet the actual needs. While we must keep the funding issues on the table in assertive and cogent ways, we need just as cogently to support methodologies, strategies, philosophies that empower us to get the job done well: collaborative, developmental, progressive, individualized means to counter the archaic "university model" that generally has nothing to do with us/our students/our work.

Chuck Annal: Louise is right: "There will never be enough money to meet actual needs," especially in public two-year institutions. I think it a little unfair, therefore, to blame unilaterally "administrators" who try to juggle funds as best they can. Indeed, the fault may as much be with us when we do not make clear to these people the importance of what we do so that enough dollars flow in our direction to make opportunities for professional development possible. If we have both the time and the dollars, then there should be no excuse for not being professionally current and aware and taking the time to give some creative thought to how we might better our plight.

JANE PETERSON: I think Mark raised an interesting point about distinguishing between changes in amounts of money available and administrative priorities—the actual allocation of funds. My sense is that few of us know as much as we should about funding on any level above the departmental one (I am thinking not only of how decisions are made at higher levels on our campuses but in our districts, counties, and states as well). As my own response earlier implied, I feel we (community college faculty in general and writing faculty in particular) need to become more proactive (and storytelling is one avenue open to us) in educating various groups who have an impact on work situations. To be effective, however, we first need to learn about the processes that create these situations and the values and backgrounds of our audiences. We also need to address the issue of the kinds of support traditionally not available to us—Paul's point about the foundation and alumni support that universities often receive.

READER:

SCENE 4

CHORUS: If you could plan the future of community colleges, what would you want to occur?

CHARLES TAYLOR: One hundred percent full-time employment is primary. I would also ask for administrators who respect teachers as people and not just parts in a machine. We as community college instructors have gone to college many years to prepare ourselves to be teachers. Can't we make our own decisions? I recognize that community colleges grew out of high schools and vocational institutions, but my feeling is that community colleges are still trying to grow out of the past.

BARBARA LEWIS-JENSEN: I'd like to see an integration of the process approach in composition, literature, and drama. Also, there needs to be more written work in subjects other than English. And we need more communication between the disciplines, more communication between junior colleges and the state university system.

LOUISE DEUTSCH: We should work to convince higher education to see community colleges as autonomous entities having identity, purpose, goals, and operational modalities. We are *not* stepsisters in higher education, nor are we the fifth and sixth years of high school or the path toward the "real" (four-year) college experience. Further, we are not the developmental/remedial dumping ground of postsecondary education. Neither are we "terminal" education preparing (i.e., "training") folks for blue-collar careers. We can and must witness to the stuff we're really doing.

MARK REYNOLDS: I would like to see faculties have a greater voice in institutional policy. I would like to see faculties given the wherewithal to become true professionals: the time and tools needed to be effective teachers and the funding for continuing professional development of their own choosing.

DAN JONES: In the future I'd like to see composition programs receive program accreditation from a national or regional agency, much like allied health programs do today. Accreditation guidelines could control class size, numbers of composition sections taught by each instructor, percentage (and training) of part-time instructors, training of full-time instructors, etc.

KEITH KROLL: There should be more emphasis on hiring full-time faculty, faculty as teacher-researchers actively involved in the governance of the college and in the profession. Empower students through pedagogy that values their knowledge. Reward excellent teacher-researchers with reduced teaching loads.

Assessment is here to stay. If we don't begin to do assessment, outside agencies will come in and do it. The role of community college faculty as teacher-researchers (who create, revise, develop the curriculum, and who assess their teaching and their students' learning) provides a genuine way to empower faculty.

RON SEVERSON: I would like to see the assessment model expanded to include a long-range assessment of the impact a two-year degree actually makes in the lives of our students *after* they leave our colleges. We might have to face some hard facts that the learning our students gain in many cases does not translate into significant life or career changes for them. I don't know. But if we found this to be true, and we analyzed the reasons why this were true, we might be able to restructure our curricula to make more of a difference in our students' lives. Or we might end up questioning whether an equal education in our society does actually provide equal access for many of our students who often face additional barriers of race, gender, or class. If so, we would need to take a lesson from Studs Terkel and help our *ex*-students tell their stories to a wider audience.

PAUL BODMER: I want community colleges to place a stronger emphasis on the value of an educated person, rather than the expediency of a trained person. Associate degrees, whether in a liberal arts curriculum or a vocational-technical curriculum, must contain the courses and pedagogies that promote reflective thinking and reasoning.

LARRY RODERER: Our future as community colleges depends on how well we perform our mission to practice the open-door policy and create opportunities in education for nontraditional students. Our teachers need security, advancement, cooperation, challenges, and variety. We need to continue to operate on a very comprehensive basis as full colleges for local people in our communities. The prison example is a good one to show how deeply we must reach into nontraditional areas of our communities and promote higher education for all those who might benefit by it, especially for those who would otherwise be a burden on themselves and society.

MICHAEL KOWALSKI: Most of all I would like to see government funds that would enable more students to devote full time and energy to their studies.

RON SEVERSON: I want to echo this comment. Many of my best students cannot reach their potential because they need to work full-time, while raising a family, while devoting themselves to a full load of courses, just to maintain the meager amount of financial aid they do receive.

KAREN LOVE: I want the same old things we have always wanted—smaller classes, fewer classes, higher pay, more professional development opportunities. Everything else will follow in the wake.

TONI ROWITZ: More money . . . more space . . . fewer students . . . and how about recognition from the four-year schools that our worth/abilities/value is equivalent to theirs . . . and finally, how about a society that recognizes the value of education and is willing to pay for it!

JO ELLEN COPPERSMITH: Greater awareness on the part of government representatives of the vital role of the community college, so they give priority to funding essential needs such as more full-time faculty and better classroom facilities in all of our country's community colleges.

JANE PETERSON: Most of our discussion here about the future seems surprisingly narrow and myopic, focusing on improved working conditions for writing teachers and increased respect for faculty, community colleges, and education in general. The subtexts I find in these responses represent feelings often articulated by two-year college faculty: anger, frustration, hope, and hopelessness.

CHUCK ANNAL: I'm surprised that only Paul said anything about the curriculum. I teach in a technical institute where students receive only a minimum exposure to English, humanities, social sciences, etc., and I am concerned about turning out a student who can write a computer program that will analyze the stress factor on a 200-foot bridge but who doesn't have a clue to why the Cambodian student sitting next to him might get depressed occasionally. I'm not sure that fewer students, fewer hours, and fewer part-timers will address such problems.

This is not to discount the consistent pleas for better working conditions, however. I agree that they need to be better. But as I said earlier, we need to be more aggressive and persistent in making our complaints known. If this means unionizing, so be it. If it means forming a strong national organization of two-year college teachers of English, amen. Finally, however, we must have the facts—we have to show that 150 students for one comp instructor adversely affects the quality of instruction. We have to show that fifty percent part-timers affects curriculum coherence and consistency. We have to demonstrate why thirty students in a comp section are too many. The people who make decisions on these matters will respond to hard evidence. But someone has to be persistent and forceful in presenting the information . . . and we're the only ones who can do that.

READER:

ACT III

A colleague who does not wish to respond to the questions as presented and who does not wish to be identified writes a personal letter to Helon and Liz. She expresses some common community college faculty attitudes and points to some important issues.

ANN ANONYMOUS: I want to talk about this whole project! I was startled by the vagueness of these questions. So, I called an emergency English department meeting to see if anyone else had any idea about how to answer them.

Only one of us had ever heard of Mike Rose, and no one had heard of his *Lives on the Boundary*. We thought it presumptuous that the questioners would assume that we had, as if to not know were to admit we were not part of some private elite. I guess we *are* more concerned with practice than theory. I have no time to read a background study just to understand the question because I have papers to grade. I have no idea whether I am an epistemic rhetorician or not. If I discovered that I were, I wouldn't have the time to do anything to remedy it anyway.

The dreamy nature of the speculation question seemed like it was meant for someone who doesn't work for a living. I picture some imaginary English teacher lounging on a chaise by the pool, popping bonbons, and pondering the meaning of work—Narcissus entranced by his own features.

We thought it presumptuous and condescending that the chapter title for community colleges is going to be called "Writing in the Margins," as if we were on the outer edges of the real action. The very title indicates the attitude of the universities toward the work going on at the community colleges where we are doing a large share of the teaching of writing in this country. Indeed the universities are on the margins of the real world.

LYNN BLOOM: Ann is too exercised about not having read *Lives on the Boundary*. Any book that's received awards from MLA,

NCTE, and *CCC* should be a household word in the profession. And, of course, it is a pedagogical book, not particularly theoretical, though philosophical.

I think, however, that Ann is appropriately offended that community colleges would be considered "marginal." The question isn't whether Harvard would consider community colleges marginal; it's where they fit into American higher ed, and they are certainly a big part of the central activity, and not at all marginal.

RON SEVERSON: Plenty of working-class people never knew they were working class until the concept of working class was created. No one is working-class because no one can be reduced to class. But the concept may have adequately represented how other people, i.e., those who did no manual labor, perceived those who did.

Now we have marginalized people. When we read professional journals about teaching composition, two-year college professors are definitely underrepresented, even though we teach over fifty percent of higher education writing classes in America.

As professionals we do need time to read, think, and write about what we do and what others do. We need to subscribe to journals, write for publication, and attend conferences. We need to demand time and financial support for these activities because they are part of the *work* we do for a living, not just superfluous activities those university nonworkers do.

If we are truly not on the margins of higher education, then we need to stop acting marginalized by being defensive about our relation to universities. Community colleges and universities have different missions. Community colleges accomplish their own mission better than univesities could. In my mind, that doesn't mean universities fail in their mission, or that community colleges would better accomplish the mission of a university. Professors from each institution might try complementing (complimenting) one another instead of competing. To do so, community college professors need to read and publish and university professors need to read what we publish. As long as we community college teachers don't define ourselves as central, others will define us as marginal. That's what this chapter is all about I think.

HELON RAINES: Yes, that is what this chapter is about. And as we suspected, we find in the culture of two-year colleges vast differences, including an absence of consensus on eradicating, ignoring, breaking, or using boundaries or margins. In fact, as we find with Ann, some respondents consider such language part of the jargon of a small group of insiders. Other more common differences include teaching loads, class sizes, students' preparations and abilities, administrative attitudes, institutional funding, individual philosophies. On the other hand, we find significant similarities including privileging students, as we also recognize their tremendous needs and abilities, valuing teaching writing, emphasizing the practical, understanding the significant role of two-year college writing teachers, and respecting the varied missions of community colleges.

We share concerns about the exploitation of community college teachers, as well as of part-time teachers, adjuncts, and graduate teaching assistants; about finding ways to meet the diverse needs of student writers in a multicultural society: and about the balance between theory and praxis.

We also share common goals, such as developing ways to eliminate exploitation in order to enhance professionalism; finding means to bring attention at all levels to the critical roles played by writing teachers; discovering avenues for teacherly conversations, inviting students' dialogue so they may assist in detemining what they will learn and how they will learn; developing curriculum, programs, and services that truly educate and enable our students; reestablishing the value of practitioner lore and rewriting the text of scholarship in composition with storytelling as a significant mode of constructing knowledge; affirming the "margin" of the composition text as a critical position from which many voices speak as contributors, correctors, questioners to generate the multivocal narrative of teaching, learning, and writing, and to constantly destabilize and shift anything like a static "center." In accomplishing these goals, we believe that the evolving text of composition will continue to resonate through constant reflection and criticism from many perspectives.

We find that almost all of the speakers in this play value difference, celebrate similarities, and affirm the necessity of talking together, working together, acting together to accomplish together our common goals.

LIZ NIST: Moreover, we see this conversation primarily as a beginning. Helon and I hope to continue this research by conducting group interviews and collecting narratives as we had originally planned. As you have seen, the responses to our written survey do invoke a conversation but as several people point out, the wording of our questions tended to foreclose our thinking about ourselves narratively, as subjects. We want to bring colleagues together in a relaxed atmosphere conducive to talking through our stories and concerns. It's possible our national and regional organizations could assist in this effort by scheduling such sessions in conference programs.

We also hope that you, good reader, have entered into this conversation as you have deconstructed and reconstructed the text. Your marginal notes, comments, observations, and questions are important for future directions in this ongoing challenge to tell our stories. Please do send us your responses—even a copy of your annotated text—anything you would like to contribute to our continuing study of the culture of community colleges.

Helon Raines
Casper College
125 College Drive
Casper, WY 82601
(307) 268-2502

Liz Nist
Anoka-Ramsey Community College
11200 Mississippi Boulevard
Coon Rapids, MN 55433
(612) 422-3308

A Beginning

Notes

1. This composite sketch is based on information from a national survey sent to all member colleges of the American Association of Community and Junior Colleges; information based on the fall term of 1987 was returned from 236 colleges. Much of the information given here also was reported by Helon Raines, "Is There a Writing Program in This College?" CCC 41 (1990) 151–65.

2. All of the responses in the play appear as written by the "characters"—direct quotation, as cited—without significant changes in the text, although in places we added transitions and condensed paragraphs.

15

Resuscitating a Terminal Degree: A Reconceptualization of the M.A. in Composition

Sheryl I. Fontaine/California State University, Fullerton

The first graduate programs in rhetoric and composition were established only a little over twenty years ago (Chapman and Tate 127). In the history and development of these and other programs, we can *read* our discipline. Any particular set of program goals, graduate courses, and faculty profiles is a concrete representation of our abstract beliefs about what it means to be a composition specialist, to study literacy, written language development, writing pedagogy, and the construction of written texts. And as composition becomes increasingly massive and diverse, the selections that we make about what to include in our graduate curricula shape the discipline by affecting students' and colleagues' perceptions, valorizing certain texts, and promoting particular viewpoints.

This relationship between our graduate programs and the character of our discipline lends special significance to the handful of books and essays that describe and/or analyze graduate study in composition. Covino, Johnson, and Feehan in 1980 and Chapman and Tate in 1987 used surveys to find out how universities were designing and implementing doctoral studies in rhetoric. Janice Lauer discusses graduate study in "Composition Studies: Dappled Discipline," as does Louise Wetherbee Phelps in "The Domain of Composition." And the 1989 Modern Language Association publication *The Future of Doctoral Studies in English*, includes Bettina Huber's "Report on the 1986 Survey of English Doctoral Programs in Writing and Literature" and essays by Gary Waller, Richard Lloyd-Jones, and Andrea Lunsford and Janice Lauer that characterize doctoral study in composition in relation to Ph.D. programs in English. Together, these works serve as useful points of reference for the discussion and analysis of graduate study in composition.

But something is missing: These discussions of graduate study make reference *only* to the Ph.D.; the M.A. is never mentioned. I must admit to having been struck by this observation only after I found myself with the opportunity to teach composition courses designated as being at the *master's* level of graduate study and to propose a *master's* degree or specialization in the field. Until this time, I suppose that I had unconsciously assumed that an M.A. program would replicate, with fewer credit hours, the doctoral program I had completed and had already cloned in a doctoral program I had helped design for a major research university: a course on research, one on pedagogy, one on theory, and one wild-card "topics" course. But now that I have a personal stake in the courses and a personal connection to the students, I find myself wondering what an M.A. program in composition *should* be. My own nationwide survey of 243 graduate programs had revealed that twenty-five percent of the M.A.-granting institutions who responded offer degrees or concentrations in composition; another fifty-three percent offer one or more courses in composition. Given the impressive number of schools with master's work in the discipline, why have M.A. studies been virtually ignored in our professional discussion of graduate study? What assumptions about the discipline, graduate students, and professional development are behind this lack of attention?

Attitudes Toward the Master's Degree

On the surface, the neglect of either M.A. programs in composition or the M.A. portion of an M.A./Ph.D. program in the field is quite innocent. Most scholars share my own initial assumption that master's study prepares students for doctoral study in the same way that most bachelor's programs prepare students for the M.A., offering courses similar to those in graduate programs, but whose intensity and concentration is less acute. In my survey, I found that the composition and rhetoric courses most often required for an M.A. degree or an M.A. concentration in the field were the same as those required in Ph.D. programs (Huber 154)—"Theories in Composition," "Rhetoric," "Teaching Methods," and "Research Methods." If we accept the most common Ph.D. program as our model, then there seems to be little reason for separate discussions about the M.A.; they are implicit in our discussions about the Ph.D.

But there may be a more deep-seated reason that our discipline—and others—have given so little professional attention to the master's, a reason rooted in the early history of the M.A. degree itself, a reason that is potentially harmful to our students and to composition. Richard J. Storr explains that in the late eighteenth century many "Americans did, of course take the Master of Arts degree, qualifying for it by staying alive and out of trouble for three years after graduating from college and by giving very modest evidence of intellectual attainments" (*Graduate Education* 1). At this time, many faculty members believed that the M.A. was customarily awarded "to all college men who three years after graduation were not in jail" (Rudolph 336). In the mid-nineteenth century, one Harvard professor was reportedly certain that there existed a faculty group that was "disposed to claim for every blockhead, who [was] a graduate of three years standing, a vested right to the title of master of arts" (Storr, *Graduate Education* 48). Even when students began to *earn* their master's degrees by completing course work rather than merely completing residency, the degrees were not considered "advanced degrees." American higher education sought to establish systematized graduate study whose defining capstone—the Ph.D.—would parallel the advanced degrees of European universities. When this finally happened, the M.A. became infinitely second-rate.[1]

I heard echoes of these nineteenth-century attitudes in my survey. Several respondents from M.A./Ph.D.–granting institutions described the master's degree as "worthless," attaining value only if it becomes the basis for Ph.D. study. This view brings to mind an officially unconfirmed but persistent perception of graduate students, one I held when I was in graduate school and have had described to me since by the graduate students I teach. Getting accepted into an M.A. program is relatively easy as compared with getting into a Ph.D. program. Indeed, the scuttlebutt among graduate students is that at schools with M.A./Ph.D. programs, the former is used to "weed out" undesirable students, that faculty have little vested interest in the students who enter the M.A. program, but the school's and, consequently, the faculty's reputations are wrapped up in the quality of its Ph.D. students.[2]

A similar, if less harsh, estimation of the master's degree is suggested by schools that offer the M.A. as their highest degree. The unspoken measure of the success of these graduate programs is the number of students who continue their graduate study at the doctoral level. While the programs' financial security may depend on the number of master's students they enroll and their intracampus reputation may rely, in part, on the number of students who complete their degrees, the prestige and status of any master's program seems to be determined by the quantity and quality of the doctoral programs it feeds students into.

This belief, inbred through decades of academic generations, that an M.A. degree is less valued by faculty than the Ph.D., that M.A. students are less valuable and less worthy of scrutiny and attention than Ph.D. students, offers another explanation for the lack of regard scholars have given M.A. studies in composition.

Consider how this belief is further revealed by the position research holds in graduate study. Historically, the doctoral dissertation, as an example of "original research," stands as the mark of distinction between the Ph.D. and the M.A. As fine as any individual master's thesis may be, on the whole, the thesis requirement in M.A. programs is not universal and when it does exist, represents, as compared with the Ph.D. thesis, a relatively small portion of the degree program.

The emphasis that Ph.D. programs initially placed on original research was as closely connected to America's desire to emulate European (particularly German) universities (Storr, *Beginning* 31) as it was to an individual discipline's desire to proliferate its intellectual territory. But once these doctoral programs were established, keeping up with the Europeans lost its appeal, and advancing intellectual territory became a primary concern. Indeed, as disciplines matured, constructing increasingly well-organized professional behaviors, the importance of having doctoral programs that would replicate—and even advance—the work of the discipline, grew commensurately. Richard Ohmann has explained that as professions take shape, they do so by controlling access to a particular body of knowledge and a particular kind of work, i.e., research (250). M.A. students are kept *just* outside the borders of the discipline. We train them in programs whose structure and content replicates the Ph.D. program, but preserve their outsider status until deemed worthy of access to our Ph.D. programs. The nearly religious regard with which graduate schools have come to hold research is reflected in Albion Small's 1905 proclamation: "The prime duty of everyone connected with our graduate schools is daily to renew the vow of allegiance to research ideals. . . . The first commandment with promise for graduate schools is: Remember the research ideal, to keep it holy" (Storr, *Harper's* 159).

And so as composition, a relatively young discipline, sought professional recognition for itself, it privileged the original research that traditionally distinguishes Ph.D. programs and has become the accepted "mark" of an established discipline. In doing this, composition is using research at once to court the approval of other disciplines and to serve as the ultimate definition of its professional membership.

These attitudes, that M.A. programs are validated only in relation to Ph.D. programs and that the original research of Ph.D. programs is the true identification card of the discipline, makes our inclination to reproduce the doctoral course of study in our M.A. programs less innocent than we may have thought.[3] By replicating the Ph.D., we award it with the validation that comes with being an ultimate model and goal for academic study, the validation that causes all other degrees to stand in its shadow and to vanish once the doctorate is earned. And as a consequence, M.A. students lose their sense of professional place in the discipline and M.A. programs lose whatever particular significance they could have for students and for composition.

Reconceptualizing the Degree Program

So what if we *do* accept that the professional attention denied M.A. studies is, in part, a result of inbred, but nonetheless harmful prejudices against master's programs and in favor of doctoral programs? Unless we change the way we actually conceptualize the master's degree and its possible contribution to and position in the professional development of our students and our discipline, then our admission of prejudice will effect little change. We can begin this reconceptualization by identifying characteristics particular to the discipline of composition and to our M.A. students, characteristics that should affect the assumptions on which our master's programs are based.

Begin with the fact that, unlike courses in most disciplines, composition courses exist almost exclusively at the graduate level. Except for students at those very few schools that offer one or two undergraduate courses in composition (this number is augmented if we liberally include courses in *doing* expository, autobiographical, creative, or other kinds of writing), undergraduates get, at most, a casual sense of the discipline from the one or two specialists in the department, freshman composition instructors who offhandedly refer to the discipline, graduate student hearsay, or the limited experience available to undergraduates as peer tutors in a writing center. But there is no established undergraduate major — or minor — in composition. Consequently, most students have no systematic introduction to the discipline until graduate school. Many master's students choose composition as a field of study only after entering literature programs. Or they do so with a very shaky, often inaccurate sense of what the discipline is (see Axelrod for further discussion of this subject). And even those literature students who take individual composition courses to complement their literature degree, often have no idea about what they are taking. I have discovered that these students tend to enroll in a single composition seminar because they believe (and probably with good cause) that it will make them "more employable" or because their graduate advisor has recommended it or because it is a required adjunct to the teaching assistantship that is giving them minimal financial support.

Now consider the diversity of student background, experience, and professional goals in an M.A. program. Students entering a Ph.D. program in the humanities generally share a common goal: to teach at a university and produce scholarly research and writing. Using my survey of M.A. programs as a source of information, I found that students entering M.A. programs across the country have many goals in addition to that of continuing their studies in a Ph.D. program: improving their position and pay as high school teachers, teaching in or administrating educational programs in community colleges, becoming professional writers, working with technical writing, satisfying their curiosity about certain academic subjects. While Ph.D. programs find themselves faced with the pressures of a diverse student body, one that has "become multilingual, multiracial, and mixed in social class" (Lanham 73), M.A. programs must add to this the diversity of professional and personal intention that characterizes their students.

The Field-Coverage Principle: Problems and Alternatives

Recall that most of the M.A. programs that responded to my survey reported a set of core courses, "Theories in Composition," "Rhetoric," "Teaching Methods," and "Research Methods."[4] I certainly cannot know from course names exactly what happens in the classroom. Nonetheless, the names result from a process of ordering and codifying the discipline, of abstracting what are perceived to be its most valuable ideas and generalizing them under a set of course names. As such, the names shape the discipline they are representing and the perceptions of others about the discipline (Armstrong and Fontaine). The names of this core set of courses, become the four separate informational categories that define composition for new students and for faculty outside the field (many of whom are members of our departments). The limits of such a definition are stretched even further at schools with only one or two composition specialists to teach all the composition courses and run all the various programs. The number of core courses must then be reduced, forcing faculty to select the one that will have the responsibility of "defining" the discipline for students.

At one time, the "grid of literary periods, genres, and themes in the [course] catalog was a clear expression of what the [literature] department was about" (Graff 8), justly representing the theory-less, ideology-free array of topics collected under its rubric. But now, in the post–New Critical era, this grid is no longer adequate to introduce students into a discipline that includes among its integral perspectives Marxist theory, feminist theory, and cultural studies. Similarly, the theory, rhetoric, teaching, and research grid, our own version of a "field-coverage model," does not adequately represent composition, a discipline bursting with ideological discussions and webbed with interconnections. As

Gerald Graff says about the literary grid, it is not the *fact* of compartmentalization that is a problem, it is the apparent *disconnection* among the compartments.

Courses selected according to the field-coverage principle, do not give to students who enter our M.A. programs with comparatively little knowledge of the discipline a true sense of what it is to study composition. That is, designing a graduate program with the intent of achieving "field coverage," we give students the impression that the discipline being "covered" is inherently and agreeably defined by a static set of informational units. By separating composition into the topics of theory, rhetoric, teaching, and research we belie its evolution and the way composition teachers/scholars have come to look at the written word, at student writers, at ways to gather information and to make knowledge. This model does not sufficiently represent the intellectual and personal positions and struggles that have become so familiar to us that we forget to identify them as distinctive characteristics of our discipline.

In reconceptualizing the master's program in composition, I suggest that we no longer use "Theories in Composition," "Rhetoric," "Teaching Methods," and "Research Methods" as our core courses. We need to reenvision the courses that invite students into composition and place the traditional "core courses" much later in our students' professional development, using them not as introductory courses but as specialized, advanced ones.

Let me explain. We would ground graduate study at the M.A. level in a "conflict model" of the discipline (Elbow, *What Is English?* 60). We would design our courses and programs with the assumption that composition is not defined by a consensus of fixed, eternally accepted set of categories, but by conflict, by various and changing theories and ideologies, by numerous moments of consensus followed by equally numerous moments of disagreement.[5] Moreover, our master's courses should take as their central purpose letting students identify this conflict and variety in the discipline and experience it as it emanates from their own histories and conceptual priorities, from their encounters with students, colleagues, and texts.

Courses in an M.A. program such as I am suggesting might, for example, include one on "Myself as a Writer." Placing students' own learning and writing processes at the center of study, this personal study could be complemented with essays, like those collected in Tom Waldrep's book, *Writers on Writing*, in which writers and composition specialists talk about their own writing habits and practices, leaving room for the reader to speculate about the connection between personal writing behavior and the professional understanding of writing. Composition was established on personal stories and experiences. Thanks to early pieces by writers like Peter Elbow and Ken Macrorie, composition remains forever grounded in the vital relationship between our personal experiences (as writers and teachers) and professional generalizations. The course I am sketching would let students explore this relationship in their own lives and in the writing of professionals, giving them a strong, essential understanding of the way compositionists view the world.

Master's students might take a writing course that would put them in the position of being novices, producing, alongside the more familiar form of academic prose, writing that is as unfamiliar to them as it will be to their students—autobiographical, biographical, or even creative writing. Students may come to a much fuller understanding of the process of writing and teaching by taking a course in which they "study" discourse by creating it, following Kinneavy's or Moffett's or Britton's or others' rubrics, and learning about peer groups by being in them and about required prewriting or journal exercises by doing them.

Another course could look at the written discourse of the discipline. This would not be the traditional course in which one beleaguered professor routinely critiques students' academic writing and assigns weekly recitations. Rather, this course could use as its texts current issues of composition journals. Students would be asked to subscribe to different journals and then to read with an eye to identifying what "story" preceded or served as a catalyst for the articles. What are the questions that are being debated? What is the context that seems to be surrounding them? What would you need/want to read next?

In experiencing—and coming to identify—the irregularities and contradictions of the discpline, its search for answers and agreements, students can *become* compositionists. For it is not by accumulating facts that we become members of a discipline; it is by embracing its ways of seeing and talking about a particular part of the world. If our M.A. programs can help students do this, then the once-benign courses that attempted field coverage, will lose their sense of consensus and inactivity, becoming enlivened by their position in a dynamic and diverse discipline. That is to say, the courses that had divided the discipline into disconnected categories of information would now be presented to doctoral students who have gained, through their master's study, a clear understanding of the problems, issues, and ways of inquiry that define composition. The original research that doctoral students must complete would become part of a slow evolution of personal, original inquiry.

Students cannot acquire this understanding of the discipline unless we reconceptualize the way novices enter composition, the way we want them to construct (and have constructed) their perception of the discipline. Unless we rename the categories of the discipline, based on a new set of assumptions about what should be the driving perception behind the courses, then we have not made any essential changes in the way we think about composition or about the master's portion of students' professional development.

Rather than leaving our programs with an accumulation of information and little change in their own way of thinking, students will leave with a vision of writing and teaching that can be shared with others in our discipline, that was arrived at through personal inquiry. Students who finish our programs and return to graduate school or to high school classrooms or business complexes or publishing houses or even their own houses, will have received a terminal degree that does not end in an intellectual "straight line." They will have acquired a way of thinking about writing that can be carried into any professional situation. And we will have designed programs that truly show the workings of our discipline, a discipline that is not about lists of topics and books but about the processes of writing, teaching, looking at written text, and understanding how these texts can change our lives.

Although the last paragraph provides the traditionally expected closure to this essay on M.A. programs in composition, it does not in any way complete discussions on the topic. The courses I have briefly described are better generic sketches than specific examples. The assumptions I outline only *begin* to delineate what might distinguish master's and doctoral levels of study. While there may be almost no formal discussion of the master's programs in composition, responses to my survey suggest that many of the faculty teaching courses and designing programs are having their own private discussions with their colleagues. My hope is that this essay will help to make these discussions public, to serve as a point of reference, disagreement, or question from which we can examine our attitudes about the master's and initiate our reconceptualization of the M.A. in composition.

Acknowledgments

I would like to thank my department for the financial support of my survey research.

Notes

1. Richard J. Storr has commented on the fact that "although the master's degree is much the older degree in the United States, difficulty in defining that degree has been perennial since institution of the Ph.D. degree. The relation between the two degrees has been constantly at issue, and the issue has not been whether the doctorate is a master's plus something added but whether the master's is simply something less than a Ph.D.—a fetal doctorate" (*Beginning* 47).

2. The real sense of the appellation "terminal" master's degree comes through in the story of a woman who passed her M.A. exams only to have her accomplishment completely diminished by the graduate committee at her school, which made determinations about whether M.A. students would be accepted into their Ph.D. program. Although this woman had not requested admission, nor had plans to enter any Ph.D. program, she received a letter from the committee informing her that, based on her performance in the M.A. program, she would not be accepted into the Ph.D. program; her master's degree would be terminal.

3. Unlike the evolution of graduate education in many disciplines, composition graduate programs established in departments predominated by Ph.D. students historically preceded those established in departments predominated by M.A. students (Huber 157). Given that M.A. studies in composition appeared *after* Ph.D. studies, *after* the discipline had established and reflected upon the nature of its graduate preparation, this unreflective replication of the Ph.D. and the scant disciplinary attention devoted to M.A. studies may be less easy to overlook than in other disciplines.

4. The names I use here are either quoted exactly from the course lists I was given or are very close versions of names such as, "The Fundamentals of Teaching Composition," "Approaches to Teaching Writing," or "History and Research Methods."

Certainly there were many other composition courses named by the eighty-seven schools who reportedly offer them, some less traditional-sounding than others. But even apparently innovative course names, like "Language Bias," "Organizational Communication," and "Contemporary Urban Problems," run the risk of defining composition for novices as a set of disconnected units of information.

5. Gary Waller describes a doctoral program that seems to be based on a principle similar to the one I am describing. Using the Carnegie Mellon University program as an example, he argues that doctoral programs should be founded on structural principles that introduce students to a set of problems and issues that faculty believe defines the ways the discipline at large should think about the study of writing. However, his list— "quantitative and empirical research, the study of the composing process, the history of rhetorical theory, invention, protocol analysis, the importance of educational computing, and discourse analysis" (113)—seems much more focused on issues and information than it does on problems or ways of thinking.

Works Cited

Armstrong, Cherryl, and Sheryl I. Fontaine. "The Power of Naming: Names that Create and Define the Discipline." *Writing Program Administration* 13 (1989): 5–14.

Axelrod, Rise. "Designing an M.A. Program in Composition: Purpose and Audience." Conference on College Composition and Communication. Boston, 23 Mar. 1991.

Britton, James N., et al. *The Development of Writing Abilities (11–18)*. London: Macmillan Education, 1975.

Chapman, David, and Gary Tate. "A Survey of Doctoral Programs in Rhetoric and Composition." *Rhetoric Review* 5 (1987): 124–86.

Covino, William, Nan Johnson, and Michael Feehan. "Graduate Education in Rhetoric: Attitudes and Implications." *College English* 42 (1980): 390–98.

Elbow, Peter. *What Is English?* New York: MLA, 1990.

———. *Writing Without Teachers.* New York: Oxford UP, 1973.

Fontaine, Sheryl I. "M.A. Programs in Composition: Existing Courses of Study." Conference on College Composition and Communication. Boston, 23 Mar. 1991.

Graff, Gerald. *Professing Literature: An Institutional History.* Chicago: U of Chicago P, 1987.

Huber, Bettina J. "A Report on the 1986 Survey of English Doctoral Programs in Writing and Literature." Lunsford, Moglen, and Slevin 121–75.

Kinneavy, James L. *A Theory of Discourse.* New York: Norton, 1980.

Lanham, Richard A. "Convergent Pressures: Social, Technological, Theoretical." Lunsford, Moglen, and Slevin 73–78.

Lauer, Janice. "Composition Studies: Dappled Discipline." *Rhetoric Review* 3 (1984): 20–29.

Lloyd-Jones, Richard. "Doctoral Programs: Composition." Lunsford, Moglen, and Slevin 15–20.

Lunsford, Andrea, and Janice Lauer. "The Place of Rhetoric and Composition in Doctoral Studies." Lunsford, Moglen, and Slevin 106–10.

Lunsford, Andrea, Helene Moglen, and James F. Slevin, eds. *The Future of Doctoral Studies in English.* New York: MLA, 1989.

Macrorie, Ken. *Telling Writing*. 3rd ed. Rochelle Park, NJ: Hayden, 1976.

Moffett, James. *Teaching the Universe of Discourse*. Portsmouth, NH: Boynton, 1983.

Ohmann, Richard. "Graduate Students, Professionals, Intellectuals." *College English* 52 (1990): 247–57.

Phelps, Louise Wetherbee. "The Domain of Composition." *Rhetoric Review* 4 (1986): 182–95.

Rudolph, Frederick. *The American College and University*. New York: Knopf, 1962.

Storr, Richard J. *The Beginning of the Future*. New York: McGraw, 1973.

———. *The Beginnings of Graduate Education in America*. Chicago: U of Chicago P, 1953.

———. *Harper's University: The Beginnings*. Chicago: U of Chicago P, 1966.

Waldrep, Tom, ed. *Writers on Writing*. 2 vols. New York: Random, 1988.

Waller, Gary. "Polylogue: Reading, Writing, and the Structure of Doctoral Study." Lunsford, Moglen, and Slevin 111–20.

16

Robert Zoellner's Talk-Write Pedagogy

Gary Layne Hatch/Arizona State University, Tempe
Margaret Bennett Walters/Arizona State University, Tempe

In 1969, Richard Ohmann devoted the January issue of *College English* to a monograph written by a teacher and researcher of composition at Colorado State University—Robert Zoellner. At the time, Zoellner's theories about the composing process and his radical approach to handling student's writing problems received extremely negative responses. In attempting to revive his work, we realize that responses to Zoellner's position might still be negative, for the "mentalistic paradigm" informing current research and theories in composition was the same paradigm that Zoellner wanted researchers and teachers to reconsider in 1969. In his introduction to Zoellner's article, Ohmann applauds Zoellner's monograph because it is not just another personal approach "in a field already littered with gimmicks, hunches, and personal strategies" but is rather "a set of instrumental concepts," a questioning of "a deep tacit assumption" underlying the field of composition teaching ("Talk-Write" 267). Zoellner attacks the idea that "the written word is thought on paper" ("Talk-Write" 269). He objects to the then-current pedagogy, which held that writing problems stem largely from a deficiency in a student's thought and that writing can be improved by improving a student's thought processes. Zoellner opposes the "think-write" metaphor, which privileges thinking over writing and focuses on the artifact of writing. Zoellner views writing as an act, a complex of behaviors, a "pattern of responses" that produce the finished essay ("Talk-Write" 272).

Zoellner's position is based on what he calls the "talk-write" metaphor by which he seeks to apply principles derived from behavioral psychology to writing problems. As we shall show, such a construct was then and is now a radically different approach to the theory and practice of composition, for, in Zoellner's words, the talk-write pedagogy "directs its efforts, not to the establishment of right *thinking*, but rather of right *behaving*" ("Talk-Write" 289).[1] Zoellner's opposition of the key words *thinking* and *behaving* demonstrates the primary opposition between his pedagogy and the traditional pedagogy he attacks.

Zoellner's objection to traditional product-oriented teaching methods is of historical interest because he was among the first to suggest what has now become a commonplace in composition theory: that it is much more useful to discuss the act of writing than to discuss the result of that act. Even before he wrote "Talk-Write," Zoellner stressed the importance of teaching writing processes (see *Strategy*). For Zoellner, writing problems are maladaptive behavior rather than problems with thinking. In his monograph, he rejects what he calls the "mentalistic" or "intellective" metaphor informing traditional composition practice. Zoellner finds this metaphor inadequate as a theoretical basis for English composition because of its focus on the product of writing rather than the process of writing ("Talk-Write" 270). Not only is the traditional pedagogy "empirically inaccessible" (274), it is also "too simple." Zoellner argues that the traditional approach does not account for the great complexity of the writing process (291).

Zoellner's use of the terms "mentalistic" and "intellective" are best explained in his response to his critics in the November 1969 *College English*. In this response, Zoellner explains the vital difference between his model and other models of composition.

Drawing on the philosophy of Thomas Kuhn, Zoellner contends that those who favor the mentalist paradigm must experience "a total shift in perception" in order to objectively critique his behavioral paradigm ("Mentalizing" 216). In *About Behaviorism*, B. F. Skinner emphasizes the profound nature of such a "shift" in perception: "As the philosophy of a science of behavior, behaviorism calls for probably the most drastic change ever proposed in our way of thinking about man. It is almost literally a matter of turning the explanation of behavior inside out" (274). At the center of the conflict, Zoellner explains, are two different views of the nature of the mind: the "Paradigm of Mentalistic Human" and the "Paradigm of Responsive Human" ("Mentalizing" 218). Zoellner contrasts the essential differences between these two paradigms with regard to their concepts of mind, expression, logic, meaning, and grammar.

For the mentalist, there is an inner agent, a sort of Cartesian "ghost in the machine" that controls the body ("Mentalizing" 218). Both person and personality, for the mentalist, denote the inner self (218). The physical body does not play a role in thinking. The behaviorist, on the other hand, denies the existence of the "mind" in this sense, arguing that person and personality consist of the sum total of observable behaviors (219). Thinking and learning, for the behaviorist, involve outward, observable behavior.

There is also disagreement in the two conceptions of expression. The mentalist conceives of language activity—either in speaking or in writing—as "the expression of an inner mental activity, a series of 'signals' somehow instituted by the agent within, which convey to the outer world the 'thought' going on in the mind" ("Mentalizing" 219). For the mentalist, there is a direct correspondence between thought and language. What is written or spoken reflects inner thought. For the behaviorist, however, language is "entirely and wholly a response" to an external stimulus, particularly that verbal stimulus provided by other speakers (219). Thought is not something that occurs before expression: "We simply speak, and the speaking (or the writing) *is the thought*" (200). Though Zoellner believes there is "something inside man anterior to expression and upon which expression is at least partially dependent," these interior states are not "thinking" in the traditional sense (220n). Knowledge of the real nature of these inner states is, he acknowledges, "hopelessly fuzzy" at this time.

Logic, for the mentalist, consists of "a set of imperatives or rules that the student 'uses' or 'follows' or 'employs' in writing or speaking" ("Mentalizing" 221). The behaviorist denies that students use rules or imperatives because logic "is simply *another* form of behavior, a set of verbal constructs which attempt to describe logical behavior" ("Mentalizing" 221). For the behaviorist, the way to improve logic is to shape outward behavior.

Kuhn points out that new paradigms often result from the observation of an anomaly, a phenomenon that cannot be explained by existing models. The anomaly that Zoellner discovered was that, for some reason, intelligent, articulate students could not communicate through writing. This phenomenon could not be explained by the mentalistic paradigm because these students clearly were not deficient mentally. Zoellner found that, when questioned, these students were able to tell him what they meant by some incomprehensible sentence or paragraph they had written ("Talk-Write" 273). Students could express in speech what they could not express in writing. The talk-write pedagogy suggests a reversal in how we treat writing problems. Instead of teaching students how to think, talk-write assumes that students are mentally competent and focuses instead on the physical manipulation of language through speaking and writing.

The advantages of the talk-write pedagogy lie in its being a viable pedagogical model: it can be used in both the classroom and the office conference and it is based upon sound behavioral principles—it is "observable and manipulatable" ("Talk-Write" 274). In Zoellner's conceptualization of the talk-write model, the teacher prompts students to say what they mean, which they immediately write down. Thus, the teacher reinforces those behaviors (that utterance or piece of writing) that take the student closer to good expression. Zoellner's aim is to produce a pedagogy in which the possibility exists "that better writing *need not* be preceded by better thought, that indeed better writing may be the necessary prerequisite *to* better thought, and that some, much, or all of the improvement that we do observe in a student's scribal performance may have its source in non-intellective areas" ("Talk-Write" 291).

The talk-write pedagogy draws upon the principles of behavioral psychology, specifically operant conditioning, whereby student behavior is conditioned, or shaped, through immediate reinforcement of "successively closer approximations to the [writing] behavior with which the [teacher] ultimately wants to work" ("Talk-Write" 276). Operant conditioning is concerned with external behavior and is "response-based": "The experimenter steadfastly views the bit-of-behavior he wishes to alter as a *learned habit*, the alteration of which involves 'reconditioning'" (292). However, Zoellner extends behavioral concepts when he bases his talk-write pedagogy upon the concept of modality and of intermodal transfer to explain the "phenomenon of modally mediated transfer, whereby reinforcement of one behavior or skill improves performance of another behavior or skill" (312–13). Zoellner feels that writing has been ignored by behavioral scientists because conditioning has proved most helpful in the vocal area of therapist-patient relationships. For Zoellner, speaking and writing are discrete behaviors which, when linked together, can move students closer to the common goal of both speech and writing: effective communication. (When we discuss applications of Zoellner's work, we will show that the linking of speaking and writing and the transfer of speaking skills to writing is the most common application of the talk-write model.)

Applying behavioral principles allows Zoellner both to critique the traditional think-write pedagogy and to provide a new direction for composition ("Talk-Write" 277). To find an answer to students' writing problems, Zoellner went to the work of B. F. Skinner, Albert Bandura, W. Horsley Gantt, and Alexander Luria. Skinner's work is based on the stimulus-response-reinforcement paradigm. In his behavioral model for writing, Zoellner sought to make an extension of the stimulus-response-reinforcement paradigm to the writing classroom. He adapts Skinner's seven learning principles:

1. Concentrate on the individual student.
2. Build on the skills students already possess.
3. Work with freely emitted actions.
4. Make sure that students repeat the action frequently.
5. Insure a low duration of response.
6. Reinforce desired responses immediately.
7. Reinforce behaviors that approximate the desired behavior.
   (See "Talk-Write" 278)

Zoellner's application of Skinner's learning principles requires a unique learning environment. Zoellner envisions a classroom devoid of desks and chairs where students stand at easels and write on large pads of paper with felt-tip markers. (According to Paul Heilker, Zoellner actually practiced this method in a large classroom in the agriculture building at Colorado State University;

the room was equipped with large blackboards stretching from floor to ceiling.) The "talk-write" part of the pedagogy comes in the interaction between teacher and student and between student and fellow student. The teacher attempts to bridge the gap between vocal performance and scribal performance by having the student talk out what he or she meant to say in some unintelligible piece of writing. The teacher then has the student transcribe that utterance on the pad of paper. The teacher makes further inquiries about the written piece encouraging the student to explain further what he or she meant to say. As students try to clarify their writing, they become models of the writing process for other students. Zoellner insists that teachers must also be willing to improvise, allowing students to ask them about their writing.

The talk-write pedagogy focuses on the outward, observable, verbal behavior of the student ("Talk-Write" 289) and incorporates Skinner's seven principles of learning. First of all, Zoellner's pedagogy focuses on the individual student. This means that teachers focus on the verbal and scribal behavior—the writing act—of the individual student rather than on the product of scribal behavior, the finished essay. Second, the teacher builds on the "naive behavioral repertoire" of the student, the vocal and scribal skills the student already possesses. The teacher begins "where the student *is* rather than where he *should be*" ("Mentalizing" 230). Third, the teacher works with "freely emitted behavior." The teacher does not coerce the student to write or speak in a certain way but rather builds upon those verbal behaviors the student freely exhibits. Fourth, the talk-write environment provides an opportunity for the student to respond a number of times. A student can react immediately to a piece of writing or a teacher's inquiry, making revisions in what he or she has written. Fifth, the emphasis on "free utterance" and spoken language allows a "low duration of response." Students can respond quickly and are in a position to respond again immediately ("Talk-Write" 282). Sixth, in the talk-write pedagogy, the teacher reinforces approximate behavior immediately. The teacher or fellow student can tell the student immediately if the revision has aided understanding. This response takes the form of both verbal cues, such as "Good! Write *that* down" ("Talk-Write" 297), or nonverbal cues such as a nod of the head or a look of comprehension. Seventh, the teacher does not only reinforce "correct" behavior but reinforces each bit of behavior that approximates the behavior the teacher desires the student ultimately to exhibit. This is perhaps the most important part of Zoellner's pedagogy. Part of his indictment of current composition pedagogy stems from the fact that teachers have a notion of what "good writing" is and that anything below that level—even though it may approximate "good writing"—is substandard ("Talk-Write" 284). The talk-write pedagogy allows the teacher to give immediate reinforcement to those verbal behaviors that move in the direction of good writing. Thus, if a student vocalizes what he or she meant to say and that vocalization is only slightly more comprehensible than what the student had originally written, the teacher would reinforce this verbal behavior as an intermediate step towards having the student write coherently.

Zoellner summarizes his views in a paper read at the 1971 CCCC. In discussing the use of behavioral objectives, Zoellner argues that teachers should form behavioral objectives on behaviors students freely emit rather than coercing students into behaviors teachers think they ought to emit. Teachers must begin with the actual verbal or scribal activity of the student and then must reinforce those subspecifications of behavior that approximate the behavior the teacher hopes the student will achieve (see "Lucy's Dance Lessons"). In a response to Richard C. Gebhardt, Zoellner admits that generalized terminal objectives of some type are necessary, but he objects to the "codification" of behavioral objectives in standard curricula that specify the behaviors that all English students will master. Zoellner has in mind objectives that allow room for improvisation and flexibility ("Improvisational Bogey" 608).

On Zoellnerism: The Immediate Critical Response

Zoellner's ideas evoked immediate response. The May 1969 issue of *College English* ran a special response section entitled "On Zoellnerism." More responses followed in the November 1969 issue, which also included a reply by Zoellner. Responses were primarily very negative, and attacks were, in some cases, extremely harsh and personal. Zoellner found the criticism "depressing in the extreme," believing that few had responded in the objective fashion he had hoped for ("Response" 667–68).[2]

Some of the early critics object to Zoellner's writing style. Kenneth Eble calls Zoellner's writing "pretentious verbiage," accusing Zoellner of "a distrust of literature, a disrespect for writing, and a whoring after pseudo-science" (652). John Hendrickson also attacks Zoellner's writing style, citing as evidence Richard Larson's critique of Zoellner's style in Larson's review of Zoellner's *The Strategy of Composition*. In the November 1969 issue of *College English*, Campbell objects to Zoellner's "flights of rocket-age-rococo prose" (208).

This attack on Zoellner's writing is, in part, justified. Although Zoellner's writing is often lively and original, it is just as often obscure and overly technical. Zoellner justifies his use of highly technical terms by referring to the need to speak with scientists in their own terms. He could have avoided much of the negative response to his original essay, however, if he had tried harder to accommodate his audience and make behavioral psychology palatable to more traditional literary scholars such as Eble.

Behind the attacks on Zoellner and his writing, however, lie attacks on the behavioral paradigm he proposes. Indeed, the initial response to Zoellner's behavioral pedagogy can be characterized as a clash between the existing mentalistic paradigm and the behavioral paradigm.

The responses by John Hendrickson and Kenneth Eble show a strong attachment to the mentalistic paradigm. Eble argues that students have writing problems because "writing is closely related to thinking, something few people do well" (653). Hendrickson defends the traditional pedagogy, pointing to many competent writers that the think-write pedagogy has produced through the years, noting that Zoellner does not cite any significant success from his talk-write pedagogy. Eble and Hendrickson show a strong resistance to new ideas, occasioned in part by Zoellner's presentation of these ideas but explained as well by their inability to switch from their own mentalistic paradigm to a behavioral paradigm.

Even those who claim to understand the new paradigm often have difficulty shedding the assumptions of the old paradigm. Christopher Boyle's response provides an example. Boyle claims to accept Zoellner's indictment of the think-write metaphor for writing but objects to Zoellner's talk-write solution. He argues that writing is not behavior and that writing problems are unrelated to what is observable. He sees little use in watching another person write to learn something about the writing act, believing that nothing can be gained by watching a person scribble on paper. Boyle sees writing as a "private art," while Zoellner sees it as a "public act" ("On 'Talk-Write'").

It is interesting that Boyle claims to agree with Zoellner's indictment of the mentalistic paradigm since Boyle's response suggests that he actually adheres to that paradigm. For Boyle the act of writing takes place within the body; it is unrelated to the physical act of recording words on paper. The behavioral paradigm, on the other hand, assumes that there is a connection between observable, physical behavior and writing, that "thinking" takes place at the point of utterance or the point of inscription.

Only one of the critics who first responded to Zoellner's article meets Zoellner on the same conceptual level: Theodore Sarbin. Sarbin supports Zoellner's talk-write metaphor but would supplement Zoellner's model to include nonverbal behavior, such as gestural and postural acts (646). It should not come as a surprise that Sarbin, a psychologist, shares Zoellner's paradigm, praising Zoellner's "revolutionary" hypothesis which recognizes "that the reified think-write metaphor lacks utility" (645).[3]

Criticism of the talk-write pedagogy continued in the November 1969 issue of *College English*, in which Charles Campbell and Lynn and Martin Bloom joined earlier critics in denouncing Zoellner's hypothesis. Campbell contends that the talk-write pedagogy would invite "mindlessness and authoritarianism," fearing that talk-write could be used as a manipulative tool to control students' minds. Campbell supposes that talk-write's "group-therapeutic elements" could be disastrous "in the hands of an unscrupulous or ill-trained teacher" (215). (In the last section of this essay, we will argue that talk-write actually provides greater freedom for the student in the classroom.)

Though Lynn and Martin Bloom praise Zoellner for his "extremely valuable contribution to English pedagogy," they express serious reservations about the applicability of Zoellner's method in their article "But Will They Answer?" They "doubt whether operant conditioning could lead to writing better than mediocre, even if it should be possible by this means to teach students to construct long chains of discrete sentences" (204). Instead of "conditioning" students, which the Blooms partially object to on the grounds that "students are much more than laboratory rats," the Blooms would teach students "cognitive organizations" called "schemata" or "central strategies" that would help students to generate writing (205).

It is clear that both Campbell and the Blooms hold to the mentalistic view of writing that Zoellner rejects. Campbell believes that "the teaching of thinking by English teachers has to be a priority" (209). Lynn and Martin Bloom also believe that the answer to improving student writing lies in improving student thinking.

Later Adaptations of Zoellner's Model

In spite of the initial reaction to Zoellner's work, some scholars have discovered imaginative and useful means of adapting Zoellner's ideas to the classroom. These scholars have generally sidestepped the theoretical issues related to Zoellner's indictment of the mentalistic paradigm, focusing instead on the practical application of Zoellner's method.

Many instructors have found talk-write a useful tool for aiding invention. Terry Radcliffe outlines a system for reinforcing speech and writing based on a talk-write model. A subject speaks for thirty minutes into a tape recorder with the aid of another person, who reinforces speaking. The subject then selects material from the taped session to include in an essay ("Talk-Write Composition"). George Douglas Meyers describes how he has adapted Zoellner's model to the business writing classroom. As students are preparing their initial drafts and still formulating their ideas, Meyers divides students into pairs to talk out their ideas. Students take turns as speaker and listener, although Meyers admits that most students actually carry on an informal conversation. After ten minutes, the students write down any ideas, words, or phrases emerging from the conversation that they feel would prove useful in their essays ("Adapting" 15). In his doctoral dissertation at the University of Maryland, Meyers reports that the use of the talk-write model improves student attitudes toward writing and that students who used talk-write show improvement in all areas of their writing. Barbara Craig tries a similar adaptation of talk-write in her 1981 Ohio University dissertation. Craig finds no difference between the talk-write group and her control group, but she also admits the need for further research. In a recent CCCC paper, Margaret Walters examines parallels between talk-write as an invention strategy and *stasis* theory from classical rhetoric. She notes that although Zoellner does not mention classical rhetoric, his talk-write pedagogy can be used to resolve questions about fact, definition, the nature or quality of an act, and even questions about jurisdiction and legal processes. Students would use talk-write as a means of identifying the important points of contention in a case.

Other composition scholars have found talk-write a useful means of teaching revision. Wilson Currin Snipes uses talk-write throughout the composing process. He takes students through the following steps: talking, retalking, writing, and rewriting. Snipes agrees with Zoellner that students are much better speakers than writers. He uses peer review to help students transfer their competence in speaking to a competence in writing ("Oral Composing"). David Karrfalt has students work in small groups, engaging in peer review and evaluation. One student writes a draft, and other students comment on the draft. The students then shift roles ("Writing Teams"). Vincent and Pat Wixon use talk-write as a means of teaching revision to high school and junior high school students. They follow the method just as Zoellner describes it. They divide students into pairs (or allow students to divide themselves into pairs). The students take turns being the writer and questioner. The writer writes on a piece of butcher paper with a felt-tip pen, and the questioner asks the writer to clarify what he or she has written. The writer answers the question verbally and then records that answer in writing. The teacher also comments on student writing, moving from group to group ("Getting it Out"). Vincent and Pat Wixon report great success with high school teachers in the Oregon area that have used talk-write to teach revision. They find that talk-write works at various grade levels and in classes other than English. In "Using Talk-Write in the Classroom," the Wixons relate the experiences of a number of secondary school teachers who have used talk-write. Although some of these teachers had reservations about the method at first, each teacher relates a positive experience with using talk-write to teach revision (133–35).

Byron Stay uses talk-write as a method for teaching invention and revision to basic writers. His method is informal. Students either work in small groups or as a class, asking nonthreatening questions about what another student has written. Students are encouraged not only to clarify what they have written but also to share their experiences with writing: frustrations, feelings of inadequacy, past failures, as well as successes (250–51). Stay has found that talk-write helps basic writers feel comfortable about writing, noting that many basic writers feel inadequate because of the lack of success in previous English courses. He has also found that talk-write overcomes what Mina Shaughnessy has called the problem of "premature closure," the tendency for basic writers to view a sentence as a discrete unit of thought rather than as part of a larger passage of thought (251).

Michael Gilbertsen and M. Jimmie Killingsworth have successfully applied talk-write in the technical writing classroom. Instead of having students produce their own writing, however, Gilbertsen and Killingsworth teach editing by having students respond to a set of sentences prepared by the teacher. Gilbertsen and Killingsworth call this method the "talk-edit" approach. They divide students into pairs, designating one student as the primary editor and rewriter and the other student as the secondary editor and auditor. With each new set of sentences, the students switch roles. The two students talk through the problems, the auditor asking questions and the rewriter verbalizing possible revisions. The primary editor is responsible for making the changes, in consultation with the secondary editor, but only the secondary editor is allowed to present the final result to the teacher. If the teacher is satisfied with the result, the teacher returns with the secondary editor to the primary editor and expresses the positive aspects of the revision. If the teacher is not satisfied, then the teacher communicates these reservations to the secondary editor, who then passes them on to the primary editor. Gilbertsen and Killingsworth have found that their talk-edit approach improves the quality of student revision and also teaches students to write in groups (110–12).

Gary Hatch has found the talk-write method useful for teaching revision in conferencing sessions. Students bring completed essays to the conference, and Hatch reads through the essay asking for clarification about sections that are ambiguous or confusing. The students respond verbally, generally supplying the detail that they should have included in the original essay. Hatch then has students write down their expression immediately for possible inclusion in a revised version of the essay. This method of conferencing has even proved successful over the telephone. Students read what they have written, Hatch asks questions, and then students answer the questions, writing down what they say immediately and then reading back what they have written.

Implications of Zoellner's Work for Research and Teaching

Few researchers in composition studies today would disagree with Zoellner's argument that composition must be viewed as a process occurring within a social context. Nor would they consider his call for the application of empirical methods in research as radical as his critics did in 1969. Although few researchers in composition today would call themselves "behaviorists," most current research entails the examination of observable behavior. This is true in the case studies of Janet Emig, Sondra Perl, and Nancy Sommers, as well as in the protocol analyses carried out by Linda Flower and John Hayes. But even though there are a number of similarities between Zoellner's work and current research on the composing process, Robert Zoellner might claim (as he did with the Blooms' work) that a "conceptual abyss" existing between his work and current research places himself and current researchers "on different planets circling different suns in different galaxies" ("Mentalizing" 224). As we noted above, most scholars who have adapted Zoellner's work have ignored Zoellner's attack on the mentalistic paradigm. Gary Hatch, however, in a recent CCCC paper, argues that in order for composition to reach maturity as a discipline, composition scholars must pay atteniton to the theoretical implications of their pedagogical methods. In particular, Hatch argues that scholars must come to terms with the implications of the mentalistic and behavioral paradigms.

Consider the work of Linda Flower and John Hayes (and others who use cognitive psychology as the model for the composing process). Flower and Hayes clearly fall within the mentalist paradigm. They consider "writing as an act of thinking," and they focus on the "inner, intellectual *process* of composing" (449). For those who follow this mentalist model, writing problems result from thinking problems. And the solution to writing problems lies in teaching inexperienced writers the cognitive strategies used by more experienced writers.

One problem with the cognitive approach to the composing process (which remains one of today's primary pedagogical models) is that it encourages the type of "authoritarianism" that Charles Campbell, one of Zoellner's original critics, claimed to find in Zoellner's work. Zoellner admits that "teaching is manipulation, pure and simple" ("Mentalizing" 229). Yet teachers with a cognitive orientation consider it "teaching" if the student is aware of what they are doing and "manipulation" (and thus wrong) if the student is unaware (229). The only question for Zoellner "is whether the manipulation should be haphazard or systematic" (229). Of course, he would argue for the latter. Zoellner, however, finds the mentalist pedagogy "culturally repugnant" because "an exclusively intellective pedagogy, based almost entirely on the 'cognitive recognition' of 'rules,' the formulation of mentalistic abstractions, and the conceptualization of learning in terms of distant and often rigid objectives is . . . utterly incomprehensible for students living in a pluralistic society" (230). Rather than promoting the authority of the teacher, Zoellner's model recognizes the absolute individuality of the student. In "Lucy's Dance Lessons and Accountability in English," Zoellner argues against teaching methods that would force "stereotypical thinking." Prescribing thought processes is contrary to the behavioral, Skinnerian view that every human being has an "absolute uniqueness" (231). Zoellner asserts that the proper objectives of teachers should be "to attend more to what a given student, or a classroom full of students, *does*, than to what he or they *ought* to do" ("Lucy's Dance Lessons" 236).

In other words, Zoellner would object to teaching students generic cognitive strategies derived from "expert" writers. He assumes that students already know how to think, but that for some reason some students are less adept at manipulating linguistic systems than others. Glynda Hull and Mike Rose, in their recent *CCC* article, show an instance in which Robert, a remedial student, provides what most teachers would consider the "wrong" interpretation of a poem. Indeed, Rose, in his transcript of his conference with the student, shows a hesitation to recognize the validity of Robert's interpretation. Only after some reflection does Rose realize that Robert's unconventional reading of the poem is consistent and logical within the cultural context that Robert assigns to the poem. Hull and Rose warn us that "the laudable goal of facilitating underprepared students' entry into the academic community is actually compromised by a conversational pattern that channels students . . . into a more 'efficient' discourse" (298). Those who adhere to the mentalistic paradigm would likely claim that Robert's unconventional reading of the poem results from inefficient cognitive processes. Behaviorists would assume that Robert knows how to think, but that he may have some difficulty manipulating written language. The talk-write method would allow Robert to express his original interpretation of the poem clearly without trying to force him to read the poem or think about the poem in a certain way. Hull and Rose call for a "richer, more transactive model of classroom discourse" (297). Talk-write may well provide that model.

The talk-write pedagogy is designed to help a student find and express his or her "voice" in the social context within which people really write, for in the talk-write classroom, students can have a dialogue with various audiences: the teacher, the teacher and other students, or a partner or group of peers ("Talk-Write" 299). Zoellner's model would give students verbal force while allowing for differences in learning styles as well as diversity in thought for different gender, race, and ethnic groups.

Conclusion

Robert Zoellner offers one of the few real alternatives to the mentalistic pedagogical models current in the teaching of writing. Many teachers have found it to be a powerful pedagogical tool. But composition theorists and researchers must also give serious consideration to the theoretical problems Zoellner raises. Researchers in English composition, Zoellner writes, cannot have "totally catholic tastes," using terminology drawn from all areas of psychology to fit their preconceptions ("Behavioral Objectives" 423), nor can they apply scientific models unless such models "are unitary, organically homogeneous, and indivisible—you buy the whole package or none of the package" (427). As James Berlin reminds us, no way of teaching is ever innocent, for "every pedagogy is imbricated in ideology, in a set of tacit assumptions about what is real, what is good, what is possible, and how power ought to be distributed" (492). Berlin suggests that cognitive psychologists are most apt to forget the ideological basis of pedagogy because of their claim to an objective understanding of "the unchanging structures of mind, matter, and language" (492). Zoellner's work is as important today as it was in 1969 for its questioning of these assumptions.

Notes

1. The emphasis in all quotations from Robert Zoellner is his own.

2. After twenty-one years Robert Zoellner is still somewhat bitter about the harsh reception he received. He still teaches at Colorado State University, but he now focuses his attention on American literature rather than on composition.

3. Sarbin characterizes himself as a "more-or-less traditional professor of psychology with an interest in certain belletristic affairs." His credentials "include innumerable scars acquired in often-lost skirmishes with students in efforts to increase their scribal fluencies" (645).

Works Cited

Berlin, James. "Rhetoric and Ideology in the Writing Class." *College English* 50 (1988): 477–94.

Bloom, Lynn Z., and Martin Bloom. "But Will They Answer? — A Critical Review of One Behavioral Attempt to Call the Creative Spirits." *College English* 31 (1969): 199–208.

Boyle, Christopher G. "On 'Talk-Write.'" *College English* 30 (1969): 648–52.

Campbell, Charles A. "Think-Talk-Write: A Behavioristic Pedagogy for Scribal Fluency." *College English* 31 (1969): 208–15.

Craig, Barbara Jay. "Oral Response Groups Before and After Rough Drafts: Effects on Writing Achievement and Apprehension." Diss. Ohio U, 1981.

Eble, Kenneth E. "On 'Talk-Write.'" *College English* 30 (1969): 652–53.

Emig, Janet. "The Composing Process: Review of the Literature." *Contemporary Rhetoric: A Conceptual Background with Readings*. Ed. W. Ross Winterowd. New York: Harcourt, 1975. 49–70.

Flower, Linda S., and John R. Hayes. "Problem-Solving Strategies and the Writing Process." *College English* 39 (1977): 449–61.

Gebhardt, Richard C. "Behavioral Objectives for English: A Reaction." *College English* 34 (1973): 603–7.

Gilbertsen, Michael, and M. Jimmie Killingsworth. "Behavioral Talk-Write as a Method for Teaching Technical Editing." *Iowa State Journal of Business and Technical Communication* 1 (1987): 108–14.

Hatch, Gary Layne. "Reviving the Rodential Model for Composition: Robert Zoellner's Alternative to Flower and Hayes." Conference on College Composition and Communication. Boston, Mar. 1991.

Heilker, Paul. "Public Products/Public Processes: Zoellner's Praxis and the Contemporary Composition Classroom." Conference on College Composition and Communication. Boston, Mar. 1991.

Hendrickson, John. "On 'Talk-Write.'" *College English* 30 (1969): 653–56.

Hull, Glynda, and Mike Rose. "'This Wooden Shack Place': The Logic of an Unconventional Reading." *College Composition and Communication* 41 (1990): 287–98.

Karrfalt, David H. "Writing Teams: From Generating Composition to Generating Communication." *College Composition and Communication* 22 (1971): 377–78.

Kuhn, Thomas. *The Structure of Scientific Revolutions*. 2nd ed. Chicago: U of Chicago P, 1970.

Meyers, George Douglas. "Adapting Zoellner's 'Talk-Write' to the Business Writing Classroom." *Bulletin of the Association for Business Communication* 48 (1985): 14–16.

———. "The Influence of Using Speaking as a Pre-writing Activity on Community College Freshman Composition Pupils' Performance in and Attitudes Toward Writing." Diss. U of Maryland, 1980.

Perl, Sondra. "Understanding Composing." Tate and Corbett 113–18.

Radcliffe, Terry. "Talk-Write Composition: A Theoretical Model Proposing the Use of Speech to Improve Writing." *Research in the Teaching of English* 6 (1972): 187–99.

Sarbin, Theodore R. "Notes on Extending the Talk-Write Metaphor." *College English* 30 (1969): 645–48.

Shaughnessy, Mina P. *Errors and Expectations: A Guide for the Teacher of Basic Writing.* New York: Oxford UP, 1977.

Skinner, B. F. *About Behaviorism.* New York: Vantage, 1976.

Snipes, Wilson Currin. "Oral Composing as an Approach to Writing." *College Composition and Communication* 24 (1973): 200–205.

Sommers, Nancy. "Revision Strategies of Student Writers and Experienced Adult Writers." Tate and Corbett 119–27.

Stay, Byron L. "Talking About Writing: An Approach to Teaching Unskilled Writers." *Journal of Teaching Writing* 4 (1985): 248–52.

Tate, Gary, and Edward P. J. Corbett. *The Writing Teacher's Sourcebook.* 2nd ed. New York: Oxford UP, 1988.

Walters, Margaret. "Robert Zoellner's 'Talk-Write Pedagogy': Instrumental Concept for Composition Today." Conference on College Composition and Communication. Boston, Mar. 1991.

Wixon, Vincent, and Pat Stone. "Getting It Out, Getting It Down: Adapting Zoellner's Talk-Write." *English Journal* 66 (1977): 70–73.

Wixon, Vincent, and Pat Wixon. "Using Talk-Write in the Classroom." *Theory and Practice in the Teaching of Composition: Processing, Distancing, and Modeling.* Ed. Miles Myers and James Gray. Urbana, IL: NCTE, 1983. 129–35.

Zoellner, Robert. "Behavioral Objectives for English." *College English* 33 (1972): 418–32.

———. "Lucy's Dance Lessons and Accountability in English." *College Composition and Communication* 22 (1971): 229–36.

———. "Response." *College English* 30 (1969): 667–68.

———. "Response: Mentalizing S. R. Rodent." *College English* 31 (1969): 215–30.

———. "Response: The Improvisational Bogey." *College English* 34 (1973): 607–8.

———. "Talk-Write: A Behavioral Pedagogy for Composition." *College English* 30 (1969): 267–320.

Zoellner, Robert, and Clarence A. Brown. *The Strategy of Composition: A Rhetoric with Readings.* New York: Ronald, 1968.

17

Gender in Composition Research: A Strange Silence

Nancy Mellin McCracken/Kent State University, Kent, Ohio
Lois I. Green/Clarion University of Pennsylvania, Clarion, Pennsylvania
Claudia M. Greenwood/Kent State University, Ashtabula Campus, Ashtabula, Ohio

Imagine a cultural anthropologist setting out to study a rather widely practiced social interaction and noting with some regularity that men and women are observed behaving differently — such that the natives themselves have invented a gender-specific label for one of the ways of behaving ("feminist pedagogy") — yet not bothering (or daring) to write about this difference. What a strange silence! This essay explores just such a silence in composition research generally and in our own particular research in the teaching of composition. Studies of teachers' responses to student writing are characterized by a persistent silence on the subject of gender. Early influential studies of response to students' writing by Sommers and Brannon and Knoblauch do not mention the gender of teacher-responders. More recent studies by Anson and Freedman, which do provide such information, fail to discuss the gender role of the responder even though their data would seem to suggest the need to do so. Regardless of the gender-specific names Anson uses and despite his allusion to *Women's Ways of Knowing*, he does not discuss gender as a possible factor in the teachers' responses he presents and critiques. Freedman similarly suggests gender as a possible factor in her study, *Response to Student Writing*: for the central ethnographic portion of the study, she selected one male and one female teacher in part because they "offered a contrast with one another along the lines of their gender" (32). Yet, like Anson, Freedman is silent on the issue of gender in her discussion of these teachers' interactions with their students. It is a strange silence.

It might be argued that the silence on gender in teacher-response studies reflects the larger silence in composition research generally. The landmark research studies on writing development and writing processes published in the last two decades was, after all, virtually silent about the gender of student writers. (Two exceptions are Graves's study of differences in topic selection of fourth grade boys and girls and Beach and Bridwell's observation that female writers revised more extensively than males.) Emig, Britton et al., Flower and Hayes, Shaughnessy, Perl, and Sommers, to name a few, focused primarily on categories other than gender: age, experience, achievement levels. Hillocks's major review of prior studies on the teaching of composition, *Research on Written Composition* does not list gender as a research factor. Yet in the past five years, this has begun to change as feminist studies of women as writers have suggested the need to study women *students* as writers. The collection of essays by Caywood and Overing and the special issues of *College English*, *College Composition and Communication*, and *Journal of Advanced Composition* reflect a research environment in which it is both important and safe to study the interplay between students' gender and their development as writers.

Strong evidence of the need for related studies of teachers' gender as a factor in teacher-student interactions comes from a variety of sources, particularly from critical theory and from discourse pragmatics. Yet, for reasons we shall explore, there has not been the same effort to study the role of the teacher's gender in student-teacher interactions as there has been to study the role of the student's gender.

Flynn, for example, invoking Culler, explores the implications for composition students of strong differences between reading as a woman and reading as a man, but she does not discuss the implications of these differences for those who read—as men or women—student papers. Recent sociolinguistic research suggests that in addition to reading differently, men and women converse differently. For example, West and Zimmerman report studies in which men account for ninety-six percent of the interruptions in conversations between male and female acquaintances. Fishman reports a study in which women asked 2½ times the number of questions their male partners in conversation asked and consistently provided supportive utterances to further the topics raised by the men, who successfully initiated conversation on their topics in twenty-eight of twenty-nine cases. In contrast, the men rarely asked questions and either kept silent or delayed supportive utterances while their partners were attempting to initiate topics. Fishman notes these women successfully initiating conversation on their topics in just seventeen of forty-seven cases. Tannen provides a full account of the ways differences in "genderlect" regularly interfere with communication. Pratt's exploration of the relationship between reading and conversation suggests that the discourse situation of reading student texts is remarkably similar to that of listening to lengthy conversational turns, and it is likely that research on differences between men's and women's styles of conversing is similarly germane to studies of teachers' responses to students' texts (McCracken, "Gender"). Clearly if men and women use language differently, make meaning of texts differently, and respond differently to efforts to initiate discourse on a chosen topic, then gender is as important to explore in studies of teachers' response to students' writing as in studies of students' writing itself.

We do not know why our colleagues studying teachers' responses to students' writing have failed to discuss the gender issue they initially raised in their reports or why research on the teaching of composition has generally been silent on the gender of teachers. We do know about our own practice as researchers, however. Each of us conducted independent research into teachers' interactions with composition students. Each of our studies included both men and women instructors. Each of us observed the men and women instructors behaving in gender-typical ways. And yet each of us, in our initial research reports, remained silent about gender as a factor in teachers' interactions with their composition students.

In the time that has elapsed since these studies were conducted, we have read each other's work, discovered important similarities in our data, and discussed our individual silences. Our collaboration and our readings of feminist scholars, particularly Belenky, Clinchy, Goldberger, and Tarule; Gilligan; Martin; and Tannen have led us to write about our troubling omissions as well as to reflect on the likely reasons for these omissions in our work. We have discovered some of the concerns that contributed to our own silences. We share these concerns here because we think it possible that the same concerns may influence other researchers and in some way account for their silences.

Obstacles to Research on Gender and Teaching Writing and How We Now Choose to Handle Them

Perhaps the most immediate obstacle to writing about gender and writing instruction is the term *gender*, which has become no less problematic in the decades since Simone de Beauvoir opened *The Second Sex* by asking, "Are there women, really?" (Introduction). In our use of the term, we are not subscribing to a biological or sociocultural determinism, which suggests there are only two genders and guarantees that all those designated as men behave in consistent patterns differently than those designated as women. We recognize, in our personal lives and in our work, persons representing a whole range of gender and teaching constructs, but following Gilligan and Belenky and her coauthors, we believe that men and women are socialized differently and that as a result, there are often real differences between men's and women's ways of knowing and of listening, as well as of speaking and writing. And in our discussion, we shall use the terms *men* and *women, feminist,* and *masculinist* in their popular senses to designate social attributes commonly attributed to men and women.

Besides the difficulty with the very use of the term *gender*, an obvious concern in writing about the relationship of gender to teaching is that if traits associated with one gender and practiced more frequently by members of that gender, say females, appear to be more successful in teaching, then those reporting the findings may appear to be criticizing all members of the other gender, say males. In our case, for instance, research in the teaching of composition strongly supports the use of behaviors long genderized as "female" and in much of the theoretical literature designated a "feminist pedagogy." That is to say, current research and theory advocates that the teacher take a less authoritarian stance in the composition classroom and work instead to nurture and support the students' developing voices in writing. Teachers are advised to abandon what Freire has called the "banking" concept of education and take on the role of what Belenky and her colleagues have called "the midwife."

We suspect that those socialized as males may have to work harder at practicing a feminist pedagogy and helping students to gain a voice in their writing than those socialized as women. We believe the data we have analyzed support this belief. However, we do not wish to offend our male colleagues by appearing to take an essentialist stance with regard to gender. We worry that our findings may be interpreted to mean that all women automatically make good composition teachers and all men are ineffective. We want to be careful to state our agreement with Martin's argument that because no human being is "gender-bound," each of us has the capacity to become not "gender-blind" but "gender-sensitive" in our teaching and our research.

A third obstacle, less obvious to us at first as a cause of our early silence about gender-related findings in our research, is the inner resistance of members of a subordinate group to speak words that will call attention to their difference and call back to life the stereotypes that operate to exclude them. In our cases, we were mature women college professors completing doctoral dissertations. Having begun our careers in the 1970s, we had learned to achieve in the academy by persistently ignoring frequent and irrelevant references to the fact that we are women. Even today, there remains the belief on the part of many in academe that women writing about gender issues are somehow less academically mature than their colleagues who "are able to see the larger picture." In designing our independent research studies and in analyzing our data, none of us went looking for gender differences. When the data began to speak of gender, we dared not listen. We wrote our findings in terms of differences in pedagogy and educational philosophy. We did not discuss gender. We return to our studies to report their gender-related findings, interpretations, and implications in this essay despite the concerns we have noted because we believe that the cumulative data from our three studies are significant and that their implications for researchers and teachers of composition and rhetoric are too important to go unstated.

Overview of the Studies

The three studies taken together represent a sampling of ten college instructors, five males and five females, working in writing programs in New York, Ohio, and Utah. All of the instructors who provided data for our studies were selected because they were perceived within their departments as being excellent instructors and because they were interested in participating in a study of teaching college composition. Of all ten instructors, there was just one instance of what we call "cross-gender teaching"—a teacher using a pedagogy that could be characterized by traits typically attributed to a gender different from that teacher's. All of the women instructors in our studies were practicing what could .clearly be described as a feminist pedagogy—transferring authority to students as writers, diminishing their own role as authorities, fostering collaboration. Four of the five men instructors were practicing what could be described as a masculinist pedagogy—maintaining their role as central authorities in the classroom and controlling their students' texts.

Were the differences between the men and women teachers in these studies merely circumstantial? It is possible, but we think it unlikely. There are really only two ways to study gender and teaching. One is to design a study that statistically controls for gender. The second is to provide descriptions of men and women composition teachers at work and permit readers to match the descriptions with their own understandings of gender and teaching. Because we are wary of efforts to control for single variables in human-subject research, we have opted for the second way, and we provide summaries of our descriptive research below.

The First Study: Men and Women Reading Student Texts

Nancy McCracken set out to study the ways teachers read student papers and formulate their responses. Four college writing instructors, two each from two different writing programs, were selected as representative of response styles used in their program and recommended by program chairs as excellent models who were also interested in composition research. Interviews with the four college writing instructors, analysis of their comments written on student papers and analysis of their concurrent reading/ commenting protocols indicated clear differences between the men and women in the study. Most notably, the men interrupted their student texts to comment almost twice as frequently as the women did, and they did not often look back in the text before continuing to read after a lengthy interruption. Faced with some reading difficulty, the women most often reread or read ahead, seeking the point they assumed the writer to be making. At similar junctures, the men stopped reading abruptly and began writing what the student had done wrong to cause the difficulty. The men rarely asked questions except rhetorical—usually sarcastic—questions that were clearly directives, while the women frequently asked straightforward questions to request more information and to probe the student's composing process. The women began each summative comment with some positive statement and always referred to the ideas in the student essays. The men meted out praise sparingly, according to perceived need of the student writer, and frequently neglected to respond to the specific content of the essays.

Excerpts from two commenting protocols will illustrate the differences in reading rhythms and commenting styles. The first is John's response to an international student writing on his highly controlled assignment to write about a "Most Embarrassing Experience" in a "four-paragraph essay with introduction containing thesis and two main points, two body paragraphs, and a summary conclusion." The student has done as she was told—written a paper about a painful childhood moment her family has never let her forget. She does a fine job recreating the scene, but John interrupts his reading every few words to correct and rewrite her prose. By the end of the paper, he notices that the writer still seems "pretty upset" about this childhood embarrassment, and he resolves to say something to her about it in his comment. He is trying to change roles from authority figure to nurturer, but that is difficult, and he does not see the contradiction inherent in his commentary:

> Marietta, When people point to you as that little girl of long ago, they are very mistaken. That person from the past was just a little girl; you are a woman, an entirely different person.
> Now for your essay, although you are improving, little by little, you still are having serious problems. Your sentences sitll tend to be overlong and awkward. Study "Stringy Sentences," p. 331.
> Oh yes, your use of idioms is improving. You made one idiom mistake here, p. 3.

Dee's commenting protocols illustrate a reading style, markedly different from that of the two men in the study. First of all, she does not write any comments at all until she has read through the entire paper. She reads long chunks of the student's text without interrupting. When she does interrupt her reading, it is to figure out what the student might be doing. When she encounters a puzzlement about the text, instead of attributing it to the student's lack of effort or skill, she solves the puzzle by rereading and instantiating what she believes the student may have in mind. An excerpt from one of Dee's commenting protocols for an international student with problems similar to John's student indicates her different style of reading and responding to student writers. The assignment for the paper was to work in groups to design a utopia, each member of the group choosing some aspect of the society to study and write about. Dee has discussed early drafts of these papers with the students and at this point she is reading and writing comments on revised, semifinal drafts. In the protocol excerpt below only the words underlined are written on the student's paper. The other words are Dee's thinking aloud as she plans the final comment:

> So, Jose . . . You've done a much better job of being specific in this paper. um—and this is a difficult topic—and this is a difficult topic to be specific about. . . . OK, I'll just start a different paragraph for that, 'cause it is sort of a different point, and I want him to think about it. How did you decide—which, or what order to discuss—um—to discuss topics in—That's sort of awkward. Um—so, I'm always at a loss what to do with him in the paper—OK, let, let's just—uh, maybe I'll just go through and sort of recap what—how his paper works. [She rereads, skimming the student's paper.] OK, the whole of the thing is to be energy efficient—right? [She skims the paper again.] Reread your paper. Are you satisfied—maybe when I go through it I can comment on it—Are you satisfied with the organization? . . . I've jotted down on the paper . . . some questions the reader may have.—uh—Continue to work on word choice.—uh—Again I've marked some examples . . . Also look at sentences.—uh—Were you in class when we worked on some examples of . . . how to make . . . sentences clearer?

While both John and Dee point out their students' errors in syntax, in general, Dee permits her students much greater freedom than John in choice of topics and in organization, and she ascribes to them a writer's purpose and control, which John assumes is lacking in his students. In another paper in the protocol set, Dee is surprised by a sudden turn in the organizational structure of the student's essay. Instead of writing a directive that the student reorganize according to Dee's expected structure, she puzzles through the reading to discover the structure in the student's writing. Once she does so, she goes on reading without written comment. During her reading/commenting protocol, she says, "Okay, so this is a little different—I told them I thought it would be easier to write if they presumed that their utopian society was already in operation, and then they just were explaining how it operated—but Cathy seems to be, instead, uh, talking about how it *will* operate. This is a *plan* for a utopia. OK." In contrast, when John encounters the only student in his class to use a structure other than his assigned four-paragraph, two-point essay structure, he writes immediately, "Don't forsake the structure!"

The women instructors in McCracken's study are clearly more flexible in their pedagogical stance toward their students. In their reading, they collaborate with the student writers, transacting with their texts, rather than simply matching them to preconceived ideal texts as their two male counterparts do. The metaphors created by the four teachers in the study shed light on the different, perhaps gender-related, ways they define their reading role. John's metaphor is military:

> I've always felt I was too damn good to waste with honors people—I was shock troops. I mean, you know, have to hit the trenches; any dummy could teach honors. I've done two weeks of these "workshops," and the people were writing the same garbage after two weeks, but when I get them close to me in conference, they don't do it. . . . Sometimes, God, it's like whippin' a dying mule up a goddam hill. You know you can get it up there. And sometimes it's like a cheerleader gone mad.

The other male instructor in the study, Alan, constructs a similar metaphor—the policeman: "The . . . errors have to be fixed . . . I feel somehow that my professional obligations are to see that these errors get stopped. . . . I think of my role as a policeman or an editor—the one with whom the buck stops."

The two women in the study create metaphors that place the students at the center with the teachers in a supportive role. Dee says responding to student writing is "like giving tennis lessons. Someone can show you a few basic things, but then pretty much you just have to practice, and then your tennis coach responds to what you do in practice . . . watching you do it, [giving] you some suggestions along the line." Laura, the other woman in the study imagines her students are "delivered like a dozen eggs . . . and each egg looks identical, and they all behave identically at first. Then I try to get them to see if they can . . . peck their way out of their shells and turn out to be pink chicks or green chicks or whatever happens to be in the shell. And a few of the eggs are infertile."

While each of the instructors in this study is unique, it is easy to see patterns—the men taking an authoritarian stance and controlling their students' discourse, the women taking a collaborative stance and attempting to help students gain control of their discourse. These differences reflect differences in the two programs represented in the study: the men were selected as leaders in a traditional program at one university; the women were selected as leaders in a process-oriented program at another university. Yet the differences among the teachers also reflect broader differences in gender roles in conversation and in the use of control. In the initial report of this research, however, there was no discussion of the possible link between the instructors' gender roles and their teaching behaviors.

The Second Study: Men and Women Teachers in Conferences

Lois Green set out to examine teacher response in conference settings. She taped student/teacher conferences and analyzed the transcripts in light of how teachers or students set the agenda and thereby controlled the conference. Two teachers, identified as Sam and Lora, provide an interesting contrast in the ways men and women respond to student writers. Both instructors had given their classes the same assignment: "Study the rhetorical style of Martin Luther King's 'Letter from Birmingham Jail,' and write a protest letter using elements of King's style—particularly parallel construction and metaphor." The first striking difference between the two instructors is in their perceptions of this assignment. Sam decided that the validity of the exercise lay in mastering the descriptive terms of the rhetorician and creating an argument about King's style. Lora's primary concern is with the student's ability to marshal the power of King's rhetoric in the public expression of ideas. Sam focuses on the part of the assignment that asks the student to study King's rhetoric; Lora focuses on the part of the assignment that asks the student to write a letter. Sam's student has written four short paragraphs about King's rhetoric followed by a letter, excerpted below, written in King's style to the state's Fish and Game Department protesting the addition of a trout stamp to the local fishing license. Readers familiar with "A Letter from Birmingham Jail" will notice how the student has made the form work for her.

> Gentlemen: I have never heard of such an asinine law as having to buy a trout stamp in addition to buying a fishing license because what is a trout, if not a fish. But with this law I have to buy a stamp in order to fish for a trout because the Fish and Game Department needs more money. Being around many fishermen I have heard them, standing on the shores grumbling and swearing about the stupidity of this law. I have seen many trout taken from the lakes, and I have seen some of the fishermen with stamps and some without.
>
> Here we are getting ready to buy a new fishing license with a law that is like going to the store to buy a ten-pound bag of sugar. Even though the sugar is marked at three dollars and ninety-five cents, when we reach the checkstand we find there is an additional dollar and eighty cents charge for the bag and there is no way we can get the sugar out of the store without the bag, and there is no way we can be sure a trout would not take our bait, even if we did not buy the stamp.
>
> I have fished for many years in beautiful lakes and streams. In the early morning sunrise and in the cool dusk of evening I have thrown my line into cool, glistening water and have yet to catch a beautiful rainbow trout that would know if it was legal or not. Over and over again I have found myself wondering "What would a person, without a trout stamp, do if they caught a trout. . . ."
>
> I do however realize you need more money because of inflation. But I do believe this is a foolish way of going about it. Why not simply raise the price of the license to cover the price of the stamp? I do believe you would get the money you need and keep the fishermen happier and honest.

Sam begins his response with "That was very good. In fact I think it was excellent. Ah, the letter's not bad." The student offers a short comment and then Sam focuses on the paragraphs about King's rhetorical devices that precede the letter. He asks, "Ah, tell me why you wrote this stuff?" He also asks her, "How would you revise this thing?" then goes on to *tell* her how. He defines what it means to make an assertion: "An assertion is making a statement and backing it up." When the student says she doesn't know how she'd go about that, he tells her to mention her protest earlier and then he says, "What you have to do is convince them that King's letter is effective in the idea of a protest letter, okay? And the reason it is effective is because of the rhetoric. You are going to have to reorient this paragraph." He goes on at length discussing

King's rhetorical devices and how to identify them, instructs the student to rewrite her first paragraph and then ends the conference with, "The letter, I think, is pretty good." The student points out, "I did use parallelism." Sam agrees that she did and observes that he "got the impression" she worked hard on this.

Sam's response to the student's letter never addresses any specific comments to her strengths. Almost his entire conference time is spent trying to shape her paper into his "ideal" text of a discussion of King's rhetorical strategies. He does not help the student focus on what she has been able to do in her own words, but instead, he maintains control over her text by demanding that she use his language and think linguistically in *his* patterns. He is following a classical male pattern, as identified by Gilligan, of making judgments on the basis of the *rules* that exist, whereas the student has been making judgments on the basis of how people are affected by the rules. Hence his concentration on rhetorical explication and hers on the case-specific example. She has carefully crafted a protest letter that incorporates King's patterns of parallel construction and uses of metaphor, but Sam insists that she repeat the rules in explication of King's essay, rather than reward her for the implementation of those rules in her own letter.

Like Sam, Lora, the second instructor in Green's study, is working with a woman student who similarly handled the assignment by writing a rhetorically powerful protest letter in the style of King on an issue of immediate personal concern to her. A registered nurse, this student has written to the editor of the local paper, asking for passage of legislation to permit a "living will." The letter is too long to quote here, but an excerpt may indicate the voice of the student and her approach to the assignment:

> But when you see someone lying in a bed looking more like a disease than a person; when you avoid talking to family members because you can no longer say, "I'm sorry, there's no change"; when you see a human body with penetrating tubes too numerous to count, see a body unresponsive except for unavoidable and untreatable seizure activity; when you pray every night for the relief of the family's agony; when you become hesitantly angry with physicians who attempt futile resuscitating efforts, then you will understand why I find it necessary to preserve human dignity.

Unlike Sam, Lora responds directly to the issue raised in the letter, saying, "I think I would send that in to the *Tribune*." She is primarily concerned that the student recognize the validity of her own voice. When the student protests, "Oh, I'm not going to send it in," Lora asks if she risks anything professionally if it is published. When the student replies that isn't a concern, then Lora pushes a little further with, "I mean, aren't we about entering the public conversation here? Assuming some responsibility as a professional health person?" The student promises to think about it.

Lora celebrates her student's prose through recognition of the power of the ideas. Sam neither celebrates his student's demonstrated implementation of the rhetorical devices, nor does he allude to any of the ideas raised in her protest. He responds only in the most general terms to the portion of her paper that analyzes King's use of rhetorical devices.

What we have in this study is Sam, "reading as a man" (to borrow Culler's term), concerned with the rules that govern the structure of King's text, unable to coach his student in a delivery of her text that is already rich with the connections of her own experience in fishing. In contrast, we have Lora, "reading as a woman," concerned with the relationship between her student's call for action to alleviate suffering and her reluctance to voice her protest publicly. As in the McCracken report, however, Green's initial report repressed all discussion of gender in the response styles of her two teachers.

The Third Study: What Do Women Writers Want?

Claudia Greenwood set out to study factors, both internal and external, that influence reentry women in first-semester composition classes. These are women who have been out of school for a number of years; typically, they have been at home rearing a family since high school. Many of them are nearly at the developmental position identified by Belenky et al. as silence: "Feeling cut off from all internal and external sources of intelligence, women fail to develop their minds and see themselves as remarkably powerless and dependent. . . . Since they cannot trust their ability to understand and to remember what was said, they rely on the continued presence of authorities to guide their actions" (28). Greenwood collected data in the form of interviews, protocols, surveys, and writing portfolios over the course of one semester from eleven women students and their four professors, two men and two women. On the way to discovering the obstacles these students face as they balance schoolwork with demands of spouses, children, and jobs and try to cope with internal factors such as fear of failure, doubt about ability to learn, and guilt (Greenwood, "'It's Scary'"), she discovered "intimidation by instructors." Although the instructors in this study behaved in gender-stereotypical ways, Greenwood assigned them gender-free names in her report ("Instructor 1," "Instructor 2," "Instructor 3," and "Instructor 4"), and gender was not identified as an influencing factor in this study of "Factors Which Influence Re-entry Women Writers in College Composition Classes."

The most noticeable difference in the data is that between the male instructors' and the female instructors' expectations of the reentry women. The men had unreasonably high expectations of the returning women students. As one of them observed: "I probably expect more of the women because they've worked harder in the past. I expect them to be more fluent, too"; and "since as a group over the years women students have delivered more valuable goods, I have come to look for superior products. They seem to sense this condition and, as a result, try harder." Yet as Belenky et al. noted, "In accepting the authorities' standards, the separate knowers make themselves vulnerable to their criticism" (107). Vulnerability in the face of unrealistically high expectations of the male instructors dominated the responses of the women in the study. In one case a student had spent hours trying to meet what she believed was an important goal in writing: an average number of words per sentence. She reported in an interview: "He said the minimum was eighteen. My average was fourteen. I guess I'll have to go to a tutor for help with sentence combining." The female instructors, both with experiences balancing private and public sphere roles and duties, had more realistic expectations of their students.

Besides having unrealistically high expectations of the women students, one of the two male instructors, "Instructor 3," took the role of the traditional male authority figure. Far from attempting to practice a feminist pedagogy, this instructor believed that class time should be devoted to his lectures rather than to peer activities of any kind and that an instructor should correct students' oral language and mark every detected error on a student's paper in red ink. Though well intended, this pedagogy did not prove helpful for the reentry women students in his class.

Differences in instructor commentary were significant in this study. The reentry women in the study valued, most of all, supportive comments that suggested an appreciation of the time and effort they had invested in the product. Particularly appreciated were the comments of the women instructors, which were perceived as "above all, humane." The two women instructors seemed to make a conscious effort to write something positive as a lead for whatever criticism might follow. One would write a brief, upbeat remark such as "Super job, super Mom" The other would observe, "Very clear and strong. What a fine paper. What a good point!" These comments worked to undermine the reentry women's fear of failure and their expectation that they would be unable to learn. They made the anxious and exhausted writers feel good and provided the energy to tackle the problematic features of their texts.

In contrast, and revealing the extent to which good intentions and bad judgment may mix, Instructor 3, in his authoritarian male role, provided more than his usual extensive negative commentary for the reentry women's papers. He explained, "I usually provide more extensive commentary because I think they can tolerate more direct and detailed judgment and conclude that the additional marginalia is evidence of their importance as class members." He did not, however, witness the telling expressions and anguished sighs of the reentry women interviewed by Greenwood upon receipt of their first graded papers.

The differences between the female instructors and the male authoritarian instructor remained consistent throughout the semester. While the female instructors asked questions of their writers and recorded observations about voice and tone (Instructor 2 wrote for example, "Your voice is clear; I feel your pain."), Instructor 3 continued to remark, "See the mechanics closely. Work to prepare nearly perfect copy," and on a paper of 435 words, "No more shortees."

By the semester's end, one of Instructor 3's students rationalized, "I just felt no matter what I did it wasn't going to please him, and I thought that this is too bad, so I just kept writing to please me, and I didn't care if it pleased him or not." Perhaps Adrienne Rich would have celebrated this solution as it demonstrates achievement of the goal of which she writes, "How can we teach women to move beyond the desire for male approval and getting 'good grades' and seek and write their own truths that the culture has distorted or made taboo?" (240). However, she surely would not have recommended such a painful process.

For most students in Instructor 3's class, the semester was disabling. Sensitivity to the potential for error and increased frustration were apparent in each interview: "It's too bad, but I don't feel I've learned anything, I really don't. I needed someone to say, if you want to write a good paper you should start in this way and build from here . . . I just don't know how." It is important to note that the women in Instructor 3's class labored to produce the required text without complaint, believing that their instructor was emphasizing what was most important in writing. They followed his guidelines faithfully, learning in the process to carefully count their words to satisfy numerical length requirements, resigning themselves to a course that focused attention on syntactic and textual features. Unfortunately, Instructor 3's behavior perfectly matched debilitating expectations of the reentry women. They expected criticism and expected not to be able to understand their professors, and that is exactly what they got.

In contrast, the reentry women writers working in the classes of instructors teaching writing as a process and practicing a different pedagogy had quite a different experience. Of formative evaluation, one student remarked, "I felt good about it because I didn't know exactly what I was doing. I needed somebody to put me on track. The comments provided the direction." Peer support at each stage of the writing process and formative one-to-one conferencing with both of the women instructors resulted in the students' sense of control over their academic fate. "I see no reason for anybody in this class not to be doing well because there is help available to them if they want it."

By the end of the semester, although none of the reentry women expressed belief in herself as an accomplished writer, the women who had experienced the pedagogy practiced by the two women instructors felt they had made clear progress and were in greater control of their writing process: "I never really knew how to write or even approach an issue in writing. After my experience with this class, I feel pleased—improvement came with every writing experience."

The women students who had explored various methods of entry, strategies for development, and audiences were most pleased with the challenge of thinking about topics they had not heretofore encountered. This, the group that had also experienced peer evaluation and conferencing, was the group that began to move from "silence" and "received knowledge" toward the "connected knowing" that Belenky et al. envision as a goal for truly educated women. As one of these women put it, "As you get into the habit of writing things down, it makes your mind more active. I've had to block all that out for some years now and just think about raising babies and raising children. I forgot how to think about other things. I am pleased that I was challenged to do so. I'm a more interesting person now." It is noteworthy, although perhaps not surprising that although Instructor 3 offered conference time to any students requesting it, none of the reentry women students ever took him up on the offer during the semester. The women were afraid of confrontation, and they hesitated to challenge the instructor's authority.

Like McCracken and Green, Greenwood failed to interpret her data in the light of the instructor's gender in her initial report. In fact at the time of her first writing, it did not even occur to her to include instructor's gender in her study of factors influencing reentry women's success in college.

Summary

Were the differences observed in our three independent studies merely circumstantial? It is possible, but we think it unlikely. As we listen to John, Instructor 3, Sam, and their colleagues responding to their students' good faith efforts to write their truths, we are reminded of lines from Helene Cixous:

> Every woman knows the torment of getting up to speak. Her heart racing, at times entirely lost for words, ground and language slipping away—that's how daring a feat, how great a transgression it is for a woman to speak—even just open her mouth—in public. A double distress, for even if she transgresses, her words fall almost always upon the deaf male ear, which hears in language only that which speaks in the masculine. (251)

When we listen to teachers like Dee, Lora, and Instructor 2 as they respond to their students' efforts to "speak" in public, we are heartened by the fact that their words do not fall on deaf ears. We observe that these women value the different forms their students write in. If their assignments elicit letters, they celebrate the students' letters, if they elicit narratives of painful moments, they respond to the pain, not the surface structure. Perhaps it is only a quirk of our sampling that these women teachers all somehow know better than to try to enable their student writers by highlighting their awkwardness. Perhaps it is mere chance that these women read in the way that West and Zimmerman, Fishman, and Tannen show women listening in conversation: questioning, supporting, sharing the work of the conversation, furthering the topics raised by their conversational partners.

It might be an artifact of our small sample that the men who wound up in our studies read in the way that the men in the Fishman study participated in cross-gender conversations: withholding supportive utterances in most cases and raising new topics of their choosing rather than asking questions that would elicit further contributions from their partners. It is possible, but we think not, and we invite readers to take up this discussion through examination of their own ways of responding to students' writing in conferences and written comments.

We think it is quite likely that the men in our studies behave as they do in their response to students' writing as a result of the way they have been socialized. The research on cross-gender conversation suggests that when men in our society are in the position of having to listen to a conversational contribution they do not want to listen to, they freely take over the conversation, interrupting and withholding supportive utterances, until the speaker gives up. But in responding to students' texts, these natural conversational dodges are ineffective. Unlike the women in cross-gender conversation research, the students' texts keep right on talking at their teachers. For many educated, white, American males, this is an alien situation. The professor has no way to take a turn in the face of a student text except to correct it, or offer discussion about a tangential aspect of the writing—stringy sentences, perhaps, or King's rhetoric, or word count.

Women instructors face the same difficult discourse situation as do male instructors—having to listen to/read long bits of discourse that are often less than absorbing without being able to interrupt and change the subject. Perhaps one reason the women in our data from three independent studies in three different parts of the country handle this situation differently than do their male counterparts is that they have had more practice at it—outside the classroom. As women, they would have had years of experience listening to conversations they were not particularly interested in, but—unable to establish new topics of their own choosing because of the pragmatics of cross-gender discourse—they would have developed *women's ways of listening*.

Women who have been socialized to converse effectively with men and children learn to make sometimes dull conversation better—not by taking over with a new topic of their own—but by helping their conversational partners tell better stories. By asking good questions and offering supportive responses, they help their coconversants to make their contributions as rich as possible. This kind of listening, collaborative rather than competitive, is particularly well suited for composition teachers whose primary role, after all, is to enable their students to create and sustain rich discourse. As Adrienne Rich explains, "In order to write I have to believe that there is someone willing to collaborate subjectively" (64).

We think it likely that another reason for the differences between the response styles of the men and women teachers arises from their expectations. Although some men acquire understandings of the needs of women and other students who have been relatively voiceless in the public domain through their own experience as minorities or through a concerted effort to learn through others, all women know firsthand what it is to be rendered voiceless when trying to speak. Surely, not all women teachers choose to act on this knowledge in their treatment of student writers, but it may be that many or most do, and that may account for the gendered differences in our findings. If so, it would seem very important to observe these women working with student writers and to report their insights and strategies so that they may be learned by those who have not already acquired them. Without such learning, those who teach composition like the men in our three studies—even those who see their role as nurturers—run the risk of unwittingly misappropriating students' texts and cutting their students off from the voices they are trying to develop.

Reflections

While we cannot speak for other researchers, we know that in all three of our cases, we felt uneasy as we became aware of gender-typical behaviors in the data we were collecting. As researchers we were able to write with ease about our findings so long as the categories we used were gender-blind: we each wrote confidently of pedagogical stance, philosophy, writing-process approaches, current-traditional rhetoric. When it came to gender, however, we experienced the same kind of silence as that experienced by the women described in Belenky, Clinchy, Goldberger, and Tarule. We were unable to see then, as we do now, that we suffered from a confusion of research paradigms that currently plagues research in writing and reading. Although we were each conducting descriptive, participant-observer studies, our training in the empirical paradigm prevented us from voicing observations about such a murky subject as gender. Clearly there is no way to claim *empirically* that any of the teacher-student interactions we observed was related in any way to the gender of the teachers—even if we could find a way to define *gender* empirically. All we have as the basis for a discussion of gender in our research is our participant-observer insights and our field notes. Today we recognize that we are working within a research paradigm that obligates the researcher as participant-observer to report all salient features of recorded social interaction. In writing our initial reports, we listened to the voices we conjured of angry empiricists responding to our gender-related observations: "But, you can't prove that! How can you be sure?"

Our experience has suggested two implications for those engaged in research in the teaching of composition. The first is that researchers—and their professors and editors, the vast majority of whom are males—need to become more fully aware of feminist scholarship. Research questions and designs should reflect this awareness. Research attempting to explore the process by which relatively voiceless people become fluent in public discourse cannot profitably continue to ignore insights from feminist research. Since the gender role of a writing teacher is likely to influence her or his interactions with students, awareness of the gender-related influences on teaching can offer important insights for teachers and researchers. Further, beginning researchers need to know that gender-related findings are likely the reflection of larger cultural influences rather than individually blameworthy "sexist" conduct.

The second implication for composition research we derive from our experience is that universities and research communities should increase support for research based on "women's ways of knowing," honoring participant-observer studies and collaborative research as primary ways to study rhetoric and composition; these "ways" are perhaps even more productive than large-scale statistically controlled studies currently favored by university research communities. Our individual research institutions encouraged us to conduct descriptive studies of teacher practice, but it was our own initiative in collaborating that permitted the additional observation and insights reported here. Support for similar collaborative efforts should be offered throughout the research community.

Works Cited

Anson, Chris M. "Response Styles and Ways of Knowing." *Writing and Response: Theory, Practice, and Research.* Ed. Anson. Urbana, IL: NCTE, 1989. 332–66.

Beauvoir, Simone de. *The Second Sex.* Trans H. M. Parshley. New York: Vintage, 1974.

Belenky, Mary Field, Blythe McVicker Clinchy, Nancy Rule Goldberger, and Jill Mattuck Tarule. *Women's Ways of Knowing.* New York: Basic, 1986.

Brannon, Lil, and C. H. Knoblauch. "On Students' Rights to Their Own Texts: A Model of Teacher Response." *College Composition and Communication* 33 (1982): 157–66.

Britton, James, et al. *The Development of Writing Abilities (11–18).* London: Macmillan Education, 1975.

Cayton, Mary Kupiec. "What Happens When Things Go Wrong: Women and Writing Blocks." *Journal of Advanced Composition* 10 (1990): 321–39.

Caywood, Cynthia L., and Gillian R. Overing, eds. *Teaching Writing: Pedagogy, Gender, and Equity.* Albany: State U of New York P, 1987.

Cixous, Helene. "The Laugh of the Medusa." *New French Feminisms.* Ed. Elaine Marks and Isabelle de Courtivron. New York: Schocken, 1981. 245–64.

Emig, Janet A. *The Composing Processes of Twelfth Graders.* Urbana, IL: NCTE, 1971.

Fishman, Pamela M. "Interaction: The Work Women Do." Thorne, Kramarae, and Henley 89–101.

Flower, Linda S., and John R. Hayes. "Problem-Solving Strategies and the Writing Process." *College English* 39 (1977): 449–61.

Flynn, Elizabeth. "Composing as a Woman." *College Composition and Communication* 39 (1988): 423–35.

Freedman, Sarah W. *Response to Student Writing.* Urbana, IL: NCTE, 1987.

Freire, Paulo. *Pedagogy of the Oppressed.* New York: Continuum, 1970.

Gilligan, Carol. *In a Different Voice: Psychological Theory and Women's Development.* Cambridge: Harvard UP, 1982.

Green, Lois I. "Three Case Studies of Teachers Responding to College Students in Individual Writing Conferences." Diss. New York U, 1987.

Greenwood, Claudia M. "Factors Which Influence Re-Entry Women in College Composition Classes." Diss. Indiana U of Pennsylvania, 1987.

———. "'It's Scary at First': Reentry Women in College Composition Classes." *Teaching English in the Two-Year College* 17 (1990): 133–42.

Hayes, Elizabeth. "Insights from Women's Experiences for Teaching and Learning." *Effective Teaching Styles*. Ed. Hayes. San Francisco: Jossey, 1989.

Hillocks, George. *Research on Written Composition: New Directions for Teaching*. Urbana, IL: NCRE/ERIC, 1986.

McCracken, Nancy M. "Gender Issues and the Teaching of Writing." *Gender Issues and the Teaching of English*. Ed. Nancy Mellin McCracken and Bruce Appleby. Portsmouth, NH: Boynton, in press.

———. "Teachers' Response to Students' Writing." Diss. New York U, 1985.

Martin, Jane Roland. "The Contradiction and the Challenge of the Educated Woman." Lecture. Kent State U, Kent, OH, 1988.

———. *Reclaiming a Conversation: The Ideal of the Educated Woman*. New Haven: Yale UP, 1985.

Perl, Sondra. "Five Writers Writing." Diss. New York U, 1978.

Pratt, Mary Louise. *Toward a Speech Act Theory of Literary Discourse*. Bloomington: Indiana UP, 1977.

Rich, Adrienne. *On Lies, Secrets, and Silence: Selected Prose 1966–1978*. New York: Norton, 1979.

Shaughnessy, Mina P. *Errors and Expectations: A Guide for the Teacher of Basic Writing*. New York: Oxford UP, 1977.

Sommers, Nancy. "Responding to Student Writing." *College Composition and Communication* 33 (1982): 148–56.

Tannen, Deborah. *You Just Don't Understand*. New York: Morrow, 1990.

Thorne, Barrie, Cheris Kramarae, and Nancy Henley, eds. *Language, Gender and Society*. Rowley, MA: Newbury, 1983.

West, Candace, and Don H. Zimmerman. "Small Insults: A Study of Interruptions in Cross-Sex Conversations Between Unacquainted Persons." Thorne, Kramarae, and Henley 103–17.

Zimmerman, D. H., and Candace West. "Sex Roles, Interruptions, and Silences in Conversation." *Language and Sex: Difference and Dominance*. Ed. Barrie Thorne and Nancy Henley. Rowley, MA: Newbury, 1975. 105–30.

AT THE RISK
OF BEING PERSONAL . . .

"As We Share,
We Move into the Light"*

Penelope Dugan/State University of New
    York at Plattsburgh

Four-year-old Hilarie, whom I've known
since she was less than an hour old, sits on my
lap. My arms are around her, and *Charlotte's
Web* rests on her lap. Underlining the words
with my finger, I begin a sentence and she
finishes it. Or we alternate reading sentences.
Her head leans more heavily on my chest, and
she asks me to read aloud without her. Speaking
in Wilbur's voice and then Charlotte's, I finish
the chapter and carry Hilarie from the living
room to her bedroom. Hilarie wakes up as I pull
back the bed covers and asks for one more story.

*From the second prayer of the morning Rosh Hashanah
service.

Sitting in the dark and stroking her hair, I make up another chapter in the continuing adventures of Hilarie and Heather.

Hilarie has told me about her imaginary sister, Heather. Sometimes Hilarie goes by the name of Heather, and sometimes Heather goes by the name of Laurel. Hilarie corrects me when I get it wrong. Eventually, she goes to sleep. I remember to leave the bedroom door open and turn on the hall light. I am glad Hilarie gave herself a sister, so she won't be alone in the night after leaving the circle of light in the living room and the embracing warmth of book and reader.

I recall when I realized Hilarie could read by herself; she was holding a box of stone-ground crackers and studying the side panel of the box. She pointed to "mono-diglyceride" and asked, "How do you say that?" I told her and she then read the list of ingredients aloud. Later that night, I mentioned to her mother that Hilarie could read. Nancy said she had suspected it for sometime but was waiting for Hilarie to let her know. Now Nancy officially knew, but she didn't know how it had happened. None of us had tried to teach Hilarie how to read, but she had learned.

For as long as Hilarie could sit up by herself, she had been read to—she had been held in the embrace of reader and book. She was surrounded by books and by women who read. She knew reading was as natural a human activity as walking, talking, eating, and sleeping—well, she wasn't that sure about sleeping. Sleeping was hard because she had to do it alone unless she stayed with me where she didn't have to brush her teeth or change out of her overalls and could have the dogs in bed with her and keep the light on all night.

Nancy worried about kindergarten. Determined to send Hilarie to public school, she was afraid Hilarie would suffer for already knowing how to read and write. Also anxious, I reassured Nancy and waited. Hilarie adored her teacher and quoted her as fervently as we had quoted Chairman Mao years before. Hilarie's teacher had the good sense to rejoice at the gift of a child who could read already and put Hilarie in charge of story time.

On parent visitation night, Nancy saw a videotape of the kindergarten with Hilarie reading to the class. Naturally, the teacher took credit for this. Fine, let her, as long as she cherishes this child and all the other mothers' children as well; as long as she doesn't stand in their way and gives them the room and the encouragement to do what is as natural as talking, walking, and eating—reading and writing.

When I first moved to Manhattan, almost twenty years ago, I substituted in the public schools until I could get a "regular" job. In East Harlem, with first graders, I saw how much they wanted to read and write. Only concentrated cruelty or neglect could stamp out that desire.

A couple of years later, teaching developmental reading in the evening division of York College in Jamaica, I was urging the class through a paragraph on photosynthesis in the reading text prescribed by the English department. One of the men raised his hand and asked what he had seen me reading on the subway. It was an advance copy of Irving Howe's *The World of Our Fathers*. He asked why the class couldn't read a *real* book like I did. I looked at the class of working adults, many of whom had recently come to New York from the West Indies, Haiti, and Central America and realized how right he was. Why not? Week by week, xeroxed chapter by xeroxed chapter we read together *The World of Our Fathers*. The class found their own experiences in Howe's pages—working to send money home, saving to bring family members to

America, dealing with bosses and landlords and night school. They started a classroom version of the *Bintel Brief*, writing and answering each other's letters about problems of living in New York. This was a developmental reading class of mostly intermediate ESL students. They weren't supposed to be able to do any of this, but they could and they did. They taught me not to accept the estimations or limitations imposed by test scores. They taught me to use "real" books that could inform and reflect their experience and inspire them to write about that experience.

I learned to learn from my students—to listen to them and to talk less, to read their writing closely to discover what they knew and what they needed to know. I learned the structures of my students' lives and dreams; I learned to ally myself with these dreams.

I learned about mothers' dreams when I taught remedial writing for the federally funded Rural/Urban On-Site Collegial Training Program in the South Bronx, where simply walking by the boarded-up buildings to the school were daily tests of courage for me and my students, paraprofessionals who worked in public schools during the day and came to my classroom with their own children in the late afternoon. I learned to build each class slowly and quietly as the women gradually came in, late from appointments at clinics or delayed trains, and the children gradually settled down in our security-guarded classroom. We joked about the fact that on the streets there was no security and that perhaps the guard was there to protect against us—women strengthening skills and learning new ones to make a better future for the children with us.

Our class text was the textures of their lives. The women fought bone-numbing, ankle-swelling fatigue in a world where they had to sleep in street clothes because of the constant threat of fire and where they had to live with a bureaucracy that threatened them and their choices by its demand for literacy. We listed the kinds of writing they had to do in their daily lives and developed models. The first thing they wanted to learn was how to write notes to their children's teachers. They were determined their children would not be stigmatized by what they felt were their own deficiencies as writers. They moved from copying models we constructed as a class to substituting words and phrases in the models to transforming the models, when they weren't sufficient for new needs, into their own texts. Working in small groups, they were often joined by their children whose crayon scribbles modeled their own texts. Growing confident in their ability to write, they became models of writers for their children.

The women, children, security guard, and I were the only people in Community Junior High School 137 in the late afternoon and early evening. After the first week, the security guard propped the classroom door open and positioned his chair so he could see the blackboard and copy from it. I never saw what he wrote since he would close his notebook whenever I got near enough to see. But we all realized the class had another, slightly distant, member, and we spoke loudly enough for him to hear. Some of the women told me Jesus was very proud, and I should pretend not to notice him. He did not want to appear to be learning with women and children. I often think of him in the darkened corridor, sitting on the margins, too proud to come into the light of the classroom. I could imagine his life, but I had no access to his dreams.

Searching for a vision that would explain my students' lives and give power to their dreams, I started attending a Marxist study group led by

Eddie Boorstein who had just escaped from Chile after the murder of Allende and the overthrow of his government. I remember little of what Eddie said about *Economic and Philosophic Manuscripts of 1844*, but I remember him and his refusal to give up hope. He introduced me to the work of Herbert Aptheker and made clear the connection between revolution and literacy. He told me about Nat Turner reading of Toussaint L'Ouverture and being inspired by his successful rebellion. The rebellion of Nat Turner led to the statutes making it a capital offense to teach slaves to read and write. He introduced me to Marx and Engels's *Ireland and the Irish Question*, so I could see how colonization robs a people of their language, their culture, and their heritage. This small man with his high-pitched voice took all questions seriously and pointed us each, with his recommendations for reading, in a direction where we were ready to go.

Eddie Boorstein continued for me the work begun by Jane Elkin, my seventh grade teacher. Miss Elkin was the only teacher in the district to have a Ph.D. I never knew what it was in and how she had ended up teaching seventh graders, but she treated us with great seriousness while laughing at or ignoring school regulations. She celebrated all the Jewish holidays and explained to us what each was about. For Hanukkah, she put a menorah on her desk and lit one candle each day. For Purim, she brought in hamantaushen and told us the story of Esther and Haman. For Passover, we read from the Haggadah and sampled matzah and horseradish. Always, she stressed the themes of liberation. These classes were like a warm embrace.

I was happily reading my way through Jack London at this time. Miss Elkin called me up to her desk one day, mentioned I read a lot, and wondered if I had thought about what I wanted to be when I grew up. I said I wanted to be a socialist. I realize now the political climate of the times. Two of the Jack London books I had tried to get from the public library were *The Iron Heel* and *People of the Abyss*. Both were locked up in a glass-fronted bookcase behind the circulation desk, along with *Forever Amber*—strange shelfmates, indeed. Miss Elkin didn't miss a beat. She said she had some books of her grandfather's I might want to read. The next day she brought in books printed in Yiddish. She laughed and said she was sorry that none of them were in English, but she gave me one of the paperbound books and told me to keep it so I would remember I was part of a long and proud tradition. Years later, I lost the book, along with many others, in a flood. But I have the memory of the spirit in which it was given, a spirit of trust and confidence.

Sometimes in my classroom, I hear the voice of Miss Elkin or Eddie Boorstein or even Charlotte coming from me. I look at my students and wonder about the mix of teacher voices they hear as they speak and as they listen to me and to each other. Which voices will be forgotten and which will resonate after our course is over? Which voices will be heard in other classrooms? Which voices will help us move into the light or drive us back into darkened corridors? I wish I knew.